NEW HORIZONS IN INDIAN MANAGEMENT

Dr. Krishna Mohan Mathur
Dr. Pragya Mathur Kumar
Shiv Shubhang Mathur
Nandita Narayan Mathur

KALPAZ

New Horizons in Indian Management

Rs. 890

ISBN: 81-7835-711-9

Published in 2010 in India by
Kalpaz Publications
C-30, Satyawati Nagar,
Delhi-110052
E-mail: kalpaz@hotmail.com
Phone : 9212729499

Lasser Type Setting by: Quick Media, Delhi
Printed at : Young Art Press, Delhi

Dedication

This book is dedicated to the almighty Lord Ganesha with the following invocation

May we worship Ganapati
the protector of the noble people,
the best poet,

the most honourable,
the greatest ruler and
the treasure of all knowledge
and wisdom
O Ganapati! Please listen to us
and take your seat in our hearts

(Rig Veda, 2.23)

Contents

Preface

An ancient civilization but a young nation, the incredible India as a nation has been constantly changing and steadfastly moving towards being a self sufficient, strong federal democratic nation. During the last few years there has been a noticeable shift in the landscape of global economy from West to East and from the well established behemoths of the corporate world to a new breed of young, confident and ambitious upcoming companies. India celebrated the 60th anniversary of Independence this year and during the last 60 years there have been many various revolutions in India. Indian economy has brought about new paradigms, new processes and new generation of leaders in various fields. There is a new buzz about India in the international business community and management people. India is rapidly emerging as a preferred destination for foreign investors, young management students and MNCs. The accelerated pace of mergers and acquisitions in sectors such as financial services, manufacturing, banking services, information technology and construction have boosted FDI inflows. While inflow is increasing outflow is also equally exciting as Indian companies are becoming truly multinational in nature. India is on the way to becoming the economic, intellectual and cultural powerhouse of the world. Indian corporates are gradually rising up to the challenges of global competition and establishing themselves as effective leaders with a global mindset. New areas of challenges and opportunities are emerging in various fields. India is gradually emerging as the world's fastest growing wealth creator, the richest in human capital and leader in Information Technology. The book is about how Indian management is witnessing new horizons, new challenges, new opportunities in the present day global economy. It is an attempt to identify the newly emerging horizons in the Indian context. There are a number of emerging modern Indian corporations with a global mindset, benchmarking with the best in the world, internationalising their operations for competitiveness and becoming truly global. Peter F Drucker once wrote "the task of transferring management knowledge and management competence from the developed countries to the developing ones, and the task of generating entrepreneurial and managerial energies fast enough to satisfy the expectations of the developing world still remains one of the major tasks ahead". This treatise is a humble attempt to at least partially attempt the gigantic and complex task. The present work has attempted to cover a few aspects of the art and science of management with reference to the Indian system of management. The book highlights various facets of the 21st century Indian economy and the challenges it throws to the managers and business leaders. The word management in words of Peter F Drucker "not only denotes a function but also the people who discharge it. It not only denotes a social position and rank but also a discipline and field of study." The term management in this book has been used in a broader connotation and has four different groups of meanings, namely:

(*i*) Management as an activity

(*ii*) Management as a team in the enterprise

(*iii*) Management as a social category

(*iv*) Management as a body of knowledge

The present work highlights the new horizons of Indian management and introduces the readers to the newly emerging landscapes of Indian business. The book is organised into ten chapters. The first chapter titled "Managing Changing India" talks about how India has changed in the last sixty years due to economic planning, democratic pressures and economic reforms. The second chapter "New Horizons in Indian Management" focuses on the emerging new realities, concerns and challenges of the Indian economy of the 21st century. The third chapter analyses the ethos of Indian management and expounds ethical conduct, values, concern for the society and Nishkam Karma (performing ones assigned duties without concern for its fruits). In India a supportive family is the bedrock upon which careers are built. It stresses on spiritual quotient, emotional intelligence and laws of success. The fourth chapter explains the various efforts towards achieving good governance of the Indian economy. The Indian government is building a new architecture of inclusive growth by uplifting the poor and people at the bottom of the pyramid. Managing and governing a big democratic country like India in a federal constitutional system is a gigantic task. The big picture of the Indian economy shows all around development and growth. Various states of India have different rates of economic growth. As India gets globalised more modern, more progressive and materially rich, people are constantly asking new questions. How much has the country progressed? How well is the economy doing? Are we getting more divided between the rich and poor? Has India achieved global status as an economic entity. The fifth chapter on Corporate Governance highlights the need for companies to adhere to impartiality in dealings with the shareholders. The goals of corporate governance are to help improve standards of governance by fostering the spirit of enterprise and accountability, promoting fairness, transparency and responsibility. The chapter on "Change Management" analyses the forces for change, indicators of change, different faces of change, implementation of change management. Organisations must pay as much attention to the hard side of change management as they do to the soft aspects. The chapter on "Spirituality and Management" throws light on the core aspect of human beings - the self - the Atman or the consciousness. Soul is the space in which the body and the mind exist and draw sustenance. Spirituality is gradually moving into the corporate world. Indian management gurus have stressed the need to rekindle the heart and soul of management by developing ethical conduct of life, controlling unbridled greed and achieving a proper balance between work and life. Spiritual rejuvenation and rekindling of the inner spirit are the answers to various problems of materialistic capitalism and its various ills and shortcomings. The chapter - Strategic Human Resource Management—throws light on the concept of human resources and the various challenges before HR managers. Various steps in HR strategy have been explained and the external/internal environment of the Indian companies have been highlighted. Strategic partnership of HR with business units is acquiring new dimensions. The new dimensions of strategic partnership include understanding the business, leadership development, building teams, executing strategy, mergers, acquisitions and outsourcing. Integrated Strategic HR model has been elaborately depicted in the chapter and the best practices as propounded by various management thinkers have been discussed. Chapter 9 "Towards Global Leadership" discusses the emerging trends of Indian economy and how India can achieve global leadership. The various models of Indian companies becoming global leaders have been explained with illustrations. SWOT analysis of India as a country has been done to assess areas of future growth. The last chapter "Preparing Leadership for Future" addresses the essential issue of leadership for future. According to Peter Drucker "the prosperity (growth) if not the survival of any organisation, depends on the performance of its leaders and managers of tomorrow" (The Practice of Management 1964). The essentials of leadership for future have been analysed and the different faces of leadership have been elaborated with illustrations. A blueprint for preparing future leaders has been made in this book. The book is about Indian management and Indian economy and the changing paradigms during the last fifteen years. This work depicts how Indian economy can achieve global leadership in the next two decades and provides rich conceptual framework of Indian economy. For general readers, it will give them a very useful insight into the new trends of Indian economy. The present book is meant for young managers, future leaders and general readers who are sure to get an overall perspective of the changing Indian economy and new horizons emerging in Indian management. In each chapter there are many references of books and journals.

When the authors were checking the final proof of the book, two important historical events occurred which are very closely connected with the emerging new horizons in Indian management. Authors have therefore decided to incorporate these two events as Appendices A and B. Appendix A deals with the US slowdown and its impact on the economy. The financial crisis which convulsed America and ensnared European economies is taking its toll on emerging markets. The crisis that has seized the global credit markets is spreading. India cannot be insulated from the global financial crisis. P. Chidambaram, the Finance Minister has said "we have built a system for the Indian people that can withstand any storm that blows across the world. The SEBI's decision to ease curbs on Foreign Institutional Investors—especially the rollbacks on caps on participatory notes is an important step. The impact of this crisis has been felt across the IT sector, and other financial institutions which have a substantial degree of exposure to the US markets. The greed of the Wall Street Investment bankers and the dangers of a totally unregulated financial system are to a large extent responsible for the current crisis.

Appendix B deals with Indo-US nuclear deal - The deal provides India access to assured nuclear fuel for its civilian reactors. It allows India to reprocess and recycle spent fuel. This agreement also called the 123 agreement derives its name from the section 123 of the Energy Act under which the US has to conclude any bilateral civilian nuclear cooperation agreement. According to the Atomic Energy Act US cannot have nuclear cooperation with a country that has not signed the NPT or submitted itself to safeguards. The Hyde Act gives US administration the waiver to reach a pact with India which has not signed the NPT. The final signing provides India the recognition as a state with advanced nuclear technology with access to more and diversified sources of energy. It breaks upon a regime that blocked India's access to high technology after the nuclear test in 1974. This will allow India to achieve its target of 2020 MW of power by 2020. US firms can partner India in high tech ventures and can cover civilian nuclear cooperation agreement for mutual benefits. India has entered the 21st century as a global player with a healthy democratic system, pluralistic society and as a strong nuclear power. The relentless forces of globalisation, the ease of communication, travel, shrinking of national boundaries, the flow of people of all nationalities and colours across the world, the swift pulsing of financial transactions with pressing of a few buttons, the cell phone, computers, internet and race for economic prosperity are some of the noticeable features of the world today where India is trying to prove its strength as a economic superpower. This work is a collaborative effort of four writers having different academic backgrounds and training but with similarity in thought and perceptions to a large extent. This work has attempted to explore the new emerging patterns of Indian management and covered the latest events which have thrown challenges and opportunities to the Indian economy. The premise of the book is that various seemingly disparate issues must be integrated into a single overarching strategy if India is to achieve its objective of being a global superpower.

The authors acknowledge with gratitude thanks to all the authors and fully recognise their valuable contributions for their originality and creative thinking. It is difficult to list all those thinkers and writers whose ideas, comments and viewpoints have enriched this book. Rig Veda says : "Let noble thoughts come to us from every side" (1-89-1). We have therefore generously taken research findings, views and ideas from various books and magazines. Feedback and critical comments from the readers are most welcome. Suggestions for improvement of the book will be gratefully acknowledged and considered for incorporation in subsequent revised editions of the book. Members of our family Prabha, Niraj, Shikha, Samvit, Shashvat, Prakhar, Prabhav, Prabhas and Yagnesh deserve our thanks for giving us excellent support in completion of the book. Thanks are due to the publisher for bringing out the book with an excellent getup within a short time. We also thank the Director and faculty members of the various institutes where we have got our basic grounding about the concepts and fundamentals of management. We feel beholden to our spiritual guru Param Poojya Paramhans Swami Iswarananda Giriji Maharaj, founder of Samvit Sadhanayan Mount Abu, for his kind blessings and constant spiritual inspiration to all of us. This book is our humble offering to the Almighty Lord Ganesha whose grace and blessings remain the divine force behind our endeavors. We are all conscious of the fact that we are only instruments for carrying out designated tasks and deserve no credit at all. We are *nimitt matra* and are only tools in the hands of Lord Ganesha.

Krishna Mohan Mathur
Pragya Mathur Kumar
Shiv Shubhang Mathur
Nandita Narayan Mathur

1

Managing the Changing India

"I am convinced that 21st Century will be an Indian Century. The world will once again look at us with regard and respect, not just for the economic progress we make, but for the democratic values we cherish and uphold and the principles of pluralism and inclusiveness we have come to represent which is India's heritage" (Dr. Man Mohan Singh, January 7, 2005) India has become the world's fastest growing free market democracy having achieved a fundamental transformation in the 21st Century. The most noticeable trends of this fundamental transformation of India are as under:

1. Mature political economy with development as its core agenda.
2. Infrastructure growth—Highways, Urban Transport, Railways and Airports.
3. Pervasive communication, satellite and cable T.V., Basic and mobile telephone, Fibre/Broad band.
4. Rising consumer spending.
5. Growth of services.
6. Indian manufacturing establishing itself on the global stage.
7. Growth in literacy and higher education - HRD ministry committed to enhance professionalism and excellence.
8. A new young breed of entrepreneurs and professionals helping transforming India.
9. Big change in Indian corporate with visionary leaders.
10. Economic Reforms and planned economic development of the country for achieving inclusive development with focus on the poor.

11. India's saving rate has shot up dramatically in recent years from around 22% of our GDP to about 28%.
12. Coalition politics has become a part of our political system.

Twenty first century has ushered in economic growth with superb economic performance in India and the over all macro-economic picture of Indian economy is very bright, colourful and hopeful. Today there is India's global recognition as an economic power. The phenomenal rise of India in the global economy has been attributed to a whole host of factors, the major ones being the focus on economic reforms; and the demographic dividend that India currently enjoys due to its demographic transition. The large pool of human capital a young, talented, well-educated workforce is one of the major drivers of economic growth in India during the last decade. India has today become a sought after destination for foreign investment.

Dr. Surjit Bhalla, famous economist and Managing Director of Delhi based Oxus Research and Investments has said that next decade will be "India's Decade". He has predicted that the Indian Economy will be as under by 2010.

Table 1 Showing Indian Economy by 2010.

1.	GDP growth	7.9%
2.	Agricultural growth	3-3.5%
3.	Industrial Growth	8-10%
4.	Service Sector	8-10%
5.	Inflation rate	1-3%
6.	Export Growth	10-15%
7.	Import growth	10-15%
8.	Rupee	Rs. 45-50 a dollar

Prof. Ashima Goyal of Mumbai's Indira Gandhi Institute of Developmental Research (IGIDR) also believes that India's time has come. A Research Report issued by Goldman Sachs has said—"the Indian economy will be growing faster than the Chinese one by 2010. India is now a fast changing economy. Managing Changing India is a big challenge and a great opportunity. India, after completion of 60 years of independence, has become a trillion dollar economy, expected to soon overtake

Japan to become the third largest economy in the world. Between 2001 and 2007, about 100 million people have moved up from the bullock cart economy to bike class economy where people have proper housing, television and telephone and can travel by train. The lowest strata declined from 83% to 76% of the population. While the Indian economy is zooming to new heights, we can not be unmindful of the many challenges that face us. Six decades after the dawn of its freedom, India is on the threshold of a new destiny, its potential as a world leader has never been brighter. S. Sainath, Magasaysay award winner Rural Affairs Editor of *The Hindu* has said that India has the world's fourth largest number of dollar billionaires, whose combined wealth makes India of today the second major economic superpower in the global economy of billionaires. Indian managers are now recognized as world class managers by companies like Egon Zelinder, Mercer, Kon ferry International, Amway India Enterprises, E.I. Dupont India, Nestle India, Standard Chartered Bank, Seagram, Cadbury India, Johnson and Johnson, Baxter, Bank of America, International Paint, Honeywell and American Express. Stories of how large global corporations are hiring Indian Managers to lead internationally known organizations are well known. Indian managers are exhibiting global mindset and indepth knowledge of working across different regions, cultures and geographies. They have abilities to take risk, predict unimaginable business trends and opportunities. Rapid strides in knowledge-based industries, especially information technology, biotechnology, and pharmaceuticals; rejuvenation of the manufacturing sector, revolution in the agriculture sector and resurgence in sports have made India one of the fastest growing economies in the world. A market-oriented approach to development, opening up of the economy and the economies of scale and scope for Indian enterprises, access to modern technology, especially information technology, growth in entrepreneurship and patronizing favourable government policies of economic reforms have given birth to an almost new economy in India. The score card of India when compared to China is not very impressive but it indicates how far we have to go to achieve world economic leadership.

Table 2. Showing India and China Scorecard of 15 years

	India		China	
	1990	2005	1990	2005
Life expectancy at birth, total years	59	63.5	69	71.8
Mortality rate, infant (Per 1,000 live birth)	84	56.0	38	23.0
Mortality rate, under - 5 (per 1,000)	123	74.0	49	24.0
Immunisation (% if infants)	52	58.0	83	86.0
Prevalence of HIV (% of population ages 15-49)	0.7	0.9	0.1	0.1
Literacy rate (% of people above 15)	49	61.0	78	90.9
Energy use (kg of oil equivalent per capita)	430	719.3	775	1064.3
GDP (in current $)	316.9	805.7	354.6	2200.0
Population total	0.849	1.1	1.135	1.3
Per capita income (current $)	373.3	75.2	312.4	1645.7
GDP growth (annual %)	5.7	9.2	10.3	10.2
Exports of goods and services (% of GDP)	7.2	20.5	16.1	37.5
Gross Capital formation (% of GDP)	24.0	33.4	35.0	43.5
Time required to start a business (days)		71.0		48.0
Market cap of listed companies (% of GDP)	12.2	68.6	0.5	34.9
Telephone subscribers (per 1,000 people)*	35.4	127.7	182.2	570.2
Internet users (per 1,000 people)*	5.4	54.8	17.8	85.1
Mechandise trade (% of GDP)	12.6	28.5	32.4	63.6
FDI, net inflows ($ billion)	1.0	6.6	3.5	79.1
Total Score	484.6	696.8	1104.2	2069.6
Average Score	30.3	41.0	65.0	121.
Development Index	106.4	144.0	228.2	427.7

Source: World Development Indicators.

When compared to China, India lags behind in many spheres. However, India still holds a lead over China in software domain. According to N.R. Narayan Murthy, at some levels, the ability to interact with the customers in English is still not as easy for the Chinese technical graduate as it is for the Indian graduates.[1] Indians have had at least a 15 - 20 years lead over the Chinese in large project management. India has advantages over China due to its great information technology skills, rule of law, English language knowledge and democratic system of governance. The Economic realities of India are the political challenges of Indian state.

1. After 60 years of Independence

India completed her 60th year as a free nation on August 15, 2007. Our young nation can be really proud of its numerous achievements although the key development challenge of all inclusive economic growth still remains a distant dream. Eight areas of Indian success are enumerated here.[2] Green revolution, which started in 1965 not only transformed India into a food-surplus economy but triggered the expansion of the rural, non-farm economy. The white revolution, initiated by Dr. Verghese Kurien has made India the largest producer of milk in the world. The economic reforms of 1991 opened up the minds of Indian corporate leaders to the power of global market, helped them accept competition at home and raised the confidence of consumers. The economic reforms have encouraged entrepreneurship and given confidence to businessmen to dream big, create jobs, enhance exports, acquire companies abroad and follow the finest principles of corporate governance. Idealistic journalists and Editors like N. Ram, Arun Shourie, Shekhar Gupta, Sucheta Dalal, and independent media persons like Barkha Dutt and Rajdeep Sardesai have made Indian media, free and independent, becoming a watchdog of democracy. The telecom revolution has brought India - the urban and the rural together and has brought fresh confidence to the people as they could reach out to anyone anywhere. The space technology has revolutionized the world by bringing television to millions of Indians. The atomic energy and Indian nuclear programmes have made possible the successful utilization of nuclear energy in defence, power generation, medicines and allied areas. The software revolution laid the foundation of India's spectacular progress, and India's Information Technology (IT) exports grew from $150 million in 1991-92 to $31.4 billion in 2006-07. The above mentioned eight areas of success have made the nation proud of it achievements. India is now one of the two markets driving the world's economic growth (the other being China). Most of the top 20 MNCs in India are Fortune 500 companies. Corporate India is gaining a lot of muscle and confidence as globalization spreads. For many MNCs Indian companies are giving tougher competition now. While Indian Management talent is increasingly recognized at the global level, it still has a long way to go. While gifted with versatility, adaptability and problem-solving skills, Indian Managers have to develop "global-mindset"- an indepth and hands on exposure of working across different regions, geographies and cultures. Indians have proved that individually they can excel and compete with the best in the world. We must be able to do so collectively. We need to do more to unleash the full potential of our people's creativity and enterprise. We need better team work and the ability to build wider social and political consensus around the ideas of change and modernity. We have to strengthen and revitalize our institutions of governance, policy-making and education so that we are able to harness the energies of our people better. For the first time in 14 years, International credit rating agency, Standard and Poors (S&P) has raised India's credit rating to investment grade, Moody's Investor's service did it in January 2004 and Fitch Rating in August 2006. The upgrade is likely to spur the flow of foreign investment into power, steel and other industries, which receive less than a tenth of the funds going China's way. The 43,700 crore India media and entertainment (M&E) industry seems to be set to outgrow the Indian economy in less than five years - between 2007 and 2011 to become a Rs. 1 lakh crore industry. The Indian Cinema exhibition industry is being revolutionised through a host of changes. Unlike the U.S. where only 35 percent of film industry revenue comes from box office collection, 57 percent of revenues in India come from domestic exhibition of movies. By the end of 2007, more than 135 multiplexes with 500 plus screens offering 1.6 lakhs seats are expected in India. By 2010, the Indian film industry is targeting a revenue of Rs. 14,300 crore. What we are witnessing is a new era of growth and an exciting stage of development. Our entrepreneurial talent and innovative capabilities are opening up new vistas for the country's future. India's ranking in world's competitiveness as arrived at by the IMD recorded a significant improvement in 2006 as compared to 2005. Among a list of 61 prominent world economies India secured 29th rank in 2006 against 39th position in 2005. According to Amartya

Sen, on the economic front the big news is not only that the average growth rate of the economy is high, but that the Indian success has come in areas of hugely competitive modernity, not in the sequestered use of traditional skills and old fashioned comparative advantage.[3] Along with rapid growth has come an unprecedented increase in government revenue and the budgetary limits for public spending are now much less severe, opening up more possibilities for much needed social development. The growth of the Indian Mutual Fund over the years has brought international recognition. In the latest awards list by Lipper - the Reuters company that tracks about 1.3 lakh mutual fund schemes in 21 countries, has recognized the following 11 fund houses of India namely, Birla Sun life MF; Can bank MF; DSP Merill Lynch MF; Escorts MF; Franklin Templeton MF; HDFC MF; Kotak Mahindra MF; Prudential ICICI MF; Reliance MF; SBI MF, UTI MF; while Reliance Mutual Fund got six awards across categories like equity bond and sectoral schemes, Lipper ranked Prudential ICICI MF as the top fund house in the Indian Industry. India's savings and investment rates have crossed 30 percent of the gross domestic product (GDP). India has made remarkable achievements in the software and business process outsourcing sectors, the explosions in telecom sources and the growth of the pharmaceutical, engineering goods and automobile industries. The line up of MNCS—Google, Yahoo, Intel, IBM, Adobe, Microsoft-who have opened their own research and Development centres in India is bound to brighten the economic growth of the country. The country has become most attractive R&D hub of the world[4]. The country is emerging as a hot destination for investment in research and development. This is bound to provide lot of employment opportunities to our scientists. IBM has two centres one each at Bangalore and Delhi. Adobe has two centres one at Bangalore and one in Noida. According to C. Ram Manohar Reddy, much of this reflects a new entrepreneurial dynamism in the private sector. Indian economy now is in the midst of an investment boom. India's telecom growth, marked by a subscribed growth from 14.8 million in 1997 to over 225 million in 2007 represents more than a "connectivity revolution".

Table 3. Showing key indicators of Indian Economy

		2002	2003	2004	2005
1.	GDP (Current US$)	506.04 billions	600.66 billions	694.70 billion	785.47 billion
2.	GDP Growth (Annual %)	4.00	8.00	9.00	9.00
3.	Agricultural land (% of land area)	60.83	60.81	NA	NA
4.	Agricultural, value added (% of GDP)	20.77	21.02	19.56	18.6
5.	Exports of goods and services (% of GDP)	14.51	14.77	18.95	NA
6.	Fixed line and mobile phone subscribers (Per 1000 people)	51.6	64.03	84.52	NA
7.	Foreign Direct Investment net inflows (BOP) current US	5.6 billion	4.58 billion	5.3 billion	NA
8.	Services value added (% of GDP)	52.56	52.54	53.16	53.78
9.	Merchandise trade (% of GDP)	21.36	24.89	28.20	NA
10.	Financial performance of Indian Railways	Year 02-03	Year 03-04	Year 04-05	Year 05-06
	Gross traffic receipts (Rupees in crore)	41068	42905	47370	54492

Source: World Development Indicators 2006 and Indian Economic Survey 2006-2007.

Dr. Man Mohan Singh has said: "India's IT sector has experienced fantastic growth in recent years." Regarding the pace of economic reforms, he admits that in a federal system the politics is the art of the possible......... We are a relatively slow moving elephant economy, but when the elephant does move, it makes a sizable difference".[5] Klams Schwab, Chairman, World Economic Forum has said: "I see a big change in corporate India. Indian Companies................ have adapted well to the opening up of the economy............ I am impressed by how well Indian Companies have moved from a management style rooted in a protected environment to (one) which is exploiting global competitiveness". Konkan Railway Corporation (KRC) holds now patent for several technologies and has won international accolades. It was the first project which relied on indigeneously developed technology and Indian technical expertise. Over the 760 km stretch, there are 178 bridges, including a two km bridge over the Sharvari river and 93 tunnels. The Karbride tunnel, nearly six and a half km long, is a technical marvel. This entire project was designed and built by Indian engineers in just seven years and India can be rightly proud of this marvelous achievement of Indian engineers and entrepreneurs. The Delhi Metro in many ways, is a development of the Konkan railway model.[6] One of the most noticeable trend in Indian management is that new Indian millennial managers are beginning to reshape the companies they are working in for many ways. The new generation managers want (*i*) global branding, (*ii*) well defined career progression, (*iii*) high remuneration, (*iv*) variety of assignments, (*v*) stability, (*vi*) learning opportunity, (*vii*) authority, (*viii*) a transparent work environment and (*ix*) high degree of empowerment. The new youngsters with MBA degrees look for stratospheric growth, huge work differentiation and a sense of entrepreneurship. Change, growth and modernity have only added to Indian complexity and changing social structure. Social change and geographical inclusion are tougher to achieve than economic change. Inclusion is about creating an enabling environment for the less privileged sections to enhance their competitiveness productivity and output to claim their due share of the growth pie. The growth of some business centres in the country has been most remarkable. The speed of the development of Gurgaon is breath taking. The sort of construction that would take 25 years in Britain, seems to have came up in Gurgaon in less than 2 years. Bibek Debroy and Laveesh Bhandari believe that while reforms have benefited the poorest, there is little doubt that inequality has increased, triggering discontent among the underprivileged.

2. Changing Role of Government

Dr. Man Mohan Singh has said: "The Government has an important role to play in not only sustaining higher rates of growth but also in making the growth process more inclusive, socially and regionally. Governments must also play an active, creative and constructive role in providing and facilitating access to modern education and good health care.[7] There are numerous challenges that the Government of India and state government have to face in order to make India a global superpower. Development must be inclusive. "It has not yet provided to crores of our SC/ST and OBC brothers their rightful share in the nation's development. It has not sufficiently addressed the problems and needs of agriculture and small scale industries. Our villages need better roads, accessible and affordable health care and better educational opportunities for their children[8]." Sanjay Subramanyam, has rightly said: "The market and capitalism will never free themselves from politics, what ever the gurus of liberalization may tell us." In every economy, policies of the government with respect to taxation, monetary and fiscal policies and over all economic policies are bound to play a very important role. Reserve Bank of India (RBI's) annual report 2006-07 contains a wealth of information and data. Twenty-six states (barring Sikkim and West Bengal) have enacted fiscal responsibility legislations. The net result is that the consolidated revenue deficit of all states put together was an unbelievable .03% of GDP in 2006-07. As many as 17 states were revenue surplus during the year, the correction facilitated by buoyant tax revenues aided by implementation of value-added taxes (VAT), higher devolution and transfers from the centre in pursuances of the recommendations of the Twelfth Finance Commission[9]. The states stepped up their capital outlays, especially for education, rural and infrastructure development. Many states have managed to bring down the ratio of gross fiscal deficit to gross state domestic product to less than 3%, two years ahead of the targets set by the Twelfth Finance Commission. Eighteen state governments have set up a consolidated sinking fund to redeem their debt: Eight states have set up a redemption fund to honour guarantees that might devolve on them. Chief Ministers of various states are now inviting foreign investors in their respective states for various projects. Narendra Modi, Gujarat Chief Minister has done very well during 2006-07. Gujarat, which was ranked No. 2 in 2005-06 with investment of Rs. 24,531 crore, has emerged as the most preferred destination during 2006-07, trebling this figure and comfortably pipping the second placed Andhra Pradesh. The latest figures of 2006-07 are as under[10].

Table 4 Showing Total Investments in Some States

S.No.	*State*	*No. of Projects*	*Total Investment (Rs. Crore)*	*Percentage*
1.	Gujarat	86	73,170	25.8
2.	Andhra Pradesh	105	25,173	8.9
3.	Maharashtra	142	24,330	8.6
4.	Tamil Nadu	157	24,299	8.6
5.	Orissa	23	14,806	5.2

* Percentage of total all India Investments pie.

The total value of all investment proposals for 2006-07 in Corporate India is placed at Rs. 2,83,440 crore. That is a 116 percent increase over the figures for 2005-06. Some of the significant central government initiatives have been as follows:

1. Five Year Plans based on planning commission reports and their implementation.
2. Economic reforms - dismantling of the licence permit Raj and return of MNÇs.
3. Bank Nationalisation.
4. Liberalisation of telecommunication sector in 1992.
5. Financial sector liberalization and allowing HDFC, UTI Bank, ICICI Bank and other banks to avail opportunities for adoption of new technology.
6. Opening up of the Insurance sector.
7. Highway Development programmes for bringing roads to prosperity and linking up the country.
8. Allowing private equity.
9. The Right to Information Act 2004.
10. Setting up of National knowledge commission headed by Sam Pitroda.
11. Announcement of a National e-government plan in 2004 and the establishment of State Wide Area Network (SWAN).
12. A well-articulate Broad band policy in December 2004 and delicensing of the use of wireless equipment in land 2.4 GHz to 2.4835 GHz.

3. Conceptual Fallacies in Indian Planning

P.V. Indiresan, Former Director IIT. Madras has pointed out the following conceptual fallacies[11] :

1. Higher education is a right and should be available to every one who seeks it. About 20 percent graduates are unemployed /under employed because they have only academic learning and no vocational training.

2. Labour has a right to perpetual increase in wages. Pay increase merely produces temporary euphoria and not productivity.

3. Central subsidies alleviate poverty. The poor do need help but the central government cannot identify the poor accurately cannot target them effectively and cannot prevent heavy leakages of subsidy.

4. House owners enjoy unearned income and deserve to be taxed heavily. Incidental corruption is collateral damage and cannot be avoided.

5. Economic expansion occurs best in crowded cities and resultant slums are unavoidable. Nothing can be worse for business and finance in a globalised realim than a climate of policy uncertainty. For India to sustain growth rate of 9 percent in the eleventh plan period, it should display greater maturity and clarity of purpose in policy-making. In the case of SEZs, the discourse on rehabilation surfaced months after the centre cleared about 200 such projects all over the country. The centre's North East report card revealed that Rs. 1267 crore invested in the region led to the creation of less than 18000 Jobs[12]. Prof. K.N. Raj found serious deficiencies in district planning and state planning. He revealed growing inequalities in per capita state incomes and worsening of the income distribution. During the last 15 years there has been a constant drift from socialistic approach to planning. Capitalism and privatization are now the more popular slogans. Labour class conditions are deteriorating and even the real wages in manufacturing fell 22 percent during last 5 years. Wealth is being concentrated in the hands of a few multi-national companies. The falling calorie consumption is clearly indicative of malnutrition and under-nutrition in India. The 61st NSSO shows that per capita calorie consumption in India has declined.

Calorie Consciousness

Table 5. All India average, per capita food intake in Kilocalories/day

All India	*1972-73*	*1993-94*	*1999-2000*	*2004-05*
Rural	2,226	2,153	2,149	2,047
Urban	2,107	2,071	2,156	2,020
Bottom 30%	1,504	1,678	1,626	N.A.
Middle 40%	2,170	2,119	2,009	N.A.
Top 30%	3,161	2,672	2,463	N.A.

Sources: NSSO 31st round, 2007.

	Rural 2002-03	*Rural 2003-04*	*Rural 2002-03*	*Rural 2003-04*
A.P.	2,103	1,995	2,143	2,000
Assam	2,074	2,067	2,135	2,143
Bihar	2,225	2,049	2,167	2,190
Gujarat	2,142	1,923	2,172	1,991
Haryana	3,215	2,226	2,404	2,033
Karnataka	2,202	1,845	1,925	1,944
Kerala	1,559	2,014	1,723	1,996
M.P.	1,895	1,933	2,229	1,954
Maharashtra	1,895	1,933	1,971	1,847
Orissa	1,995	2,023	2,276	2,139
Punjab	3,493	2,240	2,783	2,150
Rajasthan	2,730	2,180	2,357	2,116
Tamil Nadu	1,955	1,842	1,841	1,935
U.P.	2,575	2,200	2,161	2,124
W. Bengal	1,921	2,070	2,080	2,011

Sources: NSSO 61st round, 61st Round, 2007.

The per capita caloric consumption has been falling steadily in every NSSO survey between 1972-73 and 2004-05. Our industrial system, according to C.K. Prahalad is generating more goods and services than at any point in history, delivered through an ever-growing number of channels. We now need a new frame of references for value creations. According to Professor Prabhu Dev Konana the global success of "brand India and continuous reinforcement of successes cloud many perceptions of reality and fall into the trap that researcher call persuasion bias. Leaders exhibit classic self-attribution bias that successes are due to their action and failures are due to others like farmers, society or NGOs".[13]

4. Managing Changing Rural India

Rural India is rapidly changing. Accordingly to Omkar Goswami, there are two rural India's. One that has growing income and consumption and the other which remains mired in abject poverty.[4] The 61st round of National Sample Survey (NSS) carried out its quinquennial survey of consumer expenditure covering 79,298 rural and 45,346 urban households across the country. Among the key findings it has been brought out that the average rural monthly per capita expenditure (MPCE) for Kerala was 81 percent higher than the all India figure of Rs. 559 or Rs. 2730 per family of 4.88 people. The figures for Goa are 76 percent higher, Haryana 54 percent greater; Punjab 52 percent higher; Himachal Pradesh 43 percent more and Jammu 42 percent greater. There were the better off regions of rural India. Unfortunately many eastern states are much worse off with MPCE for Orissa being Rs. 399; the people living in Orissa village were 29 percent worse than the all India rural average, Bihar 25 percent poorer, Jharkhand and Chattisgarh 24 percent worse off. On the whole there are two clearly perceptible faces of rural India. The top 10 percent of the rural population was significantly well off. Over the years there has been a significant shift in consumption patterns. The 60th round survey of NSSO has estimated that upto 9 percent of males in rural areas and 8.1 percent in urban areas are unemployed. The corresponding statistics for females were 9.3% in rural areas while 11.7% in urban areas. In rural India, the chain of middle men eat away nearly 70% of the price of the farm products.

According to the Food and Agricultural Organization (FAO) the average field of rice between 2003 and 2005 was 3.034 Kilograms per hectare. For wheat the corresponding figures were 2.688 kg/ha and for mustard average 909 Kg/ha. India's agricultural sector is projected to grow by about 2.5 percent in 2007, it is a slide from the 2.7 percent growth in 2006. S.Ganesan, adviser to the consortium of Indian Farmers

Association reveals, despite India having the largest number of agricultural scientists on the Government pay roll in the world over 30,000, their research track record has been most abysmal. The reasons for China having out performed India in agriculture are three fold; technological improvements accruing from research and development, investment in rural infrastructure and an increasingly liberalized agricultural policy.[15] There is one village near Delhi, Radadhana, where the Midas touch of real estate developers turned land into gold.

In less than ten years the trickling down effect of India's economic boom is clearly noticeable in Village Radadhana in Sonepat district barely two KM off the G.T. Road, about 50 km north-west of Delhi. The total land of the village is 2800 acres of which about 2000 acres have been acquired by builders at an average of Rs. 50 lakh per acre. Barring some 200 families of landless people belonging to backward classes, every family must have a net worth of Rs. 1 Crore : says Sarpanch Manoj Saroha.[16] This type of economic trickling down effect can be noticed in many rural areas which are very near to metropolitan cities. However, on the whole the rural India is having structural inequalities. According to Montek Singh Aluwalia, Deputy Chairman Planning Commission than "too many people in India were engaged in agriculture and this was the main cause of the rural urban income divide. Poor state of infrastructure is the single biggest obstacle to growth". The biggest challenge before Indian economists is their ability to cope with the change that high economic growth would bring about. The Government of India tells us that over 112,000 farmers have committed suicide since 1993. The top 10 percent of the rural population is now significantly well. Their monthly per capita expenditure (MPCE) in 2004-05 was Rs. 1,957 or an annual expenditure of Rs. 85,500 per household of 3.64 people. Rural India therefore is rapidly changing and it needs better managing. Managers must develop interest by viewing issues holistically with the surrounds of the issue and not in isolation. The National Rural Employment Guarantee programme (NREG) has been expanded to 330 district in the country with a financial allocation of Rs. 12,000 crores in the budget 2007-2008. It promises to provide guaranteed employment to atleast one member of every rural household for 100 days. With effect from

1st April, 2008, NREG scheme will be extended to all districts of India.

5. India—a Symbol of Socio-economic Change Through Democratic System

Dr. Man Mohan Singh, has said, "India is one of the leaders in showing the world the way forward in dealing with one of the biggest challenge of preventing the so called "clash of civilizations" and enabling not just a dialogue between civilizations but creating a "confluence of civilizations." Speaking on "Is Politics overtaking the New Economy" Mr. P. Chidambaram said: "The force that is driving India is young India, the entrepreneurial inventiveness and innovational spirit of India." M.S.Vindi Banga of Unilever said: "There is an urgent need to create a socio-economic structure that will play a key role in ensuring all inclusive growth." Upliftment of the common man should be the prime concern of the government. A recent study conducted by American Express published by Mercer consulting has reported that in all there are 8300 HNIs and 7,11,000 super rich people in India. The number of affluent individuals in Maharashtra has been estimated at 200,000 and Mumbai has atleast 25000 dollar millionaires - they have atleast Rs. 4.5 crore in liquid funds that are investible and they are categorized as high networth individuals (HNI). Between HNIs and super-rich in Maharashtra alone, they have a whopping $60 billion in liquid investible funds. By 2009, India will have atleast 10 lakh super-rich people. Mumbai is home to the largest number of affluent individuals and has the faster growing affluent population in the world. Due to the nature of coalition government, things seem to be falling apart, the centre cannot hold. While the strength of Indian democracy has withstood the last six decades of social, economic and political developments, there are numerous challenges to democratic government. Rule of law is inextricably connected with democracy. Corruption, criminalisation of politics and politicalisation of crime are some of the main challenges in democratic governance. India remains united politically as well as geographically because our power elite had mastered the art of mergers and acquisitions much before India Inc. Ltd. It is ideological opportunism dictated by the exigency of power that keep India united. The state of political and economic governance of the nation is not very praiseworthy or commendable. There are many partners with in the government who have little enthusiasm for reforms. There is no political opposition to focusing on infrastructure yet the performance is abysmal. India has created a great renaissance of human creativity and ingenuity during the last one decade. The pluralistic diversity and the inherent unity of Indian psyche have been brilliantly captured in the idea of *Vashudhaiva* Kutumbakam (the world is one family) that we find the roots of this changing India. We want to build a "knowledge society" and a nation of economic prosperity with values of democracy, secularism and social equity. Swaminathan S. Anklesaria Aiyar has written: "After 60 years of independence, it is disgraceful that every village does not have a pucca road, electricity, telecom, and a functioning school and health centre. Instead of providing these basics which would have converted many villages into prosperous towns, successive governments have spent 14% of GNP on subsidies most of which benefit the non-poor." India's economic boom in the last 15 years has brought a boom in stock markets and urban real estate has added billions to the wealth of those already well off. It has also hugely benefited two categories of people-those farmers within a 5 kilometre radius of any major city and landless migrants to cities who lived in unauthorised illegal settlements which were later regularized. Mr. Jagamohan former Union Housing Minister estimated that four-fifth of Delhi's settlement areas were once illegal and later regularized. The economic boom has converted millions of small and marginal farmers who lived within a 50 kilometer radius of any major city, and made these farmers into lakhpatis and a few even crorepatis. Bangalore is now home for 10,000 millionaires. As per a study by Amercian Express, there are 83,000 High Net individual and 7,11,000 super-rich people in India. While Mumbai and Delhi account for the bulk of this numbers, Bangalore, Chennai and Kolkota had shared the third positions. India's Special Economic Zones (SEZ) are bound to create lot of investment and economic growth in the long run. India can easily solve the problem of land disputes arising out of acquisition of land for developing SEZ. Rather than forcefully acquiring land; if the owners of land of these Special Economic Zones, by government ordinance/law, directed to make land owners part stakers/part owners/promoters in the project, there will be no problem for land owners to allow their land to be converted into Special Economic Zones. Central Government should issue ordinance or pass special legislation for this purpose.

Mr. Arjun Singh, Human Resource Development Minister of Union of India, addressing the Vice-Chancellors at the conference on "Development of Higher Education" said on October 10, 2007: "Higher education is the sick child of education. It is not serving the cause of the young people of India. The academic world needs to come to terms with today's reality and the 11th plan gives us enough elbowroom for experiment..... The general education system has been divorced from the Indian reality. It is now time to redraft the entire curricula." It has now been revealed that 75% of all college and 56% universities had never been accredited by National Assessment and Accreditation Council (NAAC) on quality parameters.

Prof. K.N. Raj had advocated "inclusive growth". Prof. Raj had realized that growth had to be inclusive to be politically viable in a parliamentary democracy. Government policies such as expansion of public sector, nationalization of large industries, hostility to foreign capital and macro-economic stability. Indian entrepreneurs could attract state resources for their benefit in the form of infrastructural business below their costs and protection of small firms. Prof. Raj concluded that "the bulk of the population of this country feel that they have not been benefited in any obvious way from the development." The World Bank's India development policy review, (2006) mentioned two most pressing challenges for public action in India—the institutional reforms to enhance the capacity of public sector institutions to ensure the effective delivery of core services and sustaining rapid growth making the process of economic growth more inclusive across sectors, across region and bringing the benefits of higher incomes and living standards to more people". The Eleventh Plan approach aims at creating physical assets, human capital and capabilities and opportunities for productive employment especially for the lower-middle class and the poor, and it will help in achieving sustainable and inclusive growth.

6. Managing "the Transforming Economy"

During the last one decade, India has been described as a "transforming economy" rather than a developing economy by the United States Agency for International Development (USAID). It indicates the unique position it is gradually occupying in the world. Influential recent studies such as the ones carried out by Goldman Sachs and MC Kinsey suggest that the Indian story of the last one decade see India as a giant in the making, a crucial pole of the future world economic order. By 2006, Indian industry had proven its resolve to complete by going global. During the last one decade, every big industry ranging from auto to engineering to pharma to IT has a substantial global manufacturing and R &D footprints. In India between 1999-00 and 2004 - 05 rural poverty declined from 26% to 22%. That is, 44 million people rose above the poverty line. According to latest NSS survey, between 1993-94 and 2004-05 the following notable figures are worth reporting.[17]

1. Per capita consumption of edible oil rose by 30% in rural areas and 18% in urban India.
2. The proportion of rural households using cooking gas rose six-fold, from 2% to 11.7% while the urban proportion doubled to 89%.
3. The proportion of rural households using electricity rose from 34% to 54%. The urban proportion rose from 74% to 94%.
4. Purchase of readymade garments rose by 75% and of hosiery products threefold, in both rural and urban areas.
5. Refrigerator use increased from 1% to 4% in rural household and from 12% to 32% of urban households.
6. Between 1999-00 and 2004-06, the proportion of T.V. households rose from 19% to 26% in rural areas and from 59% to 66% in urban areas.

During the last two decades, India Inc. is gradually become richer and richer in terms of assets. Gradually over the years Indian Inc. has developed a global mindset. Leaders proclaim India's strength lies in its ability to bypass industrial economy and leapfrog from an agricultural economy to a service-based economy. The supporting argument is that most developed countries are service-based economics. India's success is due to transition to knowledge economy.[18] During the last few years, the new Indian millennial managers are beginning to reshape the companies they are working for. They are highly achievement oriented, are tech-savvy, relish an entrepreneurial work environment, are networked and importantly, have great pride in being Indian managers. Unlike that past when there was a scramble for overseas posting, today many of them are preferring domestic assignment over foreign ones. For young Indian managers, while entry-level salaries have reached stratospheric levels, the right environment, brand reputation of the firm, faster career advancement and high levels of empowerment are crucial. These generation managers are virtually forcing a revolution in Indian companies. For the young generation managers it is not just a great place to work out finding a company that is the best place to launch a career, they generally look for the following aspects. 1. Area of posting. 2. Job profile - learning on the job and autonomy. 3. great brand equity and profile of the company. 4. Money and other perks. 5. Degree of empowerment and a sense of entrepreneurship—in fact all together in the same place.

According to Bikranjit Maitra VP and Head, HR Infosys Technologies young, managers want: (1) global branding; (2) well defined career progression; (3) high remuneration; (4) Variety of assignments; (5) security; (6) learning opportunities; (7) authority (8) transparent work environment and (9) foreign assignments. Arie de gues in 1988 has said: "the ability to learn continuously may be a company's only sustainable resource of competitive advantage". According to Gita Piramal, "Be it the IT or the ITES Companies, the pharmaceutical or the automobile companies, in fact, companies in any sector you care to name, we (Indians) have a substantial number of future world-class leaders in the making. India is the biggest and the most innovative laboratory in management practice in the world today." A steady stream of innovations is gushing forth from India of the 2000s.

Public sector undertakings have their very important role to play in making India a self-reliant and global leader. In 2006-

07 the top 10 public sector undertaking had their sales as shown against each.

Sl.No.	*Name of the PSU*	*Sales in Rs. Crores.*
1.	Indian Oil Corporation	2,00,923.09
2.	Bharat Petroleum Corporation	1,07,452.3
3.	Hindustan Petroleum Corporation	96,918.15
4.	Oil and Natural Gas Corporation	56,903.7
5.	Steel Authority of India	40,291.75
6.	Bharat Sanchar Nigam Ltd.	40,135
7.	NTPC	32,631.7
8.	Mangalore Refinery and Petrochemicals	32,376.88
9.	Food Corporation of India	22,976
10.	Chennai Petroleum Corporation	74 72,57

Government Investment in PSUs has been going up since independence. But it trebled from early 1990s to 2006 after the reforms were ushered in. A comparative figure of top ten companies from 1969 to 1997 and 1997 to 2007 indicate their ranking in terms of assets as given in.

Table 6. Showing Top Ten of India Inco. by Assets

1969		*1997*		*2007*	
TATA	505.36	TATA	37,510.80	RELIANCE (MUKESH)	1,14,086.40
BIRLA	456.40	BK-AV BIRLA	19,497.94	TATA	98,233.05
MARTIN BURN	153.06	RELIANCE	19,345.50	RELIANCE (ANIL)	47,929.85
BANGUR	104.31	RPG	9,664.12	ADITYA BIRLA	45,568.89
THAPAR	98.80	ESSAR	9,593.78	ESSAR	35,138.09
S NAGARMULL	95.61	OP JINDAL	5,456.10	OP JIND AL	26,886.40
MAFATLAL	92.70	MAC	4,782.10	HINDUJA	23,196.88
ACC	89.80	LM THAPAR	4,434.09	BHARATI	20,628.72
WALCHAND	81.11	ISPAT	4,425.35	STERLITE	19,324.34
SHRIRAM	74.13	GROUP USHA	4,210.87	BAJAJ	16,960.74

Source: Dr. Gita Piramal; prowess
Figures in Rs. Crores

A young new generation of leaders came at the helm of Indian Inc-Ratan Tata became chairman of the group in 1991; Kumar Mangalam took over a larger role from 1995 and Anand Mahindra moved in M&M in 1993. It is high time to explore how the development of innovative management system and processes can utilize the large pool of talent and resources available within Indian family and set India on the road to becoming an economic superpower. The emerging realities, concerns and challenges of the new Indian economy need to be analysed and studied in depth. India's current high rate of growth seems to have robust foundations making. India is the biggest and the most innovative laboratory in management practice in the world today. A steady stream of innovations is gushing forth from India of the 2000s. Another noticeable development of the Indian economy is retail loans by the banks. Middle and high income homes in India have increased from 1.16 Crores in 1997 to 2.98 Crore in 2007. Retail loans have emerged as the biggest area of growth for Indian banking sector. Banks are catering to a new generation of young people that give on credit. Manufacturing and Capital goods lead the rampaging industrial revolution as can be seen from the following indicates.

Table 7. Indices of sectors that contributed the most

Category	*29 Nov 2005*	*6 Feb 2006*	*Growth percentage %*
Capital goods	5,608.48	7,070.14	26.06
Metal	5,927.25	7,181.44	21.15
Health Care	3,039.22	3,477.67	14.42
BSE Auto	4,128.22	4,589.98	11.19
FMCG	1,598.19	1,754.02	9.70

Source: BSE - From 9000 to 10,000.

Young people now take loans for everything, from buying an automobile to going on a holiday. There is a huge retail credit opportunity that has surfaced during the last two decades. The banking sector's home loan portfolio has increased by about Rs.63,000 crore and other retail loans such as personal loans and credit card received portfolios by about Rs. 46,000 crore in 2006-07. In the last three years 2004-2007, the number of credit cards has more than doubled and that of debit cards has almost quadrupled. There were 22 million credit cards and 70 million debit cards in India by January 2007. The development of the Indian Stock Markets over the last ten years is truly an amazing spectacle. For India, the positive factors include a consistently strong economic growth and a stable macro-economic and regulatory environment. Despite an impressive records of reforms and initiatives pertaining to the stock market, foreign players and influences seem to be the determining factors. On July 2007, there are 4910 companies listed on the BSE, with a market cap of over Rs. 46 Lakh Crore. The scams caused by Harshad Mehta forced the Government of India to set up the Securities and Exchange Board of India (SEBI) in 1993. The same year Foreign Institutional Investors (FIIs) were allowed to invest in the Stock Market. In 1994 the government approved setting up the National Stock Exchange (NSE). The mutual fund industry also took wings at the same time. In 1995 online trading was opened to brokers. In 1996 the National Securities Depository (NSD) was opened and companies with licences were allowed to open depository services. The IPO Boom of 1993-94 and the introduction of free pricing in public issues provided companies with access to cheap capital. Angel Investors and Venture Capitals started investing in India. The global liquidity overflow trickled to India, between 2004-2007 India has spent over $35 billion in global acquisitions. Dematerialization has made our life extremely simple. Indian retail investors got MNC Shares, cheap when Foreign Exchange Regulation (FERA) Act 1973 forced multinational corporations to limit foreign ownership to 40% (51% in some high technology areas) and MNCs were asked to off load the balance shares at the price fixed by (CCI) Capital Issued (Control) Act 1947. However after economic reforms, the Foreign Institutional Investments has been liberalized and flood gates have been opened and India could get FDI of $11 billion. Patrick French has said: The economic boost of the last 10 year has engineered a propulsion that has changed the way Indians think about themselves. They now have a chance to shape their destiny.

7. Emerging New Role of Private Equity

Dhirajlal Hirachand Ambani, or Dhirubhai introduced the equity culture for the corporate India and scripted the equity growth story in 1982 when 5,50,000 - 13.5% Pref. shares were issued as right to equity share holders. According to estimates of consulting firm Bain and Company, well over 100 private equity funds are swarming around for deals, making India the fastest-growing private equity market in Asia, with a 67 percent compounded annual rate since 2002. According to Prof. Talmor of LBS worldwide, there are normally three drivers of private equity: the governance arbitrage, leverage arbitrage and the regulatory arbitrage." Some private equity firms emerge winners due to the following factors:

1. Build a long term reputation;
2. Have a consistent track record of returns;
3. Ability to build the right team;
4. Manage the stars within the firm;
5. Bring on board corporate leaders;
6. Build trust and relationships with investing companies;
7. Take right decision to exit at right time.
8. Help companies make course corrections and tough decisions;
9. Manage limited partners and funders of the P.E. firm.[19]

Private equity is making a difference by not only bringing in stability and deeper pockets but by their international networking, by helping in strategic decisions and improving corporate governance. The performance track record of Indian P.E. investments is a big plus to attracting great capital. The four noticeable key trends of P.E. are as under:

1. Putting money in medium and large firms;
2. Investments in family managed business;
3. Growing interest in publicly listed companies.
4. Averaged size of investments increasing.

In 2006, about 300 private equity investments were clinched to India worth about $7.5 billion and up to March 2007, about $ 3 billion of private equity transactions are estimated to be completed. The PE deals during the last four years were as under:

Table 8. Showing P.E. deals and their value

Year	*Number of deals*	*Value ($ billion)*
2004	60	1.1
2005	124	2.0
2006	302	7.9
Upto June 2007	200	6,82

(*Source*: Grant Thomiton)

With more PE coming into India, the role of minority share holders in a company may increase. In 2007, Blackstone completed the largest buy out deal in Indian PE history with its 200 million acquisition of Intelenet. Blackstone with overseas operations, shape strategy and even use the company as its vehicle for further acquisitions in this space. "The private equity management is very different from traditional management in the sense that its time frame is five to six years and its objective is fastest growth possible," says Ranu Vohra, CEO of Avendur advisors.

Table 9. Showing Top Ten P.E. deals in India

Sl.No.	*P.E. Investor*	*Investee*	*Value ($mn)*
1.	Kohlberg Krais Roberts & Co	Flexronics Software system	900
2.	Carlyle Group	HDFC	650
3.	Avenue Capital	SKIL	500
4.	Oak Hill Capital Partners gen N×360/KLI	Vertex Data Science	426.2
5.	Providence Equity Partners	Idea cellular	400
6.	DE Shaw	DLF	400
7.	Tanasek Holdings P TV	Tata Tele Services	
8.	Black Stone	Eenadu Group	275
9.	GLG Partners	Idea Cellular	213
10.	Morgan Stanley Real Estate	Oberoi Construction	150

(*Source:* Grant Thomton).

According to Donald N. Sull of London Business School, "Leading private equity firms have pioneered a set of practices that enhance a firms's value. They typically leave their portfolio companies better than they found them. These times are more focused, leaner and better equipped to spot and seize opportunities in their market, even after becoming public companies again." Private equity major Blackstone's acquisition of 50% stake in Gokaldas exports is significant in that it is the first major buyout of a listed company. Black Stone, the world's biggest private equity investor, has set up shop in Mumbai and has invested around $525 million.

Table 10. Showing Top Asia Deals of Private Equity Market

The Asian PE market saw 316 deals worth $4.81 billion as on 5 August 2007. The top 5 deals of the past fortnight were worth about $140.65 million

Target	*Target Nation*	*Investor*	*Investor Nation*	*Deal Value ($M)*
JBF Industries	India	Citigroup Venture Capital International	Hong Kong	118.00
Aquamats Holdings	China	SAIF Partners	Hong Kong	10.00
Promac Engineering Industries	India	Undisclosed Indian investor	India	8.00
Veryad.com	China	Undisclosed Indian investor	China	2.65
Unitech Printed Circuit Board Corporation	Taiwan	CLSA Capital Partners	Hong Kong	2.00
Tech Tribe Networks	India	Canaan Partners, RB Webber	US	NA
Catholic Syrian Bank	India	Gartmore Investment, Siguler Guff & Co.	UK	NA
Sula Vineyards	India	Future Capital Holdings	India	NA
JRG Securities	India	BPEP International	UK	NA

For the first time, India has crossed China in terms of PE investments in the first six months of 2007.[20] India has seen $3.7 billion worth of private equity investments ahead of China which saw investment to the extent of $2.6 billion during the first half of 2007. PE fund for India in infra-structure will soon be based on individual asset-level funding.

8. Managing Indian Financial Sector

In 1998 Narasimhan Committee report set the tone for what came to be called second generation reforms in the financial sector. During the last ten years there has been a rapid transformation of the financial sector. Today banks, insurance companies and the capital market and its intermediaries are much better regulated and capitalized and are enabled to face global competition. Automatic Teller Machines (ATMs) and Points of sale (Pos) terminals provide convenience to the customers. By and large I.T. development in Indian banking so far has been vendor driven. Globalisation, liberalization, customer's demands, technological advances, and internet facilities have changed the face of banking in India. According to M.V. Nair, Chairman and Managing Director, Union Bank of India, Mumbai, the banking industry will have to face and address the following ten challenges:

1. Retail renaissance;
2. Seeking and reviewing new markets;
3. The decision to outsource;
4. Financial inclusion;
5. Monitoring credit quality;
6. Achieving comprehensive governance of risk management;
7. Basel II - driving enterprise - wide change;
8. Corporate governance moving to greater transparency;
9. Grooming the next generation of talents of employers and officers;
10. Consolidation resulting in synergies with regard to geographies, organizational cultures technology and other factors.

These are very interesting times for Indian banks, particularly with India Inc. now realizing its global ambitions. Indian banks have taken bold steps to go global by spreading their wings overseas; foreign banks are increasing their presence in India and are growing rapidly. The few signs of consolidation in the banking industry have become visible. For the fourth consecutive year HDFC has re-emerged as No. 1 bank in the 13th B.T. KPMG Best banks survey.[21] With the economy surging and business going global, India's best banks will need not fast world class size but new skills and operational efficiencies to remain competitive. To drive the massive changes and to manage the potential risk, India needs a much stronger banking sector. Capital account convertibility, integrated pan-India payment system and synergies with the growth in capital markets and insurance, would be among the many expected systematic changes that would fundamentally reshape the dynamics of the banking sector. According to K.V. Kamath, the financial services sector in India has played a critical role in fulfilling the needs of the growing and increasingly diverse economy, offering high quality services to businesses and individuals alike. India's financial regulatory framework is comparable to international standards. State Bank of India (SBI) is the country's largest bank and nearly 50 percent of its total business is done on core banking solution (CBS) and is on its way to being fully wired.

9. Brand Management

The criticality of building a brand, sharp customer focus and providing value for money to the customer by driving the costs down, improving the productivity and quality are essentially customer friendly approaches that are essential for sustainability of an organization.[22] Branding is the art and cornerstone of marketing which has to take care of the six well known attributes of a brand namely attributes, benefits, values, culture personality and consumers needs. The concept of branding is already under going dramatic changes - form USP (the Unique Selling Proposition) to OSP (Organisational Selling Proposition) to HSP (the Holistic Selling Proposition) Branding is all about building trust which hopefully leads to loyalty and ultimately purchases. Trust is generated over time, often over years and makes people permanent customers. According to the Economic Times 6 June 2007 the most trusted India's brands 2007 are as under[23].

HRD and Education Segment

1. Mgt Education	—	IIM
2. Engineering Education	—	IIT
3. Education School level	—	Kendriya Vidyalaya
4. Professional/ Vocational	—	NIIT
5. Public Schools	—	DPS
6. Insurance	—	Life Insurance Corporation, SBI Life, ICICI Prudential Life Insurance.
7. Mobile Handsets	—	Nokia
8. Retail/Leisure	—	Big *Bazar, Pizza* Huts, Cafe Coffee Day, Mc Donald's.
9. Consumer Durables	—	Videocon, Onida, LG, Philips.
10. Auto	—	Splendor, HH Passion, TATA SUMO, Bajaj Pulsar, TVS Victor
11. Telecom	—	Airtel, Reliance India Mobile, BSNL, TATA Indicom
12. Mutual Fund	—	Reliance Mutual Fund, SBI Mutual Fund, UTI Mutual Fund
13. Foods	—	Britannia, Tata Salt, Amul, Dabur, Maggi.
14. Home and Fabric Care	—	RIN, Ariel, Fevicol, Surf.
15. Beverages	—	Tata Tea, Bournvita, Horlicks.
16. Personal Care	—	Colgate, Vicks, Lux, Dettol, Lifebouy
17. Banks	—	State Bank of India, ICICI Bank, Bank of India
18. Chocolate/Confectionery	—	Parle, Cadbury diary milk, 5 Star, Kitkat.
19. Airlines	—	Indian Airlines, King Fisher Airlines, Air Sahara.
20. Consumer durables	—	Videocon, Onida, LG, Philips

Every brand that has been around for a decade or so has the potential to lose their appeal, loyalty and consumer's choice. Brands need constant renovation in terms of new product design, packaging, improvement or new color combinations. The brand's role is to remain instantly recognizable for credibility and distinctiveness. Good business must spend time to reconsider brand strategy. Out of every 100 brands that are born, 90 perish. Brands that are wellnurtured, well managed and kept relevant to a new audience have generally a long life. Brand building is a fairly long term and on-going exercise. Sometimes brands decline in the country of origin but become the hottest selling brand in another country[24]. Brand experts feel relatively newer brands like Amul, Titan and Brooke Bond have potential to grow into iconic brands.

10. Managing Human Assets and Developing Individuals

Government of India, Ministry of Human Resource Development has the key responsibility for adopting various strategies and innovative approaches, in collaboration with the state governments to develop the human capital. Watson Wyatt's Human Capital Index study found—that the real investment in Today's knowledge society is not in plants and machines, it is in people. India today needs global competencies, global opportunities and consequently global aspirations. Literacy rate of Indian People above 15 years was 61.0 percent in 2005 and it must be raised to almost hundred percent. A great human capital asset nation like India needs an education revolution with a massive expansion and qualitative upgrade of both higher education and professional training. National Knowledge Commission (NKC) has proposed to set 1,150 more universities and an additional 50 national universities. We need an integration of all forms of higher education, supported by massive investment in infra-structure and quality improvement for manifold expansion. Quality of education also needs India's attention - Inspite of the various pockets of excellence, none of the Indian universities ranks among the top 50 worldwide. T.V. Rao has said, "The future is going to be a competency era and it is people who will give strategic advantage to firms. The future is full of opportunities. The future is going to be the future of genuine Human Resource Development managers".[25] In order to meet the challenges of globalization, Quality challenge, people challenge, Technology challenges, Challenges of Social responsibility and high commitment to the nation are the main issues for the HRD Professional. Corporate sector has an important role to play in building a culture of learning organizations. We must give HRD a top priority both in the corporate world and the general education to all citizens. In India, it is shocking that after six decades of independence and the spending of millions of Crores, literacy is hardly 65% and most people, who complete school, cannot read simple paragraphs or do simple maths sums.[26]

H.G. Wells wrote—"If we continue to leave vast sections of the people of the world outside the orbit of education, we make the world not only less just but also less secure." A good education system must recognize the race each student runs with himself or herself and that helps students develop well-rounded personalities and global mindsets. During the last few years increasingly the jobs of white collar elites in fields as diverse as investment banking, aircraft engineering and pharmaceutical, research have begun flowing to India due to India's constant upgrading of various high value skills and knowledge related areas. Infosys devotes $65 of every $ 1000 in revenue to training. IBM by contrast spends just $6.56. Recently Airbus hired Infosys to design the part of the wing of the superjet jumbo A380 aircraft. India has to constantly upgrade training for high value skills.[27]. India is one of the pioneers in organizing course at Business School on entrepreneurs. Prof. Radha lyer at K J Somaiya Institute, Prof. Suresh Rao at S.P. Jain Institute and Prof Arya Kumar at BITS Pilani are now organizing courses on "entrepreneurship". These courses are behind many successful entrepreneurs.

11. Managing Ship Building Industry and Ports

For so many decades Indian ship building industry has not been able to exploit the international boom and the potential of sea trade with neighbours. There are 12 major ports in India, namely Visakapattnam, Chennai, Mumbai, Kolkata-Haldia, Kandla, Jawaharlal Nehru Port, Paradip, Mangalore, Mormugao, Tuticorin and Cochin. The National Maritime Development Programme (NMDP) 2006 has set the trend for public - private partnership (PPP) in the development of infra-structural facilities in major ports and empower them to achieve world class standards in their performance. While the NMDP envisages an investment of Rs. 55,58 Crore, 64 percent of which would come from private parties. According to R. Sampath,the total cargo handling by the port majors during 2005-06 was 456.20 million tons against 383.75 million tons in the previous fiscal year, registering a double digit growth percentage. Rising consumer demand from developing countries, coupled with increasing disposable income will translate into more trade and cargo movement. Ship building industry of India also needs investment and attention of the government and global investors. Ship building and ship-repairing industry has huge potential in India. India is well placed to supply cheap skilled labour. New ship builders like Bharati Shipyard and ABG Shipyard have come up with the abolition of industrial licensing in the 1990s. Sea king owned by Nikhil Gandhi is setting up a shipyard at Pipavan Gujarat to build ship of up to 300,000 dead weight tonnage. ABG has set up a major Shipyard costing Rs. 1600 Crore in Dahej Gujarat. It will build up to 25 ships a year, making it a major Asian player. P.K. Ruia is building up a mammoth shipyard at Haldia costing Rs. 3,000 Crore. It will be among the biggest in the world, building 12 ships a year of panamax size. The project will include ship-breaking and ship-repairs units, as well as a mini steel plant and captive power plant.[28] Adani group is setting up a Rs. 1000 Crore shipyard at Mundra in Kutch, adjacent to its new deep water port. Tata steel plans a shipyard at its new coast-based plant in Orissa. Tata has formed a joint shipping line with NYK of Japan.

12. Managing Stress and Managing work-life Balance

Long hours of work, high level of competitiveness too high ambitions, work overload, noisy and over crowded city-life, tight deadlines of job, air pollution, frequent traveling and Jet lag problem, insecurity of job, lack of adequate physical exercise, family problem are some of the reasons for growing stress in today life. One in every four person is suffering from stress in New Delhi.[29] Samir Parikh carried out a study for Max Health Care and found the following reasons for stress—percentage of respondents admission and reporting—(Stress-0-Meter).

1.	Inadequate exercise	56%
2.	Faulty life style/Inadequate leisure	48%
3.	Inadequate Dietary habits	30%
4.	Inadequate rest	39%
5.	Inadequate coping skills	46%
6.	Faulty time management	35%
7.	Presence of physical illness	30%
8.	Individual personality factors	20%

According to Piyali Das Gupta, more than 50% of employees in corporate India suffer from stress and the workplace efficiency of 44% corporate workers is impaired by stress. According to Psychiatrist Samir Parikh, "Corporate stress results in loss of productivity, decreased corporate profits and increased absenteeism." There is certainly a lot of performance related stress in the corporate world, primarily because organisations peg revenue targets above the output level of their employees. Late/erratic working hours and loss of one's personal life add to the stress. As a consequence, burnout and attrition rates are on the swing. According to a research study by National Institute of Mental Health and Neo-sciences Bangalore, 65% executives are victims of stress according to their own admission, 22% suffer from a lower level of stress and 11% suffer from very high stress level. This research has been carried out in 2007 based on study of 250 CEOs by Dr. Purohit of Ujjain. About 10% of Delhi kids are said to the hypertension patients—a number that is growing every year. During the last three decades there have been a spate of writings on managerial and executive stress in India and abroad.[30] In many companies, employers are working even beyond twelve hours a day and there is lack of work - life balance. Family life is being neglected. This needs to be rectified. In modern life depression, fear, anger, sense of insecurity, value disgust are all generated due to the body and mind stress. Stress and its consequent effects need to be managed effectively. The quality of your life is the quality of your communication to yourself.[31] There are many techniques and methods to reduce stress. Yoga, meditation, regular morning walk, a successful family life and balanced work-life balance and good time management can help reducing stress "there are many forms of self-help techniques which may be used to counteract stress and deal with the problems when they are recognized and controlled.[32] Burnt Out Stress Syndrome (BOSS) is a possible consequence of a high level of stress, personal frustration, inadequate coping skills in the long run, major personal, organizational and social costs in the present day tension filled world.[33] The following ten points action plan is very effective in preventing and fighting stress and burnt out stress syndrome:

1. Ensure six monthly medical check up and keep away from alcohol, drugs and unhealthy food habits.
2. Carry out regular physical exercise or yoga or games for atleast 45 minutes.
3. Ensure a good and balanced diet;
4. Devote sometime everyday for meditation, prayer or spiritual exercise;
5. Avoid long hours of hours by having five minutes relaxation after every 2 hours and keep open channels of communication;
6. Utilize psychological counselling services if afflicted by stress or burnt out syndrome.
7. Listen to good music, see good films and stay with open communication with your wife, children, friends and colleagues and lead an active social life;
8. Identity early warning signals of stress and adopt suitable coping strategies.
9. Effective time management reduces stress.
10. Take a balanced and holistic approach to deal with stress related problems or burnt out stress syndrome.

13. Managing the Uncertain Future

All India Management Association organized the flagship event, the National Management convention from 6 and 7th October 2006 at Delhi. Mark Fuller, Chairman, Monitor group, USA observed; I think the future has a great deal to do with the past and the recent years have been full of good news for the Indian economy. The future of India depends on deepening the clusters that exist and looking at challenging ones. There is a pervasive sense of optimism and confidence in India. Keep the optimism and don't let it change into lethargy. Regarding problems of acquiring land for developing SEZs creatively Dr. Edward De Bono has suggested that rather than forcefully acquiring lands of villagers, if the owners of these lands are made partners, giving them part stakes/ownership in the project, they will be happy to give their land. In the knowledge revolution lies the seeds of the future because the knowledge is the currency of business. Shiva Nadar, convention chairman said, "Now with the markets booming, no one can afford not to be in India! I think it is important to know where you are and not just where you want to go if you want to manage the future". During the last fifteen months, not only has the perception of the world about India changed, but what is significant is, that our perception about ourselves has changed. India has synergized its advantages into competitiveness and is now driving the competitiveness of major economics" say Kamal Nath. Mr. Peter Sehwartz, the Chairman, Global Business Network has said: "Keep your eyes on the horizon. There will always be problems and challenges. The biggest challenge for India is sustaining the hope and optimism of the huge population. If there are inequalities then diversive forces will raise their head". A good manager needs to think of the global world - about the other competitors, about markets, about quality of products and services and about brand management. The world expects India to play a larger role and we should live up to its expectations. According to R.A. Mashelkar the future of India is not in Indian technology but in Indian talent. Pramod Bhasin CEO GENPACT says: "The Single most important issue we face in the future is managing talent. The war for talent has just begun when too many jobs are chasing to few good people resulting in demand-supply inbalance." India has tremendous opportunities in the areas of vaccines, and biopharmaceuticals, biogenerics and traditional medicines. India can become a leader for most dramatic innovations. Innovative India should lead the world and become a knowledge powerhouse for the world. India has tremendous amount of talents in the country. Indian entrepreneurs have great strength they can adapt to changes in technology, can overcome cultural and mindset issues and can manage diversities very well. There is a great future for almost everyone in the retail sector and we need to address both urban and rural India. India must think holistically about a brand. It is time for India to take branded offerings into the global market. A global strategy is required for building a brand that include picking the domain, selecting the right market, and thinking globally about a brand name for its positioning on the world scene. Mr. L.N. Mittal, the Steel king has said, "There is still further scope in the future. The road to lined global business is long, winding one, unless you walk with care and caution, you might slip..... Indian business needs more cooperation from the government." For the success of a company, it is important to understand the following six components of changing pattern (1) Customers, (2) Employers, (3) Suppliers, (4) Banks, (5) Government, and (6) Share holders. For successful business in the global competitive era, you also need to understand the cultural, linguistic and regional diversities and the world business trends. For managing the future, the entrepreneurs and business leaders must first learn to manage themselves—their time, their health, their mind - set, their optimism, and their own commitment to universal values. We must facilitate individuals and organizations of India to realize their full potentials. With globalization, managing people diversity is one of the greatest challenges of the future. Globalization, diversification, wider customer interface, changing organizational structure and government regulation each of these result in increasing diversity and effectively managing diversity is a great challenge for the future. At present 21 of 100 global leaders were from India and till 2035 the country would supply knowledge workers and skilled labour to the rest of the world. Our educational system and HRD ministry have therefore a great role to play in searching, nurturing and empowering the entrepreneurial and leadership talents in India. The unprecedented rise in economic inbalances in the last 15 years has led to social inequalities. The withdrawal of state from sectors that mattered to the poor such as water, sanitation, education and health care, huge cuts in welfare and development spending, the slashing of subsidies and life support to the poor, Privatisation and the unprecedented rise of corporate power have increased the rising inequalities in India. Around 837 million Indian live on less than Rs. 20 a day and the landless labourers, slum dwellers, rural poor, the landless, the unemployed are suffering immensely under the present situation. Regarding effectively managing these socio-economic inequalities. Mr. P. Sainath, Rural Affairs Editor, *The Hindu* says "What raises the biggest danger to democracy is our inability to disconnect from this growing gap". India's special zones promise to become booming microcosms of industrial, commercial and residential complexes and are capable of converting rural areas into developed urban centres of development.

14. The Overall General Performance of Changing India

Business Today report about India's GeNext—An AC Nielsen Survey on how people perceived India's growth, found—that 63 percent of Indian youth feel that globalization has been extremely good and beneficial. The sample was of 1380 persons (79 percent men, 21 percent women). According to the survey reports Areas where Indian has progressed the most are as under[34]:

1. Business and Commerce - 57%
2. Science and Technology - 43%
3. Education - 19%
4. Quality of life - 15%
5. Infrastructure and Transportation - 14%
6. Arts, Culture and Entertainment - 11 %
7. Defence - 10%
8. Tourism - 6%
9. Equality of Women - 6%
10. Human Rights - 5%
11. Health - 3%
12. Poverty Eradication - 2%
13. Environment - 2%
14. Politics - 2%
15. Spiritualism and religion - 2%
16. Social Equality - 2%
17. Law and Order - 1%
18. Sports - 1%

According to the same survey areas where India needs to improve to become a developed country were as under:

1. Poverty Eradication - 65%
2. Infrastructure and Transportation - 64%
3. Law and order - 64%
4. Education - 62%
5. Science and Technology - 54%
6. Business and Commerce - 49%
7. Politics - 48%
S. Health - 39%
9. Quality of life and standard of living - 38%
10. Human Rights - 37%

India's per capita consumption expenditure, according to an Asian Development Bank study is $1,194 (Rs. 48,495). The contribution of the small and medium enterprises (SME) to the GDP is 9 percent. The number of Indian companies listed on the London Stock Exchange is 24. Top management in Indian are at No. 36 on the list with a buying power of $92,750 (Rs. 38.03 Lakh). However, India benefits from a large tier of Educated, English-speaking local talent, making management pay more, immune to fluctuations in the international market. According to T.V. Mahalingam, the IT Boom has turned Bengaluru, Hyderabad, Pune and Gurgaon into cities of opportunities, but on the flip side, it has turned these cities into urban nightmares. It is very heartening to find that philanthropy and social service have many new takers in young professionals who are giving back to the society like never before.[35] India has achieved a new paradigm - India's gross domestic product has almost doubled to about $500 billion; the market capitalization of companies listed on the Bombay Stock Exchange has roared from 77 billion to $ 197 billion and even exports have more than doubled to $44 billion. The corporate India is much more professionally run, it follows many international best products and it certainly is more global in its outlook. According to Arjun Sen Gupta, Chairman of the National Commission for Enterprises in the unorganized sector "The whole approach to planning in India should change. Only maximizing economic growth should not be the aim. Planning has to occupy itself entirely with the improvement of the poor and vulnerable sections of society through social engineering.[37] The march towards economic development has not really given adequate results because over 300 million people still go to bed each night without dinner and approx. 77 Percent of our working population earns less than Rs. 20 a (PER) day. But what has been achieved during last sixty years needs to be recognized and celebrated in some manner. High levels of inequality can disrupt social cohesion and could lead to civil war. Prime Minister Man Mohan Singh says that unless the poor participate in fast economic growth, uprisings could disrupt our nationhood-over 150 out of 600 district are affected by Maiost—Violence. We need to be optimistic and have faith in the ability, determination and courage of Indian people who are bound to usher into a new paradigm in years to come. It boils down to the strength of character of the one in leadership, can he work for a larger good? Can he restrain his ego and his greed[38] Within a decade, India will have to overcome a slew of challenges if it has to emerge as a developed nation. With half of its population under 24, India can earn a rich demographic dividend if it invests in giving its young the right skills, attitudes, knowledge and global mind-set. The Indian industry must develop—"Social responsibility". Milton Friedman, Nobel Prize Winner for Economics, in his book "Capitalism and Freedom" has said, "there is one and only one social responsibility of business—to use its resources and engage in activities designed to increase its profits so long as it stays within the rules of the game, which is to say, engages in open and free competition without deception or fraud." The last 25 years laid the foundation for India to enter the global competition by demonstrating its potential to become global power. V. Tulasi Das, Chairman and Managing Director Air India has said: "Let the employees be stockholders in the company, let them all feel that sense of ownership that is so crucial for success." India should follow this mantra for developing India as a world super economic power. Indian corporate leaders are constantly busy in new acquisitions and mergers. Acquisitions, "between 1991 to 2003 have been very fast. The number of companies investing outside India have increased from 187 to 1700—a growth of 809 percent. This growth rate is higher than the rate at which domestic firms investing abroad are have made many Indians getting into

Table 11. Showing Spending spree Global buyouts have helped Indian firms spread faster

	Global subsidiaries/ Acquisitions	*Global revenue* (Rs. Crore)*
Tata Steel	Corus	87,204.00
	NatSteet Asia	4,052.08
	Total global revenues	91,256.08
Hindalco	Novelis	36,797.20
Adani Enterprise	Adani Global FZE	1,328.98
	Adani Global Pte	3,032.27
	Total global revenues	4,361.20
Tata Tea	Tetley	3,151.00
Ranbaxy Labs	Ranbaxy Netherlands	2,503.23
Tata Motors	Tata Daewoo Com V	1,646.66
Bharat Forge	CDP Bharat Forge	903.26
	Bharat Forge Inc	116.97
	Bharat Forge Alum	153.55
	Bharat Forge Kilst	202.88
	Bharat Forge Scott	78.51
	Total global revenues	1,455.17
Dr. Reddy's	Betapharm	849.2
Crompton Greaves	Pauwels Trafo Belg	784.02

This is not a ranking. It is an indicative list and may not include all companies.

* Latest available revenues. Source: Capitaline Plus, Company Sources, BW research

the corner room in American Corporate World. Rakesh Gangwal (US Airways), Rono Dutta (United Airlines), Rajat Gupta (MC Kinsey), Raj Gupta (Rohm and Hass), Ajit Jain (head of Barkslyre's "Rupercat" Insurance business) and this is not counting Indians (CEOS in Silicon Valley or Dinesh Paliwal of ABB. Indians are surely capable of managing MNCs most successfully. Indian Economy, According to Centre for monitoring

Indian Multinational invested abroad in the following acquisitions and mergers in various countries.

Table 12. Acquisitions by Indian MNCs Abroad

Year	*Total acquisitions in the world*	*USA*	*UK*	*Germany*	*Singapore*
2001	45	25	8	2	1
2002	34	19	5	1	1
2003	57	19	8	3	2
2004	53	21	7	2	1
2005	63	20	8	2	3
Total	252	104	36	10	8

(Figures indicate the number of acquisitions in some countries and total in the world—*Source:* (MIE: Mergers and acquisitions).

A total of 12 companies made it to the third annual Forbes Asia Fabulous 50 list. Bharat Heavy Electricals Ltd, Bharti Airtel, Grasim Industries, HDFC Bank, ICICI Bank, Infosys Technologies, Larsen and Toubro, Reliance Industries, Satyam Computer Services, Tata Consultancy Services, Tata Steel, Wipro, did not have to leave home to find success and continue to outshine and dominate the annual ranking of big gap, profitable companies in Asia. These companies are reaching out to the country's rural customers and shoring up the country's infrastructure at a furious pace.

15. Managing Retail Sector

"Indian retail markets are full of opportunities—for growth, for diversification and market size" says Chairman, India Retail Forum ED, ICICI bank Limited. The growth of Indian retail has shown the world how quick it can adopt to hi-tech products and services and will again set a record of sets in setting up the world-class retail formats across the country in record time. Indian retail industry has attached investment over INR 200 billions (over $4 billion) in creating infrastructure, system and shop-fit. The additional retail space is expected to add INR 30 billion ($6.67 billion) of business to retail. Leading retailers have recorded and increase in sales between 50 to 100 percent in the year 2006 over the previous year 2005. According to Mukesh

Ambani, "Organised retail has the potential to trigger socio-economic transformation on an unprecedented scale in our country and will bring about enormous spin-off benefits to the Indian economy and its various constituents. I want to create a virtuous circle of prosperity by bringing farmers, small shop keepers and consumers in a win-win partnership. Our goal is to over haul in one swoop retailing and farming, banking them through a "state of the art" distribution system with proper cold storage and transport that will give consumer fresh food at lower prices and farmers bigger incomes." During the past three years various segments of retail growth has been shown in the table below:

Table 13. Showing Percentage of Organized Retails

Retail Segments	*% Organised 2004*	*%Organised 2005*	*% Organised 2006*
Clothing, Textiles and Fashion Accessories	13.6%	15.8 %	18.9 %
Jewellery	2.0%	2.3%	2.8%
Watches	39.6%	43.5%	45.6%
Footwear	25.0%	30.3%	37.8%
Health and Beauty Care Services	6.0%	7.6%	10.6%
Pharmaceuticals	1.8%	2.2%	2.6%
Consumer Durables, Home Appliances/equipments	7.8%	8.8%	10.4%
Mobile handsets, accessories and Services	6.5%	7.0%	8.0%
Furnishings, Utensils, Furniture—Home and Office	6.7%	7.6%	9.1%
Food and Grocery	0.5%	0.6%	0.8%
Catering Services (F&B)	5.7%	5.8%	6.9%
Books, Music and Gifts	9.8%	11.7%	12.6%
Entertainment	2.6%	3.3%	4.1%
Total	3.0%	3.6%	4.6%

Source: Images India Retail Report 2007.

Rajan Bharati Mittal, Joint Managing Director, Bharati Enterprises in his keynote address to IRF has said: "Organized retail has tremendous growth potential in the fast expanding

Indian Economy. Not only will it benefit millions of consumer but also farmers, small manufacturers and artisans. The sector will also offer enormous direct and indirect employment opportunities while attracting huge investments in building the supply chain infrastructure, adding to the economic growth of India, especially in the rural areas." Indian Retail Market 2006 is given in the table below.

Table 14. Showing Indian retail Market/in Percentages

India Retail:2006 (at current Prices) Retail Segments	*Indian Retail Market 2006**				
	India Retail Value (Rs. Crore)	*Organised Retail (Rs. Crore)*	*% Organised within segment*	*%Share in total organized pie*	*%Share in total retail Pie*
1. Clothing, Textiles and Fashion Accessories	113,500	21,400	18.9%	39%	9%
2. Accessories					
3. Jewellery	60,200	1,680	2.8%	3%	5%
4. Watches	3,950	1,800	45.6%	3%	>1%
5. Footwear	13,750	5,200	37.8%	9%	1%
6. Health and Beauty	3,800	400	10.6%	1%	>1%
7. Care Services					
8. Pharmaceuticals	42,200	1,100	2.6%	2%	4%
9. Consumer Durable, Home Appliances/equipments	48,100	5,000	10.4%	9%	4%
10. Mobile Handsets	21,650	1,740	8.0%	3%	2%
11. Accessories & Services					
12. Furnishings, Utensils	40,650	3,700	9.1%	7%	3%
13. Furniture - Home & Office					
14. Food & Grocery	743,900	5,800	0.8%	11%	63%
15. Catering Services (F&B)	57,000	3,940	6.9%	7%	5%
16. Books, Music & Gifts	13,300	1,680	12.6%	3%	1%
17. Entertainment	38,000	1,560	4.1%	3%	3%
Total	1,200,000 $270 Bn	55,000 $12.4 Bn		55,000 $12.4 bn	1,200,000 $270 bn

Source: Images India Retail Report 2007.

According to Subodh Kant Sahai, Chairman of India Food Forum and Minister of Food Processing Industries, Govt. of India has said "Besides huge export potential, organized Retail in

India needs fresh and processed food worth US Dollar 30 billion by the year 2010". At present 21 million people are employed by the Indian retail sector. The impact of the rapid evolution of modern retail would be confined to perhaps 3 to 5 lac retailers across India (largely in relatively in rural towns) coming in the district range of about 1000 hyper markets and about 3000 + super markets by 2010. Over-all the universe of small retailers will actually increase by 2010. The Future Group, Tata Group, Land Marks, RPG, Reliance, Bharati, Wal - Mart, Aditya Birla, Hero Group, Carrefour/Tesco are the prominent retailers now operating in India.

16. BPO—Coming of Age

BPO industry has provided lot of job opportunities to young educated unemployed youth. The outsourcing industry is not only about call centres; it includes non-voice processes such as finance and accounting, insurance, I.T. Services etc. The average age of the employees is around 25-35 years. Business Process Outsourcing (BPO) and Information Technology Outsourcing (ITO) are significantly impacted by offshore and nearshore resources. High attrition rate, shortage of trained manpower, wage increases and security of information are main challenges of BPO. The Indian BPO Sector is clearly going places. The acquisition of Kanlay, a US listed BPO for $1.25 billion by Capbemini is the largest deal in the BPO sector. The largest Indian BPO, Genpact, is lastly to list soon. Most BPOs have chosen to list in the US because most of their clients are there and because of their keener appreciation of BPO valuations. Indian BPOs started off by providing voice-based services, and although that remains important they are today increasingly providing a whole variety of backoffice services such as accounting and pay management. Indian' advantage is no longer cost-although that remains a compelling proposition with saving of 40% to 50%. The main challenge is to deal with attrition and tighten data-security. About 325 global deals have come for renewal in 2007 which represent over a fifth of active contracts.

17. Managing India's Infrastructural Development

Finance Minister P. Chidambaram, addressing the parliamentary consultative committee urged - the states to adopt a public-private partnership model (PPP) in view of the enormous investment needs which could not be met by public sector alone. The Government of India has set up the India's Infrastructure Project Development Fund (IIPDF) with Rs. 100 Crores as the initial corpus to provide financial support to the state development activities. The country would have to develop 40,000 km of highways, increase traffic handling capacity at ports from 737 million tons to 15,00 million tons maintain the growth momentum in freight and passenger traffic at 8-9 percent annually and enhance power generation capacity to 600,000 MW. Infrastructure development would need an investment of about Rs. 14,50,000 Crores ($320 billion) during 11th Five Year Plan. According to the economic outlook for 2007-08, macro economic policy must work to preserve and strengthen the conditions that favoured robust economic growth while maintaining monetary and exchange rate stability. Buoyed by software and outsourcing boom, India has now become the sixth largest commercial services exporter. The service exports of the 25th member European Union were ($480 billion). Japan $108 billion), China ($73.9 billion) and Hongkong ($62.2 billion). India's service exports were at $ 56.1 billion in 2006.

18. Managing Great Places to Work and Retaining Talents

In the present day competitive world, retaining talents is a tough managerial work. The companies that are good to work in stick to the following commandments.[39]

1. Hiring through referrals—Happy employees, will only refer those who fit the company's needs.
2. Being a centre for learning—providing extensive training including using internal specialists.
3. Offering cross-functional growth opportunities.
4. Always completing the feedback loop. Great work places correct the wrongs.
5. Not leaving flanks open to talent outrage. They make concrete succession plans.
6. Binding empowerment into systems. No amount of training can ensure this.

7. Ensuring fun, impromptu parties, family outings, etc. for freshers create profitable companies. Human Resource Managers have to use all possible strategies to retain the talents and good workers.

One of the most challenging task of managers today is to make work-place attractive and great to work by employing various HRM Strategies.

Table 15. Showing the Top 10 Great Places to Work 2006

Rank 2005	*2006*	*Company*	*HQ India*	*On List**	*Ownership*	*Year Founded^*	*Compar Churn(°,*
1	5	RMSI	Noida	2	Owned by Risk Management Solutions (RMS) Foreign	1992	12.75
2	16	Classic Strips	Mumbai	3	Private held Company Indian	1987	12
3	N.R.	Google India	n.a.	1	Wholly owned subsidiary Indian	2004	Not share
4	1	Federal Express	Mumbai	4	Wholly owned subsidiary Foreign	1997	19
5	6	Marriott Interna-tional	n.a.	2	Managing Company: Marriott India Foreign	1999	32.25
6	9	MindTree Consulting	Bangalore	3	Publicly held company Indian	1999	12**
7	3	NTPC	New Delhi	3	Government of India (89.5 per cent) Indian	1975	0.5
8	N.R.	SAP Labs India	Bangalore	1	Wholly owned subsidiary foreign	1998	9.6

(contd.)

Rank 2005	2006	Company	HQ India	On List*	Ownerhsip	Year Founded^	Compar Churn(°,
9	20	American Express India	New Delhi	2	Wholy owned subsidiary Foreign	2002	Not Share
10	N.R.	Freescale Semi-conductor India	Noida	1	Wholly owned subsidiary foreign	2004	11

Explanations—N.R.: Not Ranked; N.A.: Not Applicable.

Indian business has developed its frontiers in extending the concept of Corporate Social Responsibility (CSR). Meera Mitra in her book "India's Corporate Social Responsiveness in a globalized world" has reported many examples of CSR and shows how it can range from direct corporate interest to the larger community, beyond the company and its immediate environment and to the larger issues that concern society. TATAS, Infosys and Wipro are the role models in this respect. Milton Friedman has written: Companies could make as much money as possible while conforming to the basic rules of society - both those embodied in law and those embodied in ethical custom.

Summing Up

In a federal set up, the performance of various states have differed and each state has her own priorities. Those states who have addressed social issues like investment in agriculture, education and health have been able to weather the storm of change. Assam has put up a good show in 2007 in poverty reduction by trimming it down by 21 percent. Uttar Pradesh has improved the most in primary education in 2007. Punjab, Himachal Pradesh, Haryana, Maharashtra, Kerala and Tamil Nadu in consumer market have per capita incomes between Rs. 63,000 and Rs. 30,000 while in Chandigarh this figure is Rs. 71,000. Gujarat state has seen all round development and a fillip in infrastructure and investment. Between 1993-94 and 2004-05 poverty level has dropped in India by 8.38 percent, from 35 percent to 27 percent in a period of 10 years. The changing face of Indian society is bringing with it new challenges and opportunities. Managing the changing India is a most difficult task. Gender discrimination, technology, demographic structure, changing and shifting consumer pushing companies to focus on employees well being and better work environment. Dr. Man Mohan Singh has stated that economic reforms of the past 15 years had indeed produced a new class of dollar millionaires and billionaires who need to give back something to society. Capitalism could lead to a more skewed growth in society. High growth can be sustained only if all categories are equally involved, otherwise it can lead to social unrest. RBI - Governor says demographic dividend is advantage for India. The average Indian is presently only 23 years old and India has the opportunity and the ability even to drive potential reforms so that the system is reformed to reward young and dynamic leadership. Michael D.V. Rake, Chairman of KPMG International is of the opinion that "India is at the cross-roads. It has made huge progress since the reforms started in the early nineties. Today it is firmly on the global map. It is not just being talked, but it is a reality". The biggest challenge for Indian companies will be to retain their integrity and engage in developing community programmes. Companies have to simultaneously look at the growing domestic demand, while catering to the overseas market. India must promote and incentivise Research and Development; inculcate a research mind set and culture in universities; make it easy to patent innovations and strive for universities to become hubs for innovation; and ideas and not just graduate students for disseminating information. Mrs. Mira Kandar in her book "Planet India—how the fastest growing democracy is transforming America and the World", has said; One day soon when a critical mass of the talent, the money, and the market is in Asia, a tipping point will be reached and India will be joining the game or even winning the game to inventing new rules for new games.[39] In the life of a nation 60 years are not a long period; particulary for India which believes in cyclical time-frame. In last 60 years, many achievements have been made which can make any Indian proud. We are however always reminded of the memorable address of Pt. Jawaharlal Nehru on 14 August 1947 in which he said: "The achievements we celebrate today is but a step, an opening of opportunity, to the greater triumphs and achievements that await us. Are we brave enough and wise enough to grasp this opportunity and accept the challenge of the future?".

References

1. N.R. Narayana Murthy—Opportunity Enclave India-Singapore—Hindu Chennai Edition August 18, 2007, p. 15.
2. N.R. Narayan Murthy—Eight Areas of success—The Hindu-Independent India at 60, 5th August 2007. p. 6. The author has summarised India's areas of success as given in this para.
3. Amartya Sen—India in the world—Independence India at 60- Hindu Chennai special issue August 15, 2007, p. 2.
4. Sujata Dutta Sachdeva —World's R&D hub— Times of India New Delhi, SUNDAY 1/4/07.
5. Dr. Man Mohan Singh—"moving the Elephand" Fortune 53 October, 31, 2005, p. 54.
6. Dr. E. Sreedharan—New temples of modern India. The Week December 31, 2006, p. 82.
7. Dr. Man Mohan Singh India at sixty. The Nation is one of the move -The Hindu—Chennai. Independent India at 60, p. 2.
8. Atal Behari Vajpayee—getting ready for a global role—India Today—Anniversary Issue—Dec. 26, 2005, p. 257.
9. The Economic Times—Chennai. The Fine Print—RBI Annual Report has good news—4th September 2007, p. 10.
10. Krishna Gopalan—Gujarat on the Top Again—Business Today, September 7, 2007, p. 22.
11. P.V. Indiresan—Vision 2020—Failed by Fallacies—The Hindu Business fene—14 June 2004, p. 8.
12. Mahendra Kumar Singh and Nitin Sethi — Rs.1200 Crore got N.E. Only 18,000 Jobs — Times of India 1st April 2007.
13. Prabhudev Konana—Teaching professor of Texas at Austin—Need to wake up to the Realities—The Hindu—Chennai, September 22, 2007.
14. Omkar Gowami — The two faces of rural India — Business World, 28 May 2007, p. 38.
15. Pallavi Aiyar—Agriculture: Where India and China stand. The Hindy Chennai, September 3, 2007.
16. Deepender Deswal—"Almost every family's croreparti in this village." Times of India, 24 July 2007.

17. Swaminathan S. Anklesaria Aiyar—Rural Prosperity does not win elections, Times of India, 6th May, 2007.
18. Prabhudev Konana—Need to wake up to the realities—The Hundu, 22 September, 2007.
19. An IM report—Indian Management—May 2007, p. 20.
20. Sharma and R. Samson—PE Funds and India Infrastructure story, Economic Times, Dt. 14.8.07.
21. Sanjay Narayanan—From the Editor—Business Today, February 25, 2007.
22. Abad Ahmed and OP Chopra—"Passion to win"—How winning companies Develop and sustain competitive Edge". All India Management Association, Excel Books Private Ltd., New Delhi, 2004, p. 110.
23. Economic Times—India's most trusted Brands 2007—Categorywise listing of Brand Equity's most. Trusted Brands 2007 Survey—6 June 2007, p. 384.
24. Jagdish Shelth—"If time change—change your audience Indian Management, November 2005, p. 30.
25. T.V. Rao—Future of HRD—Mac Millan India, Delhi 2003. Preface, p. VIII—IX.
26. Swaminathan S. Anklesari Aiyar, Market Shump and Inequality—Economic Times, Chennai, 29 August, 2007, p. 14.
27. Anand Girdhara Das—India's edge goes beyond outsourcing, Times of India, New Delhi, 5 April, 2007.
28. Swaminathan S. Anklesaria Aiyar—Ship Building: India's next star industry—Times of India—8/4/07.
29. Kamayani Singh—Stress alarm 10% kids have high BP—Times of India, New Delhi.
30. Marshall and Cooper—(1979) Executive under pressure—A Psychological Study. MacMillan—London (1979).
31. Swami Sukhabodhananda—Oh Mind—Relax Please—Published by Prasanna Trust Bangalore, 2002, p. 75.
32. Dr. K.M. Mathur—Challenges to police, Human Rights and National Security—Kalpaz Publications, Delhi, 2003.
33. Krishna Mohan Mathur—Indian Police—Role and Challenges—Gyan Publishing House, New Delhi, 1994, pp. 47-48.
34. Business Today, September 9, 2007, p. 34.

35. Bhattacharya—The New Age Do Gooders—Business Today—August 26, 2007.
36. Anil Sachdev, Mudit Mehrotra and Priyanka Jaitly—The Talent Paradox Business World—Special Issue—23 April 2007. Table Showing the Top 10 Great Places to work given by the research team headed by Anil Sachdev.
37. M.K. Venu—Govt. and Big Business. Economic Times, 12 June, 2007.
38. Prabhudev Konana—Need to wake up to the realities—The Hindu, 22 September, 2007.
39. Shashi Tharoor—"Planet India—from wild dreams to plans", Times of India, New Delhi, March 18, 2007.

2

New Horizons in Indian Management

I want India to become an economic super-power not only for her own sake but also for the benefit of the whole world.

Mukesh Ambani
(Unleashing India's Potential)

Max Mueller once said : "If I were asked under what sky the human mind has most fully developed some of its choicest gifts, has most deeply pondered on the greatest problems of life and has found solutions, I shall point to India". Albert Einstein once said that the world owes a lot to the Indians "Who taught us how to count" without which no worthwhile scientific discovery could have been possible. Mark Twain has said—"India was the cradle of human race, the birth place of human speech, the mother of history, the grand mother of tradition." The French scholar Romain Rolland has said "if there was one place on the face of the earth where all the dreams of living men have found a home from the earliest days when men began their dream of existence, it is India". Lyn Yutang has said: "Not until we see the richness of the Hindu mind and its essential spirituality, can we understand India." The Twenty first century is witnessing dramatic changes and challenges and flood gates of change have helped India emerge as a dominant global player. From software to agriculture, medical facilities to outsourcing, manufacturing to knowledge management, India Inc. has made a mark for itself in the world. The key to all this is trained manpower and inspiring leadership, ready to take on the emerging challenges. India faces numerous challenges and opportunities and the present chapter proposes to explore new horizons in Indian management. To manage the future, it is necessary to delve into new horizons and to develop a vision anchored around India's core values and management strategies.

Indian Economy—towards "Take-off"

Implementation of various programmes of last ten five year plans and democratic commitment to development have ultimately resulted in noticeable economic growth. India's growth can be attributed to a combination of many factors, including social variables and culture. Economic progress is not about capitalising on opportunities but upholding values like trustworthiness and honesty. 1991 was a water shed year for the Indian economy when the Government of India first began the process of integrating the Indian economy with the global one. After 1991, new horizons have emerged in various sectors of economy. Indian Managers are set to conquer the world. Infosys and Wipro are among India's best global brands - they represent not just India's software competencies but also the country's ability to adopt good corporate governance practices. Tata Steel has purchased at the cost of $ 8 billion cash Corus, an Anglo-Dutuch conglomerate that is the seventh largest steel producer in the world and almost six times its size. Dr. Reddy's Laboratories and Ranbaxy have made major inroads into the US generics market. Today Indians, like Narayan Murthy, are perceived as rich and knowledgeable persons. Narayan Murthy has taught us that wealth is not for safekeeping, but for sharing. Narayan Murthy appeals to the generative capacity of a nation now moving from rags to riches. That is why he is an icon of several generations."[1] Today when many CEOs hold onto their chairs with the tenacity of a branded adhesive, Narayan Murthy decided to step down gracefully. He has built up a glorious legacy. One sixth of humanity lives in India. In this age of rising aspirations and instant communication, there can be no peace if a billion people are discontended, deprived, unhappy and therefore angry. Individuals, communities and societies in India now have the opportunity to accelerate their growth dramatically. They can create entirely new and large opportunities for advancement." We must dare to dream. And dare to dream big. India has new horizons of management to look up. India has to harness global opportunities in the food and agriculture, manufacturing, infocom and health care sectors. Companies have to function in market dynamics founded on a new paradigm of constant change. Today Indian Companies are a craze with many young Americans and other foreign nationals. (Infosys has 126 in its first batch of American trainees in 2006.) Roughly one in 10 of the 72000 employees of TCS are foreigners. Many are trained in India before being sent to one of the 35 nations where it has operations. India can be rightly proud of its many management institutes including Indian Institutes of Managements and other Business schools at Hyderabad, Bangalore and Delhi. The Infosys training centre has a bowling alley on campus, a state-of-the-art gym, a swimming pool, tennis courts and an auditorium."[3] Management is about leadership-of people, of ideas, of markets and of availing opportunities. India is gradually emerging as the world's fastest growing wealth creator, the richest in human resource, capital and leader in information technology. In 2005 the rising fortunes of various countries were as under. Table showing rising fortunes and wealth creators in 2005.

Country	*Wealth ($ Billion)*
1. U.S.	31,296
2. Japan	11,861
3. UK	6,553
4. China	2,033
5. Brazil	1,115
6. India	0,559
7. Russia	0,553

Boston consultancy group's global wealth study shows in 2005, High growth in India (15%) as compared to China's 14.8%. Henry Ford has said: "Competition is the keen cutting edge of business, always sharing away of costs". We propose to look at Indian Management in the context of the new horizons of economic growth and the building blocks needed to capitalise on various mini-revolutions emerging in technology, communication and the knowledge management areas. Rapid advances in technology have led to the dissolutions of geographical boundaries of the nation-states and reduced entry barriers for knowledge-based business in various developing and developed countries. The transformational changes in Indian economy are supporting innovation and operating efficiency in markets across the world. With the introduction of hundred days job guarantee of one member per family in rural India, the integration of rural economy into the economic mainstream with holistic development of the agricultural and non-agricultural rural economy will create new engines of growth and push—Indian economy to a full fledged "take-off stage". During the last one decade a lot of churning at the top companies is going on. In 2006 Mukesh Ambani Controlled Reliance Industries Ltd., has dislodged state run energy conglomerate Oil and Natural Gas Corporation as India's biggest in terms of company market capitalisation. India now ranks amongst the top 5 countries in Asia (excluding Japan) in terms of VC activity. Over forty four US based VC and PE firms are now seeking to invest heavily in start-ups and early-stage companies in India. Opportunities for VCS are coming in from across the board. Textiles, logistics, telecom and design are coming up as very strong focus areas. Finance Minister P. Chidambaram has approved 22 foreign direct investment (FDI) proposals totaling Rs. 896 Crore in 2005-2006.

2. Indian Economy Growing from Strength to Strength

During the last one decade, India Inc. balance sheets are positively in great shape. Strong cash flows, low capital costs and high capacity utilization form an ideal back drop for buoyant corporate activity in India. During the last one decade, India Inc is going global in a big way. Domestic companies with quality management and strong earnings performance are finding it easier to raise money in global capital markets. Three years of high speed growth have made a variety of outfits cash-rich and eager to expand abroad. The Tata group's steel unit has acquired Singapore's Nat-steel and bought a majority stake in Millennium, steela Thai Company outside steel. The Tata hunt has bagged other quarry such as Britain's Tetley Tea, US telecom network operation Tyco global, Daewoo Commercial vehicles and Boston's Ritz Carlton hotel: A variety of smaller Indian companies have also been on an acquisition spree during the years 2004-06. There have been over 125 cross-border deals out of India since 2004. Some $ 5 Billion worth of deals have been transacted during 2006. "It is truly the phase of Indian globalisation" says Rashesh Shah CEO of Edelweiss capital. World Bank data show that India's GDP has shot up by a phenomenal 16.4% per year during the period 2003 - 06. (Phone connections have increased from barely five million in 1990 to 146 million (new mobiles) by October 2006). The telecom revolution has brought unprecedented connectivity to Indians. India's merchandise exports have almost doubled in three years from $ 52.7 billion in 2002 - 2003 to $ 102.7 billion in 2005- 2006. During the last ten years (from 1995-2006) major structural changes are noticeable in the country. Latest trends in Indian economy indicate that India has become a locomotive of economic growth and has lifted it to a higher growth path towards a take off stage. Indian companies have now achieved financial and integration maturity. Today the corporate India is in a very ambitious mood. Professor Arvind Panagariya of Columbia University says that India is not merely the beneficiary of global upswing, it has made major structural adjustments that have lifted it to a higher growth path. Indian companies are now taking over foreign giants (e.g. Tatas take over of Corus) and have the confidence of global financiers who now rate Reliance Industries and Tata Steel as more credit worthy than General Motors or Ford. India can now be considered a fairly open economy and the import duty collections average only 5% of total import. Due to Export orientation the share of goods plus services in GDP has virtually tripled from 7.9% in 1990-1991 to 20.5% in 2004-05. There is a huge structural change and service exports have more than doubled between 2004 to 2006 mainly due to computer software.[4] In the year 2005-2006 big and small Indian companies in every sector have been expanding their footprints beyond Indian shores. The asset side of corporate India's balance sheet is clearly undergoing rapid change during the last few years. Joseph Schumpeter held that the essence of capitalism is the process of "creative destruction— the perpetual cycle of destroying the old and less efficient product or services and replacing it with new more efficient ones".[5] Andy Grove, while giving his business model of globalisation capitalism held the view that dramatic, industry transforming innovations are taking place today faster and faster. The speed by which these technological break-throughs are bringing latest inventions is now lightning quick, making things obsolete over night. He held that only those paranoids, who are constantly looking over their shoulders to see which is creating something new that will destroy them and then staying just ahead of them will survive.[6] India must constantly and quickly destroy inefficient companies and replace them with efficient, dynamic, innovation savvy companies. In India the innovative companies alone will thrive in the era of globalisation. During the last one decade, old economy companies are getting tech-savvy and trying to bring innovative changes. Due to its innovative character, Infosys continues to rule the roost in the I.T. Space.[7] India today is exhibiting a sense of self-confidence and optimism and it is now one of the fastest growing economies in the world. One can clearly see the impact of technology, the communications revolution, the rise of the knowledge economy and the growth in consumer demand. The Government of India (GOI) launched the Rajiv Gandhi Grameen Vidytikaran Yojana (RGGVY) in April 2005. The goal of the Yojana is to complete the rural electricity infrastructure by the end of 2010. The RGGVY is a bold master plan for completing the unfinished task of rural electrification. GOI will provide a grant of 90 percent of the estimated capital cost of Rs.16,000 crore required for electrification of all unconnected villages. However, since the rural electrification is a state function, the implementations of this ambitious project is to be done by the states. The center has made available to them the expertise and services of CPSUS like NHPC, NTPC, PGCIL (Power Grid Corporation of India Ltd) and DVC (Damodar Valley Corporation). Dr. Man Mohan Singh has said: Agriculture is suffering from four deficits: Public investment and credit deficit; infrastructure deficit; market economy deficit and knowledge deficit. Speaking on the FICCI organized Agriculture Summit 2006, the Prime Minister reiterated more initiative by his government for soliciting both public and private investment in areas such as irrigation, water needs of farmers and rural infrastructure. The Rural Electrification Corporation (REC), on the pattern of the Rural Electricity Authority (REA) in the U.S., has been entrusted with the task of channeling the grant funds and providing soft loans for the balance requirements. The RGGVY is an excellent initiative and a great measure of the Govt. of India resolve to complete the unfinished task of rural electrification. Given the high percentage of population within the reach of the national grid, healthy functioning of the grid-based distribution industry is crucial to achieving and sustaining the "access for all" target. In order to build a self sustaining rural economy, power sector reform is one of the roads that must be traveled to reach the universal access destination. China achieved close to universal access of power over a time-span of two decades and India must achieve it in one decade to take lead over China. Availability of quality power supply would help unleash the full economic growth potential of rural India and the consequent increase of rural purchasing power will not only provide a great stimulus to the economy but also enable consumers of electricity to pay for their usuage and thus make universal access sustainable.[8] Dr. Man Mohan Singh, in Parliament has recently said, "The search for an integrated policy with an appropriate mix of energy supplies is central to the achievement of our broader economic and social objectives. Energy is the life blood of our economy. Without sufficient and predictable access, our aspirations in the social sector cannot be realized. Power shortage is not just a handicap in one sector but a drag on the entire economy". The Per Capita energy consumption in some countries is shown below.

Table showing Per Capita Energy Consumption in 2001 in Kilograms.

States	*Per Capita Energy Consumption*
India	514.3
China	886.5
USA	7,920.9
Qater	26,883.3

Source: World Resources Institute.

India cannot become a superpower if there is no power. India's dreams of becoming a superpower may crumble due to its shortage of power.[9] India's gradual economic development is noticeable in many studies. Quality of life is better in Union territories than in the neighbouring states. A recent report indicates that socio-economic indicators in Union Territories are much better than those in neighbouring states. Through the

31 page report "Administration in the Union Territories", the quality of life in various union territories has been compared with some state as shown in the table below:

Table 2. Showing Economic Indicators in Some Selected States and Union Territories

S.No.	*Union Territories/ States*	*Literacy Rate*	*Below Poverty Line %*	*Infant Mortality Rate*	*Electricity Cons. (KWH)*	*Net Domestic Output (Rs.'000)*
1.	Delhi	82	8.2	32	829	51.6
2.	Chandigarh	82	5.7	21	943	57.6
3.	Daman Diu	81	NA	37	5,927	NA
4.	Pondicherry	81	21.6	24	1,876	50.9
5.	Haryana	69	8.7	61	658	29.9
6.	Punjab	70	6.1	45	907	27.8
7.	Uttar Pradesh	58	31.1	72	202	10.8
8.	Maharashtra	77	25.0	36	585	29.2
9.	Gujarat	70	14.0	53	908	26.9
10.	Tamil Nadu	73	21.1	41	713	23.3
11.	Andhra Pradesh	61	15.7	59	543	20.7

Source: Report on "Administration in the Union Territories"—placed before Parliamentary Consultancy Committee for Home Affairs—Times of India, Report 24 Oct., 2006.

In 1991, 36 percent of India's population (in the days 846 million people) lived on less than one dollar a day. In 2001, the percentage of those living on less than a dollar a day had fallen to 26 percent or some 267 million people. India has by now lifted 94 million people out of absolute poverty in last 15 years a feat on a scale that no country on earth could do, other than China. By 2007, the people below the poverty line stand at 22 percent. Leading economist Kanshik Basu, Professor at Cornell University, has said: "It is not economic policy alone but a combination of factors, including social variables and culture, which is behind India's tremendous economic growth. (Hindu, Chennai, 23 February 2007). Indian economy is on the fulcrum of ever increasing growth curve. India has 36 billionaires while

China has 15 billionaires according to the Forbes magazine. India has emerged as the world's fastest growing wealth creator, thanks to a buoyant stock market and higher earnings when the global management consultancy, the Boston Consulting Group penned a report titled "The new global challenges—out of top 100 list published, 21 Indian companies made it to the elite list". Probably at no point of time, Indian business environment and the political, economic, social and technological factors been so industry friendly. There is a greater impetus on specific competencies for business to complete and survive competition. Corporate governance will be crucial for companies in future as they gear up for a new world of tough governance standards. Indian companies will have to integrate their acquired companies with the rest of the organisation or align themselves with the larger global presence of these companies. The Indian airline companies have been shaken up inside out by cheap domestic airlines. Mushrooming low cost airlines have changed the very dynamics of the Indian aviation and tourism industry. During the last ten years the Indian information technology, soft ware, and I.T. service industry have witnessed a huge people churn. Indian industry will have to prove their mettle in global market place in the next decade. The knowledge industries, particularly the software and I.T. enabled services industry, will have to face human resource dilemma of how to retain; develop and attract knowledge workers with their HR policies. Indian economy has many key issues namely unemployment, unorganised employment, low productivity, low per capita income, poor educational standards, mismatched education system, rural-urban disparities, lower skills in women, and lack of clarity of roles of centre and state governments regarding various issues. Corruption, nepotism, poverty, lack of decision-making at government levels and lack of enterpreneurship are some of the basic challenges to Indian economy. There is a brighter side also 25 lakh NRIs from Kerala alone pump in Rs. 26,000 crore every year into the Country's economy. During the last 5 years Uttaranchal has attracted more than 20,000 crores in investment. Gujarat has received investment commitment of Rs. 4.5 lakh crores during vibrant Gujarat summit 2007.

Table Showing the Vibrant Gujarat Bonanza

Company/Group	*Details of the Project*	*Investment*
RIL	Jamnagar SEZ, Petrochemical Complex Coal and lignite gasification project	Rs. 67,000 Cr
AV Birla Group	Rayon plant, cement plant, viscose and textiles application centre, fibre plant	Rs. 2,200 Cr
Essar Oil	Expansion of existing refinery in Hazira	Rs. 10,500 Cr
ICICI Bank	Business hub in Gandhinagar	Rs. 1,000 Cr
ONGC	Petroleum complex at Dahej	Rs. 16,000 Cr
BPCL	Crude Terminal and pipeline network	Rs. 1,700 Cr
Adani Group	SEZ in Mundra	Rs. 25,000 Cr
Torrent Industries	Coal-based project at Pipavav	Rs. 9,000 Cr
Dishman Pharma	New engineering projects	Rs. 2,000 Cr
Welspun Group	Expansion of its Kutch facility	Rs. 3,000 Cr

3. Managing Housing for the People

Bharat Nirman, Indira Awas Yojana and National Urban Renewal are some of the well known initiatives that the government has taken for providing housing for all. Although budgetary allocation for the purpose is inadequate, it has set the economy in motion to gain dynamism. The centre has allocated around Rs. 2,800 crore under the Indira Awas Yojana to construct 15 Lakh houses and about Rs. 5,500 crore for upgrading urban infrastructure. The importance of the housing and real estate sector in India can be judged by the estimate that for every rupee invested in the construction of houses, Rs. 0.78 is added to the GDP of the country thus boosting the economy. Studies reveal that India currently faces a housing shortage of approximately 20 million units, half of which is urban and around 70 percent of that belongs to the low income group segment. An ASSOCHAM paper on real estate development has estimated that the demand for dwelling units will grow to 90 million by 2020 which would require a minimum investment of $890 billion (Rs. 40,05,000 crore). Housing sector management has to take care of four aspects - the financing model, regulations, infrastructure and knowledge creation and all need to be dealt simultaneously. In urban housing planning there is a need for building houses with a multi-dimensional approach encompassing quality of living and physical development. The vision of India for 2020 should include well-planned, clean cities and villages with basic infrastructure in place, affordable and energy efficient homes, a dynamic regulatory and legal framework, and involvement of the citizens in running of their houses and vicinity in a cooperative and dynamic approach. The crisis of housing, particularly in metropolitan cities and urban areas is, in fact, an economic opportunity. Improving housing can be a powerful agent in economic development. Natural disasters such as the 2005 earthquake in Gujarat rendered 3,00,000 homeless. Providing them good shelter could provide employment to large number of people in Gujarat.

4. Managing Healthcare and Healthy Living

Medical Research, IT information technology, telecommunications have increasingly vital roles to play in health care management. The Indian market is poised to provide world leadership by offering the cheapest generic drugs in the world. The Indian industry has built a globally competitive generic pharmaceutical business. India has approximately 577,856 registered doctors, and 506,628 registered nurses and large number of medical colleges. The following table shows the comparative figures about health expenditure per capita and physicians for the people in various countries.

Table Showing Number of Physicians and Health Expenditure

Country	*Health Expenditure Per Capita (PPP US$2002)*	*Year 1990-2004 per 10,000 people*
1. United States	5,274	549
2. United Kingdom	2,160	166
3. Russian Federation	535	417
4. Brazil	611	206
5. China	261	164
6. India	96	51
7. Pakistan	62	69

Purchasing power parity per capita with US $ (*Source:* Human Development Report 2005).

On 31st October 2006, Chemicals Minister Ram Vilas Paswan released a list of 886 medicines, including top-selling anti-diabetic pills, antibiotics, cough syrups, panikers and anti-hypertensions, on which drug makers have slashed trade margin substantially, bringing the prices down upto 74%.

Table Showing details of cheap drugs

	886 Cheap Drugs	
	No. of Forumulations	*Range of Price Cut*
Alembic	109	3-36
Cadila	391	2-74
Wockhardt	101	8.33-40
Ranbaxy	72	0.26 - 42
Lupin	68	6-71
Nicholas Piramal	18	2-20

These cheaper drugs will definitely benefit the common man and the poor people. Developing and maintaining sustainable health care delivery for people are indeed gigantic tasks. The various diseases and deaths causes by them indicate what ails India and need curative and preventive actions.

Table Showing Diseases their Incidence and Death in India

Sl.No.	*Disease*	*Incidence*	*Death*
1.	Tuberculosis	85	4
2.	HIV/Aids	51	NA
3.	Malaria and Vector Borne Diseases	20.37	NA
4.	Maternal Mortality	NA	440
5.	Cancer	8.07	72000
6.	Diabetes	310	NA
7.	Mental Health	650	NA
8.	Cardio Vascular	380	NA
9.	COPD and Ashtma	405.2	NA
10.	Injuries	NA	9.8

Figures in Lakh
*per 1 Lakh Births
Source: Ministry of Health and Family Welfare.

Public-private partnerships are integral to building efficient, sustainable and quality health-care models in any developing economy. India now has quite a few most modern internationally accepted health care hospitals like Apollo, Escorts hospital in a number of metropolitan cities. Future health care programmes need to rest on hygiene awareness campaigns that cover water, sanitation personal hygiene and regular yoga or physical exercises. Better health care is far away from the common man in India. The UNDP's Human Development Report 2006 shows that this growth has not translated into better public health care for the citizens. India spends 1.2% of gross domestic product value on health sector. India's private spending on health care is at 3.6% of GDP table given below shows the share of government health spending to total health care.

Table. MEDICAL MALADY—Share of government health spending to total health expenditure

HDI Rank	*Country*	*%*
160	Guinea	16.7
167	Congo	17.5
130	Myanmar	17.9
129	Cambodia	19.3
80	Armenia	20.0
12	Tajikistan	20.5
169	Burundi	22.6
126	India	25.0
97	Georgia	25.0
99	Azerbaijan	25.0

According to United Nations Development programmes in most countries including India, improvement in Human Development Index has showed down in the period 1990-2004, compares to the pace in the previous 15 years. The share of government of health spending to total health expenditure (Investment in HDI in percentage) has been shown below:

HOW THEY FARE

Share of government health spending to total health expenditure Investment in HD1 (%)

Rank	*Country*	*1975-90*	*1990-04*
138	Nepal	42	24
134	Pakistan	27	16
93	Sri Lanka	15	7
126	India	25	19
81	China	19	22
137	Bangladesh	22	26

The world health organization and private initiatives like those of Lions, Rotary and other NGOs have addressed mass immunization programmes besides providing financial aid to deserving patients, preventive health care is more sustainable than undertaking the life-long treatment of a disease that has already declared itself in a serious form. The present primary health centers of the government need to be provided motivated doctors and staff, adequate supply of medicines and equipment and regular financial assistance. A comparative study will indicate India's present situation as compared to other states.

Topic	*India*	*China*	*USA*	*Sri Lanka*	*Thai-land*
Infant morality rate per 1000 live births	68	30	2	8	15
Health expenditure as a percentage of GDP	4.8	5.8	14.6	3.7	4.4
Govt's share of total expenditure	4.4	10	23.1	6	17.1
Per capita spending on health in dollars	96	261	5274	131	321

Source: World Health Report 2005.

5. How to manage raise in India's per Capita Income and uplift the poor

It is necessary to review the growth in per capita income over the years. Some figures of per capita income for various years are as under:

Year	*Per capita Income*
1980	Rs. 2,054
1988	Rs. 5,256
1992	Rs. 9,062
1998	Rs. 17,325
2004	Rs. 27,457

India still faces challenges of poverty with 260 million people surviving on less than one dollar a day, inequality tied to a caste system and corruption and in-efficiency in the provision of public services.[10] According to one estimate a proportion of 23.6 percent of the urban population lives below the poverty line whereas rural poverty is 27.1 percent.[11] In the world's biggest economy, one in eight Americans and almost one in four blacks live in poverty. According to US Census Bureau both ratios are virtually unchanged from 2004. Some 37 million Americans or 12.6%, live below the poverty line, defined as having an annual income around $10,000 for an individual or $ 20,000 for a family of four. The per capita income is gradually showing rise in India in ascending order. This transformational change over the past decades is only the precursor of further growth as technological change development of service sector, sense of self-confidence and optimism are all exhibiting increasing possibilities of further growth. India is now highly competitive in the markets across the world. Taping the informal economy by amending anti-money laundering Act is essential for the growth of the Indian economy. India notified the prevention of money laundering Act 2002 with amendment from July 1, 2005 defining calpability related activities with the proceeds of crime and projecting it as untainted property and punishable if found guilty of money laundering, illegal forex transactions, real estate, gems and Jewellery and high value purchases. India has set up the financial intelligence units to examine reports from financial institutions - RBI, SEBI, IRDA and to coordinate with international agencies. Money laundering shatters the economy through unpredictable changes in money supply, posing risks to the soundness of the financial systems leading to loss of investors confidence and destabilizations of financial systems. By end of October 2006, over 6,000 high profile people are under Income

Tax lens for hawala links. Greater self-sufficiency in energy and a holistic economic reforms process are bound to ensure sustained growth. However, how India stacks up today in comparison to other nations is shown in the table below:

Table showing ranking of nation state and their per capita income (in $)

Rank	*Countries*	*Per Capita Income (in $)*
1	Luxembourg	69,929
2	Norway	54,521
3	Switzerland	49,305
4	Demark	44,929
5	Ireland	44,888
6	Iceland	43,576
7	United States	39,934
8	Sweden	38,449
9	Qatar	37,610
10	Japan	36,575
13	United Kingdom	35,460
69	Russia	4,093
76	Brazil	3,417
112	China	1,269
135	India	605

Source: IMF—Morgan Stanley Research.

If we analyse the GDP growth rates of various states of India the following positions emerge with Karnataka taking the lead. India has to seek new horizons in marketing, branding and service sectors as the economy goes up with growing per capita income and growth in GDP. Increased business activities in highly commercial areas (generally called Central Business District - CBD) have been broken by the new emerging markets. For example in Mumbai and Pune, we are seeing widespread distribution of new types of physical infrastructure with the help of advanced telecommunication structures while the sun has not quite set on the existing Central Business Districts (CBDs). The emergence of new business areas herald a new beginning as businesses move to new location. Real estate, retail and media and entertainment are the three emerging sectors in Indian management.

Table showing growth chart of various states in 1990s

S.No.	States	GDP growth in the 1990s
1.	Karnataka	7.25
2.	West Bengal	6.75
3.	Gujarat	6.72
4.	Himachal Pradesh	6.35
5.	Tamil Nadu	6.33
6.	Maharashtra	6.22
7.	Kerala	5.7
8.	Andhra Pradesh	5.64
9.	Rajasthan	5.50
10.	Haryana	5.24
11.	Madhya Pradesh	5.06
12.	Punjab	4.54
13.	Orissa	4.06
14.	Uttar Pradesh	3.78
15.	Bihar	3.49
16.	Assam	2.60

(The percentage annual rate of growth in gross state domestic product in the 1990s. Both state level and NSS regional level data used to calculate GSDP).

The total number of people below the poverty line is 300 million. A national sample survey organisation's study suggests that while economic growth is trickling down very slowly, poverty has declined the sharpest in the poorer states. Leading them were Assam and the north-eastern states, where people below the poverty line decreased by nearly 4% annually, followed by Jharkhand (2.51%) a year during the five year period, Chhattisgarh (2.15% a year) and Bihar (1.69%) BPL (Below Poverty Lines) population in rural areas decreased 4.68% between 1999-2000 to 2004-05 which was over twice the pace of the decrease in urban areas, estimated at 2.12%.[12] The NSSO findings reveal an increase in BPL population in Haryana, Maharashtra, Delhi, Rajasthan and Goa because migratory labour moved out of Bihar, U.P. and Jharkhand to these states in search of jobs. Orissa has the highest proportion of poor-nearly 40% of its population below the poverty line. Jharkhand has 47.4% of BPL population with Orissa has 47.15% in 1999-2000. Per capita income of the Indians can be raised by holistic economic development of the country and restricting the rise in population. In fact many dynamic chief ministers are doing their Jet-setting attracting NRIs from their states in the U.S. U.K. and the middle east, losing no opportunity to network at international business conferences, participating in country delegations and organizing trips to sell directly to over sea business and investors.[13]

Inspite of various strategies to raise the per capita income of the people, we have a large number of people of misfortune at bottom of the pyramid. Management guru C.K. Prahlad, famous for his book, "The Fortune at the Bottom of the Pyramid: Eradicating poverty Through Profits" shows that the poor, often neglected by corporations as having no purchasing power, can be converted into the fastest growing market in the world through innovations that improve affordability and tailor products to the needs of poor.[14] In a recent lecture by Prof. C.K. Prahlad on "Democratising commerce" he identified five ways to improve affordability. First, easy payments in instalments (which have revolutionized rural sales of T.V., Cellphones, two wheelers and houses). Second, dramatic cost-cutting (Some goods and services in India cost just 2-10% of the US cost). Third goods in small rather than large packings (e.g., shampoo in sachets instead of bottles). Fourth pay by use (paying Rs. 20 for internet use at an e-cafe instead of buying a computer). Fifth direct distribution cutting out intermediaries, e.g., buying directly from farmers at e-choupals and selling to them directly through Choupal Sagar Shops.[15]

6. The aspirational challenges of the nation and how to achieve them

As an independent strong nation there can be any number of aspirational challenges. Some thinkers have posed the questions as given below:

1. What will it take to empower poor farmers? (Y.C. Deveshwar)
2. "What will it take to increase the number of women in our workforce." (Anu Aga)

3. "What will it take to make India One of the world's Top 5 Tourist destinations-" (Giovanni Bisignani)
4. "What will it take to beat Aids Epidemic" - Ashok Alexander.
5. "What will it take to Rid India of corruption." N.R. Narayana Murthy
6. On what will it take to achieve universal quality education. (Azim Premji)
7. On what will it take for India to become a nation of innovators. (Vjay Govind Rajan)
8. On what will it take to make our cities truly world class. (Nandan M. Nilekani)
9. On What will it take for an Indian to win an Olympic gold. (Rajya Vardhan Rathore)
10. On what will it take to make our cities truly world Class. (Nandan M. Nilekani)
11. On what will it take to secure our energy future (Subir Raha)
12. On what will it take to ensure clean water for all (R.K. Pachauri)
13. On what will it take to ensure quality health for all. (Kiran Majundar Shan)
14. On what will it take for atleast one car for a family of four Indians to own. (Jagadesh Khattar)
15. On what will it take to raise India's Per Capita Income to $ 250 a month. (K.V. Kamath)
16. How do you manage metropolitan cities and Delhi Capital regions? Managing urban cities, like Hyderabad, Bangalore, Pune, Kolkata, requires enormous amounts of patience, commitment and planning besides vast resources and political will. Construction of flyovers, successful broad roads - widening programmes, regulations of high multi-storeys building complexes. How do you manage it?
17. Management of disasters and natural calamities like floods, earthquakes, TSUNAMI tidal waves havoc and

cyclones—all need community participation and governmental support in terms of finance, manpower and coordination. Rescue and relief operations in various disasters need special attention.[16] Railways, hospitals, airports, educational centers and public sector undertaking are other areas for effective management. Proper planning and speedy executions/ implementation are needed. All institutions need effective management. In a sense all politicians in power, all bureaucrats at central and state levels, all heads of the department and all managers of the corporate world have to pool their own efforts to achieve and sustain holistic economic growth of the nation. The above given issues are the major challenges on the horizons of Indian management which need our collaborative efforts on a continuous basis as a nation. Management of Business schools and management of education are also great challenges. To achieve self-sustained economic growth India needs FORCE financial sector growth, openness to trade, rural-urban migration, capital formation, education and environment. Indian companies are consciously trying to globalise their image, while global firms are trying to Indianise their images in order to connect to the talent pool.[17] A classical example of how Indian companies globalise themselves would be that of Wipro Infotech—A major part of Wipro Infotech's operations are based in the Middle East, South Asia and Australia. These countries are culturally extremely different from India but "the company appointed local people in client-facing roles like project managers and sales and business professionals. It puts the client at case. It is always prudent to deploy locals". Says Tapan Bhat—VR HR—Resourcing and Talent Transformation Wipro Infotech.

7. Need for Passion to Succeed and Achieve Excellence

We need will power to achieve excellence in respective fields. John Johnson has said: "Men and women are limited not by the place of their birth, not by the colour of their skin, but by the size of their hope". "Dr. A.P.J. Abdul Kalam has said: "Nations consist of people. And with their effort a nation can accomplish all it could ever want. ... I am sure on my part that India has the ability to transform itself into a developed nation .... I know that our people have the ability to achieve the best in the world".[18] There seems to be an attitude problem as if we cannot shake ourselves out of a mindset of limited achievement. Indians must generate great visions to achieve the best in every field. A nation's wealth is the young generation of the country who need good role models in various fields to get inspiration and guidance. India today need a spirit of victory, a passion to succeed and strong will power to achieve excellence in various fields. For a nation to prosper, people of the nation must inculcate right value system and passion to succeed. Friedrich Wilhelm Hegel has said: "We may affirm absolutely that nothing great in the world has ever been accomplished without passion." In the Specific context of developing winning companies and sustaining competitive edge. Five I frame as shown below can be the guiding light posts—

1. Inspiring leadership
2. Innovative strategy
3. Implementations skills and process driven execution.
4. Internal and external win relationships.
5. Identity, Purpose, Value and culture.[19]

Putting quality of life first is important for balanced growth. Integrity, Maturity, and abundance mentality are the three primary traits of greatness. India could grow at 8% plus upto 2020, if it saved more, used resources more efficiently, integrated faster with the world economy and handled land water and energy problems well.[20] India will have to create a good investment climate, infrastructure and skills in order to ride the globalisation band wagon.[21] LN Mittal after a visit to Jamshedpur recently was impressed by Tata Steel's continued care of the environment and the people around it. He said what he saw in Jamshedpur made him proud to be an Indian. India needs more value based leadership who can be role models of integrity in its complete sense. Stephen R covey has said: "Success today depends highly on our ability to gain the vision for the knowledge worker where the primary work of leadership is to release the potential of such a worker-realizing body, mind heart and spirit towards great purposes. Great leaders inspire others. They communicate to people their worth and potential so clearly that they are inspired to see it in themselves." Success has many facets and dimensions and strategies for success must be effectively used by the leaders. Success is the progressive realisation of the worthy goals. It means winning the war, not every battle. The famous 5 Cs for success are character, commitment, conviction, courtesy and courage. Goal setting must be properly done and it needs to be supported by five DS-Dedication, direction, determination deadline adhering and discipline. Goals for success must be SMART specific, measurable, achievable, realistic and time bound. Dianna Booher, CEO of Booher consultant has suggested the following 14 point plan to achieve personal excellence:

1. Define success in your own terms.
2. Assess your strengths.
3. Set goals with deadlines.
4. Develop discipline and be willing to pay the price.
5. Use time wisely and abide by natural laws.
6. Ask for advice and compliment people for their advice and wisdom.
7. Be receptive to feedback.
8. Stay Informed and read good literature, books, journals, newspapers.
9. Learn to communicate well.
10. Do quality work.
11. Take calculated risks.
12. Be dependable and personal accountability to Almighty god.
13. Be ethical and stick to your governing values.
14. Nurture relationships.

It is necessary that individuals develop a positive, "Can do" attitude with firm belief in one's capacity and efforts. For achieving success and happiness in life, the 4 Ps model

(Perception, principles, preparation and practice) is generally very effective and practical sustained success requires achievement drive, bias towards action, commitment, dedication, emotional intelligence, faultness focus, goal-setting, healthy habits, ignited mind, and many other things including zero mistake in work. Failures can be stepping stones to a future success in life. Success in organizational context leads to organizational excellence-shared values, strategy, structure, system, style, staff and skills are the famous 7S variables of the model of excellence.[22] Excellence does not happen miraculously but springs from pace-setting levels of personal effectiveness and efficiency. Nandan Nilekani, the 51 year old chief executive of the $ 20 billion Infosys, is one of India's most successful business leaders and a key figure in the new global economy.[23] Infosys continues to rule the roost in the I.T. Space. When we look at the metrics of the three main I.T. Compaines—TCS, Wipro and Infosys - it becomes clear that Infosys stands head and shoulders above the other two I.T. Giants in terms of growth and profitability as can be seen in the Table below.[24]

Table giving comparative figures of 3 I.T. companies for Q2 FY07 Financials

S.No.	*Particulars*	*TCS*	*Wipro*	*Infosys*
1.	Sales	4,494.8	3,557.6	3,451.0
2.	Growth Q . Q%	6.3	13.1	14.5
3.	Operating Profit	1,251.7	729.9	1,109.0
4.	Growth Q . Q%	17.0	8.9	24.8
5.	Contribution of Top 10 Clients	26.8	25.7	32.9
6.	No. of active clients	742.0	593.0	476.0
7.	Offshore Revenue %	41.0	5.1	72.6

Source: Company Reports - (Rs. Crore).

As far as Infosys in concerned more than the growth in sales, it is the growth in profit that has endeared the latter to investors. Infosys has much higher profit margins than any other company in its league. Infosys has consistently managed to improve margins and maintain profit growth higher than its peers. Infosys has thus maintained its passion for excellence for the last few years. In the race for material successful, persons are bound to suffer serious stress and stress induced ill health. Stress management and management of healthy life will need self - discipline, regular exercise, meditation breathing exercise and balanced food.

8. Human Resource Management and Development

According to 2001 census India's population was 1,027,015,247 with population density of 329 per square Km or 862 Per square Mile. The existing scenario in pulsating and dynamic. India's workforce has earned a good reputation all over the world by its hard work, dedication, excellence and professional commitment. Human Resource Development policies need to be designed in such a way as to equip the younger generation with sufficient knowledge, value system, skills, habits and attitudes to face the challenge of striking a balance between national interest and global requirement. The education system should undergo drastic changes in terms of primary and secondary education to all children of the nation, irrespective of their handicaps in terms of economic status, and social system. According to Sam Pitroda, Chairman National Knowledge Commission, for India and the rest of the world, the great source of hope lies in the country's 550 million people below the age of 25 who are unencumbered by outdated thinking and are eager to learn new technologies and innovate out to make a difference.[23a] Integrated approach is desirable and the reforms in the education system should be based on comprehensive approach and futuristic vision of globally oriented education. The Indian Institutes of Technology (IITs) and the Indian Institutes of Management (IIMs) are among the world's best universities according to the 2006 university marking published in Oct 206 IITs are ranked at No. 57 and the IIMs at No.68 on the list of 200 universities. JNU is ranked 183 in 2006 up nine place from 2005. Harvard University, University of Cambridge and Oxford University have first three ranking in the world. Goldman Sachs has said that not only was India growing, but its population growth was actually an asset. Human Resource planning and management need strategic vision. Strategic HR Vision must encompass the following aspects of Business—ABCDE of vision for HR—

1. Anticipate work force needs - Talent acquisition and retention, training and performance appraisal.
2. Building readiness - Agile people and processes prepared to deal with the fluctuating business environment.
3. Creating ROI - HR needs to set itself solid targets and ensure the return on investment as HR is quantified and explained at every step.
4. Design and shape culture designing and shaping a system of values, ethics, practices and processes in anticipation of tomorrow's business needs.
5. Ensure Time bound programme and no commitment can be open ended.

Education is not only the mean but also the end in itself for the cause of economic development. India needs to spent more than 6% of GDP (currently at 3.3%) on education. Focus should be on the social infrastructure health and quality manpower. In India more than 400 women form Self-help group movement in India every hour. Over a whopping 22.50 lakh self help groups (SHGs) have so far been offered minimum banking service. However "India has a long way to go in micro financing. The micro credit sector is still in infancy in India"—says Prof. Mohammad Yinus, 2006 Nobel Peace Prize winner and founder of Grammen Bank in Bangladesh. The Manpower and skill development of the youth are the primary challenges and opportunities for India. The key challenge is to re-engineer knowledge institutions and infrastructure now to respond to their needs for the future and create new eco-systems to allow and encourage them (Young Indians) to innovate and excel globally.[24] India now needs to focus on the following:

1. Change mindset to a more rational and scientific thinking in government, administration, universities, science and technology, laboratories, schools and homes;
2. Create a new eco system to integrate resources and improve interactions between universities, industries, laboratories, financial institutions and markets;
3. Respect and promote intellectual properties, patents, copyrights and trade marks.

4. There is a need for redefining Global Dynamics by looking towards East-learning from Japan, China an other eastern countries.

India needs to develop business models best suited for Indian Companies, to respond to the emerging future needs of the developing country. The number of students going abroad from India world wide has gone up from 8,00,000 in 1975 to 2.5 million in 2004. Another emerging trend is the move to vocational Straining and super specialization. A recent survey of 100 top CEOs reveal that knowledge, skills and attitudes are becoming important. India is trying to produce/breed new genre business savvy techies.[25] The IT research firm, Gartner in 2005 predicted that the manpower demands will shift from IT specialists to versatilists-people who execute multi-disciplinary assignments to fuel value due to the following reasons: (*a*) the accessibility of global organizations to world labour; (*b*) Provision of a wider pool of talent to exploit and (*c*) Cut throat competitions. In future great demand for versatilists will emerge, with the growing need to centralize and have people who can responsibility grow up to manage teams, special groups and quality control teams. In India in the field of HRD, attitude formation and competence building are two important targets for the specialists. MA Foi employment survey, according to MD Pandia Rajan, has pegged the new number of jobs in 2006 at 10.3 lakh plus. The service sector was expected to account for more than 3.8 lakh jobs while mining was expected to loose a little over 7000 jobs. Annually 86 lakh people are joining the employment market.[26] Information technology alone is likely to generate employment for 7 lakh people. Indian managers have to learn manpower policy and management in present global context.

9. Spiritualism and Management

There are many corporate leaders around the world who are blazing that spiritual path-albeit independently, providing examples to inspire and guide others to do the same. Infosys Technology led by NR Narayan Murthy is one of the best examples of corporate spirituality, who led by example and kept spirituality implicit in his leadership work. The explicit part of the business is the house holding of economic operation and the implicit part of business is to support the employees spiritual quest in opening up. The following are some of the true characterization of the spirituality soul:—(*i*) Patience to let things unfold; (*ii*) acceptance of situations; (*iii*) willingness to look closely at self and committed to changing "ego-based" behaviours; (*iv*) Belief in a higher power the self and others, (*v*) Keeping things short, sweet and simple (*vi*) Transforming the ego. Inter cultural adjustment training needs to be imparted to all the CEOs and other managers. Corporate America is now embracing Indian Philosophy in a very big way and phrases from ancient Hindu Texts such as the Bhagwat Gita and Upnishads are popping up in the management tones and on website of consultants. Top business schools have introduced "Self mastery" classes that use Indian methods of meditation, Dhyan and stress -relieving breathing exercises, to help managers boost leadership skills and find inner peace in lives dominated by work.[27] Swami Parthasarathy, Shri Sri Ravi Shanker, Swami Sukhbodhanand and many Indian spiritual masters are now teaching secrets of inner happiness and business success - concentration, consistency, cooperation and holistic art of living making a balance between life and work. In todays competitive environment, it is not at all uncommon to find people working as much as 16-18 hours a day. It is bound to affect health and stress and thereby lead to other complications such as short temper" headache, disturbed family life, social isolation and body pains, etc. Stress management through Indian Asana Pranayam Yoga system and meditation are therefore becoming popular all over the world. In foreign countries many experts and psychological counsellors are suggesting regular physical exercises, meditation and yoga exercises to fight stress related problems. Proper balance between life and work needs to be maintained in the modern day competitive world and physical health must get its due place. About 10% of the professors at eminent business school such as Harvard Business School, North Western's Kellogg School of Business, the university of Michigan's Ross School of Business are of Indian Descent, spreading Indian wisdom in U.S.A. C.K. Prahlad talks of inclusive capitalism in which corporations can simultaneously create value and social justice. A large number of vedant scholars are on a whistle stop tour of the U.S. Counselling executives on the Central message of Bhagwat Gita to put purpose before self—"There are four important aspects in us. Says Swami Sukhabodhananda, - the body, mind, emotions and spiritual being. Focusing on their growth involves

involves an enlightened vision .... When positive energy is awakened in one's body emotion, mind and spiritual domain, a magnetic culture opens up. A higher self is awakened.[28] Within the spirituality in the workplace movement a wide series of claims are made in relation to work, meaning, individual and organisational performance and motivation to work. A mini-industry has spring up in less than ten years, supported by books, academic research conferences and trading activity.[29] Inspiration from Vedantic philosophy, Bhagwat Gita, Bible, Koran and other religious books are drawn by management experts now-a-days to emphasise the importance of spirituality in the corporate world. An International Seminar workshop entitled "Spirituality in Management" was held at szeged, Hungary by the Business Ethics Centre of the Budapest University in cooperation with other faculties and NGO's in July 1-3, 2001. Scholars and practitioners from 13 countries were represented and Prof. S.K. Chakraborty of IIM Kolkata represented India. The Vedantic wisdom contained in Hindu Scriptures provide solutions to the various crises - of Character, leadership, focusing, bureaucracy, motivation and vision and thus opening a vista in management thinking.[30] Harvard University No. 1 among top global universities has recently accepted religion as a course of study at graduate level.

India, Far East and Japanese corporations, large and small, are renowned for their use of spiritual and moral education. Organisations cannot be regarded as truly successful unless they rekindle the souls of the people working. The following key initiatives are required to reawaken the corporate soul:— (1) Follow ethical conduct in all dealings. (2) Appoint ethical people, supervisors and leaders and stress on integrity honesty, compassion and work orientation. (3) Get socially oriented and corporate social responsibilities must be accepted and carried out in right spirit. JRD Tata has said: "No success or achievement in material terms is worthwhile unless it serves the needs and interests of the country and its people and is achieved by fair and honest means." Sri Sri Ravi Shankar has said: Spirituality is remaining when you are turning within. Reflect on your life and see it from a broader perspective in the context of cosmology (how small we are in the order things), commitment (to truth) and compassion (to all) and the broaden the vision considerable.[31] Corporate houses are now getting involved in corporate social responsibility projects and give on their employees an opportunity to get involved in them.

10. The Indian Economic Policy and its Impact

Dr. Man Mohan Singh, Prime Minister of India, on the occasion of *The Economic Times* awards for corporate excellence, in the presence of over 900 CEOs of India Inc. said that power is to do good and money are both means of doing and a happy end result. It is accepted that power and money are not dirty words but legitimate measures of achievement.[32] P. Chidambaram, Finance Minister of India said: "(1) If we were able to deliver over 8% growth over the last 30 months, we can deliver a higher growth rate in the next 30 months; (2) India Inc. must enter in a big way in agriculture, without disturbing the sacred relationship between the tiller and land; (3) If we achieve growth, a democratic system will ensure equity."[34] According to International Finance Corporation's Doing Business 2007 Report, India stands low because starting business is an 11 stage process that takes 35 days while it takes just 2 days and two formalities in Australia. The Position of various countries is given below.[33]

Table Showing Countries and where they Stood for doing Business

Sl.No.	*Countries*	*2006*	*2007*
1.	Singapore	2	1
2.	Newzealand	1	2
3.	USA	3	3
4.	Japan	12	11
5.	South Korea	23	23
6.	Maldives	49	53
7.	Pakistan	66	74
8.	Srilanka	89	89
9.	China	108	93
10.	Russia	97	96
11.	Nepal	90	100
12.	Brazil	122	12
13.	India	138	134

What we need is not less reforms but more economic reforms. India Inc. has taken out in the last two years $ 10 billion to acquire companies abroad and tax revenue has risen at over 40-50% in 2005-2006. At the end of July 2006, 3058 projects were under implementation and the investment in these projects was Rs. 9,20,859 crore. Fresh investment proposal till July 2006 end was around Rs. 80,000 crores. According to P. Chidambaram, "We need to find new ways of enhancing the growth rate in agriculture, technological breakthroughs, new seeds, contract farming, massive investments in drip and sprinkler irrigation, diversification and a whole lot of things which are required to push the production of food grains and other products associated with agriculture. Slow reforms and corruption at various levels make India a difficult place to do business even in 2006-2007. An investor spends 7.8% of the cost of a property to register it in India and it takes 62 days in registering property as compared to just 2 days in Newzealand and Thailand. Hiring and firing are both difficult in India. Getting 20 license in India take 270 days while in Denmark getting 7 licenses takes 70 days. The positive aspect however is that it takes 264 hours to file and pay taxes and social security in India while the average for Asia Pacific region is 290.4 hours. India ranks 134 in doing business as compared to China (108) and Pakistan 66. India must effectively regulate monetary and fiscal policies to build the foundation of a strong national economy. The Reserve Bank of India's reputation as a regulator is rock solid in the global financial system. Reserve Bank of India has to closely monitor the role of foreign banks. RBI must ensure stability and soundness of Indian economy. While the draft approach paper of 11th Five year plan has projected GDP growth rate between 8% and 9% in 2007-12, the final draft of the 11th Five Year Plan (2007-2012) has put the growth potential of the economy between 9% and 10%. The Planning Commission, in the final draft, has said that 9% growth will require an increase in total investment rate from about 30% of the GDP in 2005-2006 to 35.1% on the average during the 11th Plan. The Planning Commission has assumed that higher growth target during the 11th Plan period would mean more than doubling agriculture growth rate from 1.7% in the 10th plant to 4% during the next plan; services growing by over 10% industry by 10.5% with manufacturing growing at over 12%.[35] Dr.Montek Singh Ahluwalia has said: Many companies changed their strategies to position themselves more approaching for an open competitive and global economy. For instance, Reliance built a world class refinery, Tatas developed an indigenously designed car. The software sector came up with an absolutely outstanding performance of competitiveness in an almost totally global market".[36] We have to do better and ensure that benefits from this higher growth go beyond industry and urban areas and extend to agriculture.

11. Knowledge Management and Competitive Edge

During the last two decades, Information Technology and Internet have given a new momentum to knowledge management (KM). India must capitalize on the talents of its people in the knowledge sector and must accelerate the rate of economic growth to achieve the "take-off stage". Knowledge management in general terms, is the systematic and explicit management of knowledge related activities, practices, programmes, and policies within the organisation with a district view to leverage individual knowledge and make it easily accessible across the organisation. KM helps in identifying priority areas and building a "critical learning mass" around benchmarked, categorised and systematically mapped areas of knowledge with the goal to build and exploit knowledge assets effectively and gainfully. Ancient Indian scriptures lay great emphasis on gaining knowledge as it has played a practical role in man's survival against the vagaries of nature and has enabled him to build a value-based cultured society. According to Hansen, Nohria and Tierney, "a company's knowledge management strategy should reflect its competitive strategy: how it creates values for customers, how that value supports an economic model and how the company's people deliver on the value and the economics", knowledge management has three main dimensions knowledge creation, knowledge sharing and knowledge application. The prestigious MAKE (Most Admired Knowledge Enterprises) survey conducted by the Teleos has assessed Indian companies along the following eight dimensions— (*i*) Creating an enterprise knowledge driven culture; (*ii*) Developing knowledge workers through senior management leadership, (*iii*) Delivering knowledge based products/services/solutions; (*iv*) Maximising enterprise intellectual capital; (*v*) Creating an environment for collaborative knowledge sharing; (*vi*) Creating a learning organisation; (*vii*) Delivering value based on customer knowledge; (*viii*) Transforming enterprise knowledge into shareholder value. In India the respective ranking of companies in 2005 is shown below.[38]

Table : 2005 Indian Make Award - winners ranked by composite score (80 is the maximum score)

2005 Rank	*Enterprise*	*Score*
1.	Infosys Technologies	64.79
2.	Eureka Forbes	63.33
3.	Tata Consultancy Services (TCS)	63.00
4.	Satyam Computer Service	62.56
5.	Wipro Technologies	61.93
6.	Tata Steel	61.83
7.	I. Flex Solutions	60.00

The following Indian companies have becomc global leaders for their innovative and pioneering work: (*i*) Infosys for developing knowledge workers through senior management leadership and transforming enterprise knowledge into share holder value, (*ii*) Satyam Computer Service for creating a learning organisation and transforming enterprise knowledge into shareholder value, (*iii*) Tata Consultancy Services for maximising the firm's enterprise intellectual capital and delivering value based on customer knowledge; (*iv*) Tata Steel for creating an environment for collaborative knowledge sharing and organisational learning; (*iv*) Eureka Forbes for creating a corporate knowledge driven culture, developing knowledge workers and creating an environment for collaborative knowledge sharing. Delhi is today the world's BPO capital and Indian cities have the top seven slots in the global ranking of competitiveness of cities as outsourcing destinations. The present top ten competitiveness index is given in next page:

Table Showing Competitive Index of the Top Ten in 2006

Sl.No	*Cities*	*Index*
1.	Delhi	100
2.	Bangalore	97.8
3.	Hyderabad	94.3
4.	Mumbai	92.6
5.	Pune	91.4
6.	Chennai	90.1
7.	Kolkata	89.1
8.	HO chi Minlicity (Vietnam)	87.9
9.	Manila (Philippines)	87.7
10.	Shanghai (China)	86.4

Source: Anit Thakur—Delhi is world's BPO Capital—*Times of India* 3 Nov 2006. The Business process outsourcing (BPO) is emerging as a new industry in the horizons of the globalisation. India is one of the major players.

India's retailing boom has acquired great momentum with international giants beginning to test the waters and the country's big business groups like Reliance, Bharti-wal-mart, Aditya Birla, Hero group and Carrefour/Tesco, RPG and Tata group taking new bold steps. Clearly the wave of the retail boom is emerging bright on the horizons. In many ways, it is a new wave of retailing.

12. Corporate Leadership and Indian CEOs

India Inc's corporate leaders are as motley as they come from the flam-boyant Vijay Mallya, to the soft-spoken Narayan Murthy; from the disciplined Azim Premji to the visionary Ratan Tata. But the one thing they have in common is that they are world-beating leaders whose reputations precede them wherever they go.[39] According to Prashanth L.J., global marketing officer, Infinite Computer Solution says: "The Indian leadership talent with strengths in social values, analytical abilities and balancing diverse cultural requirements is well poised to take on the challenges of global businesses. This makes them competent to multi task, Manage risks holistically, proactively innovate and manage cross cultural workforce." India's corporate leaders have lot of emotional competence, managerial skills, effective boundary management and "adaptive thinking" capabilities. Corporate leadership of India is inspiring and capable of creating an environment conducive to the flowering of individual competencies and capabilities down the line is an organization. Due to good corporate leadership many companies have performed remarkably well in a highly competitive global market. Companies like TCS, Wipro, Infosys, Satyam Computers and many other put before our eyes a fantastic record of performance.[40] Corporate Leadership in India has a great history. While Jamshedji Nawroji Tata is remembered for laying the building blocks of a diversified conglomerate and JRD Tata for leading the group from strength to strength during the days of the licence raj, Ratan Tata would be remembered at the modern entrepreneur who led the group in its successful endeavour to become a diversified global corporation. Is the Indian CEO as accountable as the Fords or the Dolans of the world? Turn over is company leadership in India is more driven by internal politics and perceived personal gains of the CEO and less due to the (in) ability of the person to implement a business strategy that results in tangible benefits to the Company's shareholders. Investors now prefer performance over stability and there is a wake up call for non-performing leaders.[41] Clay Ford Jr, former CEO of Ford Motor Company, was relieved of his job on September 5, 2006, Tom Freston, former CEO of Viacom (one of the world's largest media and entertainment companies) suffered the same fate on the same date. In the wake of a burgeoning scandal, Hewlett Packard announced on September 12, 2006 that board chairwoman Dunn would step down. That very day, acting on the suggestion of a former federal judge who is monitoring the company's deferred prosecution agreement drug maker Bristol-Myers Squibb effectively terminated at the tenure of CEO Dolan. Naryan Murthy is one of the best specimen of Indian corporate leaders and sets a pace for others. The best Indian CEOs do compare favourably with their international counterparts and that in some areas of management they are even superior.[42] According to a study they have unique "inner strength" and "adaptive thinking" capabilities. A research study have discovered four key areas that set Indian CEOs apart from outstanding top executives in other countries.

1. A Single minded focus on growth and innovations
2. A highly altruistic business philosophy.
3. A high degree of resilience and integrity
4. A formal professional approach to people and relationships.[43]

India needs more value based leadership - people with integrity, honesty and uncompromising of values and principles: Many leaders of our times, in business and government in India and elsewhere fail this test. Unfortunately we tend to describe all those who have positions and titles, wealth and fame, such as business tycoons and film stars as leaders in our society. The media perpetuates this notion and magnifies their power, wealth and fame.[44] True leadership lies in being the person rather than having titles, wealth, positions, influence or political clout. Indian companies should constantly try to globalise their image. By 2000, according to a survey done by business historian Gita Piramal, first generation firms (started in the 1960s and 70s) have been replaced by many of the third generation firms in India Inc's top 100 list. India is moving from an inheritance economy to one which compensates merit and values the democratizations of wealth.[45] Today India has access to a world beyond Bata Shoes and Ambassador Cars. It is the democratization of wealth. A young engineer starts a world-class software company which makes even the peons and lift operators rich. A small timer from Meerut moves to Mumbai and builds an airline empire that changes the way we travel. A cycle parts trader from Ludhiana takes phones out of the house and puts them into the hands of plumbers and frint vendors. The son of a school teacher creates one of the biggest petroleum refineries in the world.[46] Managing the future is a big challenge as the forces overturning the status quo are many and varied. At the top of their list, CEOs mention market forces such as intensified competition, escalating customer expectations and unexpected market shifts. Demographic shifts are playing their part. For coping up the challenges of uncertain future CEOs must do the following (*i*) Think broadly, act personally and manage the innovation mix. (*ii*) Make the business model deeply different, flat and receptive to the new winds: (*iii*) Substantially change how you add value in your current industry or in another; (*iv*) Ignite innovation through business and technology integration, (*v*) collaborate on a massive, geography defying scale to open a world of possibilities (*vi*) Push the organization to work with outsiders more, making it first systematically and them part of your culture.[47] Entrepreneurs are no longer from the traditional kutchi, Gujarati or Marwari communities. The corporate leader's image is fast changing in India with the process of democratization and globalisation of Indian business. India is on its way to becoming a grass roots capitalist society where every one gets a chance to enjoy the fruits of entrepreneurship hard work and professional leadership.

The upsurge in consumer demand has catapulated corporate India on to a growth trajectory as can be seen below:

Table showing Sales of BSE 200 companies, which grew at 25 percent in 2005- 2006, have registered 32 percent surge in the first half of 2006-2007

	Net Sales (YOY growth)			*PAT HI*	*Sales HI*
	2004	2005	2006		
1. Metal	24.2	43.3	26.7	92.3	96.6
2. Retail	48.4	65.5	72.3	30.4	63.2
3. IT	22.8	33.2	35.2	51.6	43.8
4. Construction	12.0	31.3	44.6	41.5	37.0
5. Capital goods	12.5	22.7	31.5	45.8	35.7
6. Oil & Gas	8.8	25.3	23.1	18.9	34.5
7. Cement	13.1	19.6	8.4	140.3	33.4
8. Auto	26.8	25.6	18.5	31.3	28.0
9. Auto Ancillaries	18.8	25.3	21.4	27.0	25.1
10. Pharma	18.0	6.9	16.8	47.6	25.1

Source: Sharekhan : Pat: Profit After Tax YOY : Year one Year H1: First half of 2006 -07 All figures are in %

Indians are now heading many multinational companies and some of them are also Women. The new face of the Indian business person is like the new face of India. A period of 15 years is too short to judge the impact of economic reforms. Indian corporate leaders bring five CS-Continuity of context, commitment to the region, cultural sensitivity, connections valuable to the organization and compassionate emotional intelligence. Indra Nooyi, who is now the Pepsi - co boss, is a role model for women and young generation of Indians. IIM-C remembers her as Indra Krishnamurthy - the youngest student of the 11th batch to pass out of the Instituted Joka Campus. Chandra Kochhar, Deputy MD ICICI Bank (37 Rank) Naina Lal Kidwai CEO HSBC (41 rank) India and Kiran Mazumdar Chairman Eicon (48 rank) are the three of corporate India's women business leaders who figure in the fortune list of the world's 50 most powerful women in 2006. An economic times analysis of BSE 100 companies shows that family owned companies have reported higher growth rate as shown below:

Promoter Type	*Net Sales*	*Net Profit*	*Market Cap*
1. Family Owner cos	21	34	44
2. Govt. Undertakings	12	21	30
3. Professional Coys	19	28	41
4. MNCs	9	14	27
5. Professional COS L (Excluding MNCs)	24	35	48

(*Source*: ET-22 September 2006)
(From Financial Year 2001-2006—All figures in percentage)

Attrition is hot - button issue, particularly if it is about the CEO of the organization. A five year study, conducted across 100 companies during 2001-06 reveals that 66% of the companies have had a change of CEO in the last five years. "Not a single company sacked CEO. Clearly in India CEOs resign, never get sacked", says EMA partners managing partner K. Sudarshan.[46] Indian Corporation must focus on core competencies and acquire the ability to be responsive to change, quality and process improvement and ensure constant innovations. Corporations in India should develop a dynamic approach to strategy formulation collaborative, drawing on key signals from all quarters and constantly evolving in the light of the new circumstances and market demands. Corporate leaders must build resilience and flexibility into the very fabric of the organization, by developing a set of core capabilities and competencies. Leaders have to remain steadfast in the face of uncertainty and have the quality to manage change effectively.[48] Churning of CEOs due to global transfers is inevitable in the present day competitive world of uncertain future. The following are the main finding of the research:-

Churning of CEOs Due to Global Transfer

1. Manufacturing - 9%
2. FMCG - 29%
3. IT and ITES - 13%
4. Pharma - 13%
5. Banking - 29%

Churning can be seen at HLL, P & G and a large number of banks. FMCG and banking sectors lead in sending CEOs to man another global positions. There is far more stability at the top in family owned undertakings because most of the time it's the promoter who runs it and board run business than the headquarter driven MNCs. Coca Cola had three CEOs in the last five years. The churning in CEOs in 2005 was as under.[49]

1. MNCs - 86%
2. Family Owner Firms - 57%
3. Professional firms - 43%

Succession planning is the best in companies which are managed by professional boards and that is why they had almost zero churn. The position of outside CEOs was found as under:

1. MNCs - 37%
2. Family Owned Firms - 42%
3. Professional Firms - 0%

The sectoral CEO churning was found sectorwise as under:

1. IT and ITES - 88%
2. Banking - 70%
3. Pharma - 67%
4. FMCC - 61%
5. Manufacturing - 58%

The industry with the fastest growth has the highest churn in CEOs-understandably due to tempting offers in for the CEOs. There are many reasons for CEOs to leave an organization as can be seen below:

1.	Death	-	2%
2.	Global transfer	-	17%
3.	M&A	-	11%
4.	Resignation	-	41%
5.	Re-structuring	-	5%
6.	Retired	-	24%

Changes are generally due to global transfers or resignations. At present the CEOs of India are in great demand abroad due to their high professional commitment, and experience of a democratic multi-religious, multi-cultural society. Large batches of well trained managers generally quit for greener pastures.[50] In order to survive in global competitive world, CEOs must be most proficient in marketing management and quality control. William A Foster has said: "Quality is never an accident, it is always the result of high intention, sincere effort, intelligent direction and skillful execution, it represents" wise choice of many alternatives. Indian CEOs must be well conversant with the paradigm shift in service marketing. Booms and Bitner (1981) have suggested an extended "7-Ps"- approach that contains the following seven PS—Product, price, promotion, place, people, process and physical evidence of what we call touch point. According to Kevin Lane Keller taking care of the marketing subtleties is a huge thing, because different markets are at different stages of development. The conditions with regard to consumers, competition, infrastructure and channels of communication are very different.[52a] In India there is a need for succession plan for leaders at various levels. The greatest challenge for organizations today is developing the next generation of leaders who can not only cope with change but also drive it".[51] The average age of executives and CEOs in today's organizations is coming down and business is faced with the prospect of young, dynamic and forward looking leaders. Every leader is wired to a decision-making algorithm, the trick is to articulate it. John Kotter says: "When it comes to leadership, there is still a big gap between what exists and what we need".[52] The following useful guidelines can go a long way for the new CEOs:

1. Listen and observer, Do your home work, 2. Tread cautiously amidst crisis, No—No to comfort zone, 3. Take first stock of the existing systems, 4. Warm up before you run, the first 90 days are critical, 5. List out your priorities future directions clearly, Remember the following eight steps of John Kotters transformation process, 1. Increase urgency, 2. Build the guiding team, 3. Get the vision right, 4. Communicate for buy-in, 5. Empowering action, 6. Create short term wins, 7. Do not let up, 8. Make change stick".[53]

13. The Emerging Issues and the New Opportunities

Inspite of all efforts to raise the economic status of the Indian people, below poverty line (BPL) population counted for 27.81% in 2004-2005 compared to 35.97% in 1993-94.[54] These estimates were prepared using monthly consumption expenditure of individuals during 365 days on clothing, foot wear, education, durables in additions to their medical expenses. This method is called the Mixed Reference Period Method (MRPM). Incredible India is a great attraction for foreign tourists. India in 2005, according to world tourism organization data, earned an average of around $1,500 from every foreign tourist who visited India in 2005. As logistics and transportation assume greater importance in the globalised world, India is attracting international logistic companies to provide integrated supply chain solutions. In a globalised market economy, logistics management includes supply chain management, distribution management, transportation management, warehouse services and distribution and exclusive technology services, logistics management is one of the new horizons for Indian managers. Air conditioned comfortable bases, trucks, water lorries, movers and shakers are all needed to boost up logistics management in India. The following are the Forex earnings per tourist 2005 (US $) in different countries of the world.

World	-	844
France	-	556
Spain	-	862
USA	-	1653
Italy	-	970
China	-	626
Sri Lanka	-	984
Honkgong	-	685
Malaysia	-	520
Singapore	-	892
India	-	1462

(*Source:* Ministry of Tourism)

A foreign tourist from the top international markets for India spends an average of 16 days in India. However, India needs to build up its tourist infrastructure and genuine welcome to tourists. All over the country the aspirations of the people are rising and people are getting more interested in satisfying their luxury needs also. The Indian consumer is lapping up credit and credit card outstandings are dominating the consumer loan kitty. Credit card outstandings increased by 199% to 4539 crores and the housing loan market grew by 54% to 1,17,917 crore at the end of June 2006. The outstanding credit on various items as on June 2006 are given below:

Sl.No.	*Items*	*Outstanding as on June 06*	*Increase*	*in %*
1.	Non-food gross credit	11,87,215	3,66,174	244.6
2.	Agriculture	1,58,506	42,619	36.8
3.	Industry	4,48,494	94,133	26.6
4.	Services	45,466	30,661	207.1
5.	Personal Loans	3,24,491	1,04,058	47.2
6.	Real Estate Loans	23,633	11,957	102.4

(June 2006 Over June 2005) (Rs. in Crores)
Source: RBI. *Times of India*, 31 Oct 2006.

Future belongs to those who think of tomorrow today. Great mavericks and change masters ceaselessly peep into the future; tap new opportunities proactively, to lead the corporate milieu. The emerging corporate battles in times to come will be won not on the might of technology but on the power of human ideals and innovation quotient. Some managers see their burnt-out colleagues, running after the elusive pot of gold at the ends of the proverbial rainbow. Modern work life ends up "Squeezing" more out of each person. The price to climb the corporate ladder is too high, too demanding and too stressful. Yet there is a mad race to climb up.

14. Managing Corruption free Society

India has loads of corruption in every walk of life and is among the most corrupt societies in the world. A world Economic Forum's Executive opinion survey of 125 countries the worst and the least bribe paying countries in 2005 were as under:

The Worst	*The Least*
1. India	1. Switzerland
2. China	2. Sweden
3. Russia	3. Australia
4. Turkey	4. Austria
5. Taiwan	5. Canada
6. Malaysia	6. UK
7. South Africa	7. Germany
8. Brazil	8. Netherlands
9. Saudi Arabia	9. Belgium
10. South Korea	10. United States

Source: Times News Network London/New Delhi—The Times of India 5th Oct 2006.

The Transparency International's Bribe Payer Index (BPI) might suggest that Indian exporters have a lousy reputation as bribe givers overseas but it is just a case of pot calling the kettle black. India was not listed on the BPI in 1999 and 2001 but in its overzeal to become economic power, it has earned a bad reputation. The Research about bribe takers reveals the other side of the picture. The names of countries given below indicate their involvement in corrupt practices.

Table showing countries getting percentage of India's export and BPI score given to India and countries where India paid money as bribery in different forms to get business. LOOK WHO'S POINTING FINGERS

Country	*BPI Score given to India*	*% of India's export*
United States	6.65	16.75
UAE	6.06	8.36
China	4.34	6.54
Singapore	6.67	5.42
UK	7.29	5.01
Hong Kong	5.32	4.34
Germany	6.67	3.42
Belgium	7.50	2.78
Italy	3.85	2.42
Japan	7.33	2.39
Holland	5.42	2.39
France	4.78	1.99
Sri Lanka	5.00	1.96
S. Korea	4.09	1.77
Bangladesh	3.01	1.59
S. Africa	6.00	1.51
Indonesia	5.00	1.33
Israel	7.50	1.18
Malaysia	6.51	1.12
Brazil	4.70	1.05
Thailand	5.00	1.03

Source on a scale from 0 to 10. Lower score means perceived as more corrupt.

The propensity of Indian to bribe overseas is directly proportionate to the willingness of the host countries officials/ business people to demand/accept bribes. India is today in 2006 less corrupt than in 2005. India has earned a better ranking in the corruption perception Index released by Transparency International and this marginal improvement (70th rank in 2006 from 88 last year 2005) has been brought by the entering efforts of the Civil Society Organisations, Central Govt. led by Dr. Man Mohan Singh and the Right to Information Act (Effective from 12 Oct 2005.[56] Wharton Professor Franklin Alen says: A low level of corruption is not a significant impediment to growth because business can obtain financing and settle legal differences outside the legal system in ways that are quite effective. ISB Hyderabad Professor Sankar De says: small and medium size Indian companies have found ways to get around the limitations of the country's financial and legal systems. Indian legal system itself creates corruption by having large backlog of cases. The whole political system needs a radical change to uproot corruption from society.

15. Building and Managing Indian Multinationals

The building and maintaining Indian Multinationals is one of the newly emerging challenges in Indian Management. The Tata Group's thrust into Africa with a social conscience is a new approach that has brought rich market dividends. A global focus will be an important strategy for future growth of Indian Corporates. These multi-nations will reflect a multi-nationals workforce. For example, in Aditya Birla Group more than 12000 of its 72000 employees are from 20 foreign nationalities. With multi-national character of Indian Management, bringing harmony in diversity is the prime task. Globalisation, diversification, better customer interface changing organizational structure and governmental regulations are all new emerging challenges which are to be managed to build and maintain a sustainable global corporation. Ratan Tata chairman Tata Sons Ltd in an interview said: "We had set ourselves the task of being a $ 50 billion group in five years. It was not good enough to be globally competitive. It was important to internationalise our operations so that we were not dependent on one economic cycle. "Ratan Tata believes that business must be based on values and ethics". The Tata group has given 16 crores for the Tsunami Calamity with focus on rehabilitation. An executive's ability to study, understand and analyse global trends accurately in a rapid changing business environment can make all the difference between riding the currents of emerging opportunities and paddling upstream against them. The following 10 global trends are very crucial for the global business.[57]

1. Growing number of consumers in emerging economic/ changing consumer tastes.
2. Shift of economic activity between and within regions (E.g. to Asia and within Europe Union).
3. Greater ease of obtaining information, developing knowledge.
4. Increasingly global labour and talent markets.
5. Increasing constraints in supply of usage of natural resources (E.g. environmental regulations).
6. Increasing communication/interaction in business and social realness as a result of technological innovation.
7. Shifting industry structures/emerging forms of corporate organization.
8. Application of scientific techniques and approaches to business management.
9. More intense social backlash against business.
10. Growth of public sector.

A scan of global trends form a tangled web that can catch a company's strategy un-awares and often proves superficial or simplify the complexity of inter-acting sub-trends. Globalisation, diversification wider customer interface, changing organizational structure and government regulations—each of these results in one big change: increasing diversity. In a global economy, changing business needs are making organizational pluralities a growing reality. Indian multi-national corporation will increasingly reflect a multi-national work force.

For example, Aditya Birla Group has more than 12000 of its 72000 employees from 20 foreign nationalities. Increasing diversity comes along gender, age, regional, educational and nationality lines and managing diversity is one of the most important challenges of the future managers. The analysis should go well beyond a superficial scan of global issues not only build a detailed understanding of the trends and how they will affect the corporation in the long run good strategic planning can help companies find new growth opportunities and evaluate what they should add to on subtract from the corporate portfolio of business. Indian Bangalore based software giant Infosys has joined the likes of eBay, Yahoo, Microsoft, Google, Dell and Cisco as a member of the elite Nasdaq-100 Index on December 18, 2006. The US SEC (Securities Exchange Commission) has assigned Infosys the status of well known-seasoned issue (WKSI). More Indian companies should try to get visible branding. The Nasdaq-100 Index is one of the world's most recognized branch marks that owes this distinction to its components: Companies that are leaders in a diverse range of industries - India needs to synergize its various advantages into competitiveness and must become an International driver of competition in major world economies. In another decade India should become a major super-economic power Mr. L.N. Mittal, Steel baron of India has said, "India is now widely recognized as a major player in the global business environment." Indian companies are generally in very good financial health. This coupled with an access to significant pool of capital is driving M and A appetite. This is the result of confidence among Indian Promoters. The most important thing is that Indians have achieved competitiveness at the global level.

The basic issue is the very high growth rate we are going for, but many questions are raised about the quality of the growth, mix of the growth, how inclusive is that growth, need to be properly addressed. The Indian education system and human resource development strategies suffer from inadequacies of structure as well as content. The soaring salaries and ample growth opportunities are spoiling employee habits and job-hopping is now a common scenario not only in the IT and ITES industry but in other sectors as well, leading to high attrition rates. Environment and ecology all over the world is facing a great threat there is a very significant part of the population, particularly in rural India, which is completely left out, leading to frustration, terrorism, violence and insurgency, thereby making India a soft target due to displaced targets of grievances and hostility in many under developed areas/states. The process of globalisation is giving rise to cultural threats leading to dilution and destruction of regional and local cultures, language, indigenous heritages and so on. 90 percent of the employment in the unorganised sector is completely neglected in India. There is 300 million population which is lacking in basic literacy primary education and health. Unprecedented amounts of venture capital have began flowing in India. More than 44 U.S. Based venture capitals are seeking to invest in India. These firms are together expected to raise as much as $ 4.4 billion (Rs. 20,680 Crores) the real estate prices keep the majority of common man out of the housing market and make the dream of owning a house more distant. Inspite of all claims of economic development, the average Indian faces the problems of water, electricity, quality of house-hold oriented services and even quality education at average cost for an average young man. Lastly despite regular economic growth for nearly a decade the nutritional status of Indian children hasn't improved. Peter Drucker in his famous book "Managing challenges for the 21st Century" (1999) has said: "The most valuable asset of a 21st century institution, whether business or non-business will be its knowledge workers and their productivity". Winner of the 2001 Nobel Prize for Economics, Joseph Stiglitz in his latest book "Managing gobalisation work" (Viking 2006) has said: "Trickle-down theory of economics doesn't work. It has not worked anywhere. It hasn't worked even in the United States." Disparities are actually increasing Nobel Laureate Amartya Sen has said: "If India could implement land reforms, spread education and extend healthcare to all, it will help positively in reducing distress migration. Distress migration was a combination of involuntary aspect, where people were being forced to move, as well as a voluntary element because people could move when they wanted to Dr. Amartya Sen has said: "Do not rely on market economy for development." We need a shift in mindset to understand that economic progress and development must be seen in its human dimensions rather than in statistical terms". Private-public partnership is prescribed as a solution for the economic problems of the country and the focus of all efforts must remain the human façe of the poor.

India today is very optimistic of growth and rapid strides. Countries with greatest expectations of growth in 2007 are shown below.

Table—Countries with greatest expectations of growth in 2007

India	90
Mainland	85
Armenia	83
South Africa	82
Argentina	80
Singapore	79
Malaysia	77
US	77
Russia	76
Philippines	75
Global Average	69
EU Average	57

Source: Grant Thornton.

However, India should not become complacent with the pace of economic reforms. Economic reforms have clearly slowed down not just in banking and insurance sector but also in many other sectors. Given the compulsions of coalition politics and elections in some states in near future, the UFA government has chosen to throw good money after bad by trying to revive sick PSUS and a conservative RBI has slowed down the pace of financial sector reforms. This requires proper strategic planning for disaster management. Disaster management is emerging as a big challenge for a country like India since India is prone to earthquakes, floods, famines, cyclones, bomb explosions, air/rail accidents and other environmental tragedies. Multi-national companies opened not only their hearts but also purse strings to assist the needy in mage tragedy in the form of tsunami and other disasters. An Economic Times New Delhi study on corporate donations indicates the following figures.

Table showing top ten donors for last two years

Top Ten Donors (2004-05)		*Top Ten Donors (2005-06)*	
Company	*Donation*	*Company*	*Donation*
Reliance Inds	38.31	Reliance Inds	25.7
IOC	26.54	Infosys	17
HPCL	21.13	Jaiprakash Asso	15.2
Infosys	21.09	GNFC	11.36
Hindalco	13.53	Jindal Steel	10.13
SCI	12.22	HPCL	8.91
Grasim	9.82	Hindalco	8.71
NTPC	9.7	Bharti Airtel	7.45
Jaiprakash Asso	9.01	Bajaj Auto	6.01
Dr. Reddy's	8.78	Dr. Reddy's	6

Indian corporate sector is gradually realising its social responsibilities and becoming more dynamic, humans and compassionate to the needs of the people who are victims of natural calamities.

The emerging frontiers and trends of the business process outsourcing include tighter partnerships and joint venture opportunities, growth in offshore business processes, increased production of granular level business intelligence to improve decision making and greater involvement of IT department in strategic outsourcing decisions in India. BPO represents a paradigm shift in low companies operate in a global economy. True development is not quantifiable whether at the personal, national or global level. Development, like happiness, primarily belongs to the personal plane. A happy nation is simply an extension of happy individuals. The goal of all human endeavours, according to Indian philosophy should be *Dharma, Artha, Kama*, and *Mokhsha* and a spiritual tendency is necessary to control our greed for excessive material wealth, excessive sexual indulgence. A balanced holistic development is needed for both individuals and the nations. It is *dharma* that renders development sustainable and holistic. Indians even today prefer happiness, contentment and peace of mind rather than running for material prosperity. The happiness index of various nations can be seen in the table below.

Table showing gross GDP ranking and Happiness Index

S.No.	*Countries*	*Gross GDP ranking*	*Human Development Indicates ranking*	*Happiness index ranking*
1.	USA	1	10	150
2.	China	2	84	31
3.	India	4	125	62
4.	Germany	5	20	81
5.	UK	6	15	108
6.	France	7	16	129
7.	Italy	8	18	66
8.	Brazil	9	62	63
9.	Russia	10	61	172
10.	Canada	11	4	111

Global tech firms are now relocating top management functions to India. Some blue chip tech companies have moved important global functions to India as shown below:

Company	*Function*
CISCO	Chief Globalisation Officer
IBM	Senior Technical and Management Personnel
Accenture	Global technical heads
Yahoo	Global product development head
Adobe	Senior product executives and business unit managers

The era of multiple superpowers has ended and today the world is closely inter-dependent, in economic and political terms. India is one of the world's biggest countries; we are growing at an encouraging rate; we have the world's largest, most educated and hardest working middle class; we represent a huge market and we are the world's largest democracy. The need today is to focus on innovation and acquire the ability to be responsive to change, quality and process improvements. Today in India, a new foreign owned factory opens every 26 minutes while in China a new research and development lab opens every

43 hours. How can India achieve top leadership in management world and successfully thrive in this globally competitive economy? India must constantly develop professional corporate leaders who have the vision, courage, dedication and inspiring leadership to initiate and manage change. India, as a global player, is now committed to explore-talented management aspirants with strong social values, having potential knowledge base and holistic understanding of applied skills and emotional intelligence.

The Indian state has a split personality. At times Indian Government talks of inviting foreign investors to boost up the economy and sometimes it turns the clock back to be an inward looking country for the sake of national security. A paranoid state that puts the shutters down on business would in fact be serving the interests of those who resent a resurgent India. Before trying to focus on imaginary enemies of foreign origin, let us fix our own inner demons. India must choose a middle path that will bring harmony between national security and a vibrant global economy. India must promote innovations and translate these innovations into business profits. Gary Hamel in his latest book "Competing for the Future" rightly says—"Getting ideas is one thing. Translating them into action is another with the constant changes and shifts in contemporary business environment, fluidity in organisational structures and processes is needed to in certain organisational effectiveness". Indians are now buying like never before, helping the corporates to cross the hurdles of rising interest rates and global oil prices and giving net huge monies to sustain ever increasing growth rate. Increasing costs of manpower, raw material and higher depreciation are dewing down profit margins. India Inc has for the last three years (2004-06) beaten the streat and odds in sales and profit growth. The new horizons of India's incorporates are very bright, attractive and alluring. But the question is how long is this growth sustainable? Growth is sustainable if we Indians work hard but there is no room for complacency.

The market conditions in India are not very stable and steady and are unpredictable. The changing face of Retailing in India and the megatrends of the next decades have to be anticipated and taken care of. The key trends of the future world have to be anticipated and pro-active actions must be taken to cope with them. Corporate leaders must redesign organisations for uncertain environments of the future. In order to effectively manage the new horizons and frontiers of future, Indian corporate leaders have to develop—a vision anchored around tomorrow's industry, tomorrow's competition, tomorrow's customers, and the tomorrow's social needs, aspirations and Indian citizens.

References

1. Dr. Debashis Chatterjee—Professor IIM Lucknow—Kaun Banega Narayan Murthy—Success Sutras Times Ascent—October 18, 2006.
2. Mukesh Ambani—Unleashing India's Potential—Economic Times, 4th October, 2006.
3. NYT News Service—Americans appear in ranks of India Cos—Times of India—18th Oct, 2006. Somini Sen Gupta.
4. Swaminathan S. Anklesaria Aiyar—GDP growing at 13.4% in dollars, Times of India, 29th October, 2006, p. 18.
5. Joseph Schumpeter—Capitalism, Socialism and Democracy.
6. Andy grove "only the paranoid survive".
7. Ravi Parwan—Sector Scan—What makes It tick? The Economic Times, 23 October, 2006.
8. F.A.Vandrevala—what will it take to electrify all our villages? Business Today, January 15, 2006, p. 94.
9. Samrat—No Super power if there is no power, Hindustan Times, New Delhi, 7.10.06.
10. Joseph S.Nye Jr.—Springing Tiger, India Today, October 2, 2006.
11. Jasvir Singh—Problem of wages, The Times of India, New Delhi 26 September, 2006.
12. Mahendra Kumar Singh—Study—BPL Population up in Delhi, Maha and Haryana—The Times of India, New Delhi, October 19, 2006.
13. Adil Zainulbhai (Managing Director of Mc Kinsey and company's India Practice)—CM AS CEOS The state of the states—India's Best and worst state of India Today special issue—September 11, 2006, p. 44.
14. C.K. Prahlad—the fortune at the bottom of the Pyramid Eradicating Poverty through profits.

15. Swaminathan S. Anklesaria Aiyar "Misfortune at bottom of Pyramid" The Economic Times, New Delhi, 25 October, 2006.

16. For detailed analysis of the subject consult Krishna Mohan Mathur—Management of Internal Security and Related issues—Chapter 5, pp. 155 -180. Gyan Publishing House, New Delhi, 1995.

17. Jhinuk Chowdhury—Branding across Borders—The Times of India—Ascent. November 1, 2006.

18. A.P.J. Abdul Kalam—Ignited Minds—Unleashing the power within India—Penguin Books India 2002. Preface, pp. IX-XI.

19. Fore exhaustive treatment of the subject refer to—"Passion to Win". All India Management Association, Publication—Abad Ahmed and O.P. Chopra.

20. Yoginder K. Alagh—Bonus or Liability —Times of India, New Delhi, 5th November, 2006.

21. Swaminathan S. Anklesaria Aiyar. The advantage of Poverty—Times of India, New Delhi, 5th November, 2006.

22. Dr. K.M. Mathur—"Towards Effective Management and pathways to excellence"—Gyan Publishing House, New Delhi, 1999, pp. 152-155.

23. Amrita Nair—Ghaswalia-Nilikani to Join Renters Board in Jan 2007. Times of India, Delhi, 23 Oct., 2006.

23(a). Sam Pitroda, Chairman National Knowledge Commission, The Economic Times, New Delhi, 9 November, 2006. Emerging India.

24. Ravi Pawan—Sector Scan what makes it tick? The Economic Times, New Delhi, 23 October, 2006.

24. Sam Pitroda—Emerging India holds innovative solution for global maladies—The Economic Times, 9 November, 2005.

25. Jhinuk Chowdhury—Jack of all Traits becomes the Master. Times of India, Ascent, 30 August, 2006.

26. Surging Economy to create 10.3 lakh jobs in 2006: MAFOI— The Economic Times, New Delhi, 11 Oct., 2006.

27. Times of India, New Delhi, 25th October, 2006—Chidanand Rajghatta Latest US fad—karma Capitalism.

28. Swami Sukhabadhananda—Roar your way to excellence—self empowerment made easy—published by Prasanna Trust, Bangalore. April 2006, pp. 41-45.

29. Emma Bell and Scott Taylor Spirituality in the workplace: Management with a mission? SLIM papers.

30. Dr. Krishna Mohan Mathur—Towards Effective management-Pathways to excellence chapters 5 and 9, Gyan Publisjing House, New Delhi, 1999.
31. AIMA News—Managing Excellence—May-June, 2006.
32. The Economic Times—Corporate Dossier—Oct., 20, 2006.
33. In slows ever after reforms India is a difficult place to do business.
34. P. Chidambaram—We need more reforms for growth—(guest column) The Economic Times, 18 Oct., 2006, New Delhi, p. 16.
35. Subash Narayan—Plan Panel drafts 9% GDP growth - The Economic Times—18th October, 2006, p. 15.
36. Montek Singh Ahluwala—It's time reform touched the farms-guest column—The Economic Times, 19.10.2006.
37. Hamsen M.T., Nohria N. and Turney T. What is your strategy for Managing Knowledge-HBR-March-April, 1999.
38. A.V. Vedpurisivar—Knowledge as a computer edge—Indian Management September 2006, p. 168.
39. Nikhil Menon—Leadership Rules—The Economic Times, New Delhi, 20th June, 2006.
40. Montex Singh Ahluwala—It's time reform touched the farms guest column. The Economic Times, 19 October, 2006.
41. Shanto Ghosh—know your CEO—Times of India, 12 Oct., 2006.
42. Dr. Man Mohan Singh—The India CEO: competencies for Success summit—January 22, 2005, New Delhi.
43. Hay group study of traits behaviours and motives of 30 of India's top CEO—a research study sponsored by Bharat Petroleum Corporation of India.
44. Arun Maira—Lack of values—we need to rethink our notions or leadership—Times of India, New Delhi, 30 Oct., 2006.
45. Navineta Devi Dayal—Inheritance of Loss - Old Business order makes way for New Times of India, New Delhi.
46. Times of India—Editorial Inheritance of Loss - Old business order makes way for New—Namita Devidayal.
47. Dinesh Narayanan—CEO swear by creative destruction—says IBM study—Times of India, 14 Sept., 2006.
48. Vinod Kumar Sharma—Designing organizations for uncertain environments—Indian Management September 2006, p. 202.

49. The story behind CEO attrition—The Economic Times, New Delhi, 18th Oct., 2006. The complete data given below is based as study of 100 companies during 2001-06 by Executive search firm EMA Partners.

50. T. Surendar—The Leadership challenge—finding first among equals—The Times of India, New Delhi, 21 September, 2006.

51. Neol Tichy Judgement Day Corporate Dossier—1st September, 2006.

52. John Kotter—HC Stoops to Conquer—Corporate Dossier September 1, 2006.

52a. Phillip Kotler and Kevin Lane Keller—Marketing Management the new edition.

53. John Kotter Leading Change—The Leadership Factor and Matsushita Leadership.

54. Mahendra Kumar Singh—A National Sample Survey Organisation's Study—The Times of India, New Delhi, 19th October, 2006.

55. Atul Thakur—Have money, will splurge in India—Budget Destination myth stands shattered.

56. Times of India, New Delhi, 7 November, 2006.

57. March 2006, Mc Kinsey Quarterly Global Survey of Business Executives; I am Davis and Elizabeth Stephenson "Ten Trends to watch in 2006".

3

The Ethos of Indian Management

"The Voyage of discovery lies not in finding new landscapes, but in having new eyes". —*Marcel Proust*

There is a frantic search for a distinctive managerial ethos in Indian Managers. India can provide many paths to value-driven effective management. The ethos of Indian Management needs to be explored and conceptualized. Since every nation requires its own unique management style which has to be based on its people and its unique culture, Indian corporate sector can draw lot of valuable guidance, sutras and workable theories from various Indian scriptures and texts like Ramayan, Mahabharat, Bhagwat Gita, Kautilya *Arthshastra* and other epics and try to broadly define the pre-requisites for an efficient, honest and successful Indian Managers. During the last five decades, only a few studies have been made by Indian Scholars about management styles of Indian Managers.[1] There is enormous scope for developing indigenous management style in India based on Indian Value and culture. Indian ethos is pre-dominantly governed by our value-orientation based on *dharma* (the supportive actions and ideology in one's own life in the family and in the community), *purushartha* [(The four fold goals of life), *Dharma* (religion) *Arth* (money) *Kama* (desires) and *Moksha* (Liberation)] and *rna* (five fold indebtedness and obligations to the ancestors, to the cultural forebearers, to the living beings and the society etc.). Indian ethos expounds ethical conduct, honesty, concern for others, integrity, morality, responsibility conscience and *nishkam* Karma (action without expecting fruits of action). Actually Indian culture has absorbed numerous enriching strands from Buddhist, Islamic, Christian,

Parsi, Sikh and Jain traditions. It is generally recognized that the Vedas, Upanishads, the Smrities, the Puranas, Ramayan, Mahabharat have all blossomed on Indian soil and have served as "deep structures" of Indian ethos. A closer study of Indian ethos gives rise to a common set of ideals, which are actively practised or are subscribed to by the greater part of Indian humanity[2]. It is for various reasons that Indian ethos of Management has not been practised by the managers and entrepreneurs as they were not trained or even familiar with Indian Culture and were trained in western styles of management. Indian Management has failed to take a hard look at Indian cultural attributes - work ethics, intellectual honesty, business transparency, willingness to be fair and honest and lack of national pride[3]. Barring few exceptions, most business organizations and companies operating in India Practice American Philosophy of hire and fire management style. The sad part is that sitting in India most business managers trained from Indian business schools know well about the way Intel and Microsoft are managed and not about how Tatas and Indian Pariwar work Indian Ethos of management is not slokas and Sanskrit verses from ancient Indian scriptures or offering the philosophy of Shankara or Buddha or Vedanta. It is not preaching religion or Hinduism. Indian ethos of management implies application of ancient Indian wisdom to Managerial tasks and responsibilities. Indian ethos of management provides a holistic approach to various management concepts. Indian Management thinkers and writers must do lot of documentation and indigenous research on Indian Management styles, values, management practices and must come out with authenticated and well researched "India-centric management practices". The Indian ethos of management has to be evolved, refined, developed and documented by constant research by management thinkers and academicians of India[4]. Ancient Vedantic wisdom has lot of useful philosophy which can enrich Indian ethos of management. The matrix which is very useful for Indian Managers and has briefly given main tenets of Vedantie philosophy and wisdom which can inspire Indian managers and entrepreneurs has been given in the next page.

The Matrix of Vedantic Philosophy and Wisdom in Aid of Contemporary Management

1. Vedanta a sovereign science.
2. In Each one of us dwells divinity Atma (Soul) (KNOW THYSELF).
3. Vasu dhaiva Kutumba Kam (Entire earth is one family) concept of extended family in organisations.
4. Essential Unity of all religions and need for tolerance and respect for other religious.
5. The Soul is infinite, omnipotent and realizable Need for moral code of conduct.
6. Seven spiritual Laws of Success.

   6.1 Law of Pure Potential

   6.2 Law of giving

   6.3 Law of least effort

   6.4 Law of intention and desires.

   6.5 Law of detachment—non-attachment to power.

   6.6 Law of Dharma or Purpose of life.
7. Need for Enlightened Guru for teaching Vedanta for dealing with (*i*) crisis of character, (*ii*) crisis of leadership, (*iii*) crisis of focusing, (*iv*) crisis of motivation and (*vi*) crisis of vision.
8. Entire cosmos permeated by the Brahma (the Almighty god) and need for welfare of the human beings.
9. Vedanta science of Human energy resources (Adhyatma-Vidya).
10. Transmigration of soul and theory of Sanskaras.
11. Four *Purusharth—Dharma, Arth, Kam* and *Moksha* as goals for realisation.
12. Leadership need *Anushashan* (Self discipline) and wisdom.
13. Stress Management through meditation and mind stilling exercises.
14. Workers need wisdom action with equanimity and work ethos.
15. *Sthiti Pragyata* for Role effectiveness.

16. Human personality covered with five sheaths and soul needs identification.
17. Vedanta brings transformational effects at spiritual, personal, social and organizational levels.
18. Quality of work life and work ethics by virtuous living.
19. Managerial Ethics and Ethical Organizational climate.
20. Organizational effectiveness and Excellence. (4)

Indian Vedantic and wisdom can provide very useful aid for dealing with various contemporary management challenges. The solutions to various managerial challenges through Indian approach can be briefly summarised as under:

Figure 2

Various Crisis and Challenges	*Indian Approach*
1. Crisis of character	Control through observance of *Dharma* (religion) and righteousness—Need to learn Adhytama Vidya and get *chitta suddhi*.
2. Crisis of leadership	Need for character building and higher value system through Vedantic training and education—concept of Rajarshi and wisdom workers.
3. Crisis of focusing	Concentration of mind—ekagrata spiritual empowerment, meditation.
4. Crisis of bureaucracy and lack of commitment	Solution through *nishkam-karm yoga*—Transformation through self-management (Self-discipline) and self-dedication.
5. Crisis of motivation	Law of giving and concept of universe as one family

Various Crisis and Challenges	*Indian Approach*
	extended (*vasudhew kutumbkam*) Theory of *Rin* (debt).
6. Crisis of vision	Solution through holistic perception of life and universe and four fold goals of life Dharma, Artha and *Karm* and *Moksha*.
7. Stress and health problems	Mind stilling exercises, meditation like Vipassna, Raj Yoga, Kundalin Sahaj Yoga, Patanjali Yoga
8. Transcendental Meditation	Prekshadhyana Tm- and other such exercises and spiritual living.
9. Lack of Discipline and low productivity	Vedanta stresses on Self-discipline, Yam, Niyam and work commitment with doctrine of *Karma Yoga*.

The ethos of Indian Management stresses the welfare of all human beings—*Bahujana Sukhaya Bahnjana hitaya ca*—(the welfare of the many, the happiness of the many). The Rig veda lays down that the dual purpose of human life - atmano *Moksartham Jagat hitaya ca* - (we work for the emancipation of our souls but also for the welfare of the world).[7] One of the most important dimensions of management is the challenge of managing human resources, here the Vedantic truths - "Isavasyam idam sarvan yat Kin ca Jagatyam Jagat" - this entire cosmos is permeated by the same pervasive energy called Brahma - the spiritual correlate of the infield field theory and the concept of the *Atman -Ishvarah sarva bhut a nam hrddess tis thati* - the lord resides in the heart of all beings, regardless of their religion, their race, their colour, their creed or their ideology. Indian ethos revolves around four *purusharthas* (meaning what should be sought after by the people) and they are; (1) *Dharma*—Virtuous living or *moral* merit in the sense of discharging one's duty; (2) *Artha*—acquiring of material wealth; (3) *Kama*—gratification of desires and enjoyment of worldly pleasures; (4) Moksha—the liberation and salvation from the miseries of the rounds of existence in the cycle of birth and death. Leadership is traditionally seen "not as power, privilege and enjoyment but as a sacred trust and responsibility". There is stress on public good, on all stake holders and not just share holder value maximization. The ideology includes ethics, social responsibility and philanthropy. The leader is expected to demonstrate. "Self-Management" before being worthy of "Organisational Management"[8]. Indian Management has added a new word to the dictionary the "intrapreneur". Educated Indian Managers began as implementors of the entrepreneur's initial vision but have increasingly taken over roles of internal enterpreneur by taking the group into diversification's, acquisitions, export markets etc. There is a typical Indian Managerial ethos with distinctive strengths that need to be nurtured and developed[9]. Every Manager must remember that every human being encapsulates a spark of the divine, and fanning that spiritual orientation is the ultimate goal of human existence. In each one of us dwells the divine, concealed but discoverable. The Upanishads call human race as "Amritasya Putrah"—Children of divinity[10]. Bringing spirituality into the work place will facilitate housing creativity and management skills, bringing about a work ambience free from tension, worry and stress. The key is therefore, holistic development - for it is not enough to have faith in god alone; we need to have abundant faith in our own selves too. That's how we will grow into becoming responsible achievers. This approach will bring superlative performances from our employees and will drive us from an asset based economy to a talent based economy. Indian management thinkers urge: (*a*) the phrase "human resources" represents the worst assault on the English language since the Watergate hearings; (*b*) the conscious use of "human response development" (HRD) is more desirable instead of human resource development; (*c*) employees are human beings and should not be considered as resource like spare parts, financial reserves and the other inanimate resource we use. Let us retain the acronym HRD if we should but let us mean by it, "human response development"; (*d*) human beings need spiritual awakening; (*e*) human beings must be grounded in his or her spiritual core to be defined in universal terms (*f*) the absence of the vital spiritual link in modern motivational theories must be removed by recognizing the presence of the spiritual core of human beings[11]. Basic practical psychological works like the Bhagwat Gita or Patanjali's Yoga sutras, supplemented by edifying teachings from Koran, the Bible and Granth Sahib and other epics, need to be used at all stages of management development programmes. A company's HRD should be a movement to mine talents, skills, technologies and competencies and develop the full potentials of the individuals and groups. So, that they can manifest their skills, techniques, knowledge, competencies and attitudes by raising productivity, efficiency, and performance superlatively in their respective fields. In our ancient scriptures, stress has been classified into three categories:

1. Bhautika or Physiological
2. Adhi Bhautika or Psychological and
3. Adhyatmika or Psychic.

It was Rishi Patanjali, the father of yoga, who around 200 BC compiled, synthisized and systematized yoga by laying down eight steps which form the basis on which the whole system of yoga works and which automatically takes care of all types of stresses and diseases[12]. Klesa, Dukh and Trivida tap are the words connoting stress in ancient Indian Scriptures. Qualities such as fear, over indulgence in food and sex, obsessive compulsive disorders, work alholism, stress, anxiety can be easily overcome by better understanding of the chakra psychology (meditation on the energy centres of the human Psyche).[13] Patanjali yoga centres and Indian asanas offer a holistic life style of bliss, efficiency, emotional equipose, mental clarity, intellectual sharpness and physical well - being. Regular physical exercise through yogasanas, pranayam (breath exercises) and meditation for about forty minutes can give as holistic life style - to work stress - free at all levels, Physical, Mental emotional, intellectual and spiritual. In the third BC Chanakya (Kautilya) wrote his celebrated treatise on state craft—"Artha sastra"—Kautilya says an ideal king is one for whom—"Praja Sukje, Sukham ragyan, Prajanam the Priyam hitan." ("In the happiness and well being of the subjects, his the well-being of the kind, in the welfare of the subjects is the welfare of the king). What is desirable and beneficial to the subjects and not his personal desires and ambitions, is desirable and beneficial for the king. "The four fold duties of the king, suggested by Kautilya are Raksha (Protection), Vridhi (enhancement), palana (Maintenance) and yogakshema (safeguard)[14]. The role of the state is to protect the wealth of the state and its subjects, to enhance the wealth, to maintain and safeguard it and protect the interest of the subjects. Even the Noble laurate Prof. Amartya Sen has asserted that Indian state has to play a sober role in giving directions and shape the economy by focussing on the social sector - basic health care, education, drinking water, roads and basic infrastructure of the nation, based on the welfare paradigm.[15] India started Public sector undertakings to give a towering position and a crucial role in growth of the economy in the early fifties and sixties. Steel plants at Bhilai, Bokara, Rourkela and Durgapur provided a strong steel base to the Indian economy. However, with liberalization and globalisation need for privatisation has been recommended as strategic sales. During last 30 months (till June 2002) 12 Central Public Sector Undertakings have been actually privatised along with 12 hotels, making a total of 24 completed transactions. This has been the most remarkable achievement of N.D.A. Govt led by Shri Atal Behari Vajpayee. The affluent market is the fastest growing segment in India: It compries some 5 to 6 million people. India has leapfrogged in technology and the consumer wants the best in the world. The speed of the change the consumer demand in India is the fastest among the South-Asian countries. The Credit cards business in India is on the high. From 42 lakh in 2000 it now stands at 52 lakhs in Nov 2001 more than a 20 percent jump. The average card spend has grown to an impressive Rs. 3,500 per month. The Indian value system can be captured in one line in words of N. Narayan Murth—"The softest pillow is a clear conscience." The biggest challenge today is to recruit, enable and retain the brightest talent, leadership is all about raising the aspirations of followers and the best form of leadership is by example. The find of achievement comes from aspirations that are higher than the status quo. A well - run corporation embraces and practices a sound predictability - sustainability - profitability - Derisking (PSPD) model[16]. A good forecasting system for sales and market trends based on data gathered ensures predictability while sustainability can be achieved by motivated sale people who make sales happen, by production are delivered on time. High profitability alone can ensure the best returns for its shareholders and profitability is most crucial for the long term success of a corporation. A good derisking approach must recognise, measure and mitigate risk along every dimension so that corporation takes carefully thoughout reasonable risks. Corporate governance needs to focus on maximising share holders value while ensuring fairness to all stake holders. "The Corporate excellence is not only about selling what is produced, not just about customer satisfaction but also about commitment to the wider world outside. Excellence should always be combined with ethics. If your add compassion and courage, the quality of EECC, you get better and stronger than Tata Steel".[17] Corporations have an important duty to contribute to society in terms of "Social responsibilities". In the corporate system, it is a good practice to under promise and over deliver. N.R. Narayan Murthy has shared the following words of advice based on his own experiences:—

"1. I want to emphasise the importance of being trust worthy in your dealings. It is on such foundations that great organisations are created.

2. Fear is natural but do not let your actions be totally governed by it. Just as fear may sometimes be the voice of your institution, it must be an invitation to explore yourself and the world.

3. A Supportive family is the bedrock upon which lives and careers are built.

4. Learn how to manage yourself, separating the merits and demerits of a decision from the accompanying feeling. Infoscions call this "being transaction oriented".

5. Live your life and lead your career in a way that makes a difference to your society.

6. Choose a worthy dream for yourself. Go after it confidently but ensure that you are following your bless. All else will follow[18].

Indian ethos recognises the power of ethical management. Self-interest prompts the businessman to make profits and obey the laws, lest he gets into difficulties. Konosuku Matsushita, in his look "Not for Bread Alone" (1985) has recommended the following seven principles of Zen meditation. (1) National service through industry; (2) Fairness; (3) Harmony and Cooperation; (4) Struggle for betterment; (5) Courtesy and Humility; (6) Adjustment and Assimilation; (7) Gratitude. These values are very close to Indian ethos of management. Over the years India's oldest and the most respected Corporate houses (Tatas) have quietly transformed itself to march with the changing times. In fact Tata is a global corporate brand today, it is because of Ratan Tata who took over as the group's chairman in 1991. Technology is changing rapidly, competition is getting fiercer and share holders and customers are becoming more demanding. Industrial houses and Indian managers have to create learning systems by making their organisations learning organisations. Good leaders inbibe learning from their environment, and constantly evolve through experience introspection and self study, leader articulates a vision that is inspiring and dynamic and guides his team towards the goal.

2. Distinctive features of Indian Ethos of Management: Prof. S.K.Chakraborty has given the following ten proposition which could form the core of future management style in India:- 1. The concept of self in man has to embrace the spiritual dimension beyond his physical, social and economic dimensions. 2. Man's creative energies are derived from and rooted in the supreme creative Intelligence. 3. Managerial decision-making required the interplay of both analytic and holistic faculties. 4 In de-egoization rests the final resolution of managerial conflict situations. 5. The key to cooperation and team work lies ultimately in the progressive assimilation of the reality that it the same Atman which dwells in each one of us. 6. A full understanding and internalization of the "doctrine of Karma" is essential to improve the quality of managerial decision-making and style. 7. Intrinsic and enduring motivational strategies need to be based on the giving model of man. 8. Conscious modulation for effective leadership style (and management style) requires the understanding of the triune guna composition of the human being—"*Sattwa*", "*rajas*" and "*tamas*". (9) All managerial decisions are subjective in the ultimate analysis and depend in a large measure on the purity of the subjective of the decision maker. (10) There is need for proper balance and harmony in the quality of domestic life and quality of work-life[18A]. Indian philosophy expounds four *Purusharth, Dharma, Artha, Kama* and *Moksha*. There is great stress on the art of living and eternal values. (11) Spiritualism is the brand mark of Indian ethos of management.

There are two important aspects of management one pertaining to the organisations the systems and the people around and the second to manager oneself. The western management has more or less ignored effectively managing ourself-one's mind feeling, emotions, stresses complexes, reactions, etc. In Bhagwat Gita the yoga-shastra deals with managing oneself. The ancient wisdom especially Bhagwat Gita's karma yoga provides a unique perspective. Vedanta has many useful things to contribute in different areas of management like self development, motivation, leadership, communication, decision-making, development of an appropriate work culture, stress management and self management. Indian wisdom teaches us the "Art of living" and can guide us in the solutions of our day-to-day problems and challenges. Indian Science of Holistic living with Indian values of life are given in Fig. 3.

Fig. 3. Indian Values of Life and Science of Holistic Living

Karma Yog	*Bhaktiyoga*
1. (Secret of action)	(Path of Self Surrender)
2. -(Path of Action and Self Sacrifice)	Key is love to emotional culture and stability
3. -Key is awareness in action and Nishkamkarma	Inner Harmony
4. -Towards greater efficiency in work	Inner Motivation
5. Raj Yoga	Jnana Yoga
6. (The way of the will) (External)-Yama	(Expanding through Intellect)

Karma Yog	*Bhaktiyoga*
7. Niyama-Asana, Pranayam, Pratyalara, (Internal) Dharna, Dhyana, Samadhi	Path of self analysis is the key to Knowledge of Reality, nature of happiness and misery
8. Integrity	Service Mindedness
9. Sensitivity	Creative thinking

Indian ethos can be drawn from the Vedas, upanishads, the Ramayan, Mahabharat, the Bhagavat Gita and other ancient Indian Sanskrit scriptures.

All values are relative to time and space but some values given below are eternal:-

(*i*) The essential infinitude and divinity of all souls.

(*ii*) The essential oneness and solidarity of universe and all life. The mahavakya of ancient India as expressed in upanishads are (*i*) Aham Brahmasi (I am Brahman); (*ii*) Ayam Atman Brahmanam (The individual soul is Brahma); (*iii*) Tat Twam Asi (Thou art that). Indian Ethos of Management redefines Management as "helping ordinary people to produce extra-ordinary results". The Indian ethos of management (IEM) take a holistic approach of Advaita non-dualism. It sees a person in his totality with various different roles—as an employee, as a father, a husband/wife/a friend, a relative and above all a citizen. Subjectivity is as important as objectivity and IEM stresses the sukshama where subtle subjective, intangible factors are more important as sthula or concrete, objective, tangible factors.

(*i*) Values of life in Indian Philosophy to be included in management.

1. Consider every human being having the same atman (Soul)-divine and full of potentials. Each soul is potential god. (Ahan Brahmasmi)
2. Consider every work as sacred and take it as Duty.
3. Perform your work and duties with full commitment and dedication but do not have any attachment to their results.

4. Offer every work to the Divine within and accept the result as His gratitude. (Prasad).
5. Maintain equanimity of mind and do not react to any situation in haste. Share the material prosperity with other people.
7. Consider the "Welfare of all" in your every actions.
8. Means are equally important as the Ends.
9. Take your people/employees at higher spiritual achievement.
10. Perform your obligations and duties towards parents, teachers, followers, society and the nature as a whole.
11. Every human being, though consisting of various organs is formless, limitless, non-dual awareness/ consciousness called Atmari (Soul). In Bhagwat Gita Lord Krishna says: "Weapons cannot cut it (Atma) fire cannot burn it, water cannot wet it, even wind can not dry it. It is not subject to being cut, burned, wet or dried. It is beyond time, all pervasive, immovable and immutable (Ch. 2 : 23, 24) The Atman in uncleavable, in combustible, eternal, all-pervading stable, immovable and everlasting. This Atman is said to be ummanifested, unthinkable and immutable. (2.25)." In the epic Mahabharata, the order of values have been given as four purushartha—dharma, artha, Kama and Moksha. The epic tells us that the wise people delight in the end-values (namely dharma and Moksha) and do not care for the middle ones (viz. artha and Kama).

The Vedantic view of Karma the purpose of work is to bring out divinity and to achieve growth and development. Transfer of Organisation's members into karma Yogis is the suggestion given in the Vedanta. Vedantic education has transformational effects of spiritual, personal, organisational and social levels as shown in the Fig. 4.

Fig. 4. Transformational effects of Vedanta Philosophy and education at various levels (10)

A Spiritual Level

1. Essential unity of all religions and respect for all religions.
2. Feeling of an extended world family
3. Follow your swadharma - righteous living.

Vedanta Education

Under guidance of enlightened Acharya, and teachers

B. Personal Level

1. Faith in potentiality.
2. Chitta Suddha.
3. Faith in Karma Yoga
4. Faith in theory of Sanskara and Prakiti
5. Atma bodha (Self knowledge)
6. Stress free and tranquility
7. Self-dedication
8. Virtuous and righteous living
9. High Character
10. Right attitude to work and organisation

C-Org' and Corporate Level.

1. Social Service Approach immense
2. Ethical Vision to mgt and activity
3. Reviewing and renovating strategies for treguna leadership
4. Job-improvement and great commitment to work
5. More cooperate and good team work
6. Greater motivation to work
7. Reduced stress - sthitc pragya
8. Enriching the skills, techniques, knowledg, excellence in work.
9. Greater Innovative and creative attitude
10. Wisdom worker and welfare org. harmony

D. Social Level

1. Social transformation by values
2. Move from self centredness to collective
3. Sharing your resources to repay debts (ren.)
4. Love and consideration for human beings
5. Better social inter action and social harmony.
6. Better quality of social life.

V. Division of the three gunas and unique work culture

In Vedanta Dharma is the duty to be performed in a given situation. Work is to be performed in a pure, honest, sincere and selfless manner and is to be offered to that divinity within without indulging in future expectations. Lord Krishna says: "Seek to perform your duty; but lay not claim to its fruits, be you not the producer of the fruits of Karma; neither shall you lean towards inaction (B.C. 2:47) Desire tainted Karma gives continuity to the wheel of birth and death. These ideals have been put to extensive practical demonstrations by some of the Indian companies like Tata group companies, Gujarat Ambuja Cement Ltd., Indian Oil etc. Vedanta offer four path to adopt change, Path of action and path of mystic experience. Excellence in work in yoga and the spirit of work should be "Yoga Karmasu Kaushalam." Performance depends upon the state of mind and Indian wisdom suggest three stated Sattvik, Rajasik and Tamsik. The following details are given to identify three types of tendencies of people.[19]

Fig. 5. Three types of tendencies of people

	Sattvik	*Rajsik*	*Tamsik*
1. Action	Measured and appropriate	Forceful and excessive	Forced and limited
2. Requires	Little supervision	Key point supervision	Constant Supervision
3. Oriented Towards	Knowledge	Action	Work
4. Interested in	Creative work	Personal achievement	immediate gain
5. Characteris-tics	Insight & foresight	Target and planning	spot limited
6. Works liking	accepts responsibility; complete it in all respects team work	Independently personal achievement; collective responsibility	Supported by others; does just the required work, To be pushed.
7. Needs	Highself actualisation Medium Social Low-Ego	H-EGO M-Social L-Self Actualization and basic	H-Basic M-Ego L-Social
8. Notices	Big Frame Work	Particulars Frame work	No Framework as such

	Sattvik	*Rajsik*	*Tamsik*
9. Operates at	Institutional level	Mind level	Body level
10. Concerned with	Mission	Goal	Immediate result
11. You appeal to his	Intelligence	Ego	Basic needs
12. Result	Purity	Pain	Ignorance
13. Management Perspective	illumined	dynamic	Insert
14. Binds	Happiness	Action	heedlessness error and ignorance

For top management you need stattvik people. You will find many rajsik characteristics in young MBAS. Tamsik people are those whom one calls "dead wood." In Bhagwat Gita Chapter 14 Sloka "Says when the light of knowledge beams through all the gateways of the body then it may be known that sattva is predominant. Greed, activity, the under taking of actions, unrest, longing these arise when Rajas is predominant (14:12 Bg). Indiscrimination, inertness, heedlessness and delusion - these arise when Tamas is predominant (B.g. 14:13) In chapter 14 of the Bhagvat Gita, the detailed description of the three gunas has been given. No one's nature is exclusively sattvit or tamsik or rajasik, there is no water-tight compartment. One has to find out which one is predominating in one's nature at a particular time.

As regard work culture the Mahabharat suggests four techniques for dealing with people namely Sam, Dam, Bhed and Dand. The various techniques suggested are as under:

"1. Sam - Persuasion—The purpose is to increase the feeling of belongingness. Discussion, reasoning, reflection of good will, friendly approach and treatment as equal are the various techniques.

2. Dam - Reward - The purpose is to acknowledge one's contributions by ways of appreciation, awards, giving material benefits, giving money and developing skills.

3. Bhed - discrimination with the purposed to focus on short falls of a person in critical light by challenges, comparisons, unequal treatment, silence and showing dislikes.
4. Dand - punishment with the aim of maintaining discipline through reprimand, criticism, imposing fines, restrictions, rough talk and controlled anger".[20]

(VI) Evenness of mind and skill in action

In Bhagwat Gita Lord Krishna says: The one fixed in equanimity of mind frees oneself in this life from vice and virtue alike; therefore devotees oneself to yoga; work done to perfection is verily yoga (2:50) further "Perform action; O Dhananjaya, being fixed in yoga". (2.48). It has been asserted that motivated Karmà is far inferior to that performed in the equanimity of mind. Take refuge in the everness of mind; wretched are the result seekers. Todays Indian managers are required to develop such an attitude of equanimity to manage the situations effectively.[21] It is an advice to became Karmayogi. In one of his letters to a young entrepreur disciple at Madras, Swami Vivekanand wrote; "Try to manifest divinity within and everything will be harmoniously arranged around it."

(VII) The Bhakti Model and for self managing teams means are equally important as the ends:

(YADRISIBHAVNALIYASHA SIDDHI BHAVATI TADRISI)

In Vedanta means applied for achieving the objectives must be pure, just honest and non harming. In Bhakti Model, the central postulates are as under:

(*i*) Making the workplace sacred, clean and bringing orderliness and regularity (Karma Kshetra as Dharma Kshetra).

(*ii*) Empowering self by discovering divinity in self (Aham Brahmasim) and in others (Tatwamasi).

(*iii*) Recognizing work as an opportunity to offer divine service (Yogah Karmashu Kaushalam).

(*iv*) Recognizing mission of life as continuation of God's mission of facilitating this creation. (Isha Vasyam Idam servam).

(*v*) Working with zero errors, zero delay, zero wastage and zero accidents.

(*vi*) Caring for others by recognizing them as part of us. (Vashudev Kutuubakam) and grahak devo bhava sevadharma. Successful innovation of self managed teams was carried out with above given doctrines. The above mentioned experiment had been tried at Yash paper mills Ayodya under the guidance of K.K. Jhunghan wala the founder managing director with Shri Suresh Pandit as management Consultant.[22]

(VIII) Sharing Material Prosperity and spiritual achievements with others

The oldest Rigveda offers a comprehensive vision of corporate life thus

(*i*) Common be your prayers, (*ii*) Common be your ends, (*iii*) Common be your purpose, (*iv*) Common be your deliberations, (*v*) Common be your Desires, (*vi*) United be your Hearts, (*vii*) United be your intentions perfect be the union amongst us, (*viii*) Macro vision and individuals part of the universe—" This universe is the manifestation of the Almighty omnipotent God who created this cosmos as one interdependent, inter-related with each other, everyone having certain role to play, certain responsibilities to exercise towards the universe. **(*ix*) Indian approach to stress and its management.** Bhagavat Gita, Patanjali Yog Sutra, the Indian system of medicine, give detailed analysis of stress and its management. Stress is termed in Sanskrit expression as "duhkha" or "Klesa". The word "Klesa" derived from the root klis (uptape, to torment, to cause pain, to afflict) means an afflicted state, a condition of pain. Patanjali crystallizes the technical connection of the word while dealing with Kriyayoga. In Sankhya Yog, duhkha (stress) is tripartite in its origin; One's own physical and mental constitution (adhyatmika), outside agencies both material and human, (adhibhaultika), and factors beyond one's control or apprehension (adhidaivika). In Bhagwat - Gita, sources of stress and methods of managing this stress have been described. The battle field is the heart of each one of us; and Arjun represents every man torn between impulses and values. Indian Wisdom has given us an analytical views of causes of stress and methods to manage it. The result of an action/situation/event depends upon the quality of work and many other external/ internal factors. Meditation equanimity of mind and complete surrender to God being karma yogi, generally takes care of stress. Patanjali yoga sutra, transcendental meditation, breathing exercises, yoga exercises—all help in managing stress. The ancient Indian science of yoga, asanas and pranayams holds the key to combat the modern menace of stress anxiety depression and frustration.[23] Indian gurus teaching yoga as stress management techniques are now brand of god - gurus such as Mahesh Yogi, Osho Rajneesh, Satya Sai Baba, Shri Sri Ravi Shanker, Swami Chinmayananda, and prabhupad of ISKON to name the few. Yoga is the most global Indian brand and almost 15 million American do Yoga in 180 Iyenger Yoga school and other such yoga centers. Swami Ramdevji of Hardiwar has started a nation wide campaign in India for Yoga as a cure for all types of diseases including stress, hypertension and depression with remarkable results. Vedanta training helps individuals in becoming better leaders and better performers as workers. In some Indian universities, Yoga and Meditation are being taught in M.B.A. Patanjali Yoga sutra presents the outlines of the strategy called 'Kriya - yoga' which is calculated to reduce the number and intensity of the stressors (Klesa - Tanukarna) and to facilitate relaxed conservation of mental energy devoid of tension (samadhi bhavana).

The Seven Spiritual Laws of Success

Dr. Deepak Chopra, the new doyen of management experts in U.S.A. draws inspiration from Vedantic philosophy to redefine spiritual Laws of success: when this knowledge is incorporated in one's consciousness, it will prove the ability to attain wealth with effortless ease and experience success in every economic endeavour.

3.1 The Law of Pure Potentiality: It is based on the fact that we are, in our essential state, pure consciousness. Pure consciousness in pure potentiality, it is the field of all possibilities and infinite creativity. One way to access the field is through daily practice of silence, meditation and non-Judgement. For achieving success, one must take some time each day to commune with nature and silently witness the intelligence within every living thing. Sit silently, watch a sunset, or listen to the sound of the sea or a stream or simply smell the scent of a flower, are some of the practical tips for realizing one's own potentiality.

3.2. The Law of Giving: The second spiritual law of success is the law of giving; the more you give, the more you receive because you will keep the abundance of the universe circulating in your life. This law could be called the law of giving and receiving, because the universe operates through dynamic exchange. One's body is always in dynamic and constant exchange with the body of universe: the mind is dynamically interacting with the mind of the cosmos and one's energy is an expression of cosmic energy.

3.3. The Law of "Karma" or cause and effect: Karma is both action and consequence of that action. It is the cause and effect simultaneously because every action generates force and energy that returns to us in life kind. If we want happiness in our lives, we must learn to sow the seeds of happiness. Obviously, Karma implies action of conscious choice making.

3.4. The Law of Least Effort: Nature functions with effortless case and carefree abandon: flowers automatically bloom, fish just swim, grass just grows. The law of least effort is best observed in nature. One can wait for the appropriate season for desires to blossom into reality with nature's desires.

3.5. The Law of Intention and Desire: One should make commitment like "I will release a list of my desires and surrender it to the womb of creation." Trusting that when things do not seen to go my way, there is a reason. In the universal scheme energy and information exist everywhere in nature. In fact at the level of quantum field, there is nothing other than energy and information. Quantum field is influenced by intention and desire because the quantum field is just another level for the pure consciousness or pure potentiality.

3.6. The Law of Detachment: In order to acquire anything in the physical universe, one has to relinquish attachment to it. One does not give up the intention or the desire rather one relinquishes attachments to the results.

3.7. The law of Dharma or purpose in life: There are three components to the law of dharma. The first component says that each one of us is here to discover our true self, to find out on our own that our true self is spiritual. The second component is to express our unique talent. The third is the service to the humanity and the living creatures in general.

Management of Environment Indian religion gives great importance to the protection of our environment and eco-system.

Delhi has the questionable privilege of being among the five most polluted cities in the world. All over the country managing the environment is a great challenge. At the Rio Earth summit in June 1992, environmental issues were hotly debated and 27 guiding principles for sustainable development were recommended. The modern holistic approach for ecological balance is reflected in the most ancient of Indian scriptures, the Vedas. The prithvi sukta of the Atharvaveda especially propounds man's close relationship with nature. The earth is revered as mother. According to Atharvaveda—"bhoomili mata putroham prithivayab"—like a mother the earth is to be respected and protected. Management of environment is no longer a national concern since entire humanity needs and entire humanity should develop and have integrated approach.[24] A prayer in Rigveda says "We offer our reverence to nature's great bounties - may we not overlook any of them." The management of environment has to be an integrated part of corporate responsibilities. Environment audit implies that companies should not wait for restrictive legislation to bring about change and environmental reporting is the most useful weapon in applying the principle of pollutar pays and user pays for the depletion and degradation of natural resources.[25] There is urgent need to develop comprehensive guidelines for effective management of environment. The government by using legal and economic measures and instruments should make companies responsible to pay for the pollution and depletion by levying effluent charges, user taxes, tradable pollution permits, deposit refund system, pollution tax on includes to conserve the environment. Verghese Kurien experiment at Anand proved beyond doubt that it should be possible to bring together millions of illiterate framers, collect lakhs of litres of milk a day and market the finished products to millions of households in the country by merely leveraging the end use of technologies and processes. C.K. Prahlad called for people to dream of building a great and prosperous India by keeping to its roots. "Indigenous technology development does not mean developing better bullock carts but means to replace these altogether".[26]

Indian heritage has provided us four pillars of purusharth (human pursuit) in which the first is Dharma second is Artha, third is Kama and fourth is Moksha. Kama (desire) starts with Kalpana (thought), from this it leads to Prakalpa (project) and then Sankalpa (determination) translates it into Karma (action). In knowledge society, the entire philosophy of business and management is to be considered both science as well as art and it is the human determination (sankalpa) which alone translates this into success. By constant self-analysis, self-evaluation, total dedication and looking within ourself that India can flourish as a self sufficient, dynamic economic world power. C.K. Prahlad is his book "Managing for the future" has asserted that only those companies will survive in the future who are able to create their own future. The Indian ethos of management must survive the global competition by building various competitive advantages over other nations. In fact competitive advantage can be achieved by India in the following ways:

1. Factor conditions skills, infrastructure, available labour, capital, land.
2. Demand conditions - both internal and external.
3. Related and supporting industries by building mutually reinforcing system.
4. Performing better than other competitors on an already existing dimension of competition.
5. Establishing new dimensions to compete, firm strategy, structure and rivalry.
6. Creating a new product/market combination.

Indian management must improve its competitive edge over other countries. Today the corporate India suffers from poverty of ideas.[27] We must improve not only our creativity, originality and competitive advantages but must draw inspiration from rich heritage. India must improve its competitive advantage over other nations by its ability to create, update and deploy various factors for its advantage. India's quest for global quality has been recently recognized. It took Sundaram Clayton, ten years of relentless improvement in quality to win the Deming prize in 1998. Seating systems manufactures Krishna—Maruti, Chennai based Range Engine values and Rane TRW stearing systems was declared 2005's Deming winners.[28] Indian companies need to build marketing skills, strong infrastructure and tackle cultural issues to grab more business. Skilled manpower is India's best asset. To realize its true potential Indian must go the Japanese way which looked into its own culture for successful management style because an Indian worker is perhaps looking at a friendly management practice with moderate job security. Infosys has become a shinning example of all the good that came out of India's economic reforms. The lesson from the Indian experience is a clear clarion call for all who are willing to listen; free trade can bring great benefits to society.[29] What modern India needs is role models of good industrialists, enterpreneurs, and business-leaders. If the country as a whole builds more role models on all part of the business and enables enough infrastructure to allow more people to participate in the economy power. India must build up a culture of collaborative cooperation and team work in the corporate sector. A strong team is essential for every successful enterpreneurial experiment to succeed. A well - knit strong team brings together a set of complementary skills, experience and expertise. India needs transformational leaders who are dedicated and well versed in Indian Ethos of management. Sahara India Pariwar is a unique example of Indian Management where growth and success are achieved through sheer determination, commitment and conceptual extension of emotionally integrated family of over 6 lac members. Prof. Arindam Chandhuri has enunciated the following four principles of India-centric management theory:—

"1. Most Indian value emotional bonds and long term relations.

2. Most Indian value growth opportunities and commitment.

3. Our cultural roots (of tolerance etc) often make us complacent.

4. Lack of patriotism at the Macro level leaves us aimless".[30]

Vedic management has become the new age mantra for some of the world's leading CEOs. In the U.S. Ford has used it for understanding joint ventures, Boling fir designing executive programmes. Nearer home, Godrej, Crompton Greaves, Excel industries and MNTL are some companies that have partaken of its concepts. Vedic managements is "a way of being and leading that is in accordance with vedic principles. It helps us to see the larger design and fabric in which we operate."[31] Leadership is a change in the way you lead an organizational transformation and strive for Kaushalam (excellence) in karma (action) and do not allow anxiety and stress for result to divert your energies. The Vedantic system advocated nishkam Karma (working without expecting any results) because it is more rewarding in the long run. Spiritualism is the brand mark of Indian ethos of management. Spiritualism about being a good human being, it is about searching for the meaning of life - a constant discovery of the self, the universal consciousness and the omnipotent universal power. Inter-dependence of course is a fundamental law of nature. Today India is a nation of more than one billion, standing at the cross roads, having a quarter of the world's poor and only 46 percent of urban population having access to modern sanitation. Since Independence for the first thirty years Indian economy grew at 3.8 percent or so and our per capita income grew by 1.3 percent in the eighties the GPF hovered around 5.8 percent and rise in per capita was 3.2 percent. The GPD grew by 6.4 percent and per capita income by 4.1 percent. In India there are large disparities between the states—there are some growing at 8.9 percent and some at 2 percent and it is leading to Socio-economic tensions. According to Dr.Man Mohan Singh, our successful experiment in democracy, with over a billion people seeking salvation through democratic process and institutions, is welcomed by the world that wants to strengthen democracies and pluralistic societies. To begin with, we must increase incomes and employment in rural India, reducing the development disparity between cities and villages. Indeed, changing the mind set and attitudes of people in public life and government services is an extremely important challenge that we must grapple with, if the next 30 years have to see India transformed.[31a] According to Dr. Man Mohan Singh there are no external constraints to India's growth and whatever constraints are there, are internal'. The basic economic and social infrastructure must take a sharp growth curve. Power has to be made more affordable and easily available. The road network has to be expanded and we will have to become a global partner in a rapidly integrating world economy. The vision 2010 can be broadly as under. Every Indian would find gainful employment and every village will have water supply, literacy will rise from 65 percent to 85 percent, forest cover will go up from 19 percent to 33 percent, infant mortality rate will plummet from 63 percent to 18 percent and poverty down from 27 percent to about 10 percent.[32] By 2010 Indian People should have an opportunity basket, including education, health care, jobs, clean environment, and generally an opportunity to prosper by becoming a successful global player. Three important components of our economy - the government, the industry and the individuals must work - together adequately prepared to face the global competition successfully. Indians know what needs to be done and we must develop courage, conviction and commitment to achieve our vision. India's vision of 2020 as given by Dr. A.P.J. Abdul Kalam is as under:— "The vision is to transform India into an economic, scientific and military power. At the core of "India 2020" is the elimination of poverty—not merely by lifting the poor above the poverty line but by providing them with a fairly assured income. I personally believe that it is possible to eliminate poverty by 2020".[33] India has done well in several fields besides nuclear science, space science, information technology etc. we have made significant progress in agriculture.

In India, there are many role models who convey the message of Indian ethos of management. In all 127 final year students of 5 business management schools, including three Indian Institutes of Management across India, have given their rating of most admired business leaders of India which is as under.[34]

1. N.R. Narayan Murthy - 47%
2. The Ambanis - 26%
3. Ratan Tata - 6%
4. Azim Premji - 4%

5. Subhash Chandra - 3%
6. K.V. Kamath - 3%
7. M.S. Banga - 3%
8. Verghese Kurien - 3%
9. Ramesh Chandran - 1%
10. Others - 4%

Business school final year students rated N.R. Narayanmurthy as the most admired business leader due to the following reasons

1. Honesty, Integrity/Ethics and values - 32%
2. Simplicity - 31%
3. Sharing Wealth - 24%
4. Visionary/Entrepreneurship - 14%
5. Successful - 12%

The following ten are the most attractive employers, according to *Business Today* February 17, 2002 study.

1. Infosys - 34%
2. HLL - 23%
3. ICICI - 11%
4. Wipro - 8%
5. Tata - 4%
6. HDFC - 3%
7. Reliance - 3%
8. Tata Adni Services - 2%
9. Other Finance Companies - 3%
10. Others - 7%

Indian economy is at the cross roads today and the Indian ethos of management in the context of 21st Century has to be redefined and rediscovered-Research with adequate scientific objectivity is needed for identifying the newly emerging trends of modern Indian Management. What are the best ways to find out Indian ethos of Management of the Twenty First Century? Is if profits or market shares or astute management practices creation of more wealth or good returns to the shareholders or is it the combination of many of the above factors? One of the most striking features of Indian outstanding organisations is, according to Abad Ahmed and O.P. Chopra, extended family ethos in the philosophy and style of management. Extended family ethos means that the top management viewed the organisation and its members as part of an extended family, they related to them as if they were members of the family. They used the language, actions and other behavioural cues that reflected a family relationship and environment and utilized the family metaphor on Collective occasions.[40] Indian management is family based and karta (head of the joint family- authority figure) dependent. The family feeling is reinforced on many collective occasions such as annual days, training programmes, informal get together etc. Top management leaders even participate in weddings and other family related events of joy and sorrows of the employees.

Over the last few years India is fast realising that its most valuable brand sits not on the shop shelves but in the corporate room. A CEO is a brand that can connect with across the corporate universe, customers, suppliers, shareholders, partners, policy makers, social pressure groups and just about anybody who remotely affects the fortunes of the universe. Narayan Murthy of Infosys Rahul Bajaj, Chairman Bajaj group, Vijay Mallya CEO UB group, Anil and Mukesh Ambani of Reliance Industries, Ratan Tata, Chairman Tata group are some of the best CEO brands of India.[35] Nandan Nilekani, the present CEO of Infosys, can be a role model for Indian CEOs. Azim Premji has been working one of the most corporate transformations of Wipro by turning it from a software hot shop into a product and consulting powerhouse. Premji is a leader open to delegating power. Narayan Murthy is one of the best role models of Indian Management. For the last two decades, mergers and acquisitions (M & A) have become a way of life for Indian Corporate world. Not all consolidations have created values for the companies or their shareholders. In fact 50 percent fail to achieve any value of course there are some winners who create tremendous value. Arthur Bert, after studying 24000 companies across 53 countries in 24 different industries found that 44 percent of the M & A companies were under performers, adding to neither their topline nor their shareholder wealth. However, in India consolidation is set to happen in pharma, cellular, software and banking sectors among some others.

Spiritual Quotient and Emotional Intelligence—Keys to Successful Careers

Spiritual quotient, emotional quotient and intelligence quotient are all needed for successful careers. Human beings are basically spiritual and spiritual values have lot of meaning for motivation, commitment, honesty and integrity. Spiritual practices and development in individuals lead to six treasures namely control of mind (Kshama), control of senses (Dama), coordination of words, thoughts and deeds (Upasati), endurance (Titkha faith (Shraddha) and mental equilibrium (Samadhan).[36] (36). Business ethics is crucial for sustained economic development. Spiritual practices like prayers, meditation and interaction with religious people (Satsang) can generate constant energy, self confidence, ability to creates happiness and a peaceful mind.[37] Emotional Intelligence as measured by EQ (emotional quotient) is a better predictor of success than mere traditional measures of EQ (Intelligence Quotient). EQ is ranked at top among the core competencies that determine today's Managerial success. The combined effect of developing SQ & EQ can awaken the untapped well springs of tremendous professional growth, creativity and all round economic development of the country.

Indians have great fear of Bosses: A very close scrutiny of Indian ethos of management indicates that Indians have great respect and fear of their bosses and generally take good care of them even in personal and family matters. "Boss is always right" and "Boss is mighty" are the general impressions in the management world. Research of Indian ethos have revealed that Indians have great reverence, regard and fear of their parents, and bosses/elders. Prof. S.K. Chakraborty rightly says: "All management is finally subjective and the responsibility for the effectiveness of Indian organisations lies with the level of development of the individual managers." The cultivation and purification of man's inner field, the realms within which subjective decisions are made, is crucial to effective and successful management. The Indian problem of organisations is to be found at the root level of personal dynamics and the solution lies in surrender to love and discipline throughout management and the workforce. The major organizational blocks in India are jealously and struggle for power. Self transformation and development of the spiritual perspective are needed in Indian Managers. Values can only blossom in minds that quiet and interiorize themselves lasting change follows when people change at the attitude/value level. There is a need to ensure that managers regularly perform effectively. How do we improve upon the effectiveness of the managers to reach the state of Excellence? This will largely depend not only upon the four basic skills in management training mentioned by Dr. C.K. Prahlad but on how clean the raw, talented or the trained manager continue his "instruments" which enable the all pervasive internal cleanliness for self-development. Taitreya Upnishad has referred them as "five-sheaths" (Panch Kosha). The internal instruments, their accretion and methodology to clean up on a daily maintenance shut up schedule can be tabulated as given below:-[38]

Fig. 6. Table showing daily maintenance routine for managers

Panch Kosh	*Instrument*	*Accretion*	*Methodology*	*Time Min*
1. Annamaya Kosha	Body	Poor Blood Circulation	Surya Namashkara and daily yoga	15 minutes every morning
2. Pran-maya Kosha	Prana	Imbalance inhaling and exhaling	Pranayama	Every morning and evening 5 min each.
3. Manomaya Kosh	Mind	Anxiety	Auto-Suggestion and Meditation	5 to 10 minutes every morning and evening.
4. Vijnan-Maya Kosh	Intellect	Indecision	Japa and Dharana	5 to 10 minutes every morning and evening
5. Anand Maya Kosha	Ego	Subjectivity	Dhyana and Transcendental meditation upto samadhi	15 minutes to 45 minutes every morning.

Corporate leaders, managers and professionals have to practise above given methodology as a part of daily routine. Ancient Indian thinkers and seers recommended above recommended routine in the morning at Brahma - Mahurt (early morning first starting at 4 a.m.) and evening at dusk time as part of sandyavandanam. These daily recommended spiritual practices can help in self development, chitta suddhi (mental purification) and stress relieving strategy. Above recommended practices will ultimately tune up the mental intellectual and spiritual levels of the managers, enabling them to achieve managerial excellence. In Bhagwad Gita, Chapter XII slokas (stanzas) 13 to 19 enumerate the characteristic features of man of perfection and man of steady wisdom. By regularly following the correct mode of conduct and the way of life as prescribed above, every manager and leader will ultimately achieve the managerial excellence. President of India Dr. APJ Abdul Kalam on 22 December 2005 called upon captains of industry to turn themselves into "Creative Leaders" to address the future needs of the economy and the society with the aim of transforming India into a developed nation by 2020. There are five identified areas where India has core competence for integrated action. (1) Agriculture and food processing; (2) Reliable and quality electric power, surface, transport and infrastructure for all parts of the country; (3) Education and health-care; (4) Information and communication technology; and (5) Strategic sectors.

These five areas are closely inter-related and if properly implemented, will lead to food, economic and national security of the country. Creative leaders of the economy must focus on the following areas:—(*i*) Bring ICT sector to rural areas; (*ii*) Banks asked to play pioneering role; (*iii*) Venture capital to generate new enterprises; (*iv*) FIIS find India attractive.

We need creative leadership in Indian who can exercise the vision to change the traditional role from the commander to the coach, manager to mentor, from director to delegator and from one who demands respect to one who facilitates self-respect. India must work out a plan for a new type of venture capital to generate new enterprises. Foreign Institutional Investors (FIIs) must find investing in India attractive. Dr. A.P.J. Kalam has noticed new welcome trend in the Indian economy—an increasing number of Indian companies investing abroad and starting new business ventures. Referring to the report "From the Ganges to the Thames" Dr. Kalam pointed out that Indian FDI in London was second only to the U.S. and Indian projects in Europe have increased from just five to 119 during 1997 to 2004. The government was commited to increasing the growth rate from 7 percent to 8 percent and to ten percent in the medium run. This calls for agriculture, manufacturing and service sectors becoming globally competitive. The corporate sector has to play an important role in a big way. Dr. Pritam Singh, Former Director IIM (Lucknow) has said "Indian must overcome certain weaknesses like of the Brahmanical mind that relies more on thought than action and leverage their strengths to emerge as the global leader". 21st Century is a period of radical transformation and faster actions will decide the leader. The concept of life long learning should be a major agenda for all organisations. Human responses should be continuously upgraded through training and retraining. India is generally seen as the most-entrepreneur unfriendly nation and therefore India must evolve an enterpreneurship conducive climate to emerge by providing adequate access to capital, the right regulatory and tax environment and positive socio-cultural attitudes towards enterpreneurship. Indian ethos of management must cover the five debts mentioned in Brihadaryaka upanishad. Deva rin, Rishi rin, Pitri rin, Nri Rin and Bhuta rin, deva stands for gods/deities, Rishi stands for teachers/Spiritual personalities, Nri stands for entire humanity, Pitri stands for parents and ancestors and bhuta for all sub-human species. Human beings must repay their debt to all of them by their acts. Indian corporate, must carry out their social responsibilities and must ensure effective corporate governance. Now management experts say "You can work for two kind of companies. Those who adopt international brands for the Indian managers must charter a fresh unexplored path for themselves and must enjoy the priviledge of pioneering an Indian brand with world wide demand for it. Small and medium enterprises include companies with will known brands with turn over of Rs. 50 crore or even Rs. 100 crore and are now the real drivers of the Indian Economy. The Indian Ethos of Management takes a holistic view of motivation—"give motivation" which encompasses the welfare of the individual as well as that of society. Indian ethos of management revolves around the knowledge of self and it includes in modern terminology "SWOT Analysis—analysis of strength, weaknesses, opportunities and threats. At various levels, vedic education and training can bring spiritual, organisational, personal and Social transformations. Indian managers must understand our rich heritage of vedic knowledge. "The Vedantic knowledge presents a most authentic corpus of ideas, concept and processes for managing oneself, one's job, one's inter-relationship. There is a need to lay the foundations of the universal "Spiritual" orientation to our managerial work milien so that the quality of worklife may be amply enriched".[39] Stephen Monallack, author and communications trainer in Australia says: Indian businesses should preach "Morality" as "brand India's" ethos. India has given the world Ganesh, Krishna, the upanishads, Buddha, the spirit of Diwali and in more recent times the wisdom of Mahatma Gandhi and others. Western Business is ready to learn: what a communication opportunity for "brand India". The west is hungry for Indian ethos of Management." "The Indian ethos as contained in the Vedas, the upanishads, Bhagvat Gita, Mahabharat, Kautilya Arthashastra, Ram Charit Manas, and other Indian epics need to be taught in Business schools. Indian concepts need to be interpreted in the modern day language with adequate interpretations. Briefly the ethos of Indian Management can be reinterpreted in the following new age mantras for success in life:—

(1) Choose your vocation and activity that fires your emotions and is compatible with your nature.

(2) All employees and managers are human beings and should not be expected to work consistently with the accelerated pace without stress, anxiety and pain. They must have time for self-introspection and self-development.

(3) India's glorious tradition of tolerance must be inbibed all people with a spirit of team work. Foster team spirit and spirit of tolerance, cooperation and mutual help.

(4) Take responsibility and do not apportion blame when things sometime go wrong.

(5) Praise Counts but praise must be genuine and deserved.

(6) When you win, be humble and share the credit with others.

(7) Idea matters and practical idea power brings change and innovations.

(8) Stay calm, stay focussed and regularly practice meditation.

(9) Duality-Dwanda is the part of the World-success-failure, pleasure-pain, fear and emotions are all part of life and must be taken with faith in God.

(10) Integrity counts and means must be given due attention to achieve results.

(11) Learn to have fun and one must take break from work to recharge the energy level.

(12) One must have a holistle living. Work, meditation, and fun all must be a part of life. Human desires never end. Salaries, aspirations, expectations, work loads, dead lines all are increasingly coming under strain. Hypertension, diabetes, cardiovascular disease, obesity, nervous breakdowns, viral infections and other stress-induced ailments are making life very challenging. Therefore holistic living is needed. Yoga, transcendental meditation, prayers, pranayam, vipassana, reiki and long walks are finding wide acceptance in day-to-day working. These practices are deeply rooted in Indian ethos. One of the forerunners in gaining universal acceptance has been Mahesh Yogi's transcendental meditation and now various types of yoga-sanas and exercises (TM), companies such as ACC, Reckitt and Colman, Indian Petroleum Corporation, the Oriental Bank, SRF Ltd, TATA Tea and Tata Chemicals are some of the companies that have availed Maharishi Yogis corporate TM Programmes Sri Sri Ravishankar has started programmes of the "Art of Living Courses" for corporates such as Escot Insurance, Wipro, Dabur.

Prof. S.K. Chakraborty of Indian Institute of Management Calcutta India has established a management centre for Humar Values which is doing research work on traditional Indian Ethos and training employees of several organisations including Bhilwara group, UTI, TATA group and others. One can clearly notice spirituality in the board room now. However, the efforts are one helping less than 20% business houses of India and the message needs to be given to more Indian Corporation and business houses. G. Narayana, Executive Chairman Excel Industries, believes that a corporation has a personality and a vibrating living being (Purusha- Visham Vishnu) the shareholder paramatma (Supreme self) and the board as the antaratma (Inner self). Such perceptions can change our entire way of business. Amartya Sen believes that India's spirit of tolerance and brotherhood is an important part of Indian ethos. In his book "The Argumentative Indian" Prof. Amartya Sen draws from Hindu, Buddhist, Jain, Muslim Agnostic and atheistic strands of Indian thought to underline the richness of India's diversity; its long tradition of scepticism and reasoning. The tolerance of variation in different walks of life goes with secular, forward-looking, egalitarian and progressive, outlook of modern Indians. In the present day global context of 21st Century, India business world must display its distinct ethos which is wedded to rich culture of India. There are some emerging Modern Indian Corporations [EMICS] which operate on a global mind set, bench marking with the best in the world, internationalizing their operation for competitiveness and aspiring to become Indian Multi-nations. They are creating brand equity of quality, reliability and cost effectiveness for Indian products, services and organisations.[40] Infosys, Wipro, Satyam, Ranbaxy, Dr. Reddy's Lab, Hero Honda, Eicher, Larsen and Toubro, Sundram Fasteners (TVS), Titan, Motorola, BPL, Hindustan Lever Ltd., Glaxo-Smithkline Beecham, Tata Sons, Reliance, Hindustan Electro-graplute, ICICI and BEL are such representative Indian Companies.

References

1. Some noticeable studies on Indian managers and management ethos are as under (a) Rangaswamy and D. Helmick—"A Comparative Study of Indian and American Executive Leadership Style"; Indian Administrative and Management Review - Sept 1976, (b) P. Singh and G.S. Das: "Management style of Indian Managers—A profile ASCI Journal of Management Sept 1977, (c) P.M. Joseph and R. Keswan: A Comparative study of leader Behaviour in public and private sectors in India - Indian Management April-June 1977, (d) B.C. Jaggi Management Leadership styles in Indian Work organisation : Indian Management AP June 1978, (e) A. Ray - The Indian Manager in search of a style - Economic and Political Weekly 1970, (f) S.K. Chakraborty - Of I.M Calcutta - He has written a large number of books on Indian Perspectives of Management, (g) Dr. K. M. Mathur - Relevance of Vedantic wisdom and contemporary Management IIPA Journal, New Delhi, Jan-March 1999, (f) Abad Ahmed and O.P. Chopra - Passion to win - How Winning Companies Develop and Sustain Competitive edge-Excel Books Private Ltd., New Delhi, 2004.
2. S.K. Chatterjee, "Race movements and Pre-historic culture" in "History and culture of the Indian People" (Editor) R.C. Majumdar. Bombay Bharatiya Vidya Bhawan 1971—Vol. 1, p. 168.
3. Dr. Krishna Mohan Mathur—"Managing Human Resource Development—An Indian perspective" Gyan Publishing House, New Delhi, 2001, p. 74.
4. Dr. K.M. Mathur has given a matrix of Vedanta philosophy in aid to contemporary management in his book "Towards effective management pathways to excellence". Gyan Publishing House, New Delhi, 1999, p. 77.
5. S.K. Chakraborty—Ethics in management—vedantic perspectives -Oxford University Press, Delhi, 1995, p. VIII
6. S.K. Chakraborty—Managerial Effectiveness and quality of work life-Indian Insights—Tata Mc Grow Hill Publishing Company Ltd., New Delhi, 1987, p. 3.
7. Dr. Karan Singh—The many dimensions of management-2nd Bhilwara oration Dec 5, 1996. Indian Institute of Management, Calcutta, p. 7.
8. Dr. Mrityunjay Athreya—"Indian Managers have distinctive strengths". Indian Management, July 2005, pp. 34-40, Vol. 44 Issue 7.

9. George Skaria - editors Note - Key to becoming a great manager-Indian Management, July 2005, p. 6, Vol. 44, Issue 7.
10. Dr. Krishna Mohan Mathur—Towards Effective Management—Pathways to excellence—Gyan Publishing House, New Delhi, 1999, p. 74.
11. S.K. Chakraborty - Foundations of Managerial Work - Himalaya Publishing House Mumbai - Second edition - Reprint 2003, p. 8.
12. Dr. Krishna Mohan Mathur—Foreword to Dr. Pragya Mathur Kumar's Book—Stress in police in India—Recognition, Diagnosis and coping strategies—Gyan Publishing House, New Delhi, 1999, p. 7.
13. Swahilya - Meditation answer to all problems Hindu July 27, 2005. Chennai. Also refer Vivekananda Kendra Yoga Research Foundation—New Perspectives in stress management 1998. By Dr. HR. Nagendra and Dr. R. Nagarathna.
14. For further details consult "The Kautilya Arthasasthra Vol. I and II by R.P. Kangla and the Penguin translation of Arthasashtra. Also refer to Pratip Kar article—"Chanakya and corporate governance" Economic Times 4th August 2000.
15. Amartya Sen—Our economic policy Deccan Chronicle, October 18, 1998, p. 21.
16. N.R. Narayan Murthy—Blissful Knowledge—The Six Pillars of Corporate wisdom—Times of India. 10th August 2001.
17. Yashwant Sinha, Finance Minister key note address at the occasion of Awards for corporate excellence—Times of India 14th August 2001.
18. N.R. Narayan Murthy - Blissful Knowledge - The six pillars of corporate wisdom - excerpts from a speech made at the Wharton Business School - Times of India 10th Aug 2001.
18(*a*). S.K. Chakraborty—Foundation of managerial work-Himalaya Publishing House, Mumbai Second Edition 1998. Reprint - 2000, p. 29-42.
19. Swami Someshwarananda "placement and communication" in Indian wisdom for management MAMTAMA centre and Vivekanand Centre for Indian Management. 1996 - p. 118. Also Bhagwat Gita-Commentary by Swami Chidbhavanananda, Trichy.
20. Swami Someswaran "placement and communication" in Indian wisdom for management 1996, p. 120.

21. Swamy Someswara Nanda—Placement and Communication - Indian Wisdom for Management—1996.

22. For details of success and brief case study refer to Shri Suresh Pandit -Successful innovations (1) Self managed teams" given in Indian Wisdom for management Ahmedabad Management Association 1996, pp. 137-144.

23. Dr. H.R. Nagendra and Dr. R. Nagarallina—New perspectives in stress management - Vivekanand Kendra - yoga Anusandhana Samasthan (VK Yogas) Bangalore 1998.

24. Dr. Krishna Mohan Mathur Keynote address for the DIGP seminar at Internal Security Academy—Mt-Abu - Consults-Police, law and Internal Security—By K.M. Mathur, Gyan Publishing House, New Delhi 1994—Chapter 2. Laws for policing the Environment—Problems and Prospects, pp. 56-92.

25. For further elaboration refer to Dr. K.K. Sharma—A case for Environmental Reporting—Indian Management—May 1998, pp. 96-98. Also refer Gupta N. Das—Environmental Accounting-Wheeler Publishing, New Delhi, 1997, p. 9.

26. Prof. C.K. Prahlad. Indian Management - Vol. 38 No. 1/2 January/February 1999, p. 5.

27. C.K. Prahlad—Times of India 13/01/1999.

28. Alokesh Bhattacharyya—The Deming Champions—Business Today 18 December 2005, p. 68.

29. N.R. Narayan Murthy. The Infosys way Building a giant from scratch. Times of India, 20 June, 2001.

30. Arindam Chaudhury—"Count your chickens before they Hatch", p. 133.

31. Prasad Kaipa of the Mithya Institute of learning and knowledge Architecture—Parul Chandra—what they don't teach you at B. Schools—Times of India, 31 July 1999.

31a. Dr. Man Mohan Singh—Towards a creative and Daring India. India Today, 26th December, 2005.

32. N.K. Singh member Planning Commission—vision 2010—A Corporate Odyssey—Business Today, April 14, 2002, p. 89.

33. Kalam's Vision 2020—Times of India, 18th June 2002, p. 14.

34. Infoglent—B School Aspirations—Business Today—February 17, 2002, p. 27.

35. Seema Shukla—CEO Brand August 19, 2001. Business Today, p. 39.

36. For further details about spiritual dimensions consult— Dr. K.M. Mathur—Managing Human Resource Development— An Indian Perspective, Gyan Publishing House, New Delhi 2001, p. 66.
37. For further details see Norman Vincent Peale Vermillion, London, 1953.
38. Plenty of instructions and guidelines on the methodologies mentioned above are given in the following publications and useful reference books:- Dr. K.M. Mathur—Managing Human Resource development—See also.

    (*a*) Vivek Chudamani by Shankara Charya—(Hindi) Geeta Press (Gorakhpur), (*b*) Light on the Yoga Sutra of Patanjali—B.K.S. Iyenger Harper Collins Publishers India Limited, 7/16 Ansari Road, New Delhi-110 002, (*c*) Light on yoga by B.K.S. lyenger, (*d*) An Instruction Booklet on yoga-Vivekanand Kendra 3 Singsrachari Street, Triplicane Madras-600 005, (e) Yoga—The art of Integration—B. Rohit Mitra the Theosophical Publishing House, Adyar Chennai-600 020, (*f*) Swami Chinmayananda: Vedanta the science of life (Part I to III) Central Chinmaya Mission Trust, Mumbai, (*g*) Swami Chinmayananda—A manual for self unfoldment Central Chinmaya Mission Trust, Mumbai.
39. Dr. Krishna Mohan Mathur—Towards effective management - Pathways to excellence, Gyan Publishing House, New Delhi, 1999, pp. 171-172.
40. Abad Ahmad and O.P. Chopra—Passion to win—How winning companies Develop and sustain competitive edge—Research Study by All India Management Association—Excel Books Private Ltd., New Delhi, 2004, p. X. Preface.

4

Managing Indian Economy-Towards Good Governance

"My government is building a new architecture of inclusive growth; elements of the new architecture of inclusive growth include; Bharat Nirman, the National Rural Employment Guarantee Act, the National Rural Health Mission, the strengthened and extended Sarva Shiksha Abhiyan, the Mid-day Meal and ICDS Programmes, Jawahar Lal National Urban Renewal Mission, and all measures necessary to ensure that the fruits of development we shared equitably and backward minority groups become active participant in our growth process with development priorities for building "world class infrastructure and its preference on the "Public Private partnerships" strategy for building up Roads, Ports, airports and power generation" (Dr. A.P.J. Abdul Kalam address to Joint Sitting of Parliament on 23 February 2007).

Managing and governing a big democratic country like India, in a federal constitutional system, is a gigantic task. In this chapter concept of governance has been theoretically analysed and then various aspects of governing the Indian economy have been highlighted. Indian economy is a developing economy but in the last four years it has achieved noticeable growth. India's development in economic sphere has been remarkable, thanks to our ten five year plans. Jawahar Lal Nehru, India's first Prime Minister wanted to build a "noble mansion of freedom" and expressed his dreams in the following words: "The service of India means the service of the millions who suffer. It means the ending of poverty and ignorance and disease and inequality of opportunities. We have to labour and to work hard, to give reality to our dreams." In this chapter, an attempt has been made to examine how far Indian dream has been fulfilled. Rabindra Nath Tagore also had dream: "India will again—in the council of global nations take the most coveted seat."

1. Concept of Governance

Indians can be rightly proud of their ancient wisdom. The Jataka tales, Shanti parva of Mahabharata, Shukracharya's Nitisar, Panini's Ashtadhyayi, Attreya's Brahmana, Valmiki's Ramayan, Kautilya's Arthshastra and many other classics are replete with descriptions of the tenets of good governance. According to the "Anushashan Parva" of Mahabharat, if the ruler was unjust or oppressive or ignored his responsibilities, the people had a right to rebellion and the people were free to kill such ruler as "a mad dog." In one of the most ancient books, Yajurveda, "Assembly of Learned (Vidya Sabha), Assembly of Spiritual leaders (Dharma Sabha) and the Assembly of the Administrators (Rajya Sabha) are the three organs of government of a ruler". (Chapter XX Verse 43). The rulers should be committed to provide speedy justice and solution of problems. "O Virtuous and prosperous King, be knowledgeable about your conduct as protector and impeller towards our progress and prosperity" (Yajur veda Chapter VIII Verse 50). Regarding qualities of king it said; "We accept thee who is knowledgeable, practices yoga, full of humility, leader among leaders, expert in science and is kind. The administration is thy mainstay". (Yajur Veda Chapter IX Verse 2). In Mahabharat in Shanti Parva, the main tenets of good governance have been enumerated as under:

1. The eternal duties of king are to make their subjects happy, to observe truth and to act sincerely. (Chapter LVIII - Verse II).
2. The main purpose of a king is to protect Dharma (righteousness) and the defender of all (Lokasya Rakshinta) (Chapter XC Verse 3).

In Kautilya's Arthasastra the author has laid down the following main tenets of good govenance:

1. King must merge his individuality with duties.
2. A properly guided administration.
3. Avoiding extremes without missing the goals. State should be directly responsible for promotion of agriculture, animal husbandry, trade and commerce.

4. Disciplined life with a code of conduct for administrators, kings and ministers;
5. Fixed salaries and allowances to public servants.
6. Law and order chief duty of the king and administrators.
7. Carrying out preventive/punitive measures against corrupt officials.
8. Pursuing good governance even amidst instability.
9. Replacement of inefficient and indolent ministers by good ones.
10. Administrators must possess qualities of leadership, intellect, energy, good moral conduct and physical prowess.[1] Kautilya was an advocate for the material welfare of the people and also their moral welfare. He recommended programmes for the advancement of weaker and vulnerable sections of the society. Alexander Pope has given the touch stone of good government as under; "For forms of government, let fools contest, whatever in best administered is best." From times immemorial the search has been on for the seemingly elusive goals of good governance. Good governance is a dynamic concept and encompasses fast - changing political, social, and economic scenario along with the international environment and conditions of operational governance. The term "good governance" comprehends both the processes and procedures as well as the substantial concerns of governance and administration.

2. Constitution of India Incorporates Guidelines for Governance

India got Independence in 1947 and adopted the Indian Constitution in 1950. The founding fathers of the Indian Constitution have given us a sovereign, socialist and secular democratic Republic. Article 37 of the Indian Constitution speaks of certain principles being fundamental in the governance of the country but not enforceable by any court and remain as directive principles of the state policy. The preamble of the constitution calls to constitute India into a "Sovereign Socialist Secular Democratic Republic and to secure to all its citizens:

(*a*) Justice - Social, economic and political;

(*b*) Liberty of thought, expression, belief, faith and

(*c*) Equality of status and opportunity and to promote amongst them all.

(*d*) Fraternity, assuring the dignity of the individual and the integrity of the Nation".

On December 22, 1992 The Lok Sabha passed the 73rd Amendment to the Indian constitution to provide a constitutional base to local government ushering in Panchayat Raj System.

3. World Bank View on Governance

The World Bank has identified the following aspects of good governance:-

(1) Political accountability, including the acceptability of political system by the people and regular elections to legitimate the exercise of political power.

(2) Freedom of association and participation by various religions, social-economic, cultural and professional groups in the process of governance.

(3) An established legal frame work based on the rule of law and independence of Judiciary to protect human rights, secure social justice and guard against exploitation and abuse of power.

(4) Bureaucratic accountability ensuring a system to monitor and control the performance of government offices and officials in relation to quality of service, inefficiency and abuse of discretionary power. The related determinants include openness and transparency in administration.

(5) Freedom of information and expressions needed for formulation of public policies, decision making, monitoring and evaluation of government performance.

(6) A sound administrative system leading to efficiency and effectiveness.

(7) Cooperation between the government and civil society organizations.

Government Agencies, MNCs, large domestic firms, NGOs, and most important the people themselves should come together to solve the very complex problems of Indian economy. New and creative approaches are needed to solve complex problems and challenges that India is likely to face in the 21st Century. The entrepreneurship and inventiveness of committed public servants, dedicated managers and statesman politicians can bring a sea-change in the Indian economy.[2] After independence in 1947, there had been two major land marks in the process of our governance, the one being constitutionalism and the other planned economic development. Governance has to extend beyond conventional bureaucracies and to involve actively citizens and consumer groups at all levels to empower and inform the public and the disadvantaged groups, so as to ensure service delivery and programme execution through autonomous elected local bodies.[3] The public administration and the civil service at all levels are passing through difficult times in terms of eroded credibility and effectiveness of the civil service, growing public perception of an unholy nexus between certain elements among politicians civil servants and criminals (as elaborated in the Vohra Committee report) and increasing criticism of the low level of honesty, transparency and accessibility to the political and bureaucrative elements in charge of administration. Political instability, proliferation of political parties, criminalisation of politics, rising number of persons with criminal records in Parliament, legislature and elected bodies are the major problem areas of contemporary Indian political system. The major factors that threatens the Indian economy today are broadly; (1) Mass Poverty and unemployment; (2) illiteracy, (3) population explosion, (4) rising inequalities and disparties, (5) lack of moral values and social obligations (6) lack of accountability, (7) inefficiency and lack of appropriate performance appraisals, (8) Ineffective and defective taxation system. It is a matter of grave concern that even after 61 years of freedom and implementation of ten five year plans, India is yet to provide a minimum of basic services such as safe drinking water, health, sanitation, medical and basic economic infrastructure of road and electricity. The Indian governments, both the central and the states, share the concern for ensuring responsive, accountable, transparent and people friendly administration at all levels and proposed an action plan for initiatives in the following areas:

(1) Making administrations accountable and citizen friendly,

(2) Ensuring transparency and the right to information, and

(3) Taking measures to cleanse and motivate civil services.

In India there is a need for an independent watch-dog agency called the centre for good governance (CGG) to monitor the implementation of the various schemes, based on the premise that power in a democracy is derived from the people and government must be accountable to them. Value for money, redressal of grievances, openness and transparency, right to information, courtesy to citizen, equal access to public consultation can be some of the guiding principles for bench marking good governance.[4] Experiments carried out in Andhra Pradesh can be a model for such venture and there are several lessons to be learned from the experiment in Andhra Pradesh. India cannot remain unaffected by the global trends leading to structural changes and reorientation of economic policies. Governance includes different relationships, command, communion and contract between different stakeholders that transcends beyond the collective meaning of related concepts like the state, government and regime. Governance, as a concept includes the following generic notions:-

(1) Applicable at each of the three levels of the individual, group and organisation or company, society or nation.

(2) The rule, management, regulation, direction, control or leadership of the affairs or participants of such units.

(3) A system, pattern or structure of participants in such a way that they are a distinctive unit with some notion of a shared purpose.

(4) An acknowledgement of the autonomy and roles played by the individual participants or elements.[5]

Since the 1980s the public service organisations world wide have seen introduction of market mechanism through public sector reforms sometimes referred to as new public management. The use of market or quasi market principles by government for delivering public services included privatisation, market testing and purchaser-provider split. Governance also includes networking and commitment to a common set of values, trust in each other and subtle rules of interaction held together, the networks. Networks in public sector and voluntary organisations offer benefits for professionals and clients to share information, learn from each other and explore possibilities for further developments. Governance as a dynamic concept, finds it application in the following fields:-

(*a*) Corporate governance (e.g. private limited companies).

(*b*) The state, both central and the states in a federal setup.

(*c*) Clinical governance (National Health Service, UK).

(*d*) Global governance (e.g. European union).

(*e*) Local self governments including Panchayatraj and district level local self government.

(*f*) Public private partnership (e.g. governing projects).

(*g*) Cooperative governance system (e.g. Milk Cooperative Unions : AMUL).

4. Common Principles of Governance and Indian Economy

Regarding common principles of governance, D.W. Taylor has enunciated the following general principles:

Knowing what governance is; Achievement of strategic ends; Board - CEO relationship; Unity of Direction; Unity of Command; Unity of Accountability; Ownership needs; Self improvement; Understanding the cost of governance.

Peter F. Drucker in his famous book "Managing for Results" has said; "There are three different dimensions to the economic tasks: The present business must be made effective; its potential must be identified and realised; it must be made into a different business for a different future. Each task requires a distinct approach. Yet they are inseparable. All three have to be done at the same time today. All three have to be carried out with the same organisation, the same resources of men, knowledge and money, and in the same entrepreneurial process". Managing the economy of a nation state also requires similar approach. United Nations Development Programme refers to governance as the exercise of political, economic and administrative authority to manage a nation's affairs. Governance is the complex mechanisms, processes, relationship and institutions through which citizens and groups articulate their interests, exercise their rights and obligations and mediate their differences. United Nations Development Programme 1997 has enunciated the following characteristics of good governance. 1. Participatory, 2. Sustainable, 3. Legitimate and acceptable to the people, 4. Transparent, 5. Promotes equity and equality, 6. Able to develop the resources and methods of governance, 7. Promotes gender balance, 8. Tolerance and accept diverse perspectives, 9. Able to mobilise resources for social purposes, 10. Strengthens indigenous mechanisms[11]. Operates by rule of law, 12. Efficient and effective in the use of resources, 13. Engenders and commands respect and trust, 14. Accountable, 15. Able to define and take ownership of nationals solutions, 16. Enabling and facilitative, 17. Regulatory rather than controlling, 18. Able to deal with temporal issues, 19. Service oriented.[7] Governance not only occupies the centre-stage in the development process but is also considered as key element to be incorporated in a sustainable development strategy. In India we require an active, dynamic and progressive state to create the politico-social and economic conditions for fundamental reform in the process of good governance central and state governments have to improve their governance systems to combat institutional deficiencies, which have diluted the efficiency of the economic reforms programmes. In recent years India has embarked upon new economic policies in several directions to improve the efficiency of her resource allocation, to enhance productivity and growth of labour and capital and to make the Indian products globally competitive. There has been a marked shift in the policy thinking towards more market-oriented approach compared to the earlier ones of bureaucratic control and government interventions. India is a sub-continent and a vast country of villages where about 110 crore people live in about 6 lakh villages spread of 600 districts. The commonly used economic indices like GDP, GNP, Sensex etc do not really reflect the economic situation of rural India. Government of India is aware of a nation wide distress migration of rural people to urban and metropolitan centres due to lack of sufficient job opportunities and paucity of basic rural social infrastructure. Government of India had launched Sampoorna Grameen Rozgar Yogna (SGRY), National Food for Work Programme (NFFWP), National Rural Employment Guarantee Programme, Swarna Jayanti Gram Swarozgar Yojana (SGSY). Pradhan Mantri Gram Sadak Yojana is to connect all habitations having 1000 people and Rajiv Gandhi Drinking National Water Mission to provide good drinking water. Indira Awaas Yojana aims of building 15 Lakh dwelling units every year. The objective of Sampoorna Grameen Rozgar Yojana (SGRY) is to provide additional wage employment, food security as well as the creation of durable community, social and economic infrastructure in rural areas. Currently 150 districts of the country are covered under National food for work programme (NFFWP) in which watershed management, rain water conservation, rural connectivity and land development are priority areas.

Indian economy has thrived by growing four and half times in the past thirty years. Dr. Man Mohan Singh, Prime Minister of India, has said: "Our successful experiment in democracy, with over a billion people seeking salvation through democratic processes and institutions is welcomed by the world that wants to strengthen democracies and pluralistic societies................. A more humane and caring India, which is also a more creative and daring India, is what we need".[8] India is making a lot of progress. But the real danger at the moment is that the country, according to Dr. Amartya Sen, may be heading towards a situation where one half will be like California and the other half like sub-Saharan Africa. Because, even though there is a problem of distribution within the urban area—the modern sector of the economy-primarily the industrial and service sector—is going ahead very rapidly and they are by international standards great performers. Yet the agricultural development has been very slow in India and this is pulling back the Indian growth rate some what. The rural sector has not remained adequately dynamic.[9] The progress of the rural economy and the lives of rural people depends dramatically on making a better deal out of public education and health care. The "Economic Census 2005" says that the 61.3 percent of the country's enterprises in the rural areas are growing faster than those in the urban areas. The top three states among the best five where the enterprises are growing rapidly are in the northeast. The survey, says that Jammu and Kashmir leads in employment in industrial units despite 15 years on insurgency. Employment here is growing at a rate of 6.82 per cent annually. Of 421 lakh enterprises 258.1 lakh (61.3 per cent) are in the rural areas while the remaining 163.1 lakh (38.7 per cent) are in towns and cities. Tamil Nadu has the largest –44.4 lakh (10.56 per cent of the total enterprises), followed by Maharashtra, with 43.7 lakh (10.93 per cent) enterprises in terms of number. The order reverses in the case of employment; Maharashtra employs 118 lakh people (11.95 per cent) among a total of 989.7 lakh employed. It is followed by Tamil Nadu where 9.89 lakh (9.97 per cent) people are employed in the enterprises. In the enterprises sector, West Bengal follows, with the number of units being 428.5 lakh (10.17 per cent), followed by Andhra Pradesh 402.3 lakh (9.55 per cent); and Uttar Pradesh has 401.5 lakh (9.53 per cent). The best Five states are Mizoram (9.6 per cent) Kerala (8.93 per cent), Tripura (8.79 per cent), Tamil Nadu (8.49 per cent) and Assam (6.57 per cent). The Census says that of the total enterprises, 61 percent are loçated in the rural areas and the remaining in the urban areas. The survey suggests that enterprises have grown at the rate of 4.8 percent a year in 1988-2005, against 2.36 per cent in the previous census. On the other hand, employment has grown at the rate of 2.5 per cent per annum in the past seven years, compared to 1.7 percent in the last census period. In India, the concern for decentralized planning is as old as planning itself, with the first five year plan document itself testifying the need for local people's participation in the formulation and execution of economic plans. The Balwant Rai Mehta appointed in 1957 recommended constitution of statutory elected local bodies and a decentralised administrative system under their control which was the basis of panchayat raj system introduced in the country. The Dantwala Committee on block planning and the Ashok Mehta Committee on Panchayat Raj submitted their reports in 1978 for improving the village level bodies and the institutional set up. Due to lack of strong political will at various levels, lack of ideological commitment towards decentralisation and paucity of funds, many of the intentions associated with decentralised planning remained infractuous. The 73rd and the 74th amendments to the constitution of India suggested uniform pattern of three tier panchayats at district level, block level and the Gram Panchayat level with the exception that states having a population below 20 lakh may have the option of not constituting the intermediate ..... at block level. The Article 243 A introduced through the 73rd Amendment Act makes the provision that there will be a gram sabha for each village or group of villages. Gram sabha consists of people themselves while the gram panchayat consists of their elected representatives.[10] One of the greatest challenges with rural India is that the media only reaches 50 percent of the population. The people in rural areas live in 600,000 villages and over half don't have motorable roads, so we need unique means to communicate to them. India has embarked on the path of economic development and new economic policies has initiated the process of globalisation, disinvestment and privatisation. The Indian democracy is putting pressure on politicians to deliver benefits of economic development in rural areas. Only by ensuring development health and education in villages can India boost its growth rate to 9-10 percent and end poverty. Nirinpan Bajpai and Jeffrey D. Sachis, Economists of Colombia University have said: "India's sustained development requires sustained development of rural India. What is needed is a system of "Life line tariffs" in which below-poverty line rural citizens would be ensured a limited amount of water, electricity at zero price, to ensure that every family can atleast meet its basic needs". The importance of rural sector has been on the decline during the last twenty five years. Shortly after independence, as against 13% and 28% in the case of industry and service while agriculture accounted for 59% of the gross domestic product. Today agriculture accounts for 24% of the GDP while industry and services make up 25% and 51% respectively. The proportion of the work force in the three sectors changed from 74:11:15 to 57:18:25 suggesting a relative income advantage to the workforce in the organised manufacturing and services sectors. Although poverty declined over 70% upto 1980 to around 40%

in 1990's to about 26% in 1990-2000, we still have 260 million people (13 times the population of Australia) living below the poverty line.[14] The real daily wage of rural earners, according to NSS Data increased by an average of 5.8% per annum between 1993-94 and 1999-2000. "Delivering a lecture on science and practical reason" at the 93rd Indian Science congress Dr. Amartya Sen stressed the need for completion of land reforms. He said: "There was considerable distress in the agriculture sector due to sharp contrast it had with the upward mobile industrial and urban segments. There was considerable stagnation in the rural sector causing asymmetries and inequalities within the country. The development of social infrastructure in health and education could make a dramatic difference in rural India. The rapid growth of the country's economy in the recent past, not withstanding, India cannot become a major player in the global economy unless it completed land reforms process and built rural infrastructure". Dr. Man Mohan Singh, Prime Minister of India, has in his Inaugural address to the 93rd session of Indian Science congress at Hyderabad has given outlines of his vision of a rural India. He said: "My vision of India is of a modern agrarian, industrial and services economy coexisting side by side where people can live in well-equipped villages and commute easily to work, be it on the farm or in the non-farm economy. The strategy of rural India has to be on the improving the quality of life in villages, based on easily accessible and appropriate technologies". Prime Minister of India Dr. Man Mohan Singh spelled out the Government's economic policy thus "unless we are able to take development forward in a broad based manner, investing in social and economic infrastructure and in human capabilities, we cannot build a more competitive society". He advocated "a cluster approach" to ensure economies of scale and boom in Special Economic Zone that could put the country on the path to becoming a global manufacturing hub. The economic growth must come not just from the large scale industries but also from the organised manufacturing and services sectors small, medium and rural enterprises: Development should no be pursued as threat to people's lives and habitats. Industry must pay more attention to the rehabilitation of people displaced by the spread of industrial activity and by urbanization. It should be cost effective, environment friendly and least disruptive.[16]

Dr. Singh called for the greater research on development of affordable and appropriate technologies for water resource management and energy production. Union Science and Technology Minister Kapil Sibal said between 1996-97 and 2003-04 agricultural imports into India have increased by a whopping 375 percent in volume and 300 percent in value terms. As a result of WTO Indian farmers are unable to get remunerative prices on export of their agriculture produce and products on account of depressed global prices. The Indian economy has been undergoing a path-breaking reform process since 1991. A look at the Indian economy under the liberalisation and globalization process of the 1990s and later reveals a mixed performance of the economy partly due to the various socio-economic bottlenecks and partly due to the slow down in the reform process in the subsequent years for mainly political reasons.[17] According to the Government of India, the number showing a reduction in poverty figures - from 36% of the population in 1993-94 to 26% in 1999-2000. Most of the claims on poverty reduction are politically motivated and its credibility is doubtful. Angus Deaton, the Dwight D.Eisenhower, Professor of Economics and International Affairs at Princeton University is doubtful about the government estimates and in his opinion nearly 20% Indians are living on less than one dollar a day. The effects of economic reforms remain puzzling and have very little effect on poverty. Considering the fact that well over 60 percent of the population is dependent on the rural sector it should be clear that for this group the feasible growth rates of per capita income can at best be marginal. However, a quiet revolution is taking place under the National rural employment guarantee Act and there are clear signs of transformation.[18] NREGA is likely to have multiplier effects on the rural economy and employment opportunities.

5. The Big Picture

16th October 2003 ordinance creating the National Tax Tribunal is a milestone in the ongoing tax reforms. It will usher a new era in tax management. The ordinance envisages the creation of 25 National Tax Tribunal benches to hear appeals from the apex, direct and indirect tax tribunals. Its chair person will be a Supreme Court judge or Chief Justice of a high court. Increasing globalisation and professionalism require the speedy settlement of disputes. The NTT being an exclusive body would settle tax disputes speedily and in the process, the high courts would get spare time to deal with other cases. Various safeguard and check balance measure will ensure the transparency and independence of the National Tax Tribunals (NTT).[19] One important feature of Indian Economy has been the structure of tax revenues. Direct taxes in 2005-2006 have for the first time touched 5 percent of GDP. Gross domestic product (GDP) grew by 8.1 percent during 2005-06. Coming as it does in the wake of growth rates of 8.5 and 7.5 percentage points during the previous two years. The saving rate during 2004-05 was 29.1 percent of GDP which is a clear step up of more than 5.5 percent points from 2001-2002. There is little doubt that the recent performance of India's economy has been robust by usual yardsticks.[20] Dr. A.P.J. Abdul Kalam has said "While aggregate indicators are important, it does not make sense to achieve a "developed" status without major and continuing upliftment of Indians". India had 70,000 Millionnaires in 2004 up from 61,000 in 2003. The 14.6% surge driving by a booming economy was the second highest rise among major nations surveyed by Merrill Lynch. India was placed after Australia which recorded a 14.8% jump in millionnaires from 117,00 to 134,000. Chinese Millionnaires went up from 287,000 to 300,000—a rise Rs. 4.3%. One million is approx of 4.5 crores excluding the value of their residence. About one of every 100 Americans is a millionnaire, compared to around one out of every 15,000 Indians. Post 1991 economic reforms included economic liberalisation, consumer focus, competition for local industry and market orientation. Reforms after 1991 removed the barriers of entry and restrictions on growth of firms, bringing in greater competitive environment domestically, improving international competitiveness and giving private sector larger space to operate. In 2004-2005 with the gross domestic product (GDP) hovering between 7-8 percent, India is now acknowledged as one of the most promising and fastest growing economies in the world.[21] All big multi-national companies are treating India as a strategic market. These include Unilever, BAT, Hindustan Levers, Procter and Gamble, General Electric, General Motors, Ford, Pepsi, IBM, Intel, Texas Instruments, Microsoft, Oracle, and many others. It is the MNCs which show both commitment and flexibility in approach that are likely to succeed in India.

Disinvestment of government share holdings in Central Public Enterprises (CPEs) started in 1991-1992 as a process of economic reforms and upto 2002-2003 total realisation from 48 enterprises has been Rs. 29,592 Crores against the target of Rs. 78,300 crores. During the last fifty seven years, the mixed system of economic planning in India, by democratic persuasion combined with a broad framework of directions has led to great disparities of wealth and pushed more people into poverty. Economic growth in India is constrained by inadequate infra-structure, a cumbersome bureaucracy, corruption, labour market rigidities, regulatory and foreign investment controls the reservation of key products for small scale industries and high fiscal deficits. According to Prof. C.K. Prahalad, the economic growth fueled by the market economy around the world is not a single monolithic problem. Each country has its own road to travel.[22] When the poor at the below poverty line are treated as consumers, they can reap the benefits of respect, choice and self esteem and can have an opportunity to climb out of the poverty trap. National (Central), state government and local bodies have an important role to play in this process by implementing various rural development schemes. Voters registration card issued by the election commission provides one form of identity in a vibrant democracy like India. In order to understand Indian economy, it is necessary to get the big picture of the economy. Growth rate, Industrial Production, food grain production and other essential components of the big picture need to be seen in the context of last three years record. Women can be vanguard of social transformation and entire development process.

Table Showing The Big Picture of Indian Economy

	Items	*03-04*	*04-05*	*05-06*	*06-07*
1.	Growth rates (%)				
	GDP (at factor cost), 99-00 prices	8.5	7.5	9.0Q	9.2A
	Industrial production (IIP)	7.0	8.4	8.2	10.8^
	of which Electricity	5.0	5.2	5.1	7.5^
	Foodgrains production	22.0	-6.9	5.1	0.3+
	Exports (In terms of US $)	21.1	30.8	23.4	36.3^^
	Imports (In terms of US $)	27.3	42.7	33.8	36.3^^

	Items	03-04	04-05	05-06	06-07
2.	Foodgrains prodn/(mn tonnes).	213.2	198.4	208.6	209.2+
3.	Electricity generated (bn Kwh)	558.3	587.4	617.5	493.1^
4.	Average exchange rate (Rs/US $)	45.95	44.93	44.27	45.48@
5.	Gth rate of money supply (M3)	16.8	12.3	17.0@@	21.1 (5)
6.	As % of GDP at current market prices:				
	Gross domestic savings (GDS)	29.7	31.1	32.4(Q)	—
	Gross domestic investment (GDI)	28.0	30.5	33.8	—
	Central Govt. expenditure	1.0	15.9	14.1(P)	13.8(BE)
	Central Govt. Revenue receipts	9.5	9.8	9.6 (P)	9.8 (BE)
	Gross fiscal deficit of central Govt.	4.5	4.4	4.1 (P)	3.6 (BE)
	Exports fob (BOP)	11.0	12.2	13.1	-
	Imports cif (BOP)	13.3	17.1	19.5	-
	Trade Balance	-2.3	-4.9	-6.4	-
	Invisibles Balance	4.6	4.5	5.3	-
	Current account balance	2.3	-0.4	-1.1	-
	External debt	17.8	17.3	15.8	-

Managing Indian economy throws complex challenges to the Government in a democratic country. India the second most populous country with a population of 1.03 billion, has 26 percent of the population in India living below the poverty line. The process of economic liberalization has led to increasing concentrations of wealth, income and economic power, dominance of the MNCs in the domestic economy, accentration of disparity between incomes and asset holding and sharp deterioration in human development. The economy is having no respite from piracy and pillage.[23]

Defining development as the process of improving human lives is not something Indian planners have done. In India policy makers have, in the past looked at aggregates of income and assets, ignoring the severe inter-household disparities, and stressing national gross output and macro-economic variables like investment, outlays and outputs. Prof. Amartya Sen's

Perception of development as "a process of expanding the real freedom that people enjoy" is not understood by many Indian planners. Besides lack of educational facilities, poor health care, inadequate infrastructure and congestion, the unprivileged lives are undernourished, inadequate provided even shelter and their capabilities and potentials are stymied by the system. Amartya Sen's capability approach looks beyond economic and monetary measures and offers a flexible framework for recording improvements, disparities and potential within a family, region and parts of the country.[24] India must move from the utilitarianism of welfare economics to the capability approach. There is a pathetic mismatch between vision and mission, philosophy and practice, dream and reality. As fifth central pay commission observes: "Today it is the perceived wisdom that government should confine itself primarily to the core functions that cannot be performed by the market. Everything else must be left to private initiative contemporaneously, there is no one who advocates an all—pervasive role for the government" Indian economic growth does not really fit in the various frameworks provided by theories of economic growth. We have evidence that the reforms in the country have tended to liberalise only the new economy sectors. (Primarily telecom) without doing much to liberalise old economy industries such as power and road sectors.[25] W.W. Rostow's stages of growth theory describes the transition from underdevelopment to development as a series of stages the traditional society, preconditions for take off into self sustaining growth, the take off, drive into maturity and the age of mass consumption. Unfortunately due to various bottlenecks, slow democratic decision-making processes, unbalanced growth, corruption and lack of innovations, India could not enter into the take off stage and the economy failed to notice of forward, backward and multiplier effects of the economy. Structural models (primarily Lewis' model) of growth focus on transfer of labour from agriculture to tertiary industries could not bring desired results and there were not many labour-related incentives that were given to industries in India.[26] The International Dependence Model aptly describes India's growth during the 1990s as supply side macro economics. It calls for dismantling of state's planning, public ownership and reducing government control over industries that imply reduction in tax rates.

6. The Employment Problems

Unemployment, under employment and disguised unemployment are complex challenges of Indian economy. Unemployment of working force creates poverty, squalor, disease and undernutrition. Although unemployment has been one of the serious impediments to economic growth, various five years plans have so far not solved the problem to a large extent. The figures below show the estimated figures of unemployed Indians—

UNEMPLOYED INDIANS

Though the rate of unemployment has gone down, it is not very significant

	8th *Plan (1992-1997)*	9th *Plan (1997-2002)*	10th *Plan (2002-2007)*
Unemployment**	7.00	7.00	4.10*
Rate (%)	1.87	1.66	0.86

Source : Ministry of Planning and Programme Implementation.
*Estimated **Figures in millions.

The Sardar Sarovar, the inter-linking of river project, gigantic industrial mining, creation of SEZ economic zone, give rise to three sets of questions concerned with (*a*) national interest (*b*) sustainability and (*c*) justice and equity. Development must adequately focus on the differential and unjust incidence of costs and benefits (both terms being defined comprehensively) on different groups of people. We can and must adopt more humane and enlightened policies on displacement and rehabilitation. Does the Sardar Sarovar controversy underscore the failure of centralized planning? Is it driven by a politics that overly privileges economy over society, instead of envisaging them as one integral whole. In the case of Sardar Sarovar, there has been lack of commitment in rehabitating. No town and country planning has been done and adequate fair compensation-cum-rehabilitation has not been done over the years. The problem with thus paradigm of development, is that it demands that the state find the capacity, will, sincerity and respect for the humanity and rights of the projected affected oustees. The current paradigm of development has created the dispensable citizen.[27]

7. Foreign Companies in India

A recent study by A.T. Kearney claimed that India is currently the second most attractive investment destination in the world after China and is ahead of the United States - quite a contrast from the 1970s and 1980s when this country was perceived as an insular (almost Xenophobic) country. In India the number of foreign companies are increasing over years and foreign companies generally prefer Mumbai, Delhi, Bangalore, Hyderabad, Chennai and Kolkata as their corporate country offices. The following figures show the number of foreign companies in India.

Number of Foreign Companies in India

Year	*Foreign Companies*
1960	565
1665	582
1970	561
1975	510
1980	315
1981	300
1985	324
1990	469
1995	619
2000	1045
2001	1141
2002	1285
2003	1497
2004	1754
2005	1840

8. Newly Emerging Economic Countries

The U.S., E.U., China and India currently account for about 47% of the global population and 56% of the global GDP. The following table gives the comparative figures of the newly emerging leaders of the pack.

	Global GDP		Per Capita Income		Population	
	2005	2020	2005	2020	2005	2020
USA	20.9	19.2	100.0	100.0	4.6	4.5
Euro	15.3	11.6	70.3	65.0	4.8	4.2
China	13.2	19.9	14.3	24.7	20.4	18.8
India	5.9	10.5	7.6	14.0	17.1	17.6
ROW	44.2	38.5	18.3	19.1	53.2	55.0
Rest of the world						(In %)

Source: BONNY Thomas quoted by Alok Sheel in Decline of American Power?—The Economic Times, 23rd April 2006.

The annual publications of the U.N.gives a good analysis of the current issues and trends in the world economy. According to the 2006 issues, global economic output has grown at a modulate pace of 3 percent in 2005 and is projected to grow at around the same rate in 2006. China and India continue to have fast rates of economic growth and increasingly these two countries are setting the pace for the world economy.[28] In India post - 1990, investment growth has been sluggish despite the fast rate of economic growth. I.M.F. has projected that during 2006, China and India the worlds two most populous countries accounting for nearly 40 percent of the world's population are expected to grow by 8.2 percent and 6.3 percent respectively. Reserve Bank of India predicted for the fiscal year ending March 31, 2006, that India should witness a growth rate between seven percent and 7.5 percent during 2004 - 05 India's GDP has grown by 7 percent against 8.5 percent in the previous year.

From a $20 billion India's Information Technology Industry, the turnover of India's I.T. Industry is projected to more than double to $50 billion, in less than a decade. By the middle of this Century India would become the third largest economy in the world. India's demographic profile gives the single biggest reason for optimism. India is not merely the world's biggest democracy but also the youngest nation state; nearly two thirds of the population would be in the 15-65 working age grant over the next decade. However, to presume that India's problems of corruption and under development, mal-nutrition and unemployment will disappear, will not be a correct forecast. India has still a very long way to go and all type of obstacles, problems and challenges are bound to come. In India there is great disparity in performance of various states as can be seen from the growth rates of various states while Himachal Pradesh, West Bengal, Karnataka, Maharashtra and Tamil Nadu did very well, other states could not perform so well.

Table Showing the Outperformer and the Underperformer

State	*% growth due to growth in physical capital*	*% growth due to growth in human capital*	*Growth in excess of potential*
Himachal Pradesh	3.49	2.87	1.33
West Bengal	3.49	2.89	1.00
Karnataka	4.73	3.01	0.77
Maharashtra	3.61	2.80	0.60
Tamil Nadu	3.48	3.09	0.44
Rajasthan	4.15	2.59	0.09
Haryana	3.68	2.85	0.06
Madhya Pradesh	3.74	2.63	0.04
Punjab	3.03	2.85	0.01
Andhra Pradesh	3.55	3.10	-0.03
Kerala	3.65	2.73	-0.13
Gujarat	4.99	2.42	-0.20
Bihar	2.77	2.51	-0.44
Orissa	3.07	2.80	-0.92
Uttar Pradesh	3.83	2.42	-1.13
Assam	3.50	2.47	-2.03

India's external debt was $123 billion in 2004, up from $ 111 billion in 2003. The World Bank plans to double aid to India to almost $ 3 billion a year with focus on health, infrastructure, education and rural livelihoods. There is a need to maximise employment and exports, not land acquisitions. Development needs to be more wide-spread-a multiplicity of dispersed SEZs are needed, spreading employment and economic growth across the country.[29] India's economy is poised to growth - stock markets are booming, the culture of plastic money is spreading rapidly, banks are receiving more and more home loan applications in urban areas, shopping malls are mushrooming and middle class people are travelling to enjoy holidays. These are all healthy signs of development but it is only one side of the picture—Life-expectancy, literacy, infant mortality ratio, sex ratio, nutrition, health, equity should be considered the major indicators of human wall being. Kerala by these standards is far ahead of many states. The question that arises is whether express highways, flyovers, enclave smart cities, malls and multi-storeyed buildings should be considered yardsticks for development. Network of small dispensaries are far more vital to public health - than the giant corporate hospitals "Why treat a scratch with a band - aid when you can do an organ transplant? We are at the point where medical tourism is going to earn someone a lot of money. Why not fight malaria through preventive measures, good sanitation, and better public health. Should we distribute - as the touts advise bed nets inpregnated with anti- mosquito repellant. That way there is technology contracts and rewards for corporate, consultants and corrupt bureaucrats.[30] The small and medium enterprises are important components of the Indian Economic system due to their employment generating potential, contribution to exports and flexibilities in operations. The following facts of the small and medium enterprises give us the bird's eye view.

Year	*Total SSI Units*	*Fixed Investment*	**Production**	**Employment**	*Exports ***
99-00	97.2	139,982	170,709	229.1	54,200
00-01	101.1	147,348	184,428	239.1	69,797
01-02	105.2	154,349	195,613	249.1	71,244
02-03	109.5	162,533	210,636	260.1	86,013
03-04	114	170,726	228,730	271.4	NA

in Lakhs *in crores NA-Not Available
Source: Ministry of Small Scale Industries.

The largest companies or the most efficient, at the end of the day, rely on a host of smaller entities for their final products. Over the last five decades, the small scale segment has acquired a prominent place in the socio-economic development of the country. The fourth report of the National Commission of Farmers (NCF) submitted in April 2006 contains a National Policy for Farmers. For the purpose of this policy the term farmers includes land less agricultural labourers, share croppers, tenants, small, marginal and sub-marginal cultivators, fishermen, people involved in animal husbandry pastroralists, tribals engaged in shifting cultivation and people engaged in agro-processing and farming related occupations. Farmers indebtedness is increasing and poor agricultural output is having following major consequences—(*a*) rural discontent and agrarian distress; (*b*) Expansion of the Naxalite type movement (*c*) returning to a "ship to mouth era" and the erosion of national sovereignty in foreign policy, (*d*) Poor soil health enhancement, (*e*) lack of water harvesting and (*f*) Widening gap in levels of rural and urban economy. M.S. Swaminathan has suggested the five point plan to deal with the situation.

"(1) Undertake soil health enhancement through integrated measures in improving organic matters and macro and micro nutrient content as well as the physics and the microbiology of the soil. (2) Promote water harvesting, conservation, efficient and equitable use by empowering gram sabhas to function as "Pani - Panchayats" for fostering as establishment of community managed water banks and the recharge of the aquifer. (3) Initiate immediately credit reforms coupled with credit and insurance literacy. (4) Bridge the growing gap between scientific know-how and field level do-how both in production and post-harvest phases of farming. Knowledge connectivity as proposed under Bharat Nirman should be accomplished by establishing village knowledge centres or "gyan champals" throughout the country. (5) Scientific strategies should be evolved in launching an integrated rural farm and non-farm livelihood initiative by revamping and integrating numerous non-farm employment and income generating agencies like Khadi & Village Industries Corporation, Small Farmers' Agri-business Consortium (SFAC) texile, leather and food parks, agri-clinics and agri-business centres."[31]

9. Special Economic Zones

The special economic zone (SEZs) scheme was introduced in April 2000. The Act was passed in 2005 and in February 2006 the government notified the rules. The existing of export processing zones have been converted into SEZs. Special Economic Zones were intended "to provide quantum jump to production for exports and consequently employment opportunities. Exports from SEZ in 2004-2005 were as under:

Zone (SEZ)	*2004-2005 (Rs. Billion)*
Kandla	10.60
SEEPZ	82.98
Noida	42.66
Madras	13.76
Surat	15.39
Others	16.61
Total	183.69

(*Source:* Ministry of Commerce) Business and economy - 10 February to 23 Feb 2006, p. 56.

In 2003-04, while existing SEZs contributed to only 4.71% of total exports of Rs. 293.37 billion, their contribution in the succeeding year grew by a paltry 0.4%, to crawl up to 5.1%; with SEZs like Jaipur SEZ being able to earn foreign capital of a meager Rs. 50 million. In 2004-05, the Santacruz SEZ contributed 45% of total export from SEZs, while Nodia SEZ registered approximately a threefold increase in exports. Performances of the remaining SEZs were not up to the mark; barring the Surat SEZ (that had about 77% growth). 200 SEZs proposal have reportedly been cleared by May 2006. The idea behind the scheme is to facilitate exports through special taxes and substantial concessions will be granted both in income tax and indirect taxes meant to make exports from these zones competitive. These are also intended to be sops for foreign direct investors to set up shop in India. These rules are so framed that practically any type of entrepreneur foreign, domestic, government whether central or state can start a unit.[32] SEZ units will enjoy 100 percent tax exemption for the first five years. SEZ developers (promoters) too get income tax concessions for ten years within a block of 15 years. They can provide all types of support services utilities, housing, restaurants, and security on commercial terms and will enjoy exemption from service tax. However, from the practical point of view the concept and the execution of the SEZ has been faulted. These are likely to aggravate regional disparities. Poor infrastructure and multiplicity of regulations have been hampering these SEZ. These are likely to widen regional disparities and affect tax buoyancy over the medium term.

10. Disinvestment of Public Sector Undertakings

"Disinvestment of public sector undertaking is considered as a part of economic reforms in India. Disinvestment can be justified on economic grounds so as to lessen the burden on government finances, to have faster economic growth by facilitating technology upgradation by allowing investment by the private sector in the public enterprises. It is also to encourage professionals on the board of enterprises and to free the enterprises from bureaucratic interference". Disinvestment would enable government to mobilise funds which could be used to reduce debt burden or to take up projects of social and community welfare. Disinvestment is also argued on economic grounds that it would kick off economic growth and then postponement of disinvestment makes the economy and the stock market sluggish. Disinvestment, in particular, strategic sale had been justified on economic grounds that "the benefits are real and not illusory" as the expected earnings from the disinvestment proceeds, if put in a bank at 10 percent interest would have yielded much higher returns than the annual return even from dividend declaring enterprises. Government's policy towards public sector was amplified and reflected by the budget speech for the year 2000-01 which emphasised on disinvestment/ privatization /Public Sector restructuring as:

1. Restructure and revive potentially viable PEs;
2. Close down PEs which cannot be revived;
3. Bring down government equity in all non-strategic PEs to 26 percent or lower, if necessary; and
4. Fully protect the interest of workers.

In a suo-motu statement laid before the Parliament on December 9, 2002, The Policy announced was that "the main objective of disinvestment is to put national resources and assets to optimal use and in particular to unleash the productive potential interest in our public sector enterprises.[33] "The disinvestment of CPEs over the years 1991-92 to 2002-2003 yielded Rs. 29,592 crore against the target of Rs.78,300 crore and a greater part was realised in the later years with the adoption of the policy of strategic sale of enterprises. The Supreme Court in its order dated December 10, 2001 validated BALCO disinvestment and remarked that "Thus, apart from the fact that the policy of disinvestment cannot be questioned as such, that the facts herein show that fair, just and equitable, procedure has been followed in carrying out this disinvestment". This disinvestment of central public enterprises from 1991 to 2003 is given below:

Table 1. Disinvestment in Central Public Enterprises (CPEs)

Year	*Target (Rs.Crore)*	*Achievement (Rs.Crore)*
1991-92	2,500	3,038
1992-93	2,500	1,913
1993-94	3,500	2,291
1994-95	4,000	2,629
1995-96	7,000	367
1996-97	5,000	380
1997-98	4,800	912
1998-99	5,000	5,371
1999-2000	10,000	1,829
2000-01	10,000	1,869
2001-02	12,000	5,633*
2002-03	12,000	3,360
91-92-97-98	29,300	11,530
98-99	5,000	5,371
99-00-01-02	32,000	9,331
	66,300	26,232

*Includes amount realised by way of control premium, special dividends and transfer of surplus cash reserves prior to disinvestment.

Source : Economic Surveys, Government of India.

11. Foreign Investment in India

Foreign investment in India is gradually increasing over the last 15 years. Table showing foreign investment in various countries—

Host Countries/ Economy	*2003*	*2004*	*2005*
1. Africa	17.2	18.7	28.9
2. Latin America and the Caribbean	48.0	68.9	72.0
3. Asia and Oceania	106.9	155.5	172.7
4. South, East and South East Asia	94.7	137.8	146.2
5. China	53.5	60.6	60.3
6. Hongkong (China)	13.6	34.0	39.7
7. India	4.3	5.3	6.0
8. Singapore	9.3	16.1	15.9
9. South East Europe and the CIS	24.0	37.2	49.9
10. Russia	8.0	12.5	26.1

Figures in Million.

12. The Challenges of the Rural Sector

Sitaram Yechury CPI (M) leader has asserted that investment must be directed to areas that will allow the poor to be brought into the market process. Union Agriculture Minister Sharad Pawar says:- "The Indian farmer is facing a serious crisis. The farming community has been ignored in this country over the last ten to fifteen years. It is surprising that in the budgetary provision, not more than two percent money has been allocated for agriculture where more than 60% percent of the population works." (The Hindu Chennai 18 Nov. 2005.) The average monthly per capita expenditure (MPCE) of farm households across India was Rs. 503 in 2003. On the average Kerala's MPCE is Rs. 901, Punjab Rs. 828, Orissa Rs. 342, Jharkhand Rs. 353, Chattisgarh Rs. 379 and Bihar Rs. 404 only, Madhya Pradesh is Rs. 225 (MPCE). These figures relate to NSSO's 59th round survey only 6 percent of the rural household have telephones only 0.6 percent of the rural house holds have a computer. In 1991, 26 percent of the farm households were in debt. India, where 70 percent of the people live in rural areas, should have a vision to transform itself into an economically developed country before 2020."[35] According to Dr. APJ Abdul Kalam the transformation of India will need the transformation of 600,000 villages. This will need the creation of programmes for urban facilities in rural areas (PURAS) spread over different parts of the country with physical connectivity, electronic connectivity, knowledge connectivity leading to economic connectivity. The genius of India lies in grass-root entrepreneurship. Prof. Tarun Khanna of Harvard and Prof. Hwang of MT in a research report have argued in India's favour vis-a-vis China. There is a need for national level debate on broad public policy aspects especially those relating to equity, regional balance, decentralization, SEZ scheme and employment generating schemes in rural areas. The latest economic survey talks of demographic dividend, referring to a larger and younger labour force in coming years. But, according to Pulin B. Nayak, Director Delhi School of Economics, there is an India where significant sections of the youth in remote villages and tribal belts have only a bleak landscape before them and no gainful employment along with a steady and unprecedented growth in aspirations. This combination can hardly be salutary for stable and equitable economic development of the 70.9 lakh jobseekers. 60 lakh people have been given employment under the National Rural Employment guarantee scheme as announced by Union Rural Employment Minister on 23rd May 2006, in Lok Sabha—making a Suo Moto statement on the NREG Act, the Minister said that 24477877 applications for registration had been received and 17089915 job cards have been issued and final operational guidelines have been formulated. On 8th September, 2007, the Union Government has announced extension of National Rural Employment Guarantee Act (NREGA) which guarantees 100 days of wage employments to rural households to all the districts of India with effect from 1 April, 2008 and it will cost exchequer Rs. 20,000 crores per year. The recent 60th round of National Sample Survey Organization reveals that unemployment increased during the period 1993-1994 to 2004. Unemployment rate for males increased from 5.6 percent to 9 percent in rural areas and from 6.7 percent to 8.1 percent in urban areas. 285 million or 27.75% of India's population lived in urban areas. In 2001 there were 5161 urban centers in India of which 37 were metropolitan cities. According to official figures there are 67.01 million poor in urban areas (23.62%) in 1999 - 2000. Urban poverty is largely concentrated in the small and medium towns. In the year 2000 just 15% of the population were below poverty line whereas in small towns it was 33% and in medium sized towns and cities it was 23%. Urban development is a state subject and there are a few centrally supported urban development programmes. India's economic development needs a proper direction and holistic approach. Check up how the bottom 30 percent of population in each of our states is doing or has done during the last 5 to 10 years and you might get a very different view of development. India accounts for 57 million of the world's 146 million malnourished children. Malnutrition rates among children of 0-3 years vary greatly across states, from Madhya Pradesh (55.1%), Bihar (54.4), Orissa (54.4), Uttar Pradesh (51.7), Rajasthan (50.6), Goa (28.6), Manipur (27.5) and Kerala (26.9). Each year 6,00,000 under 5 year child deaths could be averted if simple health interventions along with correct feeding practices were adopted, in India - insufficient quantity of food is less to blame for child under-nutrition than poor food quality and safety and women's low social status. In India lot of research needs to be done in various facets of Indian economy. According to Prof. C.K. Prahalad, The real source of market promise is not the wealthy few in the developing world, or even the emerging middle income consumers. It is the billions of aspiring poor who are joining the market economy for the first time".[37] The future research would have to focus on issues of market efficiency, the costs and benefits of free capital movements, the role of derivative instruments, corporate governance and practices of Indian companies, mergers and acquisitions in the banking sector, quality of investment, banking services, developments in micro-financing in the context of the growing role of the private sector and effectiveness of various schemes for poverty allevation. Indian Economy needs authentic and reliable data based on ground realities. Physical potential and growth chart showing position of different states are given below: Gujarat, Karnataka, and Rajasthan, lead in physical potential but the growth chart shows Karnataka, West Bengal and Gujarat leading the other state.

Table showing physical potential and growth chart of states

Physical Potential		*Growth Chart*	
State	*% growth in physical capital in the 1990s*	*State*	*GDP growth in the 1990s*
Gujarat	3.91	Karnataka	7.25
Karnataka	3.70	West Bengal	6.75
Rajasthan	3.25	Gujarat	6.72
Uttar Pradesh	3.00	Himachal Pradesh	6.35
Madhya Pradesh	2.93	Tamil Nadu	6.33
Haryana	2.88	Maharashtra	6.22
Kerala	2.86	Kerala	5.77
Maharashtra	2.83	Andhra Pradesh	5.64
Andhra Pradesh	2.78	Rajasthan	5.50
Assam	2.74	Haryana	5.24
Himachal Pradesh	2.73	Madhya Pradesh	5.06
West Bengal	2.73	Punjab	4.56
Tamil Nadu	2.73	Orissa	4.06
Orissa	2.40	Uttar Pradesh	3.78
Punjab	2.37	Bihar	3.49
Bihar	2.17	Assam	2.60

India is changing with a speed that is astonishing but much still remains untouched. There is uneveness in the boom India is experiencing and great disparities between rich and poor, educated and uneducated, urban and rural people. "India is still associated with a lumbering bureaucracy, corruption, lax law and order and the slums of Mumbai and Kolkata."[38] Prof. Prahalad's approach to development gives interconnectedness of economic development to social transformation. Prof. Prahalad has through a number of case studies suggested social transformation and scaling innovations for creating enabling conditions for development of the private sector. Through various strategies the very poor gradually move to the middle class and process can be accelerated by well designed economic policies and strategies.

It is revealed from data that rural areas of Haryana, Punjab, Gujarat and Maharashtra are having a large number of crorepatis and gradually rural demand will be the key to future industrial growth as is shown in Table below:

Rural demand-key to Industries Growth

(Market share of rural areas in percentage)

Items / Year	*1985-86*	*1992-93*	*1997-98*	*2001-02*
1. Mopedes	42.0	39.6	46.7	48.4
2. Motorcycles	52.0	47.7	51.0	52.9
3. Scooters	36.0	27.8	34.5	40.1
4. Refrigerators	14.0	18.1	26.3	28.0
5. Colour T.Vs.	11.0	31.1	34.7	36.0
6. Washing Machine	12.0	9.9	15.3	14.0

Source: NCEAR—Indian Magt. Sept. 2004, Vol. 43 Issue 9.9.12.

13. India : Great Power or hollow Power?

Nowadays Indian people, particularly the intelligentia increasingly ask whether India is going to become a global power in a decade or so. Economists and social thinkers are divided sharply on the issue. The 2003 Goldman Sachs report on BRICs (Brazil, Russia, India, China) emphasised the huge economic growth potential of the four countries, suggesting that by 2050 China would be global leaders in GDP (though not GDP per capita) followed by the US with some way behind. Arvind Virmani, the director of ICRIER, in a paper published in November 2005 used a mix of economic, technology and strategic parameters to formulate an index of power which he has called Virmani Index of Power (VIP) to analyse the global power from the 18th to 21st Century. Virmani defines countries with a VIP of over 20% as global powers and with over 5% as regional power with relativity to the USA which has the bench-mark rate of 100%. The table given below gives estimates for VIP for the top 13 countries for the year 2003 and 2005.

Virmani Index of Power

Countries	*2003*	*2005*
Global Powers		(In Percentage)
USA	100.0	100.0
Japan	28.0	27.0
China	22.0	25.0
Regional Powers		
Germany	18.0	17.0
France	13.0	12.0
United Kingdom	13.0	12.0
Italy	12.0	11.0
India	7.8	8.5
Canada	8.0	7.8
Russia	6.0	6.5
Spain	6.5	6.4
Brazil	5.7	5.8
Korea	5.5	5.5

To attain number three states, says Virmani, India needs to persuade the US to supply military, nuclear and other techno-strategic inputs, needs to acquire tehnology from all other economic partners, even while developing its own research and development division and should seek a strategic partnership with democratic, multi-polar fringe countries such as Japan, UK, Germany, France and Russia.[40] Having nuclear weapons is useless when India cannot control corruption in its own country. Having nuclear weapons is an illusion of power when it cannot dictate terms to Nepal, Sri Lanka, Pakistan and Bangladesh. Being a regional power in South Asia is useless, in attaining even small regional aims by getting Bangladesh to provide road transit from Tripura to West Bengal and persuading Nepal to build big dams to supply hydro-electricity to India or to even persuade Tamil Tiger to lay down arms. India has so far failed to do anything whatsoever to prevent Pakistan from sending armed terrorists into Kashmir for a country where criminal justice system has practically failed to deliver justice, where criminals dominate Parliament and legislative proceedings, where criminals and naxalites dominate 150 out of 600 districts, to talk of being a regional power is simply laughable. A government that steadily loses control over its own regional trouble regions, that cannot control terrorism, insurgency, militants and even powerful common criminals, simply cannot claim a regional or global power.

The latest 57th round of the National Sample Survey (NSS) pertaining to the year June 2001 to June 2000 provide the following statistics which indicates that there is chronic hunger haunting the false claims of economic prosperity.

Figures Showing National Sample Survey Reports for June 2001-June 2002

•	Monthly per capita consumer expenditure	(Urban) : Rs. 933
•	Monthly per capita consumer expenditure	(Rural) : Rs. 498
•	Of per capita spending in rural India :	
	(*a*) On Food	Rs. 276 (55.5% of total spending)
	Cereals	Rs. 96
	Milk, Milk products,	Rs. 93
	Vegetable and Edible Oil.	Rs. 222
	(*b*) Non-Food	Rs. 44
	Fuel and light:	Rs. 40
	Clothing and Footwear:	
•	Of per capita spending in urban India:	
	(*a*) On food	Rs. 402
	Cereals	Rs. 99
	Milk, Milk products, Vegetable and Edible Oil	Rs. 531
	(*b*) Non-food	Rs. 83
	Fuel and light:	Rs. 68
	Clothing and Footwear :	
•	Living Conditions:	
	(*a*) Rural households in own house	94%
	(*b*) Urban households in own house	60%
	(*c*) Urban households in rented house	34%

(*d*) Urban households homeless	6%
(e) Urban households with access to electricity	91%
(*f*) Rural households with access to electricity	52%

- Employment:

Rural population employed:	43%
Urban population employed:	36%
Workers in male urban population:	55%
Workers in male rural population:	55%
Workers in female urban population:	14%
Workers in female rural population:	31%

One in every one thousand households in towns go "chronically hungry" not getting enough to eat in any of the months. In India in 2001-2002, six percent of the urban dwellers were homeless or living in shanties and only 60 percent households lived in houses they owned. Only 52 percent in villages had access to electricity as compared to 91 percent in urban India. Only over two-fifths of the populations in villages and more than one third in towns were employed. Among males around 55 percent people were employed while 31 percent of rural women were part of the work force, only 14 percent of the urban women fill in this category. India continues to spend more than half of the total consumption expenditure on food.[41]

14. How to Manage India to Achieve Status of Economic Super Power

Economic survey 1996-97 says: "fifty years after achieving independence, poverty, illiteracy, diseases and lack of minimum social services continue to affect hundreds of millions of our people". Mixed economy at work has resulted in inward looking import substitution plans, massive and monopolistic public enterprises, over-regulation of the private enterprises, discouragement of foreign capital, pampering of organised labour license permit raj and colossal level of corruption. The 1991 crisis of Indian economy brought up wake up call and urgent need for reforms. To achieve the status of economic super power in the world, Indian must develop entrepreneurial capabilities and develop a network of powerful radar mechanism for spotting trends and development in every market around the world, provide effective leadership in industry and business. Indians must develop global mindset and global leadership qualities and attributes. India will face the following main challenges if it has to achieve a position of global super economic power in the face of intense competition from China, Japan and may other countries.

1. **Basic Infrastructure:** India will have to build national integrated network of good roads, integrated transportation system and self-sufficiency in energy, civil aviation and railway network. Basic Infrastructure should be adequate to cater for both domestic needs.
2. **Savings and Investment:** India must not only increase its GDP but also its ratio to savings and investment. There is a gap of over 15-20 percent of higher proportion of GDP that has been saved and invested in China compared to India over the last 15 years.
3. **Bribery and Corruption:** India has to take effective legal and socio-economic measures to reduce bribery and corruption in various economic transactions and must achieve a top 10 ranking on the global transparency index. Every citizen has a moral responsibility to fight corruption by lodging a complaint with the Chief Vigilance Commission, government of India furnishing information regarding the corrupt practices, abuse of power for personal gains by employees of central government and corporations and companies of the central government. Citizen doing so would be entitled to protection if the complaint is made under the Public Interest Disclosure and protection of Informers Resolution 2004. Shortly whistle blowing informer protection law is also likely to be enacted by ministry of law.
4. **Agricultural Productivity:** India must increase its productivity per acre in areas such as Rice, Cotton - Seed, Vegetables, Fruits, through effective research and utilisation of available latest technology.

5. **Education:** Today both IIT and IIM have become global brand names with a very high equity cache that reflects several top-of-the line academic qualities - such as numerical abilities, analytical skills, leadership quotient among others. We, in India, have to build such world class educational centres. Rajrishi Singhal asserts that Don't let the branding Iron go cold.[42] India must achieve near hundred percent education target within a span of ten years so that India may produce human resources capable of providing global leadership and innovative abilities to sustain economic development of the country.
6. **Eradication of Poverty:** Various socio-economic measures must be initiated for eradication of poverty, and mal nutrition.
7. **Discipline and Commitment:** India can achieve the status of super economic power only if its citizens are energised and committed to take the country to such heights by discipline, hard work and patriotic feelings.
8. **Evolving with Global Environment:** India is bound to have a bumpy road to economic super power status and therefore its leaders and workforce have to prepare themselves to face a full range of responses from punitive tariffs and export restrictions to more farsighted attempts to collaborate across industrial sectors and develop in partnership with the economically advanced nations.
9. **Complex Challenges from Environment:** Natural disasters also throw a big challenge to India. India has to utilize its scientific technological and environment capabilities to meet the challenges of water shortage, famines, floods, earthquakes, environmental degradation and climatic changes. Disaster management must be learnt and pro-active measures need to be taken whenever necessary. At all levels in education and training, disaster management has to be an important part of training and preparedness.
10. **Educating the Masses:** India has to learn what Sir Winston Churchil said "to educate its masters". In

democracy common citizens are the masters but these masses must understand their constitutional duties as a citizen of India and faithfully discharge those duties in every day life. Fundamental duties under Indian Constitution are contained in Artice 51A of the Indian Constitution. Indians must be educated and ignited to their obligations to the nation.[43]

11. **India needs Better Governance:** India's internal security problems need to be handled with a more long term strategic planning and implementation. The Govt of India responses to various problems of insurgency, terrorism, corruption, naxalism, and even law and order, continue to be limited to knee-jerk deployments, fund allocation, and vacuous rhetoric only. In mature democracies, internal security and law and order administration should be independent of political control but accountable to the law, courts and the people. If India has to become a super economic power, it must radically improve its governance in various fields by having long term solutions to the problems. Unless the political leaders find the willingness and imagination to reclaim their traditional role as moulders of collective ideals and aspirations, the India polity will be gradually be taken over by anti-democratic voices and forces. Governance does not seem to have a strong correlation with the level of economic development of political party in power since economic development is a end-result of many other factors like national resources, state of education and HRD policies over decades, level of literacy, industrial development over the years. A study by India Today in 2006, indicates that Tamil Nadu is a clear winner.

Table Showing Governance Rank

Governance Rank		*Govt. Index*	*Legal Index*	*Governance Index*
1.	Tamil Nadu	0.33	0.76	0.54
2.	Madhya Pradesh	0.33	0.61	0.47
3.	Haryana	0.32	0.55	0.44

Governance Rank		*Govt. Index*	*Legal Index*	*Governance Index*
4.	Andhra Pradesh	0.41	0.43	0.42
5.	Gujarat	0.52	0.31	0.42
6.	Karnataka	0.37	0.40	0.39
7.	Kerala	0.27	0.46	0.37
8.	Rajasthan	0.25	0.47	0.36
9.	Himachal Pradesh	0.29	0.43	0.36
10.	Jharkhand	0.25	0.18	0.35
11.	Punjab	0.31	0.37	0.34
12.	Uttar Pradesh	0.28	0.40	0.34
13.	Chhattisgarh	0.23	0.43	0.33
14.	Maharashtra	0.39	0.22	0.30
15.	West Bengal	0.37	0.18	0.27
16.	Orissa	0.18	0.35	0.26
17.	Jammu & Kashmir	0.21	0.31	0.26
18.	Uttaranchal	0.14	0.28	0.21
19.	Bihar	0.31	0.10	0.21
20.	Assam	0.28	0.13	0.20
	All India	0.20	0.28	0.24

Source: September 11, 2006, India Today, p. 43.

12. **Corporate governance needs to be effective and concerned with social responsibilities:** Corporate governance in India received a boost with the new SEBI norms for publicly held companies taking effect from January 1, 2006. Corporate governance is the way in which firm/companies and small/medium enterprises are to be governed, managed and controlled. It is about supervising and holding to account those who direct and control the management. It is putting checks and balances to prevent abuse of authority and to ensure ethical conduct as well as carrying out social responsibilities. The main doctrines of corporate governance include accountability to share holders, discipline in operations, transparency in dealings and disclosures, fairness in dealings,

responsibility of the consequences of the firms action and social responsibility. At a macro level, it demands a system of internal controls and fair reporting of accounts. Good corporate governance practices have resulted in efficient capital utilisation, strong operational results and above all a strong corporate brand image. The main reasons for corporate failure are: poor strategic decisions, over-expansion, especially through (ill- judged) acquisitions; the dominant CEO or "one man hand"; the greed, hubris and power lust of CEOs and other "star" performers; poor risk management and weak internal controls, particularly with regard to cash; and most importantly, ineffective boards and their audit committees."[43a]

Corporate social responsibility should not be just an eye wash, a commercial stunt or a publicity strategy. CSR includes strict quality control, product safety, consumer care, the ratio of profit making and resource sharing, double entry book keeping to minimise corruption and exorbitant expenses on extravaganza. Corporate social responsibility is neither charity, philanthropy, hospitality or social work but it is a moral compass for any business operation. Since companies are part of a society, these companies owe their existence to the society and must realize their obligations and contribution to the well being of the society—in terms of health care and well-being, human rights and community welfare, environment and ecology in many positive ways. Corporate contribution to charity in India are likely to grow from 22000 crores during 2006-07 to Rs. 30,000 crores in 2007-08.

13. **Social Security Scheme for 362 million unorganised workers:** In May 2006 the National Commission for Enterprises in the unorganised sector, under the chairperson of economist and Rajya Sabha Member Arjun Sengupta submitted its report to the Prime Minister of India.[44] It seeks to provide social security to 362 million workers including domestic workers. There is a legal provision under the Social

Security for unorganised workers bill to ensure employer's contribution. In the first year one fifth of the workers will be covered, the contribution of the centre and the state plus the administration cost will be Rs. 7637 crores that is approximately 0.20 percent of the gross domestic product (GDP). Of this the centre contributes Rs. 6384 crore and the state Rs. 964 crore. In the Fifth and final year when the scheme will cover the last worker, the total cost of the centre, states and administrative expenses would be Rs. 25000 crore (0.48 percent of the GDP) of which the states contribution would be Rs. 5,400 crore. The scheme entails hospitalisation benefits for workers to the tune of Rs. 15000 per year, maternity benefit of Rs. 1000 per delivery and personal accident cover in the event of death of (the) earning head of the family. The merit of the scheme is that it is for the first time anywhere in the world that a social security scheme of such a magnitude for the poorest of the poor has been drafted. This will be an example for the world. The report is likely to be sent to group of Ministers (GOM) before going to the union cabinet.

14. **Rein in strikers with Iron hand:** In a bench of justices Doraiswamy Raju and Arijit Pasayal of the Supreme Court, the highest court of India has called for a strong action against those indulging in hooliganism during strikes in the name of hartal or bandh.[45] The court held that employees of government and the private sector had no legal or moral right to strike. Unless such acts are controlled with an iron hand, innocent citizens are bound to suffer and they shall be the victims of the high handed acts of some fanatics.

15. India Vision 2020: Planning Commission report has given the following vision of India 2020—

1. India 2020 will be bustling with energy, entrepreneurship and innovation.
2. Productivity revolution in agriculture, coupled with agri business and ecology management works will generate abundant rural employment.

3. Success in I.T. will be followed by other emerging fields.
4. Inequalities in terms of gender, income, communities and regions will come down dramatically.
5. Urban traffic will be motorized as never before.
6. Computerisation of education will dramatically improve the quality of instruction and the pace of learning.
7. Environmental issues will remain serious concerns.
8. India will be much more integrated with the global economy.
9. Rising level of education, employment and income will help stabilize internal security and social environment.
10. A better educated electorate and more transparent and efficient government will characterize India 2020.

It is believed that India's economy will be the third largest after China and the USA in the next 30 years. "The world in 2050" states that India has the potential to become the fastest growing large economy in the world by the year 2050. By 2010, the work outsourced to India will quadruple to $ 56 billion a year. Even today India is among the world's most preferred out-sourcing destinations. In India we, however, require an active state to create political conditions for fundamental reforms in the process of good governance. There is a growing realisation and policy acceptance of the role of private sector in infrastructure development and service delivery.

Concluding Remarks

Nobel laureate and economist Joseph Stiglity has underlined the importance of India continuing to maintain its programmes for the weaker sections and the poor, health and education projects and rural development measures. In his latest book "Making globalisation work" (2006) Prof. Stiglity has challenged the general belief that free market leads to efficient outcome and that the role of government should be limited. He has suggested that India should use part of its foreign exchange reserves to fund infrastructure development. According to him the focus ought to be on sustainable, equitable and democratic development. Containing India against going in for capital account convertibility and allowing short term capital into economy, he said, the move could create instability. The experience of Mexico offered crucial evidence that opening up the banking sector did not work well for developing countries. Performance of governance in India on economic, monetary and fiscal fronts, is a matter of perception and opinion. Prof. Pranab Bardhan of University of California in a lecture at the annual India Policy Forum on 1 August 2006, at the annual India Policy organised by NCAER and Brooking said: "In India we face a paradox. By many measures governance is worsening, yet economic growth has averaged a record 8% for three years (2003-06). Record sums of black money are being spent by corrupt politicians, crime violence and lawlessness are all on the increase. Violence in J&K, Northern States and even other states is on the rise. Naxalite attacks affect 165 districts and Islamic terrorists attacks on innocent people, with criminal records have entered the Parliament and the legislatures and even in state/ central cabinets enmasse. Murders, criminals, economic offenders with political clout escape scot-free from judiciary. The quality of public services like public health, education, electricity and water supplies are extremely inadequate, water supply on the average is most inadequate in Chennai, Bangalore, Delhi, and many other cities. Electricity supply in many states is terribly unsatisfactory and more than 30 percent of it is reported by stolen with impunity.

There is another picture of the governance and reforms have ensured ample supplies of telephones and computers. Narayan Murthy admitted that it took him one year to get a telephone connection and another year to get an import license for a computer in the 1980s. Economic and financial liberalisation had ended that scarcity and the new technology has spread very fast. Competition has made suppliers more accountable to consumers. "Tortuous, bribe-laden procedures have been abolished or pruned for industrial licensing, import, permission, technical tie-ups foreign investment, MRTP clearance, and much else. This has aided economic growth.[46] A recent ICRIER working paper estimates that between 1999-2000 and 2006, the number of private engineering institutions rose from 669 to 1478, teachers training institutions from 1,050 to 5,190; pharmacy institutions from 204 to 629 physiotherapy institutions from 52 to 205 and management institutes from 875 to 1650. Although the quality may be spotty in many cases financial liberalisation has empowered consumers with access to housing loans, credit cards, ATM facilities and better banking facilities, mobile telephones have revolutionized the common man's life. Economic liberalism has revolutionised the capital market facilitating dematerialisation of shares and giving India an electronic exchange (NSE) superior to London's exchange. E governance initiatives in Andhra, Karnataka, Maharashtra and Central Governments have brought many revolutions in governance.

Since India is gradually opening its power, telecom, commercial real estate and retail sectors to foreigners, the pace of institutional and economic changes will be fast. India, according to William T. Wilson would surely develop as economic power and may bring economic growth in various sectors. India, as a nation, appears to be on the threshold of take off today because of the innate resilience of the people, their ambitions, aspirations and capacity to work hard to achieve their goals. India must capitalize on the talent of its people in the knowledge industries.[47] On going global transformations need guidance, to avoid very negative looming consequences and realise very positive potentials. Markets, Civil society etc., however important, cannot be relied upon to provide the needed guidance, normatively and realistically only governance can do so. However in order to adequately fulfil crucial future-building tasks, politics must be revitalised, democracy must be refocused, and governance must be radically redesigned".[49]

References

1. For further details consult R. Shamasastry, Kautilya's Arthasastra (1929) Mystore-b Meslevam Mission Press, Book 1—Chapter 19. Also K.P. Jayaswal-Hindu Policy-Bangalore (1968) Bangalore Printing and Publishing Co.
2. Peter Blunt, "Cultural Relativism, Good governance, Decentralisation and Development"—Public Administrations and Development—Vol. 15, 1995, pp. 5-7.
3. Govt. of India—An agenda for Effective and Responsive Administrator, New Delhi. Ministry of Personnel, Public Grievances and Pensions, November, 1966.

4. C.K. Prahalad—The fortune at the Bottom of the Pyramid.

5. Cutting B. and Kouzmim A. (2001) Formulating a metaphysics of governance: Explaining the dynamics of governance using the new JEWEL Synthesis frame work : Journal of Management Development Vol. 2, No. 6, p. 27-28.

6. D.W. Taylor (2000 Facts, Myths, and monsters; understanding the principles of good governance, International Journal of Public Sector Management. Vol. 13, No. 2, p. 108.

7. U.N.D.P. (1997) Good governance for sustainable human development; A UNDP Policy document, January 1997 UNDP New York; Volume 6, November IP. 19.

8. Dr. Man Mohan Singh—towards a creative and Daring India—India Today—Anniversary Issue—Momentous years 1975 - 2005 - December 26, 2005, p. 11.

9. Dr. Amartya Sen—We have to create a climate of intellectual dissidence—India Today—Aspire, March 2006, p. 56.

10. Planning Commission, Report of the working group on Decentralised planning and Panchayath Raj Institutions, Govt of India, November 2001.

15. Abusaleh Shariff and Aditi Pany—Don't Romanticise the village-company exaggarate rural economy achievements, Times of India, 26th May 2005. (Writers are with National council of Appiled Economic Research).

16. Dr. Man Mohan Singh—Development not at the cost of habitats - Hindu, 19th June 2006, Chennai.

17. T.N. Srinivasan and Suresh D. Tendulkar—Reintegrating India with the world economy Oxford University Press, New Delhi, 2003, pp. 167, Rs. 395.

18. For a detailed case study—refer Nirmala Lakshman Article-Employment guarantee signs of Transformation—Chennai, Hindu, May 11, 2006.

19. M.N. Verma—A New Era in Tax Management, Times of India, 2nd January 2004.

20. Pulin B. Nayak—Director Delhi School of Economics—In the shadow of growth—Poor, unemployed require purposive intervention. The Times of India, New Delhi—7th April, 2006.

21. A.V.Vedpuriswar—The new rules for MNCs Indian Management, May 2006, p. 67.

22. C.K. Prahalad—The fortune of the Bottom of the Pyramid, p. 82.

23. D. Bandyopadhyay—"Administration Decentralisation and good governance", Economic and Political Weekly, November 30, 1996.

24. Bini Agarwal, Jane Humphries and Ingrid Robeyns (Editors) Capabilities, Freedom and Equality—Amartya Sen work from a gender Perspective.

25. Montek Singh—"Infrastructure Development in India's Reforms" in Ahluwalia I.J. and I.M.D. Little (ed) India's Economic Reforms and Development: Essays Dr. Man Mohan Singh, Delhi Oxford University Press, 1998.

26. Todaro P. Michael—Economic Development—New York Oxford University Press, 1984: Kala S. Sridhar "Who is to be Blamed" The Economic Times, November 29, 2000—B.M. Besai (Ed) Agricultural Development paradigms for the Ninth Plan under New Economic Environment, Oxford & IBM, 1997.

27. Usha Ramanathan—Does Development entail deprivation. The Economic Times, Chennai, 25 April 2006, p. 11.

28. World Economic Situation and prospects 2006—UN academic foundation. Daryaganj—New Delhi-110002, Rs. 595.

29. Kiran Karnik—Don't make SEZ real estate Scams—The Economic Times, Chennai, 6 May, 2006.

30. P. Sainath of hi-tech, low efficiency and malls—Hindu, Chennai, 3rd May, 2006.

31. M. Swaminathan—Agriculture cannot wait. The Hindu—Chennai, 24 May 2006. The authors thankfully acknowledge the five point plan elaborated in this para to Shri Swaminathan.

32. CRL Narasimhan—SEZs Many unanswered questions—Hindu, Chennai, 22 May, 2006.

33. Nand Dhameja, Disinvestment of Central and state enterprises-Indian Journal of Public Administration, Vol. XLIX No. April-July, 2003.

34. Economy Survey 2002-03. Government of India.

35. APJ Abdul Kalam Umbilical connectivity and societal change The Hindu. Chennai, 26 Jan 2006, Valedictory Address at the Pravasi Bhartiya Divas 2006 in Hyderabad on January 9, 2006.

36. Pulin B. Nayak, Director, Delhi School of Economics,—In the shadow of growth—Times of India, New Delhi, 7 April, 2006, p. 14.

37. C.K. Prahalad—The Fortune at the Bottom of the Pyramid Wharton—Wharton School Publishing, 2005.

38. Hasan Suroor—"Seduced by an elusive idea of India" The Hindu, Chennai, 26 May 2006, p. 12.

39. C.K. Prahalad and Stuart Hart 2002—The fortune at the Bottom of the Pyramid strategy + Business Issue 26, 2002.

40. Swaminathan S. Anklesaria Aiyar—India : great power or hollow power. The Economic Times, Chennai—4th January, 2006.

41. 57th Round of National Sample Survey—Various figures and details given in this para are extracts from the above survey report, Times of India, New Delhi, 18 Dec., 2003.

42. Rajrishi Singhal—Don't let the branding Iron go cold. The Economic Times, 14 June 2006, p. 80.

43. For a comprehensive treatment of the subject please consult Krishna Mohan Mathur's book Indian Police—Role and Challenges, Gyan Publishing House, New Delhi, 1994 Chapter 9 pp. 192-212.

43a. Stewart Hamilton : Understanding the real reasons for corporate failure Sarbanes-Oxley will make title difference: Indian Management—November 2006, pp. 49-50.

44. For details of the scheme—Refer Arjun Sengupta report. The Hindu, 18 June, 2006, p. 13.

45. Times News Network—Rein in strikers with Iron hand says S.C., Times of India, New Delhi, Dec. 18, 2003.

46. Swaminathan S. Anklesaria Aiyar, Falling, governance, rising growth. The Economic Times, Chennai, 2 August 2006.

47. Pawan K.Varma—being Indian Viking—Penguin Books India, New Delhi, 2004, p. 211.

48. Yehez Kel Dror—The capacity to Govern, p. 3.

5

Corporate Governance

"Governance is the function of the ruler in order to protect the state from the wicked and nourish the good".

Somadeva —Nitivaky amrite

If economic reforms have to gather mass and speed, it is imperative that the country addresses the fundamental issues of governance:

P. Chidambaram, Finance Minister, Govt. of India. (C.D Deshmukhi Memorial lecture 2002)

Corporate governance basically deals with power and accountability for the safety and performance of assets and resources entrusted to the operating team of the firm. The ultimate objective of corporate governance is to attain the highest standards of procedures and practices followed by the corporate world so as to have transparency in its functioning with an ultimate aim to maximise the value to the various stake holders and the society. Corporate governance is the well laid out system of governance by which companies are directed and controlled by the government and the society in the best interest of the stake-holders and others, ensuring greater transparency, full disclosure, independent monitoring of the state of affairs and timely financial reporting to the Board of Directors, who are directly responsible for governance of their companies. Good governance means achieving goals and delivering results while working through various ties, checks and balances. The system must have the capacity to craft the right economic policies and once the policies are in place, the system must have the capacity to implement those policies and achieve the stated goals.[1] The more national economies get integrated into a seamless global economy, the greater does corporate power expand beyond the reach of any state power. From a historical perspective, the seeds of corporate governance were laid during the Water Gate Scandal that shook the Presidential House in the United States of America. In 1980s there were many high profile business failures due to lack of proper controls and absence of independent internal and external audits. In order to prevent recurrence of such corporate failures Sir Cadbury Committee was constituted to address the various issues related to the corporate governance in United Kingdom. In USA, Sarbanes - Oxley Act 2002 was enacted by the American Senate in July 2002 which addressed various issues associated with corporate failures to achieve quality governance and to restore investor confidence. Five hundred of the world's largest corporations account for nearly 50 percent of the international production of goods and services. Between 1980 and 1993, these 500 top corporation of the world reduced their manpower by 4.4 million, while increasing their business volume by 1.4 times and multiplying their assets by two and a half times. The new reality of unprecedented and untrammeled Corporation power cannot be easily controlled because it transcends national boundaries, and does not even come under the ambit of any state authority.[2] Developing nations should seriously consider effective mechanism to make sure—that the Bhopal gas leak tragedy like incidents do not recur and public interests are not the casualty of the aggressive pursuits of business interests by the leviathans of these multi-national corporations. During the period 1992-96 the following scams came to light in India as given in the table below:

Table Showing Scams and Amount Involved

S.No.	*Name of Scam*	*No. of Cases Registered*	*Amount Involved*
1.	Letter of Credit (Assam) scam	12	Rs. 112.00 Crore
2.	Bank Securities scam	71	Rs. 9130.75 Crores
3.	Housing Scam	16	Rs. 1,54,000/- per month Govt. has been cheated directly and according to rough estimates the Govt. stood to lose at least Rs. 1,54,000 per month.

S.No.	Name of Scam	No. of Cases Registered	Amount Involved
4.	Area Scam	01	Rs. 133.00 Crores
5.	AHD Scam	48	Rs. 750.00 Crores
6.	Telecom scam	2	Rs. 34.68 Crores
7.	Ayurved scam	33	Rs. 26.00 Crores
8.	Scam relating to allotment of petrol pump	01	—

Corporate India has gone global. Reliance Industries, Ranbaxy Laboratories, Sundaram Fasteners, Arvind Mills, Bajaj Auto, Infosys, Tata Steel, Videocon, BPL, TVS, Cipla, Wipro are all changing the face of the Indian economy. The newly emerging corporate India is at the cross-roads today and needs guiding principles for corporate governance. During the year 1999 there were a few alarming reports about lack of financial accounting in corporate sector as we can see the following reports:-

1. Half of the BSE members default in submitting returns (The Economic Times, 21.2.1999).
2. "IDBI has asked Essar Steel to bring back Rs. 245 crores diverted to group companies. Essar wants bailout but what about those funds?" (Indian Express, 23-03-1999).
3. Over 49,000 investors still stuck with Constar, face Rs. 67 crore gap -SEBI says Constar schemes is beyond its jurisdictions (The Financial Express, 30-10-1999).
4. Promoters protest against FIs divesting stakes in open market. Ask FM that they be given first right of purchase -FIs say they have right to exit at any point of time.

There are a number of vanishing companies. There are about over 250 vanishing companies in the country and there are approximately 40 such companies from Gujarat alone. Foreign Institutional Investors (FIIs) who have been granted registration are more than approx 482 and the FII investment figure till Oct 1999 amounted to US 9676.1 million. The above-referred scenario points out to the need for corporate governance. Integration of Indian Corporate sector into the world economy demands corporate governance. Need for professionalism and assertion of rights by the shareholders, whose role has become marginalised over time demand effective corporate governance. The need for corporate governance is also felt by the lending institutions which are themselves being subjected to more rigorous accounting norms, particularly with regard to non-performing loans. The advent of Multi National Corporations (MNCs) and Trans-National Corporations (TNCs) operating across national boundaries point out to the need of corporate governance. The concept of corporate governance derives its relevance in the context of mis-governance which includes non-feasance, over-feasance and malfeasance. Misuse of power, frauds, chicanery and embezzlement of funds are some of the common aspects of failure of corporate governance. Accountability in relation to public satisfaction and responsive delivery of service is a vital determinant of good corporate governance. For ensuring transparency and ethical conduct in corporate governance, it is necessary to scrape off the dead wood of old rules and regulations of precedents and red tape. Even before the recent problems in the United States of America, a wealth of theoretical and empirical work had begin to pose a question mark over uncontrolled corporate governance - Whether based on internal controls or on market mechanisms such as takeovers and firm performance.[3] Corporate governance practices include a complex mosiac of laws, regulations, institutions and implementation capacity in the government and the private sector. These are imposed not with the objective of shackling corporations but rather to balance the spirit of enterprise with greater accountability. In corporate governance, role of accountants and auditors cannot be easily estimated. Independence accountability and transparency are needed for auditors and accountants to bring excellence in corporate governance.

The Corporate governance Truism that boards must govern but not manage is swiftly being reinterpreted in an age of board room empowerment.[4] It seems that United States of America's Corporate boards are finally getting more and more demanding and active Chief Executives are now being churned at a record rate. Lucent, Gillete, Mattel, Compaq, Maytag and Campbell soup are some of the major companies whose boards had pushed out many chief executives during 2000-2001. Lee Iacocca has said: "There are two ways my directors can vote : yes or I Resign." During the last two decades things in USA, have changed drastically. The new era of empowered boards has indeed arrived in USA. Corporate Boards can now not only insist on results from management but also demand that management (sell them) on the strategy for achieving those results. CEO's tenures are now uncertain and shrinking. If projections are not met, if strategy in flagging, if a turn around does not turn and quickly - American corporate boards are quite happy now to spring the trapdoor under the corner office. In USA of 21st Century Corporate boards have lost their qualms about committing mutiny, they are even more accepting of general insubordination around the board-room table. CEO's words are no longer being the last word. So monumental have been the failure of corporate governance in the world's most efficient market, the United States, that the very expression threatens to become a hallow cliche.[5] US financial crisis of September - October 2008 shows failure of corporate governance.

The goals of corporate governance are to help improve standards of governance for their corporations by fostering the spirit of enterprise and accountability, promoting fairness, transparency and responsibility. In the words of Sir Adrian Cadbury, "Corporate governance is concerned with holding the balance between economic and social goals and between individual and communal goals. The governance structure is there to encourage the efficient use of resources and equally to require accountability for the stewardship of these resources. The aim is to align as nearly as possible the interests of individuals corporations and society. The incentive to corporations and to those who own and manage them, to adopt internationally accepted governance standards is to achieve their corporate aims and to attract investment. The incentive for their adoption by states is that these standards will strengthen the economy and discourage fraud and mismanagement".[6] In USA corporate scandals are sparking a revolution in corporate governance. The USA market is driving reforms. Investors shun companies that are seen as having lax oversight boards, want curmudgeons who will act as watchdogs, not lap dogs. Broadly principles of good corporate governance can be enumerated as under:

1. **Independence:** Not more than two directors should be current or former company executives and none should do business or accept consulting or legal fees from it. The audit, compensation and nominating committees should be made up solely of independent directors.
2. **Activism:** Boards should regularly meet with management and the evaluate their own performance every year. Boards should be decisive when planning a CEO succession, diligent in oversight responsibilities, frugal on executive pay and quick to act when trouble strikes. Audit committees should meet atleast four times a year.
3. **Director Quality:** Boards should include atleast one independent director with experience in the company's core business and one who is the CEO of an equivalent size company. Fully employed directors should sit on no more than four boards, retirees no more than seven. Each director should attend atleast 75% of all meetings.
4. **Stock Ownership:** Each directors should own an equity stake in the company worth at least $1,50,000 excluding stock options. New board members can be only exceptions who haven't had time to build a large stake.

In India, Shri Kumar Mangalam Birla Committee was constituted in May 1999 to promote and raise the standards of corporate governance in the wake of globalisation and economic reforms. The debate on corporate governance started formally with the release of the CII code in 1997 which was followed by a number of other committees and task forces. The initial debate was extended to PSUS for the first time in the Dr. YRK Reddy Committee Report 2000. The Kumar Mangalam Birla Committee Report resulted in the specific clause in the Listing Agreement as prescribed by the SEBI. Mandatory recommendations of Birla Committee are as under:—

(*a*) Applies to Listed companies with paid up capital of Rs. 3 crores and above.

(*b*) Composition of Board of Directors—Optimum combination of executive and non-executive Directors.

(*c*) Audit Committee—with three independent directors with one having financial and accounting knowledge.

(*d*) Remuneration Committee.

(*e*) Board procedures - Atleast 4 meetings of the board in a year with maximum gap of 4 months between 2 meeting to review operational plans, capital budgets, quarterly results with minutes of committee meetings.

(*f*) Director shall not be a member of more than 10 committees and shall not act as chairman of more than 5 committees across all companies.

(*g*) Management discussion and analysis report should cover industry structure, opportunities, threats, risks, outlook and internal control systems.

(*h*) Information sharing with share holders.

Non-Mandatory recommendation of Birla Committee are briefly enumerated below:-

1. Role of chairman.
2. Remuneration Committee of Board.
3. Shareholders right for receiving half yearly financial performance.
4. Postal Ballot covering critical matters like alteration in Memorandum etc.
5. Sale of whole or substantial part of the undertaking.
6. Corporate reconstructing.
7. Further issue of capital.
8. Venturing into new businesses.

On implementation of recommendations of Kumar Mangalam Birla Committee, clause 49 has been introduced in the listing agreement with stock exchange. Clause 49 requirements include management discussion and analysis report to cover outlook, risks and concerns, internal control systems and its adequacy discussion on financial performance and disclosure by director on material financial and commercial transaction with the company. Clause 49 requirements also include share holders investors grievance committee under the chairmanship of independent director and minimum two meetings in a year. Clause 49 also stipulates report on corporate governance and certificate from auditors on compliance of provisions of corporate governance. The corporate governance basically encompasses the issues of :-

(1) Ownership of the corporation.

(2) Relationship between owners and managers in controlling, directing and managing the corporation.

(3) The national and international laws, norms, systems and traditions by which corporation are controlled, directed and managed.

(4) Relationship between the corporation and the society and all stakeholders.

(5) Role, responsibilities, rights and privileges of investors, board of directors, CEOs and other stakeholders.

(6) Issues of accountability, transparency, safety and performance of the assets and resources and role of professionals.

(7) Institutional, legal and procedural arrangements containing legal procedures, practices and implicit rules that determine corporate governance with the object of maximising long term shareholder value and safeguarding the interests of all stakeholders.

(8) Who exercises powers on whose behalf and how in this exercise of power controlled?

Corporate governance is a very broad concept and has to take into account corporate laws and regulations of the nations, corporate crime, corporate ethics, corporate political activities, corporate code of conduct, corporate government relationship, social responsibilities of the corporation and role of international governance

> practices. The confederation of Indian Industries (CII) has defined Corporate Governance in the following words; "Corporate governance deals with laws, procedures, practices and implicit rules that determine a company's ability to take managerial decisions vis-a-vis it claimants in particular, its shareholders, its creditors, the state and employees. There is a global consensus about the objective of "good" corporate governance: maximising long term shareholder value. Since shareholders are residual claimants, this objective follows from a premise that in well performing capital and financial markets, whatever maximises shareholder value must necessarily maximises corporate value must satisfy the claims of creditors, employees and the state."

The Bhagwat Gita's Philosophy of action with detachment gives invaluable lessons for corporate governance. It provides a code of Ethics to the CEO and the Board of Directors. Thieving, adultery, causing injury to others, lying, duplicity, chicanery, violence, partaking of certain types of food and idle occupations are forbidden. In the context of corporate world they could be interpreted as thieving (Tax avoidance/Tax stealing), buying/duplicity (lack of transparency), idle occupation (lack of customerisation), chicanery (bad and false accounting practices), etc. Bhagwat Gita's practical philosophical inputs would definitely suit the code of ethics of global companies. But it requires a lot of self-introspection, change of mind sets and courage to ensure fair play and ethical conduct in corporate management. Corporate governance is like an Oxymoron in the Indian Context. There are many Indian Companies which have voluntarily established high standards of corporate governance. New age companies like Infosys, follow practices comparable with the best in the world. In 2000, Infosys was presented with the National award for excellence in corporate governance instituted by the Finance Ministry.

At the top level many corporations are following rules of good governance. Godrej group, the Vardhaman group, Indian Oil Corporation, Excel Industries, Yash Paper, Eicher are some of the organisations following Dharma and principles of

Corporate Governance. Infosy Technology and Wipro Corporation have been steadfastly promoting corporate governance. Mr. N.R. Narayana Murthy of Infosys Technologies describes the core of corporate governance by the simple statement: "A Clear conscience is the softest pillow". Infosys has the motto : "Powered by intellect; driven by values." Corporate governance activism has been given the following new issues to the corporate world:

1. Social Investing and social responsibility.
2. Governance Code and self imposed regulations.
3. Shareholder Consciousness and awareness of the corporate activities.
4. Shareholders involvement in management.
5. Shareholders' candidate for election in the board.
6. Corporate take overs.
7. Management buy out.
8. Eco-balance sheet and social responsibilities of the companies.

Corporate governance can be referred as "Enlightened Rule" of independent and powerful board of directors. Good corporate governance is the corporate manifestation of the personal beliefs and values of its chief executive which go to configure the organisational values and culture and influence the thoughts, beliefs, and actions of its employees leading to sustained delivery of quality service and value to every constituent of the company".[7] A democratic society cannot tolerate for long a capitalist system where there is too much inequality of wealth and resource. A society in which the top one percent earn more, collectively than the bottom 40 percent will not be tolerated by any developing nation where people have democratic rights. The following quotation from David Korten's book - "When Corporations Rule the world" scares all those who are concerned with the welfare of the Masses:-

1. "In 1989 the top 1 percent of Americans earned an average of $559,795 each, receiving as a group, more than all the bottom 40 percent.
2. In 1992 the top 1000 CEOs in America received on average 157 times more salary, as the average worker.

3. Forbes' top 400 richest people, had a net worth in 1993 of $328 billion, equal to the combined GNP of India, Bangladesh, Nepal and Sri Lanka.
4. 70 Percent of the World trade is managed by 500 corporations".[8] Above given statistics proves that there is something basically wrong with the corporate governance system in USA. Peter Drucker has said: Corporate Capitalisim - that is, the establishment of a management accountable only to itself has made management and companies exceedingly vulnerable. They have no constituencies to come to their succour when attacked".[9] Inflation distorts. It distorts values. There are structural changes within the economy that make a good many companies of yesterday's most successful companies no longer appropriate to todays economic realities. Corporate governance and capitalism cannot provided satisfaction to the "Hungry Spirit" and the developing societies have to move away from the myth of share holder value to community value. In many ways, the current phase of globalization and corporatisation has an in-built structural tendency towards making the entire process unsustainable. Job less growth and sharp accentuation of economic inequalities have lead to a shrinkage of the global market. The focus of economic reforms must shift, from being solely pre-occupied with corporate profits towards enhancing peoples welfare.[10]

Political leadership of a high order with strong political will is needed to effectively tame corporate governance and ensure economic liberalisation with a smiling human face. The quality of corporate governance has direct bearing on the stake-holders, community and environment as well as competitive sustainability. Transparency and professionalism in corporate governance built up a corporate culture with distinctive frame work of values, purpose and identity. Corporate governance must be guided by the stakeholder theory of corporate management with due emphasis on corporate social responsibility.[11]

Corporate social responsibility has gone beyond merely financial aid and donations. More and more corporations are building institutions to work with communities. Corporate participation and involvement is very important in all national socio-economic activities. Corporate social responsibility include the setting up of Charitable Trusts and educational institutions or environmental protection by planting trees or checking levels of pollution or producing eco-friendly products. Corporate governance in India is different for private sector and public sector undertaking at the central and state levels. In a company, under the concept of limited liability, each investor is obliged to share proportionate risk and equally to share proportionate reward. Companies, by definition, are governed by the company Act, companies have shareholders, listed companies are legally liable for compliance of the listed agreement. ONGC chairman Subir Raha has said: "A public sector company is owned in entirety or in majority by the people. The fiduciary responsibility of a member of the board of a company is not waived if the company is in public sector, and this is the law of the land".

The corporate world is in turmoil all over the globe because of corporate governance issues triggered by events like the Enron melt down. Similarly, problems keep arising because of lack of sensitivity on the part of companies to the community and environmental issues that damage the goodwill of the community towards the business world in general and the concerned company in particular.[12] Examples of good corporate governance are some of the outstanding Indian companies like Ranbaxy, Tata Sons, HLL, Wipro, Infosys, and Titan. Corporate governance comes from leadership and philosophy of the organisations. Mr. Bhaskar Bhatt of Titan has articulated this philosophy thus: "All stake holders including share holders, employees, the people whom we buy from the people whom we sell through and of course the most important, that is the customer and the community they serve. Win / win paradigm of external and internal relationships must be maintained to ensure fair and equitable share to everyone concerned. Corporate governance has assumed great importance in the 21st Century. In the context of globalisation, privatization and economic liberalism, the subject of corporate governance has acquired great importance in the present uncertain and turbulent times. The quality of corporate governance has a direct bearing on the stake-holders community and environment, as well as on the sustainability of the enterprise itself".

Just as the Central Government is accountable to four different levels of powerful institutions namely the people of India, the Parliament, the Controller and Auditor General of India and the Central Vigilance Commission, to whom the corporate institutions are accountable? Surely corporation in India must be accountable to regulators like Securities and Exchange Board of India (SEBI), the Department of Company Affairs (DCA), to the share holders and of course to the government. In May 1999, The Kumar Mangalam Birla Committee on Corporate Governance submitted its report to SEBI. A little later over three years, the regulators has appointed a committee headed by N.R. Narayan Murthy to not only take stock of the implementation of the earlier report but to revisit the entire preposition and provide a fresh look at corporate governance taking into account the big picture emerging out of globalisation of Indian economy and emergence of MNCs on the scene. Companies like Infosys developed credibility and confidence of stakeholders by listing in US stock markets, which require high level of transparency in accounting and financial reporting practices. The corporate governance tripod-three entities management, the board of directors and shareholders, play important roles to ensure good corporate governance. Each country adopts its own corporate governance principles that are appropriate for that market and which contain the general socio-economic requirements of the country. The rules of corporate governance as are understood in the global economic arena, cannot be easily imported by the newly developing countries because these rules are the first and foremost routed in people of a specific country. Corporate governance all over the world has spawned an increasingly hostile, unforgiving environment for CEOs and investors during the last three decades. Corporate governance guidelines need to be reviewed on an ongoing basis by companies, institutions and shareholders in order to assess their responsiveness to the prevailing corporate governance climate to ensure that they remain truly beneficial for all. A recent Supreme Court of India Bench Mark judgement has announced that companies can be tried and punished. The

Supreme Court has held that "a corporate body can be tried and punished with a fine for committing financial irregularities including tax violations. Companies could no more claim immunity from persecution and courts could impose fines on them even though they can not be sentenced.[13] Legal analysts feel that companies could be tried and punished for committing financial irregularities, including tax violation. This judgement could open a plethora of cases against many corporation like ANZ, Grindlays Bank, Standard Chartered Bank and other financial institutions which were allegedly involved in 1991 securities scam. Even AB Bofors, facing trial in the Rs. 65 crore Bofors, pay-off case could face trial and if found guilty be fined. According to the Supreme Court judgement referred above, there was no blanket immunity for any company just because at the end of the trial, the juristic person (Company) could not be sentenced to a jail term. It was further held that since these cases had an adverse impact on the economy as well as the society, it was necessary that companies face prosecution along with those who perpetrated the crime. Therefore, there is always need for transparency and professionalism in corporate governance. "The Criticality of corporate governance has come to the forefront after a major shake up in the corporate world by the collapse of companies by Enron. In August 2002, a committee headed by Shri Naresh Chandra was constituted to examine corporate audit, role of auditors and relationship of company and auditor. The most salient recommendations of Naresh Chandra Committee are as under:—(1) Recommended a list of disqualifications for audit assignments like direct relationship with the company; any Business relationship with client, personal relationship with Director; (2) Audit firms not to provide services such as accounting, internal audit assignments etc to audit firms; (3) Auditors to disclose contingent liabilities and highlight significant accounting policies; (4) Audit committee to be first point of reference for appointment of auditors; (5) CEO and CFO of listed company to certify on fairness, correctness of annual audited accounts; (6) Redefinition of independent directors—does not have any material, pecuniary relationship or transaction with the company, (7) Composition of Board of Directors; (8) Statutory limit on the sitting fee to non-executive directors to be reviewed. The recommendations of the Naresh Chandra Committee have formed part of the companies (Amendment) Bill 2003, SEBI has constituted a committee headed by Shri N.R. Narayana Murthy to review existing code of corporate governance and its main recommendation are briefly as under: (1) Strengthening the responsibilities of Audit Committee; (2) Improving a quality of financial disclosures; (3) Utilisation of proceeds from IPO; (4) To assess and disclose business risks; (5) Formal code of conduct for Boards; (6) Whistle blower policy to be in place in a company, providing freedom to approach the audit committee; (7) Subsidiaries to be reviewed by audit committee of holding company.

Corporate world is quite familiar with its two important constituents namely, the investors and the lenders. During the last two decades, the FIIs sought to bring about the subtle change by communicating to companies through their dis-investment and investment decisions, the need for increased transparency and greater disclosure. In keeping with the current focus on corporate governance, financial and investment institutions have sought to appoint nominee directors on the board of several well managed companies to act in the best interests of the shareholders of the company.

A recent study by professors Millstein and Mac Avoy provides empirical evidence showing a high correlation between superior corporate governance and superior corporate performance. Corporate governance must demonstrate concern for corporate social responsibility (CSR) as an enlightened self interest. Corporate governance has to include concern and initiative for boards socio-economic and environmental issues as a part of corporate social responsibility. Openness, transparency, meritocracy and professionalism have to be the distinctive part of corporate governance. Corporate governance can influence corporate culture. Corporate culture is just one among several important elements in any organisations make - up and success-along with vision, strategy marketing, financials and the like corporate Governance in due course of time can mould and build cultures. Most companies say their culture is outstanding customer service, excellence, team work, shareholder value, responsible corporate behaviour and integrity.

Corporate Governance needs to govern corporate staff people/bureaucrats who "provide Coordination among disparate line organisations; establish and enforce corporate wide strategies that allow the enterprise to avoid duplication, confusion and conflict; and provide highly specialised skills that cannot be duplicated because of the cost or simply the shortage of available resources".[14] Corporate governance is a very macro envelop sort of thing, it is concerned about taking care of all stakeholders interests. Sustainability, stability, competitive edge and reliability reflect quality of governance. The underlying belief of the corporate governance should be to pro-actively take initiative in societal and environmental issues that develop goodwill for them in the community as well as protect the environment and improve the quality of life and well being of the people in the community.[15] Infosys, one of the best known IT Indian Companies is known for its distinct identity, under the leadership and membership of Mr. Narayan Murthy and is today one of the most respected "World Class Company", as it is regarded as "a company by the people, for the people and of the people". Wipro is a value-led company known for its four key values—"human values, integrity, innovative solutions and value for money". Three important factors namely transparency, professionalism and meritocracy form the basic quality of corporate governance in Indian corporate world. Policy makers of different nations have to develop their own legal and regulatory frameworks for corporate governance reflecting their own economic, legal and cultural circumstances and market participants have to develop their own practices. More over corporate governance is a complex phenomenon which has to be implemented through close cooperation between the public and private sectors and a combination of statutory regulations and self-regulation. To safeguard the economic interest of the owners and shareholders, corporate governance norms stipulate adherence to certain guiding principles like having an independent chairman, having a majority of independent non-executive directors, allowing share-holders to participate effectively in shareholders meetings with voting rights, provision to replace managing professionals in the case of certain failure or lapses. United States of America has taken the lead to put in place a legal framework in the form of Surbanes-Oxley Act 2002.

In many countries the corporate boards have been in a slumber and the Chief Executive officer has been calling all the shots in the game. The larger than life CEOs have been generally dominating the board. Corporate boards are generally dominated by "insiders" and do not take an independent and objective view of the management. Generally corporate governance demands that companies abide by the various provisions ensuring certain safeguards for shareholders and investors. For example, SEBI recent guidelines on corporate governance generated an immediate demand of 4000 independent directors on the boards for several blue chip companies and compliance was required by April 2002. Indian companies, are, by international standards, at least 10 years behind their global counterparts on corporate governance. In India Mandatory Compliance is the main driver for change.[16] Corporate Governance, in principle, demands to the joint responsibility imposed on the board of directors and management to protect shareholders value. Four factors globalisation, consolidation, competition and technology—are necessitating from the Indian view point need to adopt better corporate governance practices. Corporate governance need to be more effective if increasing incidence of frauds are to be stopped—One 6 June 2005, Ministry for Company Affairs Govt. of India sent out a stern message to Corporate India to decide whether it wants more controls or a freer hand in its functioning. If corporate frauds, continue, then government interference will be much more. India Inco needs to make the distinction between ambition and destructive greed and frauds and day light robbery. Some of the incidents indicating failure of corporate governance are reported below.

1. Daewoo Motors—21 prosecutions under Cos. Act filed on 17.2.2005.
2. DSQ Software—Investigation restarted after HC order vacated on 28.05.2005.
3. Design Auto Systems—Investigation stayed report being examined by MCA.
4. Bonanza Biotech—Investigation stayed report being examined by MCA.

5. Vatsa Corporation—55 Prosecution cases under Cos Act filed against officers of Co.
6. Ketan Parekh group—(16 entities) petitioner has four weeks time for filling SLP.
7. Mardia Chemicals—Investigation under progress.

Recently, Minister for Company Affairs said : "There are about 50,000 prosecutions pending under the Companies Act for many years. Instructions have been ordered in 109 companies with over 100 FIRS having been filed and as many as 91 cases having been registered, prosecutions have been launched in 177 and 157 cases in two different categories. Twenty one promoters and directors in seven companies - Frontline Financial Services, Komeon Communication, Lyous Enterprises, Srijo Dye Cherm, Keshar green field, Protect Circuit Breakers and Thirth Plastic Company have been arrested. Investigations in 26 cases have been handed over to serious fraud investigation office." The World Bank has told the government to encourage institutional investors to exercise their ownership rights more actively in the ethical conduct of the companies they help. Institutional investors are better positioned than retail investors to monitor the way their portfolio companies are run. FIS need to disclose their voting policies and records as well as material conflicts of interests which may affect exercising their ownership rights. Mutual Funds in the country play a very passive role in corporate governance of the companies they have invested in. Foreign Institutional Investors (FIIs) are more active in their exercise of voting rights.[17] Insurance Corporate and banks are more active than mutual funds but not to the extent of FIIs who regularly attend shareholder meetings, vote, meet the management informally and even consult other institutional investors. The World Bank feels that the experience in developed countries where shareholders activism is vibrant endorse the fact, that the active monitoring of the ethical practices of the companies by institutional investors can make their books more rosy and corporate governance more vibrant. The globalisation of the Indian economy has resulted in a serious concern in the public and the government in the corporate governance and their conformity to the international norms of ethical governance. The key issues for corporate governance emerging out of present international trends are as under:—

(1) Maintaining continuity by succession planning.

(2) Identifying opportunities.

(3) Facing challenges and managing change within the business.

(4) Allocation of resources towards the right priority.[18]

Corporate Governance is now giving more importance to accounts and financial management. Many corporations in their eagerness to increase their earnings and accelerate their growth, exploited the weaknesses in the accounting standards to inflate profits and understate liabilities. Accounting control go haywire if corporate governance is not effective. All over the world corporate governance could not be effective because insiders have been able to manipulate things to their advantage-through anti-take over measurer, non-voting shares, limitations on voting rights and by dominating the board itself. In India, the situations is very different because in the family managed business majority of shares are held by the business family and their relatives, dependent people. "The governance problem in India is not the classical Ends and Means problem of dispersed shareholder not being able to control management. It is the problem of preventing the expropriation of minority shareholders by the controlling shareholders. The recent recommendations of the Naresh Chandra Committee have suggested improvements in standards of good corporate governance, including the suggested criteria for determining independence of directors on listed company boards. Recently the following tighter rules are being recommended for independent directors for corporate boards:-

(1) "A Majority of independent members;

(2) Former partners or employees of outside auditors are not considered independent for three years;

(3) A former employee is not considered independent until five years after employment has ended;

(4) Atleast one audit committee member must have accounting or related financial management expertise."[19]

Good corporate governance is a part of strategic management for survival, consolidation and growth. There is therefore a demand for simplification, greater accountability and transparency, necessitated by increasing investor awareness and competitive market forces. There is an urgent need for an effective legal system that will enable commercial disputes to be resolved quickly except in the chartered High Courts of Madras, Bombay, Calcutta and Delhi High Court, all original suits are required to be instituted in the lower courts. It is imperative that we set up a commercial division in each High Court so that commercial cases belonging to certain categories can be resolved through these commercial courts.

The split of Reliance Industries has badly exposed the corporate governance in India. When allegations are made about misgovernance in India's largest corporate empire by those very persons who are running the show, should the government have allowed the situation to fester for seven months and in the end endorse the sad outcome? Should Departments of Company Affairs (DCA) and the Securities and Exchange Board of India (SEBI) have slept over controversies for such a long time? Don't they have certain statutory obligations towards corporate governance and accountability?[20] We have to move from the era of individual misgovernance to corporate governance. The time has come to create fresh norms governing splitting of a corporate empire and for corporate governance in general. Well attended board meetings in the first step toward good corporate governance. The regulator should set an example in corporate governance. Indian corporates have still a long road a head before they become leaders in the international market and confident of becoming models for corporate governance. The role of the government should be that of a facilitator. The whole issue of fiscal responsibility and about level of fiscal deficit, Parliament must look with prudence and Reserve Bank of India should have a larger degree of autonomy. By redefining the role of the three branches of the state, by empowering the executive government, by decentralization and devolution of powers and functions, by inducting knowledge and talent in administration and by enlarging the role of market and the corporate sector, we should try to bring about a qualitative change in the governance of the country, particularly the economy. Pressure of public opinion and investors groups, including large foreign institutional investors, will lead to increased disclosure of financial data, other strategic non-financial informations and compliance of various corporate laws and regulations. India Corporations will have to:

1. "Learn to cope with lesser and lesser freedom of strategy and management;
2. Learn to operate outside the comfort zone in a tough and competitive environment;
3. Become fast but flexible;
4. Cope with increasing complexity of world markets;
5. Protect and develop invisible assets namely, intellectual property, Human resource Brand Equity, Corporate Image etc.."[21]

Effective and meaningful reforms of corporate governance require that space needs to be created on boards of directors who can be truly independent of management. The starting point can be to set aside majority seats on the boards and on nomination, audit and remuneration committees for independent directors, nominated by institutional investors. Economic offences must be quickly investigated, effective prosecution of offenders must be done and courts at all levels must dispense justice quickly and cheaply in a limited time frame. The Kumar Mangalam Birla Committee has recommended that institutional investors should effectively safeguard their interests by disinvesting their holdings in a given company and by using their voting power at general body meetings. This option is somewhat cumbersome and may not be possible due to lack of timely response or non-availability of vital information, If financial institutions had their nominees on boards, they would be exposed to charges or insider trading. However, the same argument also applies to family owners as well. Institutional investors can entrust the job to independent professionals. The problem is that as long as independent directors owe their presence on the board to management, their independence would be questionable. According to Prof. T.T. Ram Mohan, institutional activism itself is absent in India and you can understand why the controlling shareholders are hardly ever removed for non-performance. All the tenets of governance amount to nothing where the ability and the willingness to penalize non-performance are missing.[22] The debate in India has inadequately focused on matters of board composition and structure. The debate on corporate governance should focus on the following main questions.

(1) "What is independence? How is it to be identified and developed?

(2) How the overall board independence to be perceived, nurturned, defined, articulated and institutionalized?

(3) What contributions would regulators or stock-exchange make to the public policy on corporate governance?

(4) Do the promoters government of private really appreciate, understand and wart better corporate governance?

(5) Does the top management of the corporate world and PSUs have any idea of the existing numbers and potential sources of independent directors?

(6) Is there any agreement on the training needs of independent of independent or other directors? Have we developed any agency to train them?

(7) What will be the role of independent directors?

(8) As a community of trade and commerce, are we preparing ourselves for improved corporate governance? Good corporate governance cannot be ensured only by regulatory and legislative framework unless the human material including independent directors and audit committee membership have certain inherent value system and the community provides conducive atmosphere for it to flourish. SEBI recent guidelines on corporate governance has generated an immediate demand on 4000 independent directors on the board of various corporations. It needs long planning and well designed HRD programmes to build up an army of experienced independent directors suitable for corporate board rooms. The recent trends

in corporate governance can be briefly enumerated as under:

1. Demands for greater transparency and accountability.
2. Clear demarcation of roles and responsibilities.
3. Performance Appraisal of Board Members and Management.
4. Succession planning.
5. Concept of social welfare and corporate social responsibilities.
6. Ethical and moral behaviour and attitude of corporate sector as a whole.
7. Democratization and one member one vote principle in corporate boards proceedings.
8. Corporate governance to be made a way of life through continual improvement on internal systems and customer satisfaction.
9. A more effective legal system to penalize and reform those who violate corporate governance rules and procedures. Commercial division of high courts and Supreme Court to deal with corporate disputes and governance lapses within a given time frame, need to be created.
10. Money is generally considered the major source of power and one person, holding both the CEO and chairman post, becomes the most powerful person in the corporate circles.[23]
11. Lack of communication, ignorance of shareholders and the public about the boards role, inadequacy of information and lack of proper feedback mechanism are important factor which hinder effective control of the Board of Directors.
12. The exact legal duties of the board of directors are rather ambiguous. The following main issues emerge in this context:—

    (*a*) What are the legal duties, responsibilities and role of the board?

(b) What is the information available? What type, frequency and the format of information's are required by the board?

(c) What is the tenure of a director and what is the desired behaviour of directors?

(d) How can boards create competitive advantage for the corporates and whether members of the board can openly open a dialogue, debate and give their dissent?

(e) Are there any procedures or processes to review and assess the performance of the board itself.

Directors are generally and traditionally been hand picked by the CEO or selected from a list provided by the CEO. Most of the time boards ratify the strategies and decisions relating to major policies of the working directors on the board. Many of the directors and the CEOs may be working together on different boards (interlocking directorships) and follow a policy- "You scratch my back, I will scratch yours". There is a general tendency to agree with the decisions of the CEO. All corporations need a government that has power, has continuity and has legitimate right to rule. Corporate governance, as a first step, need an independent and strong board of governors (directors). Independent Board of Directors are "Trustees for the best balanced interests of stock holders, employees, plant community, customers and suppliers alike.[24] In a corporation the board of directors is the supreme body and the board functions in good part through its committees. Most important committees are the finance, Executive, audit and Bonus and Salary, each of which are composed exclusively of directions authorized to exercise the powers of the board in the management and affairs of the corporation. The finance committee and the executive committee are the central authority for policy determination.[25]

The scandals of Enron, Arthur Andersen, World cam, Adelphia and other former high flyers of USA demonstrate not only lapses of ethics but also a disdain for the rule of law. Therefore the selection of a well qualified and ethical CEO is the most important role of a Corporate Board.[26] Executives need to avoid not only impropriety but even the appearance of impropriety if they are to recover peoples trust. It is not enough to implement the Naresh Chandra Committees recommendations on corporate governance, there should be a ban on persons sitting on board of companies in similar lines of business. Germany's concept of Corporate Governance covers the entire gamut of relationships between all the institutions and individuals directly or indirectly involved in decision making in an enterprise including owners/shareholders, managers, employees, launders, suppliers and customers. Corporate Governance is accountable to not only shareholders but their accountability extends to all stakeholders like employees and the society in general. Margrete Blair in his book "Ownership and control : Rethinking corporate governance for the Twenty first century (1995), has stressed residual claimant theory where the shareholders are only residual claimants and there are numerous others who make investments specific to a given corporation. The Treadway report and the Cadbury Report advocate and recommend the needs of their country and are culture-specific documents related to local circumstances and needs of the nation. In Canada the Toronto stock exchange guidelines require the boards of directors to assume responsibility for the stewardship of the corporation including strategic planning risk assessment, succession planning communication policy and internal control system." Corporate governance is very important for all developing countries and it basically encompasses the following issues:-

1. The rights of the shareholders and investors including FIIs;
2. The equitable treatment of shareholders;
3. The role of stakeholders in corporate governance;
4. Disclosure and transparency;
5. The responsibilities of the board of directors and CEO;
6. Corporate laws, government regulations, corporate culture and financial/economic development of the country.

Several studies have asserted that quality of corporate governance practices are positively related to the need for external financing and the protection of investors rights. Corporate Governance are bound to differ from countries to countries and corporations to corporations. Research findings suggest that some governance mechanisms e.g. outside directors and the separation of CEO/Chairman are effective strategies. For Corporate governance of family owned business houses, the compositions of the board of directors and need for independent directors are very important issues. Amit and his co-author Belen Villa Longa of Harvard Business School, after studying more than 500 companies over seven years have came up with the following surprising results. "Our findings about family ownership and control suggest that despite the costs associated with the family's excess control, the benefits of family ownership make minority shareholders better off than they would have been in a non-family firm, because these families go overboard in terms of trying to be better governed simply because they want to alleviate concerns of minority shareholders about (the family members) appropriation of private benefits which is the key to unlocking greater value.[27] Corporate governance in recent years has gained much importance and a regional conference on Managing Corporate governance in Asia was held on April 7.8.2005 at Bali, Indonesia which was very well attended. The challenges of Corporate Governance are very complex, multi-faceted and need constant review analysis. There are operational benefits too in investing in Corporate Governance as it brings better returns on equity. 80-90 percent of the investors are willing to pay a 20-30 percent premium for companies that have good corporate governance.[28] Corporate governance refers to the control and organisation of private corporations. It is an issue of relevance to human resource management for two reasons. First it is argued with increasing frequency that national systems of Corporate Governance shape the pattern of employment relations within the economy. Corporate governance encourages an opportunist or adversarial approach to work force management by downsizing and redundancy strategies.[29] The concept of corporate governance is highly helpful in resolving the executive remuneration. The Kumar Mangalam Birla Committee on corporate governance has recommend the formation of a "remuneration Committee, which will determine, on behalf of shareholders, the remuneration to be provided to executives. Corporate governance has become important because of corporate mergers, take overs and massive reorganization to fend off hostile take over bids. Corporate governance need to be controlled by Indian company law amendments which emphasis self regulation and greater accountability through disclosures and not be a blind imitation of the Sarbanes-Oxley Act (SOX) of the US. The law will ensure that businesses are "enabled and not besieged." Indian company law requires greater vigilance on the part of the Chartered accountants and Company Secretaries. By January 1, 2006, all corporations will need independent Directors on the Corporate boards including public sector undertakings. The government has to notify 29 accounting standards. Inaugurating a seminar on "good corporate governance practices", organised by the National foundation for corporate governance (NFCG) and confederation of Indian Industry (CII) Komal Anand, Secretary, Department of Company Affairs said that the Company Affairs Ministry would launch shortly a World Bank funded e-governance project known as MCA - 21, to open a chain of 53 "front offices" of the Registrar of Companies (ROC) where the companies and professionals would be able to file returns and documents in the electronic mode on a 24 × 7 basis and also get trained for the purpose. The whole project would be completed in three years. Legal pundits of world renown have acknowledged that governance regulations in clause 49 of the listing agreement are comparable to the best in the world.[30] The Indian law entails penalties including criminal liability for violation of prescribed norms. Clause 49 of Sebi's listing agreement specifies wide ranging framework for risk management, internal controls assessment, compliance measures and governance practices for companies to adopt. This includes undertaking some additional internal assessments (including enterprise wide risk management) in addition to achieving the desired levels of independence in the constitution of their boards and audit committees JSW steel, Revathi Equipments and Bilcon are some of the companies who have taken positive steps to ensure compliance. Govt would be more strict with companies who do not file annual returns and reports in time. The penalties under the proposed new law are expected to be much higher than the existing ones and provide incentives to file reports in time. This is likely to improve corporate governance in India and can serve as model for developing countries.[31]

References

1. P. Chidambaram - Failure of Governance - Economic Times, New Delhi, 24th January, 2002.
2. S.H. Venkataramani - The Corporate Society, Hindustan Times, New Delhi, May 27, 1997.
3. T.T. Ram Mohan - A fresh book at governance - The big picture -Economic Times, New Delhi, 21 November 2002.
4. Ralph D. Ward - Twilight of the gods - CEOs were once thunderbolt -tossers; now they are being tossed from board rooms at record rates -Economic Times, 8th April, 2001.
5. T.T. Ram Mohan - A fresh look at governance - The big picture -Economic Times, New Delhi, 21 November, 2002.
6. Sumathi Mehta - corporate governance and excellence - Economic times, New Delhi, 2 June, 2001.
7. Deepak S. Parekh - The real meaning of corporate governance Indian Management - the Journal of the All India Management Association, Vol. 38, No. 8, August 1999, p. 100.
8. David Korten - "When corporations rule the world" quoted in Charles Handy - "The Hungry Spirit" - Hutchison, London.
9. Peter Drucker - The frontiers of Management - Butter Worth Heinemann Oxford, 1987, Reprint 2003, p. 235.
10. Sitaram Yechury - Feeling upside Down - Disenhancement against Neo - liberal economics is being felt beyond the developing world - Hindustan Time, Jaipur, 23 September, 2005.
11. R.E. Freeman and D. Reed' - Stock holders and stake holders. A new perspective on corporate governance in C. Hinzinga (Ed) corporate governance. A definite exploration of the issues (Los Angels VCLA Extension Press, 1981.)
12. Abad Ahmed and O.P. Chopra - "Passion to win how winning companies Develop and sustain competitive edge". Excel Book Private Ltd, New Delhi, 2004 F 205.

13. Supreme Court of India - Justices K.G. Balakrishnan, D.M. Dharmadhikari and Arun Kumar - Ref. Times of India, New Delhi, Friday 6th May, 2005.

14. In - Who says elephants can't dance - Inside IBM's Historic Turn around -Harper Collins Publishers, 2002, p. 181.

15. Abad Ahmed and O.P. Chopra - Passion to win - How winning companies Develop and sustain competitive edge - Excel Books Pvt Ltd., New Delhi, 2004, p. 207.

16. Poonam Barua, Study on corporate governance - quoted by Shalini Singh-SEBI Guidelines Set companies on Board Room Hunt - The Economic Times, New Delhi, 5 June 2001.

17. The Economic Times - FIS should be more pro-active in corporate governance - World Bank - Delhi Bureau, 19 Dec. 2005

18. K. Gopal - Emerging trends in corporate governance - Indian Management. All India Management Association - Vol. 37. No. 10, October 1998, p. 14.

19. Kemba J. Dunhan - The Wall Street Journal - new Rules prolong search for corporate directors - The Financial Times, New Delhi, 31 August, 2002.

20. Bishwajit Bhattacharyya - Reliance split is a bad omen - Times of India, New Delhi, 28 June 2005.

21. K. Gopal - Emerging Trends in Corporate Governance - Indian management - The Journal of the All India Association - Vol. 37 No. 10 Oct., 1998, p. 15-16

22. The Dr. J.J. Irani Committee report (2005) T.T. Ram Mohan - A fresh look at Governance - The Big Picture - Economic Times, New Delhi, 21 Nov. 2002.

23. Satheesh Kumar T.N. Reinventing Boards - Corporate Governance -Indian Management - The Journal of the All India Management Association - Vol. 44. issue 9. Sep 2005, p. 120.

24. Peter F. Drucker - The frontiers of management - Butter worth Heineman - Oxford, Reprint, 2003, p. 254.

25. For exhaustive details of various' Committee their role in corporate governance consult Alfred P. Sloan, jr, "My years with general Motors-Currency Doubleday, New York, 1990, pp. 186-200.

26. Constance Bagley—Sharing the Responsibility of corporate governance working knowledge—Harvard Business School.

27. (Theme) Business Families—Professor Amit of Wharton and Belen Villag Longa of Harvard—Indian Management—The Journal of all India Management Association, Vol. 44, Issue 8 August 2005, p. 42.

28. Vivek Gupta—"Corporate Governance four Prospectives and an Imperative". Business Today, 27 February, 2005.

29. Edmud Herry and Mike Noon—A dictionary of Human Resource Management, Oxford University Press, 2002, pp. 62-63

30. Self regulation to be the focus of company law amendment the law will entail penalties for violation of norms, Hindu, 22 December, 2005.

31. The companies Bill 2008 would be tabled in the coming session of Parliament. It contains various provisions aimed at bringing in a flurry of changes for the corporate sector. The bill proposes to do away with promoters buying shares at a discourt. It lays down higher and stringent penalties for corporate offences. It provides special courts to deal with corporate offences, regulation of insolvency winding up and liquidation. It aims to bring in "self-regulation but with accountability."

6

Change Management

- Change is the law of life. Those who only look to the past or the present are certain to miss the future.

  —*(John, F. Kennedy)*

- "To exist is to change, to change is to mature, to mature is to go on creating oneself endlessly"

  —*(Henre Bergson)*

Alvin Toffler in his well known book "Future Shock" (1984) has argued - that "the humanity is constantly threatened by future shock which occurs constantly due to various types of changes and the society itself is in a state of flux". Change is so frequent that there is no stability and even values come to reflect this. Globalisation of markets, technological changes, political realignments, changing demographics, changing customer preferences, organizational restructuring, economic growth are all causing change. Change today is continuous and intrinsic, extrinsic and discontinuous, complex and unpredictable. The rate of change is faster than our ability to comprehend and cope with it. Change consciousness is the understanding of the need and necessity for change. Individuals, organizations and societies are all constrained to keep pace with change and develop better techniques for change management. The movement from one state of existence to another is change. The reasons for change to occur could range from "the old shoe being worn out" to a desire to upgrade, modify or improve. Planned change involves activities that are goal oriented and intentional. The goals of planned change in an organization mostly are : improving the behavior of individuals and groups in the organization. People who act as catalysts and assume the responsibility for managing change activities are Change Agents. As is true of the new Shoe, change usually hurts/pinches and creates a sense of discomfort.

That is why in organizations as also elsewhere, people resist change. Forms of resistance to change could be overt and immediate (such as voicing complaints, refusing to comply with new methods of work); or implicit and deferred (such as loss of employee loyalty and motivation, increased errors or mistakes, increased absenteeism). The individual is likely to resist change because there is a fear of the unknown, a sense of insecurity and selective information processing. The organization also experiences a threat to established resource allocations, established norms, established power relationships compounded by structural inertia and there is a need for adopting tactics to deal with the resistance to change. The major tactics for dealing with resistance to change are education and communication participation, facilitation and support, negotiation, manipulation and cooptation and finally, coercion.

Change management is the continuous process of aligning an organization with its market place and its people. Dr. Dan Gottliet has given a favourite aphorism : "change is like a manure, it smells terrible, but it makes things grow."

Peter F. Drucker has suggested the following five major areas to be considered in change management.[1]

1. Managing smallness or bigness—that is the management requirement of size by itself.
2. The second major area is the management of complexity and diversity and the limits of the family owned business.
3. The third area is the multi-national corporation with complexities of multiple political and governmental relationships and restraints.
4. At what point in change and growth does management have to change its characteristics, its structure, its behaviour and how to prepare itself for change and growth without overloading the organization.
5. Managing innovation is a topic in itself change management involves mammoth efforts and time consuming campaign.

One of the key responsibilities of HR as a change agent is to be the champion of change management in the organization.

It must demonstrate the importance of activity guidance to senior executives and managers and supervisors. The need for change management and use of change management techniques to avoid project failures or embrace and thrive during change. Many changes fail in organizations that do not appreciate and manage the people side of change. For it to become a valuable partner, four principal HR goals are:

(*i*) Work as an integral member of the organization change team

(*ii*) Interpret and advise upon personnel laws and regulations

(*iii*) Apply HR processes

(*iv*) Help minimize potential negative impacts to affected employees.

2. Forces for Change

In India, liberalization, privatization and globalization have been the major triggers for change. Change has been variously defined as making a material difference in something compared to an earlier state, transforming or converting something, or simply becoming different. Organizational change may mean changing technological infrastructures (e.g. moving from a mainframe environment to distributed computing), marketing strategies (targeting a new customer base), or management and decision making practices. Organisational change is not new to the business landscape. The greater the technological developments and the greater the amount of products and information generated, the more necessary it becomes for corporations to provide effective management and develop solid organizational practices. The ultimate challenge for most organizations is to change corporate climate and culture. An organisation's climate can be defined by how its employees view the organisation's fundamental reason for being, specifically, the company's overall mission and goals and how important the employees' sense of well-being is to those goals. The corporate climate then breeds an organizational culture that consists of what employees see as management's beliefs and value systems. These two things, climate and culture, then determine how each manager and employee shapes his or her own performance, usually in order to most successfully meet company goals and hopefully ensuring his or her own success as well as the company's. These factors affect every aspect of each person's job including decision-making processes, communication patterns within the organization, and individual accountability and responsibility. Coping with change is a permanent part of every manager's job: mergers, acquisition, new strategic partnerships, evolving processes and full-blown restructuring have become common milestones in the life story of most organizations.[2] In the life cycles of organizations there is a change stage when the organization needs to reinvent itself to adapt to changing market conditions or new opportunities and should not logged down to its own bureaucratic life, rules and regulations that it can no longer meet and anticipate the needs of the targeted customers. In their article titled "The Psychology of Change Management", Eimly Lawson and Colin Price list out four conditions required for changing mind sets:

1. They need a purpose to believe in and would be inclined to change their behaviour to serve the purpose.
2. Adults must have the skills required for change and need to use information experimentally and integrate it to their existing knowledge apart from listening to information.
3. The reward and recognition systems must be in tune with the desired new behaviours.
4. They need role models.

3. Indicators of Change

Change could occur in different areas, for different reasons, due to different triggers. There are four primary indicators of major work-place change : a change to the organizational structure, a new product or service, new management or a new technology. Organisational change may change through major downsizing, outsourcing, acquisitions, or mergers. These actions are often accompanied by layoffs, particularly as certain positions become redundant. A new product or service has implications for changes in production, sales and customer service. Additionally, by changing product or service the organization may face new competitors or new markets. New management such as a change in chief executive officer or president, often brings a period of transition during which upper-level managers are likely to alter existing business processes and personnel policies. Finally, new technology can create vast changes in the organization. Technology can change the production process or the working conditions (i.e. telecommuting) and these changes may influence the skills that employees use on the job. In addition change can also be categorized specifically into four categories: structural change, cost change, process change, and cultural change. Structural change occurs when there is an alteration to the company's organizational structure. This reorganization may occur due to a merger or acquisition, or it may be the result of a restructure. For instance, an organization that is intent on increasing its innovation may reorganize its traditional functional structure into a more flexible matrix structure that uses small, self-managed teams. Or, an organization that is expanding into new markets may adopt a divisional structure in which different geographic locations operate nearly independently of one another. Striking a balance between the global and local geographic and cultural factors would call for a major contribution from the HR. Cost changes are those that occur when an organization attempts to reduce costs in order to improve efficiency or performance. Major adjustments may be made to departments to cut costs; reducing budgets, laying off employees in redundant positions, and eliminating nonessential activities may all be a result of cost change. The HR needs to play an important role particularly where the cost cutting measures involve laying off large number of employees. This may occur in production settings; there may be changes to how a product is created, assembled, packaged, or shipped. Or, in a service organization, there may be changes to the procedures used to accomplish work; new computer systems may create the need to change how paperwork is completed, or a new manager may modify the process used to handle customer complaints. In India, certain banks introduced computerization in operations without taking into account the need for training the employees. As a result, not only was there stiff resistance from the employees who felt threatened and insecure, but even the desired impact on consumer satisfaction was not achieved. Cultural changes are the least tangible of all the types of change, but they can be the most difficult. An organization's culture is its shared set of assumptions, values, and beliefs. A prototypical culture is its shared set of assumptions, values, and beliefs. A prototypical culture is the very bureaucratic, top-down style in which stability and standard processes are valued. When such an organization tries to adopt a more participative, involved style, this requires a shift in many organizational activities. With the advent of MNCs and global influences, the organizations of today are grappling with the reality of the culture shock. Calling the boss by his first name remains a tricky issue in India where traditionally, people older in age would never ever be addressed by their names. When manager-employee relations are altered with a change in culture, HR needs to fill in the gaps as and when necessary.

4. The many faces of Change

Arthur Achopehauer says, change alone is eternal, perpetual and immortal. Change management is generally faulty. Strategic failure, communication gap and resistance to change all act as standing blocks in the transformation process in many organizations. John P. Kotter, author of the best selling "Leading change" asserts "the problem is that most companies handle change very poorly. It happens slower than they want, it creates more pain than they want and it does not meet their goals." Successful companies that make leaps in strategy or technology do it through effective leadership. Kotter insists that "three-quarters of all change activity has to do with leading, not managing, leaders need to engage the execution team to ensure that strategy translates into action. Serious views change process as consisting of three steps—unfreezing, moving and refreezing. Planned change efforts can be characterized as falling along a continuous lime ranging from incremental changes that involve time tuning the organization to quantum changes that entail fundamentally altering how it operates. The pace of global, economic and technological development makes change an inevitable feature of modern life.

Not every change that occurs in the organization is a cause for concern. There are changes in organizations that are routine (e.g. they are commonplace and often expected), and there are those that are not routine (e.g., unique and unexpected). Examples of routine changes are organizational turnover and staffing replacements, small changes to products or services, or changes in human resources policies. Routine changes are the easiest to manage, and employees are somewhat accustomed to routine changes. However, if not handled properly by management, even routine change can prove to be difficult. The key lies in effectively communicating to the employees the need/ benefits of the intended change prior to its execution. If changes are not implemented properly or not well communicated, problem may arise. For example, a small change in the work timings of the company may seem insignificant to management, but if employees are not properly apprised of the change it could result in considerable difficulty. The employees may refuse to follow the new policy. Non-routine change is much more difficult than routine change; it can be unpredictable, significant, or even radical, and employees are much less likely to adapt well to non-routine change. In general, a non-routine change is seen as threatening, and employees are likely to be resistant. For instance, if a company announces a merger with a former competitor, this non-routine change is very likely to create anxiety about compensation and job security.

5. People are the Real Engines for any Organizational change. Effective HR is the Driver

As a general rule, it is not the proposed changes the people resist, but the impact that the change will have on them, personally. People become comfortable in their jobs, in their areas of expertise, and in their relationships with coworkers and managers. Even when employees are not very satisfied with the current workplace and therefore welcome change, they may find change to be stressful. Helping employees anticipate difficulties and informing employees of how these changes will be handled can be a source of comfort to them. When an organization proposes large-scale change, those affected begin to worry about how their jobs will change, what new skills they will need if their responsibilities will change, how established lines of communication will be altered, and how working relationships will change. The most successful members of a company may feel threatened because they were able to perform so well under the old organizational structure. Some common employee reactions to change include confusion, denial, loss of identity, and anger. And this resistance is not limited to employees - managers and executives may be just as prone as employees to experiencing problems with radical organizational change. For HR to become more effective as a change leader and sponsor of change, it must be able to manage employee resistance to change, build change competency into the organization, avoid unnecessary turnover or loss of valued employees, and increase the probability that the business changes produce the desired results. T.G. Connings and C.G. Worley has suggested a five phase approach to effective change management as given in Figure 1 below:[4]

Figure 1. A Five Phase Approach to Effective Change Management

1. Motivating change
   (*a*) Creating readiness for change.
   (*b*) Overcoming resistance to change
2. Creating a vision
   (*a*) Mission and the core ideology
   (*b*) Valued outcomes
   (*c*) Valued conditions
   (*d*) Mid-point goals
3. Developing political support
   (*a*) Assessing change agent power
   (*b*) Identifying by stake holders
   (*c*) Influencing stake holders
4. Managing the Transmission
   (*a*) Activity planning
   (*b*) Commitment planning
   (*c*) Management structures
5. Sustaining Momentum
   (*a*) Providing resources for change
   (*b*) Building a support system for change agents
   (*c*) Developing new competencies and skills
   (*d*) Reinforcing new behaviours.

Organizational change management is the application of a systematic process for managing change across an organization. It is the top-down, manager's approach to taking an organization through the transition from today to a new future state. Research shows that the greatest obstacle to change management is "employee resistance." This resistance impacts the project team and its success. HR can play a vital role in managing resistance to change and helping the team succeed. The 2005 Best Practices Report identifies the top five reasons front line employees resist change as:

(*i*) Employees were not aware of the underlying business need for change.

(*ii*) Lay-offs were announced or feared as part of the change.

(*iii*) Employees were unsure if they had the needed skills for success in the future state.

(*iv*) Individuals were comfortable with the current state; they wanted to maintain the personal rewards and sense of accomplishment and fulfillment provided by the status quo.

(*v*) Employees felt they were being required to do more with less, or do more for the same pay.

HR could handle all the reasons for resistance by doing a few things such as:

- Being proactive and getting involved from the start
- Communicating and ascertaining a two way flow of information to create awareness
- Planning, identifying and coordinating the needed resources
- Providing necessary training
- Defining the new goals and objectives clearly
- Empowering the employees and playing the role if a strategic partner.

6. Implementing Change.... hands on

To properly implement change, management must take a number of steps; involving key people, developing a plan, supporting the plan, and communicating often. The people side of change must be kept in focus all along. The successful execution of any organizational initiative depends on the human capital. That is why HR, the people's people, have a critical responsibility in implementing change.

- The first step in implementing change is involving the key people. This typically means upper-level management and other executives whose processes and employees will be affected by the change. For instance, if a new computer system is to be installed in all areas of a company, key people would be not only top managers, but also lower-level managers who supervise the employees' use of the new technology. A different set of key people would be involved in a cost-cutting change. If the company is reducing its operating budget in a specific division, the managers of that division and also human resources personnel should be involved. Psychologically also, being involved in the change process from the beginning itself would result in more active participation and a positive approach of the employees. In any circumstance in which there is a change to personnel policies or in which demotions, transfers, or layoffs occur, the human resources department should be involved to manage this change smoothly. For managing change in a global economy, managing diversity is important. Diversity includes not only cultural and ethnic diversity but also age, gender, sexual orientation and physical abilities on primary categories of diversity. Changes in culture and management system would include recruitment, orientation, performance appraisal, compensation and benefits, promotions, training and development and other human resource management tasks. Effective recruitment and management of a diverse workforce can enhance a company's competitive advantage by adding expertise relevant to addressing increasingly diverse market; expending creativity in problem solving; and increasing organizational flexibility, goal achievement and profitability.[5] Warren Benmis tied executive leadership to strategic change[6] Edgar Schein, who developed process approaches to organizational development, has highlighted the key role of organizational culture in change management[7] while Richard Beckhard focused attention on the importance of managing transition[8], Robern Tannenbaum continued to sensitize OD to the personal dimension of participant's lives.[9]

- After key personnel have been identified and properly involved, the second step in implementing change is to develop a plan for effective transformation. The plan should help to define the responsibilities of the key people involved while also laying out short-term and long-term objectives for the changes. This would be a responsibility of the HR wherein the job description would be clearly defined and a suitable person would be placed at the right place at the right time. In practice, it would often involve training the incumbents for their new roles. Because change can be unpredictable, the plan should also be flexible enough to accommodate new occurrences.
- The third step in implementing change is to support the plan; this means that management follows through on the plan it created. Key to this step is enabling employees to adapt to the change. Periodically, counseling and other such assistance may have to be provided to employees facing the challenge of change. Employees may need training, reward systems may need to be adapted, or hiring may be required. If the organization does not provide the support necessary for the plan to take effect, it is unlikely to succeed. Since you cannot hire just the hand, the whole person always comes with it-organizations would have to provide support and help the employees to cope well and perform effectively.
- The final step in successful change implementation should occur throughout the change process. Communicating with employees about what is occurring, why the changes are being made, and how they will develop is critical. Communication fulfils the

following functions; it control members behaviour, fosters motivation for what is to be done, provides a release for emotional expression and provides information needed to make decisions. Because change can create a lot of fear, increased communication can be used to calm employees and encourage their continued support. In addition to downward communication, managers should pay attention to any upward communication that occurs. They should be available to take suggestions or answer questions that employees might have. Creating opportunities for employee feedback, such as holding meetings or having an open door management policy, may facilitate change more successfully. Michael Ussem, Director of the Wharton Center for Leadership and Change Management advocates the implementation of "Uward leadership" where middle managers would be critical change agents in guiding the top management in leadership and strategic issues. That way there is a greater chance that the change process is sustained and becomes successful.

7. Making the new Shoe fit well.. .Change Management

There are generally three types of organizational change: (1) developmental change; improving and/or fine tuning skills, methods or conditions to improve what already exists; (2) transitional change, implementing interventions in which changes evolve more slowly towards a new state (e.g. mergers, acquisitions, new systems/services/techniques); and (3) transformational change, introducing new and radically different forms of the organization's mission, culture and leadership. Transformation may involve both developmental and transitional changes and may be managed as a series of transitional changes.[10] Change agents, who help plan and implement the changes, may be executive managers, employees, or internal or external consultants who are skilled in organizational development techniques and interventions for assisting change activities. Change agents diagnose, plan, implement, monitor and support systems and human factors before, during and after a change.[11]

Change management is the process, tools and techniques for managing the people-side of change. Resistance to change, as put forth by Kurt Lewin, affects managers and employees equally when systems undergo change. As such, resistance is a naturally occurring phenomenon that can be dealt with in a constructive manner. In a sense resistance is a sign that radical change is indeed occurring and that an organization is not just redefining the status quo. HR can help management by anticipating common reactions and using them to their best advantage. For instance, if an employee is able to make requested changes to his or her performance but not willing to do so, some negotiation might be all that is required to convince that person to follow along with the company's new direction. For those who buy into the need for change but lack some of the necessary skills, targeted training could be all that is needed to quell the fears of those people. Whatever the resistance an organization encounters, it is almost a guaranteed part of change, which has become a constant in the business landscape. With the globalization of markets and speeding technological innovation, an organization cannot afford to rest on its laurels. Change management is a method for reducing and managing resistance to change when implementing process, technology or organizational change.

'Eight Steps to Successful Change'

John Kotter's highly recognised books 'Leading Change' (1995) and the follow-up. "The Heart of Change" (2002) describe a helpful model for understanding and managing change. Each stage acknowledges a key principle identified by Kotter relating to people's response and approach to change, in which people see, feel and then change—Kotter's eight step change model can be summarized as:

1. *Increase urgency*. Inspire people to move, make objectives real and relevant.
2. *Build the guiding team*. Get the right people in place with the right emotional commitment, and the right mix of skills and levels.
3. *Get the vision right*. Get the team to establish a simple vision and strategy, focus on emotional and creative aspects necessary to drive service and efficiency.

4. *Communicate for buy-in.* Involve as many people as possible, communicate the essentials, simply. Appeal and respond to people's needs. De-clutter communications—make technology work for you rather than against.
5. *Empower action.* Remove obstacles, enable constructive feedback and lots of support from leaders. Reward and recognise progress and achievements.
6. *Create short-term wins.* Set aims that are easy to achieve - in bite-size chunks. Manageable numbers of initiatives. Finish current stages before starting new ones.
7. *Don't let up.* Foster and encourage determination and persistence. Encourage ongoing progress reporting. Highlight achieved and future milestones.
8. *Make change stick.* Reinforce the value of successful change view recruitment, promotion, new change leaders. Weave change into culture.

For motivating change the following three methods can help generating creating readiness for change:- (1) Systemize organizational employees to pressure for change; (2) Reveal and highlight the discrepancies between current and desired rates; (3) Convey credible positive expectations for the change. For overcoming the employees resistance to change; the three major strategies can be as under: (1) empathy and support; (2) communication; (3) participation and involvement.[12] In order to manage change, change agents must be effective and powerful in the organizations. Grimer and Scheim have identified three key sources of personal power, in organization (in addition to one's formal position); knowledge, personality and other support including social networking[13] charismatic leaders can inspire devotion and enthusiasm for change from subordinates. Bringing leadership down to frontline and middle management, the change process in Indian companies can take a truly new meaning.[14] Change management can be successful if all members of the organization develop right motivation for change, and are empowered to became change agents.

Change management is the application of many different ideas from the fields of engineering, business and psychology. As changes in organizations have become more frequent and a necessity for survival, the body of knowledge known as "change management" has also grown to encompass more skills and knowledge room each of these fields of study. The most common barrier to successful change in organizations was a lack of change management. They fell short when managing the people side of change and encountered several challenges. Not managing the people side of change impacted their success and introduced risk into their projects. Change management can not only mitigate these business risks, but in many cases avoid them entirely. Business leaders have the potential to not only manage resistance once it appears, but to prevent it in the first place. Unfortunately, many business leaders and project teams do not appreciate their role in managing the people side of change until after resistance impacts the success of their change. As enumerated in the book "Change Management: The People Side of Change" (edited by Jeff Hiatt and Tim Creasey) the key concepts are:

- Change agents must be conscious of both a sender's meaning and a receiver's interpretation.
- Employee resistance is the norm, not the exception. Expect some employees to never support the change.
- Visible and active sponsorship is not only desirable but necessary for success.
- Value systems and the culture of the organization have a direct impact on how employees react to change.
- The size and type of the change determines how much and what kind of change management is needed. Just because a change is small does not mean that change management is not required.
- The 'right answer' is not enough to successfully implement change.

Employees go through the change process in stages and go through these stage as individuals to put these principles into practice, two change management approaches are necessary; the employees' perspective and the managers' perspective. Managing change from the manager's perspective is called organizational change management. Individual change management is often overlooked by many change management models. Individual change management includes the tools and processes that supervisors use with their employees to manage individual transitions through change. This employee-oriented component of change management is the critical ingredient that allows a project team to:

1. Help employees through the change process
2. Create a feedback loop to business leaders and identity points of resistance
3. Diagnose gaps in communications and training
4. Implement corrective action.

To be more effective as a change leader and sponsor of change, HR would have to: manage employee resistance to change, build change competency into the organization, avoid unnecessary the turnover or loss of valued employees and integrate the changing leadership paradigms. Understanding and applying these principles will help in the application of techniques and process for individual and organizational change management. Organizational change management is the application of a systematic process for managing change across an organization. It is the key to taking an organization through the transition from today to a new future state. Many changes do fail in organizations that do not appreciate and manage the people side of change. HR must tackle the challenge that the dynamic environment of 'changing organizations' has thrown open. The challenge for HR is, to employ all the resources at its command and facilitate a smooth transition, manage the process of change in such a way as to maximize the benefits and minimize the cost in the interest of organizational growth. Once the new-shoe fits well, winning the race would be the next thing to follow.

8. Retaining top Performers

Amidst all the challenges of managing change, one crucial issue is often overlooked; retaining top performers.[15] The following steps can help managers in retaining top performers:

(*i*) Provide clear information.

(*ii*) Make your stars part of the planning.

(*iii*) Present a united front.

(*iv*) Approach resisters.

(*v*) Pay attention to personal concerns.

(*vi*) Pre-test details of the change.

Tersa Robinson, Senior Manager of Best Practices and Risk Management for Insurance provider Aflac says "I give as much information as I possibly can, to help to performers understand the reasons behind the change." Involving top performers in planning and implementation of change makes success of the change management. The leadership team and front line managers must present a united front. Betty Barley says "The leadership team has to sell the future. If they cannot or are distracted by performers will smell that a mile way. If they are leaders fighting, they will conclude that the change is doomed in the worst case and will be messy in the best." Aron Ain, says "we aggressively sign up leaders and managers long before we communicate a significant change to those who are impacted. We want to make sure our frontline leaders have all the data they need to support the change. For retaining top performers they must be made to understand the change and must be encouraged to advocate the change. Zigarmi strongly advocates approaching top performers particularly those resisting change. "Go to them, listen to them, solve a problem if you can. They may become mental or even advocates for change. Top performers need to be assured that the change would not transform work they enjoy into a daily grind and the quality of their work will continue to be recognized and respected. Top management must keep their top performers on board when the organization is negotiating the waters of change and bolster their confidence in the organization's future and their role within it. Communicating the change is different from selling it and therefore top performers must be given as much information as possible and the reasons behind the change. Specific attention must be paid to the personal concerns of the top performers. Capalli suggests that personal concerns of star performers should be thought through and communicated carefully. "You want to show that the organization is paying attention to career paths and has a structure in place to handle these purposefully."

9. Change Management Structures

Organisations need special change management structure including people who have the power to mobilize resources to promote change, along with interpersonal and political skills to guide the change process. After native management structures may include the following :[16]

1. The chief executive or leader manages the change effort.
2. A project manager temporarily is assigned to coordinate the transition.
3. The formal organization manages the change effort in addition to supervising normal operations.
4. Representatives of the major constituencies involved in the change jointly manage the project.
5. Natural leaders who have the confidence and trust of large numbers of affected employees are selected to manage the transition.
6. A cross section of profile representing different organizational functions and levels manages the change.
7. A "Kitchen Cabinet" representing people whom the chief executive consults with and confides in manages the change effort.

It is important to sustain momentum and special efforts are needed for sustaining energy and commitment for implementing the change. The following five activities are required to sustain momentum for carrying change through to completion:

(*a*) providing resources for change
(*b*) building a support system for change agents
(*c*) developing new competencies and skills
(*d*) reinforcing new behaviours and
(*e*) staying the course - a steady focus on change implementation.[17]

Charles Darwin said: "It is not the strongest of the species nor the most intelligent that survives. It is the one that is the most adoptable to change."

10. Success Factors for Change

There are some standards of excellence that organizations can use as a benchmark to measure their change efforts. Fortune magazine annually asks companies to rank firms in their industry on the following eight attributes:

1. Quality of management
2. Quality of product or service
3. Innovativeness
4. Value as a long term investment
5. Financial soundness
6. Ability to attract, develop and keep talented people
7. Community and environmental responsibilities and
8. Use of corporate assets.[18]

There are a number of other success factors which are characteristic of organizational effectiveness. Some factors are given below-

1. Externally focused: market driven
2. Customer centred
3. Strategically net worked with business alliances
4. Mobilized towards a shared vision
5. Focused on creating value in products and services
6. Committed to positive continuous learning and continual change
7. Determined to fulfill ethical responsibilities to all stakeholders (customer, employee, suppliers, society)
8. Committed to measuring progress against world class standards of excellence.[19]

Change agents help and implement the change and these change agents may be executives, managers, employees or internal or external consultants.

11. Change management through Human Resources

It has basically three aspects -

1. Change management dealing with people
2. Change management dealing with group and
3. Over coming organizational resistance to change.

Schein has said: Leaders create and change cultures while managers live with them. Organisations with adaptive cultures can initiate incremental changes in their strategies and practices in the context of environmental change. During 1950s and 60s Hewett Packard culture stressed serving everyone having stakes in the business with integrity and fairness, encouraged collegial behaviour, avoided employee Pay off and was paternalistic. In 1970s and 80s the firm shifted its focus from instruments to computers accompanied by change in organizational culture. The new culture of professionalism was a logical response to as new set of conditions.[20] Cultural change is an extremely difficult and long term process, since it requires an understanding of the cultural dimentions (artifacts, norms, values and basic assumptions). Since an organisation's culture and its mode are closely related, a significant change in one will induce the change in the other. Mental modes are characterized by time (past, present and future) stability-instability (homoestasis — heterostasis, inadequacy — adequacy (or depletion vs repletion) and reality -unreality. Mental modes are related to organizational goals.

Human response to change may vary from individual to individual, group to group and organization to organization. Change to many individual and working group, means learning new skills, and new routines and acquiring new relationships. According to Senge (1990) Individuals may not resist change, what they resist is being changed. Basic to managing change is the need to develop change consciousness and create a culture where employees seek change. Change resistance can be due to negative attitudes, lack of involvement, personal criticism, loss of status and authority, inappropriate timing, cognitive rigidity, challenging authority or threat to job security, reduction in salary, pay benefits and overtime allowance, pride and satisfaction etc. Training is important to manage change. Motorola provides one with the example of a company who successfully changed the organization in improving quality through the six sigma approach (i.e. zero defects and the elimination of variability) by effectively training the employees and allotting 2.4 per cent of budget for employee training (Denton 1995). Participation management is another useful device. An example of participative management is IBM's PRIDE programmes that refer to people, Responsibility Involvement, Development and Excellence in quality control (Kirkpatrick 1993). Employee empowerment can help in managing change through people. Some of the organizations that have successfully implemented employee empowerment are Hewlett Packard, Levi Strauss, Intel, Nordstrom, Xerox etc. employees tend to give positive support to change when they get partnership in the organization. Example of companies that have profited by the stock ownership plans are Lucent Technologies Inc., Cadbury Schweppes PLC, John Lewis Partnerships, Infosy etc. Group approaches to organizations change can be brought through sensitivity training, team building and creation of self-managed teams. The techniques to align employees with change processes/ efforts should focus on tasks, roles, teams and HRD systems to get desired changes. Change in organizations general demand linking strategy, structure, people, processes, culture and technology with the purpose and successfully transformational planning for change. Prof. K. Harigopal has suggested aligning employees with change through HRM techniques[21] as shown in the Box given.

Box — Aligning Employees with change: HRM Techniques

Task Focused change	Role focused change	System focused change
• Employee education and training • Employee counseling • Cross training for multiple skills	• Role clarification • Individual role compatibility	• Salary and Incentives • Compensation systems • Employee—appraisal and career path

• Behaviour Modification • Commitment to change • Employee elasticity-stretching the potential	• Team building • Employee empowerment • Monitoring and modeling • Winning Employee Commitment	• Management by objectives • Clarifying contractual obligations

Change Management at ICICI—A case study—ICICI was established as a public limited company by the Govt. of India in 1955 to promote Industrial development in India with the basic objectives to—

1. assist in creation, expansion and modernization of enterprises
2. expand the investment markets.
3. take up the ownership of industrial investment and
4. encourage and promote the participation of private capital both internal and external.

In 1988 ICICI promoted India's first venture capital company - Technology Development and Information Company of India Ltd., (TDICL). In 1996, K.V. Kamath became CEO of ICICI and introduced massive changes - from a development bank mode to that of market-driven financial conglomerate. The change programme was started within the organization, the first move being the creation of the Infrastructures Group (I.G.), Oil and Gas Group (O&GG), Planning and Treasury Department (PTD and the Structured Products Group). These groups were seen as thrust areas. To take the problems of customers, ICICI set up three new departments. Major Cliente Group (MCG), Growth Client Group (GCG) and Personal Finance Group (PFG). Though employees within the organization showed resistance but the customers were happy about this new arrangement. Training programmes and seminars were conducted for around 250 officers by external agencies and during 1995-96 around 35 offices were sent for overseas training programmes. ICICI organized reward system for group performance. After a year employee showed significant improvement in accepting the programme. The employee behaviour pattern after two years showed relief, employment, liking and acceptance of business development activities. A 360 degree appraisal system was put in place whereby an industrial was assessed by his peers, seniors and subordinates. By 2000 ICICI had emerged as the second largest financial institution in India with assets worth Rs.582 billion. ICICI faced change challenges in December 2000 when ICICI was merged with Bank of Madura (BoM). There were large differences in profiles, grades, designations and salaries of personnel of the two entities. ICICI bank was nearly three times the size of BoM, its staff was only 1,400 as against BoM 2500. The ICICI - BoM merger drew up the HR blueprint having -

1. A data base of entire HR structure;
2. Road map of career
3. Determining the blueprint of HR moves
4. Communication of milestones and
5. I.T. Integration—

People integration - business integration Hewitt Associates were appointed consultants to help in working out a uniform compensation and work culture. Areas of HR integration focused on :

1. Employee communication
2. Cultural integration
3. Organization structuring
4. Recruitment
5. Compensation
6. Performance management
7. Employee relations

By June 2001 the process of integration between ICICI and BoM was started. Training programmes were conducted with stress on knowledge on attitudes, skills and technology upgradation. Effective communication channels were established to ensure employee participation. By the end of 2001 change was effectively achieved and HR aspects were successfully handed. By 2001 the employee strength rose to 8275. A win/win situation was created and change management was effectively carried out by various HR initiatives. In March 2002 ICICI Bank and with

K.V. Kamath still heading ICICI the change over was again successfully completed. The integration of various operation of both the entities were managed in a most successful manner. Managing change requires five adjustments and orientation of the attitudes and behaviours of employees towards the intended change both at the individual level and at the collective level as groups / teams. The case study presents the initiatives taken by the change leaders. Massive changes were organized at the organizational level and effective management with proper HR initiatives proved beneficial to the organization. The change leader Shri K.V. Kamath once said, "we do put people under stress by raising the bar constantly. That is the only way to ensure that performers lead the change process."

13. Concluding Remarks

According to Michael Useem, the need of the hour is to bring in the significant part of any corporation into the larger change management process. That way there is a greater chance that the change process is sustained and successful.[22] Managers all over the world today recognize the inevitability of change, that the only constant is change itself. The changes surrounding the world are not mere trends but the working off large, unruly forces: the globalisation of markets, the spread of information technology and computer networks; the dismantling of the hierarchy and diversification of the working force. Change management is a critical challenge to the global world. The following common sense guidelines are suggested to have successful change efforts.[23]

1. Do not promise that all employees undergoing a change effort will be winners.
2. Do not blame those who lose out for their negative attitudes.
3. Do not focus only on the new and forget the old.
4. Avoid symbolic or pseudo-participation in the change effort.
5. Avoid destroying the old culture without building a new one.
6. Do not launch human resource management programmes in the context of a major change without the necessary time and resource to support them.

Change management is a complex process where effective leadership, building successful teams in the midst of transitions, monitoring, feedback are all very important.

The success of a corporate change effort depends upon the understanding the role of "perception" in change management. Perception is the process of acquiring, interpreting, selecting and organizing sensory information and involves both the recognition of environmental stimuli and actions in response to these stimuli. Our perceptions reflect our emotions, needs, expectations and learning. Many change management gurus have focused on soft issues such as culture, leadership and motivation. In 1994 Boston consulting group research have suggested four DICE factors for change management and have used these hard side of the change management initiatives is more than 1000 change management efforts world-wide. Harold L. Sirkin, Perry Keenam and Alan Jackson have come to the research conclusion that the following four factors (DICE) determine the outcome of any transformation initation:[239]

1. D—The *duration* of time until change programme is completed if it has a short life span; if not short, the amount of time between reviews of milestones.
2. I—The project team's performance *integrity*; that is, its ability to complete the initiative on time. That depends on the member's skills and traits relative to the project's requirements.
3. C—The *commitment* to change that top management (C1) and employees affected by the change (C2) display.
4. E—The *effort* over and above the usual work that the change initiative demands on the employees.

Organisations can determine if their change programme will succeed by asking executives to calculate scores of the DICE framework—duration, integrity, commitment and effort. Prof. S. Ramanarayan has conceptualised change management as the ability to cope with SCUDS (an acronym for simultaneously, complex, uncertain Dynamic situations). In all organisations change management is very complex because it really involves a whole bunch of variables and so when you touch one thing, many other things also need simultaneous handling, uncertainty is always there and sometimes uncertain things may not be easily managed as planned. Futurologists have been predicting large scale technological changes which human societies are now confronted with. Triggered by the IT revolution and more specifically the internet revolution, robotics, intelligent sensors, digital imaging, super conductivity, nano-technology, gene therapy and biotechnology have helped in the emergence of the intelligent society global business with explode once language barriers are technologically dealt with. The process of globalisation have received an immense boost owing to the emergence of I.T. enabled networks which provide instant reach and real-time interaction. The twentieth twenty first century has brought changes in the corporate world in the following dimensions:

1. Emergence of intelligent society (knowledge society);
2. Dehumanisation at work;
3. Strategy: Top down to bottom up;
4. Growth—wealth extracting to wealth creating;
5. Organisation: Pyramid to web;
6. Style: Stability to change;
7. Reach: Domestic to global;
8. Structure: Thick boundary to thin boundary;
9. Operations: Vertical to virtual;
10. Product: Mass production to mass customisation;
11. Financial disclosure: Quarterly to real time;
12. Inventories: Months to hours;
13. Quality: Affordable best to no compromise;
14. People: Employees to nomads;.
15. Job expectations: Job security to employment security.
16. Leadership: Transactional to renaissances.[24]

The concept of scuds (simultaneously complex, uncertain, dynamic, situation) can be best illustrated by the speed of change we are witnessing today. Radio reached fifty million homes in fifty years, the telephone in thirteen years and the internet in four years. Today news reaches billions of people world-wide instantly. Multi-nationals are invading developing economies, established businesses are losing their hold; large companies are disappearing because of the pressures from larger ones, leading to acquisitions and mergers; thus destabilising the balance between economy and manpower. Massive restructuring exercises, technology-related developments, outsourcing models are leading great job losses. Managing change in such a fast scenario is a big challenge for leaders. In an economy where the only certainty is uncertainty, the one sure source of competitive advantage is knowledge when markets shift, technologies proliferate, competitors multiply, and products become obsolete almost overnight, successful companies are those that consistently create new knowledge, disseminate it widely throughout the organisations and quickly embody it in new technologies and products."[25] Knowledge management is typically implemented as any other change management programme. Whatever the challenges of change, Wipro is clear about its value-based stand. To quote Azim Premji "To meet the future, we are prepared to change everything about ourselves except our beliefs as they alone guide, govern and find us together as an organisation".

Prof. S. Ramnarayan has suggested the following stages for solving an organisational change problem.

(*i*) You need to formulate and understand the problem and need to first improve your understanding of opportunities and needs.

(*ii*) Concept development by finding out what are the alternative ways of approaching the problem.

(*iii*) You have to develop workable alternatives.

(*iv*) Evaluate—You need to look at the benefits, costs and so on.

(*v*) Implementations: which means installing the plant or executing the best workable alternative.[26]

Implementations takes too long period because we do not anticipate a whole set of things in the planning stage with the result—that all those stages go wrong in the implementation process. We must move away from a directive approach and move towards learning approach or participative approach. In order to manage change, top management has to evolve and communicate a concrete and clear vision and seek cooperation of every member of the organisation and help make the necessary mind shifts. Skillful and continuous communications, using the state of art, has to be made to all concerned, inside and outside the organisation. Credit must be shared with all members of the organisation and sustained efforts must be continued.

References

1. Peter F. Drucker: Management Tasks, Responsibilities, Practices, Allied Publishers Ltd., New Delhi, 1996, pp. 642-43.
2. Judith Ross Report—Retaining top performers—Harvard Management update, distributed by New York Times Syndicate, Hindustan Times Power Jobs 14 March, 2006—Jaipur, p. 2.
3. D. Nadler, Organisational Frame—Bending—"Types of changes in the complex organization" in Corporate Transformation eds. R. Kilmann and T. Covin (San Francisco Jossey Bass 1988), pp. 66-83.
4. T.G. Cummings and C.G. Worley: Organisational Development and Change—5th edition (Minneopales/St. Paul West 1993, p. 145.
5. T. Cox; Jr-Cultural Diversity in Organisations—Theory, Research and Practice, San Francisco Berrett—Kochler 1993, pp. 3-40.
6. W. Nennis—Managing People is like herding cats: Warren Bennis on Leadership—New York: Executive Excellence, 1997.
7. E. Schein—Process Consultation Revisited: Creating the Helping Relationships—(Reading, Mass: Addison—Wesley 1999). E. Schein—Organisational Culture and Leadership—San Francisco: Jossey Bass 19997, 2nd ed.
8. Rickard Beckhard—Agents of change San Francisco: Jossey Bass 1977. Also Beckhard and Harris: Organisational Transition 1992.
9. R. Tannenbaum and R. Janne—"Holding on, Letting go and Moving on—understanding a Neglected perspective

on change in Human systems development eds. R. Tannenbaum & others, San Franscisco: Jossey Bass 1985—pp. 95-121.

10. L. Ackerman—Development, Transition or Transformation: The Question of Changes in Organisations O.D. Practitioners—December, 1986, pp. 1-8.
11. Joseph W. Weiss—Organisational Behaviour and Change: Managing Diversity Cross-Cultural Dynamics and Ethics, Vikas Publishing House, New Delhi, 2000, p. 411.
12. D. Kirkpatrick ed. How to Manage change effectively—(San Francisco, Jossey Bass 1985).
13. Greiner and Schein: Power and Organisational Development.
14. The changing leadership Paradigm—All India Management Association—Indian Management, p. 19.
15. Judith Ross Reports—Retaining top performance—Harvard Business update distributed by New York Times Syndicate-Hindustan Times—Power Jobs—Jaipur, Tuesday, 14th March, 2006, p. 2.
16. R. Beckhard and R. Harris: Organisational Transitions: Managing Complex Change 2nd ed. (Reading, Mass: Address-Wesley 1987).
17. Thomas G. Cummings and C.G. Worley—Organisation Development and Change—Thomson—South Western 2001. Reprint-2004 Eastern Press Bangalore, pp. 168-171.
18. E. Brown, "America's Most Admired Companies" Fortune 2, March 1999, p. 68.
19. Joseph W. Weiss—Organisational Behaviour and Change, Vikas Publishing House, New Delhi, Reprint 2001, p. 402.
20. Kotter J.P. and Heskett J.L. (1992) Corporate Culture and Performance, Free Press, New York.
21. K. Harigopal—Management of Organisational Change. Leveraging Transformation—Response Books, New Delhi, 2001, p. 108.
22. The Changing Leadership Paradigm—Indian Management—The Journal of the All India Management Association. February, 2006, Vol. 45, Issue 2, p. 19.
23. Jeffery K. Liker, David B. Roitman and Ethel Roskies: "Changing Everything All at once: Work Life and Technological Change" Sloan Management Review—Summer 1987, pp. 43-44.

23a. Harold L. Sirkin, Perry Keenam and Alan Jackson—The Hard side of change management, Harvard Business Review—October 2005, p. 111.

24. Pritam Singh and Asha Bhandarker—Leadership in Twenty-first Century—Towards Corporate Renaissance—Paper incoporated in Transformational Leadership—Edited by Shivganesh Bhargav—Response Books—New Delhi, 2003, pp. 36-37.

25. Nonaka, I. (1991) The knowledge-creating company—Harvard Business Review—Nov-Dec., 96-104.

26. Managing organisational change by Prof. S. Ramnarayan in Managing Organisational Change—Edited by Ahmedabad Management Association, 1999, p. 9.

7

Spirituality and Management

"The poverty in the West is a different kind of poverty—it is not only a poverty of loneliness but also of spirituality."

(Nobel Prize winner—Mother Teresa)

"I have never doubted that this is a spiritual universe; and if I can not understand exactly how that can be and how God works, it must be because God has chosen to have it that way."

(Upton Sinclair—Pulitzer Prize Winner American Author)

"The Vedanta appears among explicit doctrines as one of the most direct formulations possible of what makes the very, essence of our spiritual reality"

(Schuon Frithjof—"The language of the Self.")

"Spirituality refers to the ancient and abiding human quest for connectedness with something larger and more trustworthy than our ego-with our own souls, with one another, with the worlds of history and nature, with the individual winds of the spirit, with the mystery of being alive."

(Richard Wolman—"Thinking with your soul")

Spirituality implies:- (1) a pure mind, a pure heart; (2) a calm head, a cool brain; (3) well regulated breathing system and nervous harmony; (4) self awareness; (5) ethical conduct and honest, simple and religious way of living. The basis of spirituality is simply knowing ourselves better. Religion is the banana skin and spirituality is the banana. By spiritual we mean the abiding human quest for connectedness with the mystery of being alive and having cosmic connected ness. The spirit of the man is the candle of the God - the Lord. Swami

Vivekananda's message to the management people is: "Can you give back men their lost individuality? Tell every one about his/her real nature and see how the sleeping soul awakens. Power, glory and purity will come, all that is excellent will come when the sleeping soul is aroused to self-conscious activity by the power of words, by the power of behaviour." As Chhandogya Upanishad says: "When a man realises the self, he does not depend on anyone but the infinite power, bliss and excellence of the self. Man is infinite in spirit." As Jesus Christ has said: "I am the spirit and he that worships me as spirit, worships me in truth." Lord Krishna, Incarnation of Lord Vishnu, in Bhagwat Gita says: "First find your true self, then go out into the field of action and success is bound to be yours." In modern day life which is full of tension, stress, struggle for existence and survival of the smartest human beings, Lord Krishna in Bhagwad Gita assures that "(*i*) We are all spirits, divine beings; (*ii*) Bliss, peace, abundance and immortality lie within us." "Not only many famous physicists and other scientists have for quite some time been openly admitting of the compelling necessity to consider the spiritual/metaphysical aspect of man; even some social scientists and one or two high priests of management thought in the USA are also just beginning to use words like 'spirit' 'spiritual' etc. in some of their lectures or writings".[2] The spiritual core of human beings is the pure, uncontaminated, truly free, luminous consciousness within. On 30th June 2006 Sri Sri Ravi Shankar, the charismatic spiritual guru and the founder of "Art of Living Movement", spoke the following words "Spirituality is not running away to the Himalayas or from responsibility. It is remaining where you are and turning within. Reflect on your life and see it from a broader perspective in the context of cosmology (how small we are in order of things), commitment (to truth) and compassion (to all). .... The first law of spirituality is to stop blaming yourself. .... Spirituality performs miracles in management .... positive vibration is a form of spirituality and a tremendous phenomenon. Somebody who has this in him can be made a good manager".[3] Religion has generally three components theology, rituals and spiritual contents. Spirituality, according to Peter Pruzan of Copenhagen

Business School (Denmark) refers, to a search for meaning, which transcends material well-being, a focus on basic, deep rooted human values and a relationship with a universal source, power or divinity. Spirituality deals with basic human emotions. Spirituality is one's belief in religion. Spirituality is soaring in inner self and ultimately getting enlightened. Spiritualism implies a certain regard and complete adherence to the basic human values and ethical principles. Spiritualism embraces the key ethical principles, such as compassion, tolerance, a sense of caring, consideration of others and the responsible use of knowledge and power - principles that transcend the barriers between religious believers and non-believers and followers of various religions.[4]

Spiritual and ethical development of human beings has always been part of the general practices of various religions. Every person requires some values and ethical conduct to live in a civilized society. Man is spirit or pure consciousness which is encashed by his bio-chemical body or physical constitution. The spirit is not a part subordinate to the bio-physical/ bio-chemical self but independent. There are four important aspects in human beings; the body, mind, emotions and spiritual being. Spiritualism is the brand mark of Indian ethos of management. It encompasses conscience—that still small voice within human beings that assures them of what is right. Bhagawad Gita contains the essence of the spiritual science. Spiritual science is the science of the self, soul or Atman. Man is like the musk deer that goes around the jungle looking for the source of pleasant smell, while not realising that smell comes from his navel.

According to Swami Vivekananda, This self or soul or substances is all that exists in the universe. It is not in the brain but in the heart that Atman (soul) possessed of knowledge, power and activity has its seat: The human being is composed first of this external covering the body; consisting of the five elements and (subtle) body consisting of mind, intellect and ego. Behind them is the real soul of man which is self-luminous. In Bhagwad Gita, it is called the supreme purusha in this body. It says "The supreme purusha in this body is also called the spectator, the permitter, the supporter, the enjoyer, the Great Lord and the supreme self." Human beings are all eternal spiritual beings, but because of spiritual amnesia, we are misidentifying ourselves with our temporary physical body. Devoid of the spiritual learning, man is like any other creature, being born to live mechanically manipulated by nature and die. There is an unconscious inward movement of every human soul towards the spiritual quest".[5] In management science a fundamental proposition needs to be made that the concept of self in human beings has to embrace the spiritual dimension. Human beings have God (soul) with themselves." Explaining the self Sri Sankaracharya has said: "There is one self existent, eternal, who is the base of all body that "I am" and who is the witness of the three states of consciousness—Jagrat, Swapna, and susupti and who is separate from the five sheaths .... who sees everything, but whom none sees; who enlightens the intellect but whom nothing can enlighten .... from whose nearness, the intellect, mind, senses and the body work, as energised by Him; who knows all, from body to ego but whom none knows......... This is the Atman indivisible, eternal, blissful, knowledge, even-uniform-understood in the understanding only; and engaged by whom, all senses and organs work".[6] The basis of spiritualism is the conviction that spirit is the essence of life and that it lives on after the body dies. In Bhagwad Gita, Lord Krishna says; An external portion of myself, having become a living soul in the world of life and abiding in prakriti, draws (to itself) the five senses, with mind for the sixth. This soul (spirit) cannot be cut, nor burnt, nor moisted, nor dried out. It is eternal, all pervading, stable, immovable and ancient.

The human body goes on changing; new cells are born and die but the soul (spirit) the real self, provides the space for it to happen: Soul is the space in which the body and mind exist. Carl Jung in his famous book "Modern Man in search of a soul" has talked about four stages that people go through to reach maturity. The highest stage is the stage of the spirit. This is when you finally recognize that you are not an athlete, a warrior or a statesman, that you are in this world, but not of this world. You recognise that you are not a human being but a spiritual being with a human experience. Human life is like a garage where we park our souls for a time but our inner spirits are not so confined. In Quran it is said; "He originated the creation of man out of clay, then He fashioned his progeny of an extraction of mean water, then he shaped him and breathed his spirit in him." Spirituality is expressed in many ways. For different people, it means different things. For some, it is about surrendering themselves to the ultimate eternal power. For some others spirituality implies following eternal values of life and listening to one's little voice. For some it is simply leading an ethical and virtuous life and for some it is devotion and meditation of their Isht Deb (God of choice). Acharya Rajnesh, "Osho" reminds us:- "Bring a little more awareness to your existence. If you are walking, let each step be taken in full consciousness. Try it in small acts. Eating, taking a bath, swimming, talking, listening, cooking, washing your clothes— Deautomatise all processes. Suddenly you are enlightened" meditation leads you to enter to the inner most shrine of your being that is your inner treasure. The Spiritual aspect of human beings is very clearly depicted in the following stanzas:-

"I have a body, but I am not the body;

I have a mind, but I am not the mind;

I have an intellect; but I am not the intellect;

I have the senses, but I am not the senses;

I am the self-luminous, Pure consciousness the poorna"

Spiritual knowledge is to be experienced, by transmission from an enlightened master who gracefully and willingly transmits it to his pupil or disciple after ascertaining his purity, shraddha and keenness to learn. Spiritual knowledge happens in the silence of one's mind. Meditation is the way to silencing the mind. To go beyond ego, to go beyond mind, to go beyond chatter, meditation is the answer to spiritual knowledge called wisdom. The places of worship are positive energy fields of spiritual vibrations. The spiritual fields like temples, holy rivers, holy places uplift consciousness leading to harmony, peace and feeling of spiritual fulfilment "Be still and know that I am God".

Know yourself as light, self-luminous and exercise it in meditation by technique of Raj Yoga Karma Yoga Bhakti Yoga or Gyanyoga. Deep within each one of us there is an inner longing to live a life of greatness and contribution to really make a difference. The man who rejoices in the self, is satisfied with the self and in centred in the self is a man blissful, peaceful and in satchit—Anand (eternal joy), he is called Brahma-jnani. One of the signs of the enlightened man is that he always enjoys boundless bliss within himself.

Spirituality moving to corporate world

Spirituality has ultimately arrived at the shop floor, corporate office and board room. The management students at Wharton, Kellogg, Harvard and Standford are now getting uplifting doses of spirituality by management guru like Deepak Chopra. "Now it's time for spirituality to come out to the board room, factories, business places, parliament, assemblies, hospitals and labour unions............. Spirituality is "Bhav Roga Nidhan" the remedy for all worldly ills. It is spirituality that brought freedom to the country and it is spirituality that has woven the diverse fabric of the country." Spirituality is not just a practice but an attitude which gets woven into one's life. If a nation upholds spirituality, spirituality would uphold the nation. The soul has seven innate positive qualities—peace, joy, love, bliss, knowledge, purity and power. One who is a spiritualist and meditates on "Aum" for his life maintains, the indispensable attributes like truth, abstinence from sensual pleasures, non-injury, non-acceptance (of gifts), renunciation, sanyasa, cleanliness, cheerfulness, absence, from fraud, and many other kinds of control external and internal. The non-physical soul is intimatery connected with the cells of the physical body. These qualities of the soul flow as spiritual energy to each cell and nourishes them. The mind acts as a sieve between the spiritual energy (soul) and the body. When the mind creates negative thoughts, the sieve of the mind gets blocked, thereby blocking the flow of this spiritual energy. In the spiritually "magnetised" or "soul-conscious" state, the soul is in its rightful place as a ruler of the body, sitting on its throne between "the eye-brows."

Recent management thinkers like Arie de geus and Peter Senge talked about how the companies should treat their enterprises as "living work communities" rather than economic machines. Vijay Govindarajan of the Tuck School of Business says; "Reengineering has its value. But the rounds of re-engineering have stripped organisations of their heart and soul." The constant recurring waves of corporate scandals—Martha Stewart, Enron, Worldcom, and the recent phone-tapping at "Haorlett Packard" have further corroded the corporate world's unethical core. Indian gurus like Swami Parthasarathy of Vedanta Institute, Sri Sri Ravi Shankar, Deepak Chopra, Maharishi Mahesh Yogi and Yoga Acharyas are now most sought after persons the world over. *Wakhlu* had nearly 400 clients todate including several from South Africa, Dubai, Finland, France, Malaysia and India. India's CEOs—from the UB group's flamboyant Vijay Mallaya to Yash Birla and Mukand Ltd Suketu Shah—they are all turning towards spiritualism for their organisations. "The Art of a Living" sessions of Sri Sri Ravi Shankar are becoming more and more popular in the corporate world. Mantra Science with gayatri Mantra, Mahamritunjay mantra and others are now becoming more popular and needed for peace of mind. "The results of mantras don't come over night but they create a sense of well being, positive thinking and bind people together to a common thread. Even leading management thought leaders are walking the spiritual highway. At XLRI in Jamshedpur, there is an Indian philosophy module that is always hugely over subscribed Dedna Miller, cofounder of the global Dharma centre says: "Wealth creation is no longer the goal. It becomes a means of enabling and sustaining the society. Business leaders should promote the spiritual fulfilment of every one touched by the business, employees, customers, suppliers, share holders and society." The whole world is now realising that spirituality is one of the important needs of the human society—what ever may be the levels of economic development or prosperity.

Need to rekindle the heart and the soul of management

Many sociologists Anthopologists and management thinkers have noticed a steady deterioration of the quality of working life in many modern business organisations. In the corporate world with negative emotions our inter-personal relationships tend to get tensed up .... particularly on the work-front. Instead of producing results we become busy managing our negative emotions with people. We are busy keeping internal accounts and settling score with each other. "People are liabilities" mindset, down sizing spiral, mechanistic culture, lack of genuine leadership, lack of value, numerical myopia, lack of human sensitivity, unethical conduct for quick results are some of the well known ills of the many modern business organisations. Leadership behaviours that are commonly noticed that sap the energy and enthusiasm of the people include:-

1. "Pre-occupation with self-promotion and self aggrandisement rather than focusing on organisational health and the well being of all members.
2. Using people as "Stepping stones" and discarding them subsequently without the rewards due to them.
3. Divide and rule tactics to secure one's own position.
4. Stealing credit from those who actually deserve it for their work or ideas.
5. Excessive control over professionals who have the capability and the desire to work independently; not empowering them to perform their roles effectively.
6. Whimsical, adhoc decisions making; inconsistency in thinking; lack of clarity about long-term direction;
7. Management by fear.
8. Unrestrained ambition and greed; lack of financial integrity and intellectual dishonesty.
9. Keeping people in the dark not communicating regularly and clearly with them.
10. Insufficient attention to the development of the people one works with".[7]

A senior manager of a renowned large industrial enterprise, in a letter to IIM Calcutta has admitted......... "My own story has been .... that I have been doing almost everything I would rather not do: talking lies, mis-representation of facts, giving bribes, taking illegal short cuts etc, in the name of furthering the company's objective of increased business." Most of the employees in business organisations complain of meaningless work, excessive stress, long hours of work, lack of human compassion and increasing insecurity—all leading to hypertensions, cardiac problems and stress induced diseases. "No nation is immune today from unethical activities, corruption and moral disarray. Buffected by the conflicts, tensions and anxieties, temptations and frustrations of world around them and at the same time finding only a great emptiness within himself, Man today is in the midst of a serious multi-dimensional crisis of working life in corporate sector leading to a parching of the human spirit, having traumatic, humiliating experiences and mental ill health. Studs Terkel, most appropriately prefaced his seminal book titled "Working" with the acerbic observation that "work is, by its very nature, about violence—to the spirit as well as the body .... It is about daily humiliation". The present organisational studies indicate that the quality of work life in most business organisations is sub-standard and there are broadly the following maladies—

1. Resentment and disillusionment with promotion criteria and performance appraisal system.
2. Widespread frustration and unhappiness due to comparison with other organisations.
3. Frequent fits of anger and misbehaviour amongst top level officials, entrepreneurs and managers.
4. Unrealistic personal expectations and sale targets.
5. Unlimited addiction to luxurious things and lower order material needs, greed for more money, fame and power.
6. Glorification of speed, fashion and excitement as against serenity, harmony and simplicity.
7. Groupings and cliques hampering open and frank communication.
8. Too long hours of work and emphasis on quick results.
9. Regional prejudices, undivided subjectivity and power games.[8]

The cumulative effect of corporate misdemeanours and spate of scandals, frauds and gross misrepresentation is that for the common man, it has become a synonym for unrestrained exploitation, greed and economic manipulations. *Hindiry*, CEO of network, in his book "The good, the bad and the overpaid" describes the dastardly actions of executives of Enron, Worldcom, Adelphia and makes the observation that "many of today's crop of chief executives are irresponsible or criminal or both". One of the more interesting ideas to emerge from America's soul-searching after the turn of the century corporate scandals is that its leading business schools may have neglected to teach students about the moral dimensions of being a CEO. Harvard Stanford and others have since scrambled to introduce business ethics classes. What directors, managers and others need to remember is that ethics matter and must be demonstrated from the top; that it is better to manage market expectation rather than to manage earning to meet expectations; and it is false economy to scrimp on information and control systems. For those who are victims of down-sizing spiral, it is a traumatic and humiliating experience leading to financial insecurity and loss of respectability in the eyes of their family members, professional peers and society in general. Restructuring and down-sizing moves are just frauds when in many cases there are unjustified increases in executive compensation even upto 400 times the compensation that is paid to the lowest paid employees. In effect people are turned out ignominiously and even most committed, loyal hands are dispensed with so callously and cheaply. In the corporate sector the fetish for measurement or "numerical myopia" is being pursued at the expense of organisational loyalty, experience, commitment and competencies.

4. Work-Place Spirituality and Managements

Swami Someswarananda has enunciated the following basic principles of management based on Indian spiritualism

1. Each soul (spirit) is a potential god: Aham Brahmasmi- I have immense potentialities and I can make the impossible possible. Tatwamasi - Every body can make himself a genius.

2. Why work? Atman Moksharya, Jagat Hitayah Ch. for my own salvation (upliftment) and for the good of the world. (Synchronise your private benefit with public benefit).
3. What is work? Yajuaryat Karmanaha Parasparam Bhavayamtaha : Karma is to be done with the spirit of Yajna; Nurture, each other.
4. How to work? Seva + Tyag: Serve/ Others and give your best for the good of others.
5. Spirit of work: yoga Karmasu Kaushalam; excellence in work is yoga.
6. The resources : Sukshma > Sthul : subtle/subjective factors are more important than gross/objective factors.
7. Advaita—the non dual or the Holistic approach - Every person is not only an employee in an organisation but he is a father, a husband, a friend, a relative and above all a citizen.
8. Sthita-Prajna-emotional stability and high emotional quotient.
9. Redefinition of various management concepts in the light of the above mentioned principles.[9]

All over the world there is a movement during the last twenty year about work-place spirituality. Roots of such movement can be traced back to India and Hindu Vendanta philosophy. Britain, U.S.A., Japan have also taken many initiatives regarding work-place spirituality. In Britain early industrialists such as Josiah Wedgewood and 19th Century Paternalists such as the Cadbury, Lever and Rowntree families-actively sought to manage employee spirituality and religion. The work of industrial missions in the later half of the 20th Century has maintained a spiritual or religious presence. Far Eastern and Japanese corporations, large and small, are renowned for their use of spiritual and moral education. In India following ethical conduct, recognising social responsibility and appointing ethical people has been a long tradition of good organisations. Tata Steel is undoubtedly the best example of social responsibility. Rishi Patanjali has done seminal work in giving the world 195 sutras and he has given eight steps for human development through spiritual eight fold path. (Eight limbs of Yoga).

1. Yama—Social virtues recommended by Patanjali are Satya (truth), Ahimsa (Non-Violence) Brahmacharya (Continence or Chastity), Aastheya (non-stealing), aparigraha (non-covetousness). His vision is not to deprive others of what legitimately belongs to them. These are governing principles of social life.
2. Niyamas—Personal virtues are austerity, self study, cheerfulness, purity of mind (motives and intentions and surrender to god (synergy with the cosmic intelligence). Internal and External purification, contentment, study and worship of god.
3. Asana—Asanas are basically, physical exercises of body to feel fit and healthy.
4. Pranayama—controlling the vital force breath (prana) and nervous system with scientific breathing so that the whole physiological activity is well regulated.
5. Pratyahara—It is the turning mind inward on the self and judgement free watching of thoughts and vital energy. It is removing the blocks from the process.
6. Dharna—It is focussing the mind's attentions to a limited space of an inspiring object or theme/mantra and focussing on the light of the self (Chittasya desa bandhata). It is concentration on the key points of the project.
7. Dhyana—Focussing the mind on the chosen theme without destracting dissimilar thoughts (tatra pratyaya ekantanata). It is taking a holistic approach to system and process.
8. Samadhi-egoless state of excellence leading to the perfect illumination of the consciousness. You bring out best in this state. You totally abide in your own self. It is realisation and achievement of the goal[10]. According to Patanjali as soon as all impurities have been removed by the practice of spiritual disciplines—"the limbs of yoga"—a man's spiritual vision, opens to the light giving knowledge of the Atman. When one gains the Atma knowledge due to spontaneous

enlightment, he also obtains super natural powers of hearing, touch, sight, taste and smell.

In the context of industry/management these eight steps signify conservation of energy, settling down, regulating the life force, withdrawing the mind from destraction, retention of the mind, concentration, taking a holistic approach and ultimately realising and Achieving the goals/targets. Bringing spirituality in the work place has facilitated housing creativity, bringing about a work ambience free from tension, worry and stress. N.R. Narayan Murthy has emphasised trust worthiness in dealings, a supportive family, and leading a career - that makes a difference to the society.[11] Infosys is a living example of workplace spirituality. Work place spirituality has the following postulates in Indian context:

1. Making workplace sacred, clean and bringing orderliness and regularity; (Karma Kshetra as Dharma kshetra).
2. Empowering self by discovering the divinity in self (Aham Brahmasim) and in others (Tatwamasi).
3. Recognising work as an opportunity to offer divine service (Yogah Karmashu Kaushalam).
4. Recognising mission of life as continuation of God's mission of facilitating this creation (Isha Vasyam Idam Servam).
5. Working with zero errors, zero delay, zero wastage and zero accidents considering work as worship and efforts to bring perfection.
6. Caring for others by recognizing them as part of the family (Vasudhaiv Kutambakam).[12]

Spirituality is that advanced stage of mind in which peace, felicity, spiritual bliss, sato gunas-truth, equanimity and cheerfulness, large heartedness, universal love and knowledge of self become spontaneous and natural. To be in constant company of spiritually evolved persons who by their practical wisdom, can inspire peace and tranquillity within you.

Human beings are basically spiritual and spiritual values have lot of meaning for motivation, commitment, honesty and integrity. Spiritual practices and development in individual lead to six treasures namely control of mind (shama), Control of senses (Dama), coordination of words, thoughts and deeds (uparati), endurance (Titiksha), faith (Shraddha) and mental equilibrium. Indian spiritual practices can be very useful for Indian Managers who now-a-days suffer from stress, ill healthy, anxiety, indecision and subjectivity. Indian ethos of management, which seeks to give importance to human beings and spiritual values of life, has redefined the various terms of management below:[13]

Term	*General Western Definitions*	*Indian definitions*
Management	Getting things done by others	Helping ordinary people to produce
Productivity	Related to plant capacity	Related to man's capacity
Planning	MBO	MBS (Strategy)
Leadership	Produce results	Produce performers, help the subordinates to develop leadership qualities.
Effective Supervision	Concern for task and work	The growth of subordinates in their workplace.
Motivation	Maslow's theory of needs	Self motivation helping subordinates to have ananda (Creative joy) and Mukti (Autonomy) in their work.
Resources	External	Inner
Health of the Org	Balance Sheet (Profit)	People oriented Programme
Profitability	In term of money	In terms of good image, of veridibility and trust of customers.
Hygiene Factor	Job enrichment	Mind Enrichments
Structure	Hierarchy	Organic evolution
Growth	Turn over	Coordinating private and public benefits.
Manplacement	According to academic qualifications	Jnana (Bhakti) Yoga (Karma orientation)
Training	Development of functional skills	Balanced view of life and stress on yoga.

Taitreya upanishad has referred to five sheaths (Panch Kosha) in human body and various methods have been suggested by our ancient Indian thinkers to keep human beings physically sound, mentally alert and psychologically positive and full of zeal/motivation. As a daily routine if human being perform the following routine, they are found to remain healthy, happy and physically fit. The daily routine suggested is given below:[14]

Figure—Showing Daily Maintenance Routine

Panch-Kosh (Five Sheaths)	*Instrument*	*Accretion*	*Methodology*	*Time*
Anna Maya Kosh	Body	Poor Blood circulation	Surya Namashkar and Asanas	35 Minutes every day morning
Pranmaya Kosh (Life force)	Prana (Breath)	Inbalance in inhaling and exhaling	Pranayam and breathing exercises	20 minutes morning
Manomaya Kosh (Mind)	Mind	Anxiety	Meditation and praying Auto Suggestions	15 Minutes per day can be done in evening
Vijnana Maya Kosh (Awareness)	Intellect	Indecision	Dharma and Jap	10 to 20 minutes
Anand Maya Kosha (Happiness and Inner Joy)	Ego	Subjectivity	Dhyana and Transcen-dental meditation	30 minutes per day. (Morning and Evening)

Spirituality in the work place can at times result in surfacing various paradoxes and the conflict between appropriate ends and means. Spirituality in work place is more than a passing fancy; it is changing the fundamental nature of work. Individuals are searching for meaning in their work, a meaning that transcends mere economic gain. According to many authors maintaining an organisation spirituality is no easy task. About two decades back the Steel Authority of India had launched a concerted work culture drive with the following key features:

1. Stoppage of overtime payments.
2. Special effort to identify and act on habitual absentees.

3. Cessation of regularization of back-date absence.
4. Periodical surprise check on shift change delays, man to man relieving etc.
5. Stoppage of crowding by hordes of people when an accident occurs in the work-place.
6. Vigilance over unnecessary loitering about in the plant or going out of the factory gate during duty hours. Above basic ground rules are an eloquent proof of absence of chitta suddhi in managers and workers. The Bhagwat Gita has given the doctrine of Karma Yoga-work without hankering for its fruits.

In organisations an effective work culture based on spirituality needs to be created. This spiritual work culture involves fearlessness, purity, self control, sacrifice, straight forwardness, self-denial, calmness, absence of fault-finding, absence of greed, gentleness, modesty and absence of envy and pride. Mere work ethic is not enough; what is needed is the work ethic conditioned by ethics in work. Spirituality and service orientation in work can result in sound mental health of the managers and the workers. Some of the impediments to sound mental health are:

1. Greed—for power, position, prestige and paisa (Money) (4 PS).
2. Envy—regarding others achievements, success and rewards.
3. Egotism—about one's own accomplishments, qualification, and expertise.
4. Suspicion, anger and frustration.
5. Anguish through comparisons.

In the famous book "Is the American Dream killing you? How the market rules our lives", the author Paul Stiles says that what is needed is a global shift in consciousness—away from conspicuous consumption and towards a more meaningful balanced way of life. "Moderation" Stiles says "arises from a spiritual awakening, and elevation of consciousness, an awareness of the way things truly are" Human-kind lacks a universal spiritual solution. An elevation of consciousness can come from meditation, and spiritual lessons from Bhagwat Gita. Spiritual knowledge is the knowledge of the Atman the eternal truth of Brahma or self. Spiritual knowledge transcends the material and the transient to the enduring and the eternal. Albert Einstein once said; "When I read the Bhagavad Gita and reflect about how God created this universe, everything else seems so superfluous." Only through regular meditation, appropriate value system and correct perception, people can rise above the external vagaries of economic life in the modern age. In modern age people are generally suffering from Asuri work culture (Demonic work culture)—involving egoism, delusion, personal desires, improper performance, self-advancement and pride. In Katha Upanishad it is said : "Fools dwelling in darkness, but thinking themselves wise and erudite, go round and round, by various tortuous paths." In Chandogya Upanishad, it is said: "As one not knowing that a golden treasure lies buried beneath his feet may walk over it again and again, yet never finds it, so all beings live every moment in the city of Brahma, yet never find Him because of the veil of illusion by which he is concealed." People of this world are running after material and physical pleasures. In pursuit of Spiritual self awareness and realization, Indian scriptures have given four paths:

1. Jnan (gyan) Yoga - Vigilant discrimination to preserve nirdwandic poorna self.
2. Bhakti—Yoga-devotion to God.
3. Karma Yoga—work commitment with complete detachment from their results.
4. Raj Yoga—to practice psychic control through disciplined breathing and other exercises.

There is erosion of moral fibre and temptation to adopt immoral means—Tax evasion, illegitimate financial holdings, deliberate oversight in audit, improper financial reporting, money laundering and all kinds of economic offences for personal gains. This all needs to be corrected. Conducting meditation sessions or prayer meetings in office are not the only way to deal with spirituality. It needs to create a divine work culture and right leadership at all levels, whose beliefs are spiritually rooted and who believe in the dictum of work is workship. Spirituality is inherent in management decision making because all decisions are subjective. A more inclusive, holistic and peaceful approach of spirituality to management is needed for the upliftment of environmentally degrading and socially disintegrating world of our age. Spirituality is the art of living according to Indian sanskars and traditional oriental living. Spirituality encompasses a wide range of values including faith, coverage, compassions, integrity and justice and has an important place in management. Dalai Lama's book "Ethics for the new millennium" is a very popular book among business executives and the book, at one place says: "Spiritual audit of corporate America, indicates that 60 percent of the respondents believed that spirituality in the work place can be beneficial and righteous if it is not promoting a particular religion." Spiritualism in the work situations creates some of the following main issues:

1. "Can a person work for a tobbaco company while at the same time be a non-smoker and convinced of the ills of smoking?
2. Should orders about fake killing of terrorists/insurgents be obeyed by the police, can a policeman work in a terrorist infested area and kill some suspects when so ordered by his superior officers, realizing well that some of the suspects may be innocent?
3. To get customs clearance speed money is made by material manager?
4. Dronacharya's spirituality when he asked Eklavya for his thumb?
5. Do ends justify the means? Should we become rich by bank robbery?
6. What is the logic for an American soldier fighting in Iraq or should Indian soldiers fight in Sri Lanka against LTTE?

5. Organisational Leadership and Spirituality

An individual Leader whose beliefs are spiritually rooted can bring about transformational change within the organization. Mahatma Gandhi's life is a living example of how one leader can bring change in big country like India and inspire thousands of people to die for Indian independence. Romani Rolland has said about Mahatma Gandhi.

"Mahatma Gandhi has the spirit of religious faith and clarity seeking to find a new humanity. He was a saint who was often spoken about with veneration .... with Gandhiji everything is nature, modest, simple, pure—while all his struggles are hallowed by religious serenity." The Mahatma, an incorrigible idealist, was a revolutionary leader of men and was obliged on occasion to over-dramatise a situation and exaggerate certain aspects of it to rouse adequate mass favour. Mahatma Gandhi gave India non-cooperation movement and Quit India movement. His movements were based on principle on non-violence. C.F. Andrews has said Mahatma Gandhi's marvelous spiritual genius has appealed to me in a very different way. For his character, in his own way he is great and creative. It is of more ascetic order. He has an air of religious faith. Organisational leaders have great responsibilities in the context of workplace spirituality. They have to keep an eye on the bigger pictures. They should remain calm in the eye of the storm and act with courage. They must integrate spiritual dimension with the organisational work. They should always listen to their inner-voice and set example of work as worship. They should always follow the path of righteousness. Depree (1989), Etzioni (1993), Fairhohm (1997), Green Leaf (1977), Hawley (1993), Keifer (1992), J. Maxwell and Vaill (1989) are well known authors who propounded theory of spiritual leadership. Leadership involves influencing people's souls rather than controlling action. Leaders should commit to the care of the whole person, they must include spiritual care into their practice.

Organisational leaders, besides having knowledge about markets, technology, strategic planning and human behaviour in organizations must have knowledge of Brahma Vidya or the spiritual knowledge. They must realize that the same spiritual power (Atma/soul) resides in all his employees. Leaders must recognize their social responsibilities and ethical values of life. He should be well-versed in turn-around management and empowerment of his subordinates. Leaders must learn to build up permanent and powerful organization and must learn to share power with others. Successor planning is an important task for the leaders. Mahatma Gandhi was a great organizational leader who had clear vision and mission, was a great strategist and was always leading from the front. He was a good mentor, organizer, planner, effective communicator and great team builder. According to Jawahar Lal Nehru "The amazing thing about Gandhiji was that he adhered, in all fullness to his ideals, his concept of truth and yet he succeeded in moulding and moving enormous masses of human beings. He moulded a whole generation." Dr. Debashis Chatterjee, Professor at IIM Lucknow writes. "I am proud I belong to a rich country that NR Narayan Murthy calls his home. He has left behind a glorious legacy. He has taught us that wealth is not for safe keeping, but for sharing" NR Narayana Murthy, mentor of Infosys appeals to the generative capacity of a nation now moving from rags to riches. That is why he is an icon of several generations. In about 30 years Infosys has earned international recognition as a MNC due to its leadership who had spiritual orientation. The mission statement and the concern for the common man is quite evident in working of Infosys. About 10% of the management teachers at best business schools like Harvard Business School, North Western's Kelkogg School of Business and the University of Michigan's Ross School of Business are now of Indian descent. Indian born strategists are helping transform corporation. C.K. Prahalad, Ramcharan, and Vijay Govindrajan are among the world's hottest business gurus advising some of the tops US Companies. Organizational leaders and executives should be motivated by a broader purpose than money. According to Prof. C.K. Prahlad corporations can simultaneously create value and social justice. According to Prof. Ram Charan, "the key point is to put purpose before self. This is absolutely applicable to corporate leadership today." Many of these management gurus are linking some of their theories to or deriving them from Indian Philosophy contained in Bhagwat Gita and Upanishads. In the Bhagavat Gita the nature of a perfect man who is spiritually evolved in full is fit for providing inspirational leadership. Only such persons should be the leaders, who has subdued their self, from whom desire has fled, through "renunciation", attains the supreme state. Leaders should be endowed with pure intellect, abandoning hatred, having abandoned egoism, power, arrogance, anger and aggrandizement. An organization leader who has spiritual orientation should have vigour, forgiveness, fortitude, purity absence of hatred and absence of pride.

Spiritually oriented leadership must aim at upliftment of the human spirit and soul by his ethical conduct and good decision making policies. He must re-kindle the hearts of the employees by respecting their skills, talents and performance, and by appointing the right persons, whose value systems are correct. They must treat people like great assets and not liabilities. They should themselves follow ethical conduct and get socially oriented to a open culture which enriches or contributes to the well being of all who come in contact with them. The organization leaders must build a human culture which can fulfill the inner aspirations and motivations of the people, getting the best performance out of them and make them feel wanted and enhance their self esteem. Dave Packard, the legendary cofounder of HP believed in a value system where employees are able to accomplish something collectively that they could not accomplish separately and also "make a contribution to society" a phrase which sounds trite but is fundamental. It is this kind of underlying philosophy that drives several hundred centers of Rama Krishna Mission which are doing excellent work under leadership of saffron clad swamijis. One important task of an organization leader is to choose wisely and utilize scarce resources optimally. During the curtain raiser before the Mahabharat war, Duryodhana choose large army of Lord Krishna as his help while Arjun selected Shri Krishna for his support. This episode gives us a clue as to the nature and decision-making of an organizational leader the former chose numbers, the latter wisdom. Decision making by leaders must be done with great care and long term strategic planning. The true investment in the knowledge society is not in machines or tools but in the knowledge of the knowledge workers. It is the Bhagwat Gita which considers each human being as infinite, omnipresent, omniscient spirit—the Atman-eternally pure, eternally perfect. Like any other knowledge, spirituality needs to be taught, the soul can receive impulse from another soul. That soul from which this impulse comes is called the guru, the teacher and the soul to which the impulse is conveyed is called the disciple. It is mysterious law of nature, that as soon as the field is ready, the seed must come, as soon as the soul wants religion, the transmitter of religious force must come. There is nothing higher and holier than the knowledge which comes to the soul transmitted by a spiritual teacher. Bhagwat Gita gives us insight into (*i*) turn around management, (*ii*) transformational management, (*iii*) empowerment, (*iv*) learning organizations, (*v*) vision, (*vi*) internal and external management and, (*vii*) ethical values. The turn around must first occur in mind. The Punjab Petro Chemicals Ltd. was in for three crore loss. By positively tackling the situation through teachings of Gita, the company was turned around in six months and it started earning profits. We find that Arjun was transformed by the sermons of Lord Krishna and as Mahabharat indicates he stood steady on the ground with bow and arrows in hand, lessons of Karma Yoga transformed him. Bhagwat Gita contains main tenets of Bhakti Yoga, Karma Yoga, Gyana Yoga and Dhyana Yoga. Bhagwat Gita gives us insight into internal and external management. Right speech, right work, right earnings, right exercise, reality, right meditation, right intention and right vision constitute internal management. Love and dedication, work and recognition, knowledge and learnings trust and responsibility are the areas of external management.

Swami Vivekananda was a great spiritual leader who built up Ram Krishna Mission with its branches all over the world. His organizational ability, communication skill, team building and setting example by his own deeds are all ideals for managers and leaders to imbibe. Kathopanishad offers an excellent definitions of the art of living. The art of living is nothing but the art of choosing wisely. Dipak Jain, Dean of the Kellogg School of Business prides himself on introducing an elective programme called "Soul of Leadership" at Kellogg in 2002-03. Quoting instances from the Mahabharata, Jain elucidates. "We tell our students that having an exit plan for business project is as important as having an entry plan." Abhimanyu's chakravyhu hence finds relevance in the present context." The economic boom as well as the gradual emergence of Indian MNCs drive this interest of western business people in Indian Philosophy. The Bhagvat Gita makes a penetrating analysis of the human psyche and the process of human motivation. The penetrating insight it creates helps us to think in terms of self motivation as an instrument not only for achieving organizational goals but also for injecting vitality and dynamism in it. Vinoba Bhave, Mahatma Gandhi, Swami Vivekananda, BG Tilak, Aurobindo and Rama Krishna have lived and demonstrated the practical wisdom before our own eyes.

6. Global Shift Towards Spiritualism

Today there is a global shift in consciousness away from conspicuous consumption and towards, a more meaningful, balanced way of life. According to Paul Stiles, moderation arises from a spiritual awakening, an elevation of consciousness, an awareness of the way things truly are human kind seems to have finally evolved a universal economic solution (the free market) and a universal political solution (democracy) on a global basis but what it still lacks is a universal spiritual solution. The "Atma-Brahman equation" has been described as the solution in modern quantum mechanics in atleast eleven best selling books in the world, all written by western scientists. One book "TAO of Physics" by Fritjoj Capra, another book "Mysticism and the new physics" by Michael Talbot, the third book, "The eye of the Shiva" by Armory de Reincourt, are most inspiring books on Spiritualism. For Franke, since spirituality is in its essence self-transcendence, it brings with it human freedom. When a person exercises spiritual freedom and responsibility, there follows a host of effects: Peace of mind, good conscience and contentment. The second truth "This universe is connected not spiritually but physically" has been discovered in 1965 after EPR Paradox. J.S. Bell of Bell Laboratory discovered the Bell's theorem, which showed that I and you, are basically connected. In 1985 with all the perfections of Bell's theorem experiments, it was found that a star near the sun and you and I are all at this moment physically connected instantaneously. Management science is learning from ancient Indian Wisdom. There is a historic shift from effective control to self management. This historic shift to self management offers organizations four main ways to best develop and motivate knowledge workers; (*i*) Know people's strengths; (*ii*) place them where they can make the greatest contribution; (*iii*) treat them as associates and (*iv*) expose them to challenges.

7. The Universal Laws and Spirituality

According to Swami Vivekananda universe is an ocean of matter. This in an ocean of ether, in which we find the sun, moon, stars and ourselves in different states of solidity; but the continuity is not broken, it is the same through out. This universe is a unit of Pran, and Akasa, force and matter. Unity is the law, physically, psychically, mentally, morally and meta physically, it is all one". Natural laws, based on principles, operate regardless of our awareness of them or our obedience to them. Natural laws or universal laws are part of the human condition, consciousness and conscience. Those who live in harmony with such basic principles as fairness, equity, justice, integrity, honesty and trust, progress and become successful. Dr. Deepak Chopra, the doyen of management in USA draws inspiration from Vedantic philosophy to redefine spiritual laws of success. When this knowledge is incorporated in one's consciousness, it proves the ability to attain wealth with effortless ease. It is our limitations which compel us to search for the soul and this is the starting point of spiritual quest. There are two things: waves, which compose our knowledge and that which is beyond the waves. The starting point of spiritual quest lies between these two. Bhagwad Gita keynote is the spirit of Nishkam Karma which implies the following:-

1. Work is sacrifice.
2. Work is necessary for Chitta Shuddhi (Self Purification- Purification of Spirit).
3. Work is to be done as a homage to the indwelling supreme-work is worship.

Spiritual Laws of the Universe

1. The Law of Pure Potential—According to Swami Vivekanand "Each soul is potentially divine. The goal is to manifest this divinity within, by controlling nature, external and internal. Do this either by work, or worship or psychic control of Philosophy by one or more or all of theses and be free". For achieving success, one must take sometime each day for his self-realization by any of the means mentioned above.
2. The Law of Giving—The second spiritual law of success is the law of giving; the more you give, the more you receive because you will keep the abundance of the universe circulating in your life.

3. The Law of Karma or cause and effect—Karma is both action and consequence of that action. It is the cause and effect simultaneously because every action generates forces and energy that returns to us in like kind. If we want happiness, we must learn to sow the seeds of happiness. In spiritual terms the efforts we put into seeking divinity becomes our sadhana or spiritual discipline. Sadhana is essentially a code of self-imposed discipline and practice for spiritual upliftment. Sadhana raises the consciousness from the physical to the meta physical, conferring peace, tranquility grace and divine bliss. Our worldly activities earn us a living and our sadhana earns us the bliss of enlightened life.
4. The law of least effort—Nature functions with effortless ease and carefree abandon; flowers automatically bloom, fish just swim, grass just grows. Joseph Campbell puts it; "We must be willing to get rid of the life we have planned, so as to have the life that in waiting for us". We must listen to soft whispers at cross-roads moments.
5. The law of intention and desire—In the universal scheme energy and information exist everywhere in nature. In fact at the level of quantum field, there is nothing other than energy and information.
6. The Law of Detachment—In order to acquire anything in the physical universe, one has to relinquish attachment to it.
7. The Law of Dharma or Purpose in Life—There are three components to the Law of Dharma. The first component says that each one of us is here to discover out true self. The second component is to express our unique talent. The third is the service to humanity and to serves one's fellow human beings. Hyrum W. Smith has given the following ten natural laws for successful Time and Life management :
    1. You control your life by controlling your time.
    2. Your governing values are the foundation of personal success and fulfillment.

3. When your daily activities reflect your governing values, you experience inner peace.
4. To reach any significant goal, you must leave your comfort zone.
5. Daily planning leverages time through increased focus.
6. Your behaviour is a reflection of what you truly believe.
7. You satisfy needs when your beliefs are in line with reality.
8. Negative behaviours are overcome by changing incorrect beliefs.
9. Your self esteem must ultimately come from within.
10. Give more and you will have more.[15]

According to Swami Vivekanand, the greatest help to spiritual life is meditation (Dhyana). In meditation we divest ourselves of all material conditions and feel our divine nature. The less the thought of the body, the better. For it is the body that drags us down. It is attachment, identification, which makes us miserable. That is the secret to think that I am the spirit and not the body. I am the witness." According to Holy Quran, Allah is always ready to guide the one who submits to him in all humility, earnestness and gratefulness. Every follower must be able to realize the depths of his growing spiritual consciousness that he is an inseparable part of universal consciousness. The Holy Quran says. "Eat your Lord's Provision and give thanks to Him." Every follower of Islam should be a true embodiment of spiritual and social stability and harmony. According to Swami Madhavananda work done in the spirit of sacrifice can accelerate this gradual cleaning process—*i.e.* Chitta Shuddhi, which according to Sri Shankaracharya is a pre-requisite for true understanding of the Atman (Soul). If an individual violates the spiritual laws for his own development, he will cause injury not only to himself but to the society. Spiritual life always implies something higher than itself towards which it is ascending, ethical existence is the highest manifestation of spirituality. We find many drug barons, mafia leaders and terrorist leaders who are simultaneously ruthless and immoral while being a devout follower of a religion or sect. Spirituality is not the same as religion although frequently used synonymously. While religion deals with rituals, beliefs, religious symbols and prayers, spirituality refers to non-material matters that concern the spirit, mind and consciousness of the individuals, it is personal and individual. Spirituality can encompass a wide range of values and ethical practices including compassion, integrity, justice, wisdom and honesty. Patanjali Yoga sutra has given us spiritual values of life namely Maitri (friendliness) Karuna (Compassion) Mudita (Delight or sympathetic joy) and Upeksha (indifference or disregard for the wicked). The philosophy of total spiritual transformation of the perceiver (drusta), the feeler and the thinker, all at once, is the prime contribution that the Gita has to make to this timeless tradition of the Hindu Culture.

8. Spirituality-Ethical Conduct and Management

Spiritual and ethical aspects need to be given great importance today in view of the clashes of personalities, succession feuds, top level manipulations and board room fights in the corporate sector. Many successful business executives, who can identify their organizational mission, do not think about the purpose of human life. Prof. S.K. Chakraborty of IIM Calcutta, Ahmedabad Management Association, and a number of Vedantic Scholars have developed a series of concepts, programmes and case studies to inculcate ethical conduct and spirituality based on concepts and Theories derived from ancient Indian Vedantic literature particularly the Patanjali Yoga Sutras, Bhagavad Gita, Upanishads, Mahabharat and traditional Indian Literature. Conferences, seminars and short training programmes are being conducted for managers with some of the following topics.

1. Promoting a spirit-centred leadership style to generate happiness, in the work place performance.
2. Role of spirituality in transforming contemporary management theory and practices and emphasizing Karma Yoga work is worship.
3. Developing ethical values and an open organizational culture for integrating perception of self and identity into management context.

4. Introducing various asanas and breathing exercises for executives and employees to cure their stress, instability and dizziness and make them lead a balanced healthy life.
5. Ethical conduct and corporate culture.

In managerial role before taking a course of action many times one should ask at least some of the following questions to determine whether it is truly ethical:-

1. Is it reasonable? 2. Is it responsible? 3. Is it fair? 4. Will I think well of myself after this action? 5. How will some one look up to do it? 6. Is it honest?

Above mentioned questions can guide corporate world to follow ethical conduct and be able to listen to one's little voice within. Ethical decision making can help the corporate world to follow fair practices. As a corporate leader one must act in accordance with ethical values and should give only legal and ethical orders to subordinates to carry on. Stanley Mingram has said "Once you accept another person's authority, you become a different person. You are only concerned with how will you follow out given orders rather than whether it is right or wrong." Only one third of even significant minority do not want to carry out unethical or illegal orders. They constitute a power center which no authority can influence because of the integrity of their moral composure and spiritual strength of character. Therefore corporate world must charter its course of action based on ethical values following the moral code of conduct. In one of the international seminar on life management, Swami Sukh Bodhananda has said; "Proceed positively, prepare prayerfully, plan purposefully and pursue persistently." An organizational leader must possess the following five values namely integrity, sensitivity, creative thinking, confidence and service mindedness. Sri Aurobindo talking about Indian mind has said: "The instinct of the Indian mind was that, if a reconstruction of ideas and of society was to be attempted, it must start from a spiritual basis and take from the first a religious motive and form." In the corporate world there are many leaders who are blazing that spiritual path, albeit independently—providing examples to inspire and guide others to do the same. "We have interviewed spirituality inspired leaders around the world and have found that for some, leading by example and keeping spirituality implicit in their leadership, works best. A European Corporate executive said: "The explicit part of business is the house holding or economic operation and the implicit part of the business is to support the employees' spiritual quest in opening up. "Kyocera, a Japanese company that makes cell phones, prominently displays various spiritual covenants on their website Corporate Motto : Respect the Divine and love people; preserve the spirit to work fairly and honourably, respecting people, our work, our company, and our global community. In 2002 four international business organization began sponsoring "International spirit at work" with the intention to bring to public recognition organizations whose spiritual based practices, policies and procedures help to make the world a better place. In India their are very large number of companies which are in their modest way supporting spirituality based business deals. Spiritual intelligence has three main components; first Integrity being true to one's values, convictions and conscience, and having a connection with the infinite, second, meaning having a sense of contribution to people and to causes; and third voice-aligning our work with our unique talents or gifts and our sense of calling.

9. India the Citadel of Spiritualism

According to Swami Chinmayananda the road sign "U Turn" could be taken as an indicator that we ought to turn the direction of our life towards spirituality instead of trying to change others." In India, from time immemorial, people took up spiritualism in right earnest. They contain all that is needed to guide human beings on the holy path of spiritualism. The majority of Indian People, even illiterate and poor villagers, are highly spiritual, God fearing and religious by their sanskars and pattern of living. Even when they are not able to read and write, but they have learnt religious practices from their ancestors and elders. India is the land of spirituality and universal tolerance.

Spiritual leadership involves influencing people's souls rather than controlling action. Spirituality in the unique, personal significance of the inner voice of the soul which has at the nexus of talent (your natural gifts and strengths), passion (those things that naturally energize, excite, motivate and inspire you), need (including what the world needs enough to pay you for) and conscience (that still, small voice within that assures you of what is right and that prompts you to actually do it). Muhammad Yunus, founder of the Grameen Bank of Bangladesh and Nobel Prize winner in 2006, could establish the system of micro-credit to the poorest of the poor, by just trying to help someone very poor and the vision was evolved. Today Grameen bank works for more than 46000 villages in Bangladesh through 1267 branches and over 12000 staff members. Great vision comes as people see human needs and respond to their conscience. One can get a vision of the soul (Atman) by sravana (listening to religious discourses), manana (pondering over and analysis of what has been heard) and nidhidhyana (meditation and devotion). Spiritualism has created many missionary organizations which are doing great service to the humanity like Ramakrishna Mission and Chinmaya Mission, which have opened many educational schools, hospitals and other service institutions. The following managerial issues can be scanned, and resolved, using the concepts, principles, and processes from Indian Psycho-Philosophy of Spiritualism: (1) Creativity, (2) Concentration, (3) Team work, trust and cooperation, (4) leadership, (5) Conflict-resolution, (6) Counseling, (7) Managerial/ business ethics, (8) Stress/burnout syndrome, (9) Top Executive loneliness, (10) Inner harmony, (11) Motivation and (12) Theory and method of work etc. Indian Institute of Management Calcutta had started a course on "Managerial effectiveness and value systems" in 1983 and a number of officers/managers have been benefited from such course. Quality of life should be termed as quality of domestic life (QDL) and there should be harmony, peace and virtuous family life of managers and all employees of the organization. Indian business leaders are now emphasizing spiritualism even in the realm of corporate sector and business organizations. There are many reported case studies how spiritualism has helped the organizations and a few example reported are as under:-

1. Productivity miracle at Jalandhur—Standard Electricals Company which had only Rs. 2 Crore monthly sale and Rs. 5 lakh monthly profit, on the average, in the first ten months of the financial year, catapulated to an average of Rs. 4 crore (double) sale

and Rs. 50 lakh (Ten Times) profit in the rest two months of the same financial year (Suresh Pandit report in Indian Wisdom for management).

2. Breakthrough in industrial relations and productivity through Bhakti model (Menon Piston Ltd Kolhapur an ISO 9002 company).

The four magnificent parts of human nature consist of body, mind, heart and spirit. Spiritual intelligence represents our drive for meaning and connections with the infinite. Spiritualism and ethical code of conduct are needed to reduce the following chronic problems of globalisation:-

(*i*) Back biting, infighting, victimism, defensiveness, not sharing information.

(*ii*) Ambiguity, hidden agenda, political game and chaos.

(*iii*) Apathy, moonlighting, boredom, anger, fear.

(*iv*) Misalignments, hypocrisies, inter departmental rivalry.

Spiritual awakening and rekindling of the inner spirit is the answer to these problems.

From 1983 onwards Indian Institute of Management Calcutta has been conducting a course on "Managerial Effectiveness—The Indian Ethos for the second year post graduate students. Many batches of IAS coming to IIM Calcutta were also exposed to various ideas described above and it found very good response even from Muslims, Sikhs, Christians and others. Indian scriptures detail the path of the inner ascent, the inward journey by which the individual soul gets at the ultimate reality. It is only when one's gaze turns inwards, away from the worldly attractions, can absolute truth regarding the mysteries of life since the real at the heart of the universe is reflected in the depths of the soul. Regarding practical spirituality, the first and foremost task before us is to control the vast mass of sunken thoughts the control of the unconscious and the next is to go beyond the conscious when the super conscious state is reached man becomes free and divine. The great help to spiritual life is meditation (Dhyana). Swami Sukhabodhananda is a corporate management guru who has infused management science with the much needed dose of ethics and spirituality. In India, USA, U.K. and Switzerland, his self development programmes have benefited many leaders of the corporate world. Spiritualism helps us to a peaceful and better living one needs eyes of spirit (divya chakshu) to behold the ever-luminous self and guides us to the divine knowledge which enables a seeker to embark on an inner voyage of self-realization and a life of perfect harmony, peace and bliss.

> "Like the winds of the sea
>
> are the ways of fate;
>
> As we voyage along through life,
>
> 'Tis the set of a soul
>
> That decides its goal,
>
> And not the calm or the strife"
>
> Ella Wheeler Wilcox

While science and western materialism get us physical comforts, spirituality brings us mental calm. We need to create a balance between material comforts oriented science and spirituality. In Katha Upanishad it is said: "Know the self (Individual Self) as the master of the chariot, and the body as the chariot. Know the intellect as the charioteer and the mind as verily the bridle. They call the organs the horses the organs having been imagined as horses, (know) the objects as the road. The discriminating people call that self the enjoyer when it is associated with body, organs and mind (Kath I. III. IV) Arise, awake and learn by approaching the excellent ones (Spiritual teachers). The self is a smokeless light of the size of a thumb. One of the India's great spiritual guru Shri Aurobindo Ghosh has talked about the special spiritual responsibility of India; not only to create material prosperity, but to lead towards the next stage of evolution of life forms in this world towards what he calls the "super-man" concept.

Spirituality as a Way Towards Better Work-life Balance

Corporates who inculcate a spiritual ethos at workplace, gain a more satisfying way towards better work-life balance. Spirituality is the inner journey of leading to compassionate doing, it reinforces the notion of universal inter-connectedness. Spiritual intelligence is our ability to experience, acknowledge and discern a sense of invisible order in worldly disorders. A host of organisations including South West Airlines and Lucent technologies are tapping the human spirit at work to attract and maintain a motivated, performance boosting workforce. A Google search on spirituality and Management throws over six million hits while the number of hits for spirituality and Business were over 16 million and spiritual and organisation over five million on the internet. There seems to be a sort of spiritual renaissance as the fourth wave of the spirituality after the technological "third wave" through out the world. Books about the ensoulment of corporate life have been hitting best-sellers lists. Mitroff, II and Denton E.A. (1999) book. "A spiritual Audit of corporate America" Jossey Bass Publishers Sam Franciso CA., Naylor T.H., Willimon W.H. and Osterberg R (1996) "The search for meaning in the workplace", Abington Press; Mashvilla T.N., Renesch J (1992), New Traditions in Business. Spirit and Leadership in the 21st Century", San Francisco; Elkins, David, "Beyond Religion: A personal program for building a spiritual life outside the walls of traditions and religion;" Manzz C.C., Manz K.K., Marx R, and Neck, CP., (2001). "The wisdom of solomon at work. Ancient virtues for living and leading today"—published by Barrett Kochiler San Francisco, are just some of the most popular books today. Mitroff and Denton (1999) offer a spirited case that companies fostering a spiritual environment tend to have employees who are more creative, adaptive and productive to change. Companies such as ACC, Reckitt and Colman, Indian Petrochemicals Corporation, the Oriental bank, SRF Ltd., Tata Tea and Tata Chemicals, Birla group of companies, Mahindra and Mahindra, Arvind Mills, Escort, Dabur, Bajaj, Hero Honda, DCM Sriram, Ashok Leyland, Ballarpur Industries, Eicher Kinetic group, Infosys, Reliance, Ranbaxy, Wipro are now all committed to corporate social responsibility and are organising various programmes like Art of Living programmes for conducting Yoga and meditation classes. It is now well accepted that an organisation must foster a culture that facilitates realisation of the worker's craving for belongingness, self-actualisation and meaningfulness aiming at holistic integration between the organisation and its employees at the level of soul, based on a strong foundation of values. The Bhagvad Gita has always propogated the principles of Karma Yoga in which results are supposed to be provided by God. Stephen R. Covey (2004) in his book "The 8th Habit - From effectiveness to greatness writes—Gandhi is a beautiful example of a person who developed enormous moral authority through vision, discipline and passion governed by conscience - and the world is different because of him. India, the second largest nation in the world, with over a billion people, is an independent democracy because of him". Business, management, organisations all are parts of life and deal with human beings, they all need to reinforce themselves with spiritual strength. Successful organisations will have to know how to nurture spiritual development in others. Hindu Philosophy speaks of the four purusharthas—dharma (Religion), artha (economic activity), Kama (craving for sex, wealth amd lust for sensuous pleasures) and Moksha (liberation and spiritual illumination). Spirit is at the back of and beyond all religions. Lust, anger and greed, egoism, defeat and victory, loss or gains pain and pleasure, grief and joy are all essential parts of human life. The health of the human body is very important and therefore it is folly to neglect it. The road to spirituality comes from desire to surmount major crises successfully. Peter B. Vaill, in his book "Spirited Leading and Learning" has observed that we are searching for new ways of grounding to sustain us through very turbulent times." Corporations are now seeking to inculcate spirituality in work place by providing meditation rooms, beginning meetings with moments of silence, inspiring core value statements, inspirational saying or multi-faith prayers, providing employees training to encourage spiritual development, and providing leadership in living spiritual values.[17] Spirituality originates from inside, but it also involves a feeling of being connected with one's work and with others.[18] Infosys and Wipro are the two most well known companies who have steadfastly promoted and practiced ethical precepts in management by always listening to their inner conscience. Spirituality in the work place ensures that employees find nourishment for both vertical and horizontal dimensions of their work in a conducive work culture. According to Thompson, "In some cases more spirited companies out performed the others by 400-500 percent in terms of net earning, return on investment and share holder value."[19] In the present day globalisation race, there is a definite need to attend to the spiritual aspects of the employees and catering to their spiritual needs to survive in the long run. The World Bank, under the leadership of Richard Barrett, launched the Spiritual unfoldment Society in 1993 and Danah Zohar and Iam Marshall advocated. Spiritual Quotient (SQ) as the ultimate and unique human intelligence towards the beginning of the 21st century. Spiritual Quotient is "Uniquely human and linked to humanity need for meaning, our longing and capacity for meaning vision and value. It allows us to dream and to strive. It underlines the things we believe in and the role our beliefs and values play in the actions we take. It is in essence, what makes us human."[20] Stephen R.Covey in his book the 8th Habit—from effectiveness to greatness (2004) has propounded that the whole person of human nature (Body, Mind, Heart, Spirit, Soul) can give us an uncommon ability to explain, predict and diagnose the greatest problems and challenges. In the table given below he has summarised the personal and professional (organisational) challenges.[21]

Table Showing Challenges

Personal Challenges	*Professional / Organisational Challenges*
1. Finance, Money	1. Work load, deadlines-inability to reach goals.
2. Life Balance—not enough time	2. Insufficient time and resources.
3. Health	3. Financial survival
4. Relationships-Spouse, Child/teen, friends	4. Low trust
5. Driving Raising and disciplining children	5. Disempowerment
6. Self doubt	6. Change and uncertainty
7. Uncertainly, change	7. Staying current with technology
8. Lack of skill, Education	8. Confusion-lack of shared vision and values
9. Lack of Meaning	9. Job satisfaction-don't enjoy work
10. Lack of Peace	10. Lack of integrity in boss/top management.

Once a person takes the whole person approach—body, mind, heart and spirit in a synergistic manner, life is driven by a higher wisdom, by a divine conscience whose ethic is finding oneself through the service to others, doing well by doing good. Winston Churchill has said: "To every man there comes in his life time that special moment when he is figuratively tapped on the shoulder and offered a chance to do a very special thing, unique in him and fitted to his talents. What a tragedy if that moment finds him unprepared or unqualified for the work which would be his finest hour." Every human being is precious, endowed with enormous, almost infinite potential and capacity. When a person exercises spiritual freedom and responsibility, there follows a host of effects:- peace of mind, good conscience and contentment, a sense of fulfillment and a blessed Joy. In Yoga sutras of Patanjali it is said, "when you are inspired by some great purpose, some extraordinary project, all your thoughts break their bounds. Your mind transcends limitations, your consciousness expands in every direction and you find yourself in a new, great and wonderful world."

References

1. Authors are deeply indebted to their spiritual guru and mentor Param Poojya Swami Iswarananda Giri founder of Samvit Sadhnayan Mount Abu for spiritual guidance and directly imparting spiritual training. This article is dedicated to his lotus feet.
2. S.K. Chakraborty : Foundations of Managerial Work—Contributions from Indian Thought—Himalaya Publishing House, Mumbai, Second edition 1998, Reprint 2003, p. 7.
3. Sri Sri Ravi Shankar mesmerises management Fraternity- Mumbai, 30 June 2006. AIMA News—Vol. 10 Issue 3. May- June 2006, pp. 5-6.
4. The Dalai Lama-Science and Spirituality, Times of India - New Delhi 10th Dec., 2006. Extract from Inaugural address at a conference on Science and spirituality in Modern India.
5. Swami Iswarananda Giri, The call of the divine—Discourses by Swami Iswarananda Giri, Published by Samvit Sadhanayana, Mt Abu, 2004.
6. Viveka Cudamani of Sri Sankaracarya—Translated by Swami Turiyananda—Sri Ram Krishna Math—Madras, 1991, pp. 54-57 Sloka 124-132.
7. J. Singh Rekindling the Heart and soul of management Interfaces—Vikalpa, Vol. 29, No. 2, April-June 2004.
8. Prof. S.K. Chakraborti—Foundation of Managerial work - Contribution from Indian thought—Mumbai Second Editions 1998 Reprint 2003, pp. 24-45.

9. Swami Someswarananda—Basic Principles in Indian wisdom for management MAMTAMA Centre, Ahmedabad, 1996.
10. Patanjali Yoga Sutra—Swami Prabhavananda Sri Ramakrishna Math-Mylapore-Madras 2004, p. 96.
11. N.R. Narayan Murthy—Blissful knowledge—The six pillars of Corporate Wisdom—Extract of speech at the Wharton Business School, Times of India—10th Aug., 2001.
12. Shri Suresh Pandit—Successful Innovations—Indian wisdom for Management—Ahmedabad Management Association, 1996, pp. 137-144.
13. Swami Someswarananda—Basic Principles in Indian Wisdom for Management MAMTA—AMA Centre for Indian wisdom for management Ahmedabad, Management Association Ahmedabad, 1996, pp. 19-20.
14. Consult for guidelines D.K.S. Iyenger—Light on Yoga, An Instruction Book on Yoga—Vivekanand Kendra Madras; Swami Chinmayanand a manual for self unfoldment Mumbai. Dr. K.M. Mathur—Managing Human Resource Development—An Indian Perspective, Gyan Publishing House, New Delhi, 2001.
15. Hyrum W. Smith—10 Natural Laws of successful time and life management (Warner Books).
16. Stephen R. Covey—The 8th Habit—from effectiveness to greatness. Simon and Schuster. London 2004, pp. 348-349.
17. Srinivas, Kalburgi, "Workplace Spirituality. An American Affirmation Chinamaya Management Review, Vol. 3, 1999, pp. 33-46.
18. Ashmos D.P. and Duchan D. (2000) "Spirituality at Work—Conceptualization and Measure", Journal of Management Enquiry. Vol. 9, No. 2, pp. 134-45.
19. Thompson W.D. (2000) "can you train people to be spiritual?" Training and Development Vol. 54 No. 12, pp. 18-19. Also India's most respected Companies—Business World, 27th January 2003.
20. Danala Zohar and Ian Marshall : SQ: Connecting with our spiritual Intelligence (New York and London: Bloomsbury 2000).
21. Stephen R. Covey—The 8th Habit from effectiveness to Greatness, Sinon and Schuster—London 2004. A viacom Company, p. 311.

8

Strategic Human Resource Management

Companies die because their managers focus on the economic activity of producing goods and services, and they forget that their organisation's true nature is that of a community of humans. *Arie De Gevs (The Living Company)*

The objective of this chapter is to indicate the significance of the business context in developing an understanding of the meaning and application of strategic human resource management and to analyse the relationship between strategic management and strategic human resource management. Alfred Chandler has defined strategy as: "the determination of the basic long term goals and objectives of an organisation, and the adoption of course of action and the allocation of resources necessary for those goals". Strategy is often viewed at three levels: firstly at the 'Corporate' level which relates to the overall scope of the organisation, its structure, financing and distribution of key resources; secondly at a 'business' level, which relates to its competitive positioning in markets/products/services, thirdly at an operational level, which relates to the methods used by the various functions; marketing, finance, productions and of course human resources to meet the objectives of the higher level strategies. However the rigid separation of strategy from operations is no longer valid in a knowledge based age. During the last 25 years, management of people within the organisations has moved from the sidelines to centre stage. It has evolved from *being highly critical of the personnel functions' contribution to the organisation as being weak, non-strategic and lacking a theoretical base* (Drucker, 1968; Watson, 1977; Legge, 1978; Purcell, 1985), through the development of human resource management models and frameworks (Beer et al., 1948; Fombrun et al., 1984; Schular and Jackson, 1987; Guest, 1987), to critics of the HRM concept who question the empirical, ethical, theoretical and practical base of the subject (Legge, 1995; Keenoy, 1990; Blyton and Turnbull, 1992; Kennoy and Anthony, 1992), to a wave of strategic human resource management literature focusing on the link or vertical integration between human resource practices and an organisation's business strategy, in order to enhance performance (Schular and Jackson, 1987; Kochan and Barocci, 1985; Miles and Snow, 1984), and on the relationship between best-practices or high-commitment HR practices and organisational performance (Pfeffer, 1994, 1998; Huselid, 1995; MacDuffie, 1995; Guest, 2001). R. Whittington (1993, 2001) has very briefly identified the various typology of strategy as given in Table 1.

Table 1.1. Whittington's Typology of Strategy

	Classical	*Processual*	*Evolutionary*	*Systemic*
Strategy	Formal and Planned	Grafted and emergent	Efficient	Embedded
Rationale	Profit maximization	Vague	Survival of the fittest	Local
Focus	Fitting internal plans to external context	Internal (Politics)	External (Markets)	External (Societies)
Processes	Analytical	Bargaining/ Learning	Darwinian	Social/ Cultural
Key Influences	Economics/ Military	Psychology	Economics/ Biology	Sociology
Emergence	1960s	1970s	1980s	1990s

(*Source:* Adadpted from Whittington (2001:39).

Above framework (Whittington, 2001), is grounded in empirical work and recognises that "Integrating HRM and business strategy" is a highly complex process, much dependent on the interplay and resources of different stakeholders'. Whittington typology has analysed the different approaches to 'strategy-making' experienced by organisations and considered the impact on the development of strategic human resource management. Porter identified three key bases of competitive advantage; cost leadership, differentiation through quality and service and focus on 'Niche' market. Schular and Jackson (1987) used these as a basis for their model of strategic human resource management, where they defined the appropriate HR policies and practices to 'fit' the generic strategies of cost reduction, quality enhancement and innovation. Business performance will improve when HR practices mutually reinforce the organisation's choice of competitive strategy. In Schular and Jackson's model given in the Table 2, the organisation mission and values are expressed through their desired competitive strategy. This in turn leads to a set of required employee behaviours which would be reinforced by an appropriate set of HR practices.

Table 2. Business Strategies and Associated HR Policies

Strategy	*Employee role behaviour*	*HRM Policies*
Innovation	A High degree of creative behaviour	Jobs that require close interaction and coordination among groups of individuals.
	Longer-term focus	Performance appraisals that are more likely to reflect long-term and group-based achievement.
	A relatively high level of cooperative interdependent behaviour	Jobs that allow employees to develop skills that can be used in other positions in the firm.
	A moderate degree of concern for quality	Pay rates that tend to be low, but allow employees to be stockholders and have more freedom to choose the mix of components that make up their pay package.
	A moderate concern for quality; an equal degree of concern for process and results	Broad career paths to reinforce the development of broad range of skills.
	A greater degree of risk-taking; a higher tolerance of ambiguity and unpredictability.	Relative freedom experimentation.

Strategy	*Employee role behaviour*	*HRM Policies*
Quality enhancement	Relatively repetitive/ predictable behaviours immediate focus	Relatively fixed and explicit job descriptions employee participation in decisions relevant to immediate work conditions and job itself.
	A moderate amount of cooperative interdependent behaviour	A mix of individual and group criteria for performance appraisal that is mostly short term and results oriented.
	A high concern for quality	Relatively egalitarian treatment of employees and some guarantees of job security.
	A modest concern for quality of output	Extensive and continuous training and development of employees.
	High concern for process; low risk-taking activity; commitment to the goals of the organisation.	Job training on continuous basis.
Cost reduction	Relatively repetitive and predictable behaviour	Relatively fixed and explicit job descriptions that allow little room for ambiguity.
	A rather short-term focus	Narrowly designed jobs and narrowly defined career paths that encourage specialisation, expertise that encourage specialisation, expertise and efficiency.
Activity	Primarily autonomous or individual appraisals	Short-term results-oriented performance.
	Moderate concern for quality	Close monitoring of market pay levels for use in making compensation decisions.

Strategy	Employee role behaviour	HRM Policies
	High concern for quantity of output Primary concern for results; low risk taking activity; relatively high degree of comfort with stability.	Minimal levels of employee training and development. Emphasis on expertise and professionalism.

(*Source:* Schular and Jackson, 1987).

In an expanding economy, a clear road-map is needed on what Indian companies should do to manage people in the growth phase and how HR managers can best respond. Strategic human resource management is needed in India fundamentally at various levels; managing scale, risk, execution and diversity. In India all information technology companies are ramping up numbers in a big way and it brings with it a set fresh of challenges in aspects of hiring, retention, motivation, productivity and training. According to Hema Ravichandar there is a war for talent across companies, geographies and industries. There is an increasing stress on referrals from B schools and focus on expats or returning nationals. According to Dagit Singh "In an expanded economy there are lot more opportunities for people and this actually leads to higher attrition. Even the salary levels in the industry can escalate to unrealistic levels."

Strategic management of the work force is an essential requirement for successful management of globalised, continuously changing business environment of the 21st Century. New and emerging markets will require different skills, i.e. multi lingual, cross cultural team building, negotiation skills and effective management of work force diversity in the context of fostering a diverse corporate culture. Today there is a "war for talents" and organisations have to evolve and implement a strategy that will give them a stable, committed and capable work force required to achieve a competitive business advantage and to survive in the newly emerging global competitive economy as a winner. Strategies are needed for building trust among employees and get a distinct perspective : "people are our greatest assets". All other resources one organisation commands to exactly the same extent as does any other, of all resources, people are the least utilized and that little of the human potential of any organisations is tapped and put to work. But while managers proclaim that people are their major resource, the traditional approaches to the managing of people does not focus on people as a resource but as problems, procedures and costs. Strategy is an extension of a company's capabilities and behind a farsighted strategy, there is or ought to be an ever vigilant organisations with a committed leadership and a competent team. Its people the human resources, its style of functioning its structure and system set the limits to the strategy it can put into practice. HR strategy has to be a part and parcel of strategic planning. According to Sumantra Ghosal and Donald Sull, a company succeeds by developing a coherent and mutually supportive configuration of its strategy, its resources and its management processor all three held together by a set of values-explicit or implicit that are shared by its management. In December 2004, a work attitude survey by Watson Wyatt titled work Asia Survey, came out with the following findings about employees attitudes:- (1) Job satisfaction and leadership had the highest impact on employee commitment; (2) Indian employees were least satisfied with compensation, supervisions and training; (3) Compensation is the No. 1 reason why employees leave their companies; (4) Over 80 percent said they understood how their work impacted customers and their company's goals; (5) Over 64 percent said they understood the measures used to evaluate their performance. (6) More than half the employees felt their companies didn't share information with them adequately. The above finding are related to a survey conducted in India, Japan, China, the Phillipines, South Korea, Thailand, Singapore, Malaysia, Australia, Taiwan and Indonesia covering over 115,000 (One Lakh Fifteen thousand) across 515 companies in the Asia Pacific. This survey of work Asia study by Watson Wyatt world wide points out the need for strategic human resource management.

The leading organisations of the world today believe that people or human resources are their most precious asset and the success of their strategy is ensured through the skills, knowledge and competencies of their people, people who formulate strategies and people who implement them. People constitute the intellectual social and creative capital and constitute the crew in the voyage of excellence. When someone looks at the world scene, he finds that companies like GE,

Seimens, Honda, Coca-Cola, P & G and Johnson and Johnson have become universally known cases of business success and all of them have been strong on the strategy form. A Strategic organisation travels with the support of a route map which will show in advance various alternatives routes, by-passes, shortcuts, dangerous, terrains and unpredictable factors. Every organisation must do spotting of opportunities and threats thrown up by the environment, analysing its own shortcomings and strengths and forgiving the strategies required to achieve the organization mission vision and objectives. Alvin Toffler has rightly said: "Change is the process which pervades our life and it is important to look at it closely, not merely from the grand perspectives of history but also from the vantage point of the living, breathing individuals who experience it[3]. In the present day scenario of globalization liberalization and competitive economy there is an increasing need to cope with the ever changing forces of technological onslaughts, the growing realisation of knowledge management and ever changing competitive environment. The twenty first century world is globally facing a great shortage of motivated, well educated, highly creative loyal people.

The Concept of Human Resources

Human resources refer to the workforce with a wide variety of qualities and differences in many ways (but not limited to) age, sex, language, race, religion, education, ethnic, background, economic and social status. The human resources are the greatest assets of any organisation. Human beings become resources in organisations, when they are empowered with knowledge skills, techniques, methods of work. Human beings have intellectual, emotional and social capitals. Human beings are capable of acquiring various competencies, capabilities and capacities through training and HRD interventions. Life - long learning can help human resources, on an ongoing basis, stay creative, fresh and more productive, and contribute to real assets to the organisations. Human resource have both soft and hard skills. Technical knowledge, skills in handling equipment and hard work will constitute hard skills. In understanding human resources; soft skills are those skills that are psychological and help in staying ahead in competition. Team work, communication initiative, vision, problem solving, adaptability passion for change, fast decision making, innovation, creativity and leadership are soft skills. Human resources can be helped to acquire capabilities required to perform their present and future expected roles and develop general capabilities and competencies through various HRD interventions. Human resource management must nurture Senior level, Middle level and Junior level Managers and plan their careers in an appropriate manner. Proper succession plans must be made in all organisations. Corporate boards must do proper screening of candidates before selecting a successor CEO. Strategic HRM must empower people groups and teams to realize their full potential.

In the age of dynamic change, human resource strategy becomes essential for survival, growth and success. "Strategy is a unified, comprehensive and integrated plan that relates the strategic advantages of the firm to the challenges of the environment. It is designed to ensure that the basic objectives of the enterprise are achieved through proper execution by the organisation".[4] Strategy enables an organisation to determine the alternatives available in achieving its objectives and mission and the selection of the alternative to be pursued to fulfil its vision. HR strategy is a long-term direction of human resource (HR) function in an organisation and is a comprehensive approach covering the vital issues such as change management, competence building and cultural change. In any business strategy is possible only with motivated people".[5] HR strategies to be viable, they must not be insulated from the reality and problems of the organisation. Any HR strategy must be formulated and implemented keeping in view the corporate objectives and goals, vision and mission and the broad competitive strategy adopted by the organization. To quote Michael Porter, every firm competing in an industry has a competitive strategy, whether explicit or implicit. The strategy may have been developed explicitly through a planning process or it may have evolved through the activities of their various functional departments of the firm".[6] The HR strategy is a strategic look at HR functions and includes a case for change, the vision, the mission of the functions, definitions of the customers, the design criteria, relationships, the transitions process and the implications for stake holders. Strategic formulation and implementation can be highly problematic with some of the following: -

1. "The long-term direction of the organisation;
2. The scope of the organisation's activities;
3. The matching of organisations activities to the environment;
4. The matching of the organisation's activities to its resource capability;
5. Strategic decisions are likely to have major resource implications;
6. Strategic decisions are likely to involve a higher degree of uncertainty;
7. Strategic decisions are likely to demand an integrated approach to managing the organisations;
8. Strategic decisions are likely to be concerned with sustaining change".[7]

India has great demographic advantage over other countries of the world. At current rate of growth India is facing an estimated 19 to 37 million unemployed by 2012, the largest share of which will be educated youth. A study carried out by All India Management Association (AIMA) and Boston Consulting Group, India estimates that the net workforce shortage in developing countries will range between 32-39 million by 2020. The inbalances of estimated work force trends by 2020 will be as under.

India	-	+47 Million workers surplus
U.S.A.	-	–17 Million Shortage
China	-	-10 Million Shortage
Japan	-	9 Million Shortage
Russia	-	6 Million Shortage

France - 3 Million Shortage
Spain - 3 Million Shortage
U.K. - 2 Million Shortage
Australia - 0.5 Million Shortage

These shortages in other countries present an opportunity to the Indian work force. More than 65 percent of Indian Population will be in the working age group 15-60 years. Like the uncertain weather, business is a chaotic system in which small differences in stalling points can translate into a large divergence in final outcomes. Strategies have to be opportunistic and smart and must forecast where the organisation should be in next five years time and must focus on medium and long term planning. The corporate plan must provide projections of sales, revenues, costs, profits and human resource competencies and future needs. The need for HR strategy arises out of the following issues:-

1. Retention of employees
2. Need for competent employees
3. Complex structural problems of the organisation
4. Ad hoc allocation of human resources.
5. Employees dissatisfaction with the organisation
6. Conflict management and change management by top management
7. Whether organisation undergoing any major business changes affecting human resources?
8. Whether the organisational HR processes are linked up to the mission and goal of the organisation.
9. Whether the physical resources are given equal importance towards HR functions.
10. Whether the HR function are treated as a cost or a profit centre?

Challenges for HR Managers

There is a wake up call for HR managers in India. A recent national wide survey of HR managers has brought out the following key findings: (1) Human resources in the future will have to move towards a more strategic and facilitating role; (2) Priority is now being given to key areas like performance management, talent acquisition, measuring HR performance, leadership development and potential assessment; (3) The line manager is increasingly getting involved in HR decisions and he needs to be properly trained and supported; (4) Ten top activities in terms of priority for HR professionals are (1) Performance management system; (2) Talent acquisition; (3) Measuring HR performance leadership development; (4) Potential assessment; (5) Induction of new entrants; (6) Integrated human resources; (7) Information Systems; (8) Retaining employees; (9) Multi-skilling and (10) Knowledge management. The top ten activities which can be outsourced are as under: (1) Out bounding training; (2) Compensation surveys: (3) Salary administration; (4) Psychometric testing; (5) HR Audit; (6) Attitude surveys; (7) Assessment centres; (8) E-learning; (9) Human Resource Accounting; (10) Competency mapping, HR managers will have to develop managerial competency, functional competency, specific skills and attitudinal change to be successful in the globalised Indian Corporate world. As an organisation becomes larger and its mission broadens, the process of monitoring and effectively managing the organisational health becomes uncertain. HR strategy is a long term direction of the HR functions and describes the best options suitable to an organisation for managing its human resources is line with the available systems and processor, resources, environment and its vital issues like change management. In India L and T and SAIL are among the first organizations to talk of HR strategy. Absence of an HR strategy for the organisation may lead to a mixed bag of individual motivation or alienation, growth or regression "Human resource management needs to become even more strategic in the way it operates. In fact it needs to be driven by the business needs of the organisation but without losing sight of the critical value and importance of people in making strategies a reality. Top management also needs to give greater consideration to HR issues at the strategy formulation stages." The fundamental basis of competition has begun to change. The scare resource, and the primary source of competitive advantage, is no longer physical or financial capital but human capital. According to

Sumantra Ghosal, there are three kinds of resources that people possess which collectively constitute their individual human capital. The first element is intellectual capital knowledge skills and expertise. The second is social capital the structure and quality of relationship network both inside and outside company. The third is emotional capital change and resilience for taking action can do spirit. It relates to self confidence based on self-esteem, courage and resilience to convert knowledge and relationships into effective action.

Global communication, changing composition of work force, increased international competition, technological advances, changing expectations about work and performance, shrinking pool of skilled and loyal workers, internationalization of corporate managers are important factors in bringing up need for HR strategies in the present day business environment. HR strategies have to be closely linked to business processes in the fields of customer orientation, productivity improvement, product development, culture building, corporate restructuring, cost reduction and control, transformational leadership and strategic alliances/mergers and acquisitions. The need and importance of human beings as an asset to the organisation is gaining awareness in the present day global economy. Knowledge explosion, increasing organisational complexity, change and conflict management, an increase in the living standards and expectations of human resources. Decreasing loyalty of the people to the organisations, impact of information technology and complex demands of global society·all these significant factors explain the need for HR strategy. The HR strategy process is a sequential process of integrating alternative HR practices with business processes to provide a competitive edge to the organisation in the present day scenario. The practice of the strategic HR management is about aligning the five Ps, philosophy, policies, practices, programmes and processes with the corporate strategy.

Various Steps in Human Resource Strategy

The HR strategy is a pre-planned mechanism that gives long term direction to the organisation through the following six steps.[9]

"Step One - Build the HR Vision
Step Two - Scan the environment
Step Three - Audit your competencies and resources.
Step Four - See other strategic business plans.
Step Five - Define Objectives;
Step Six - Integrate Action - Plans"

HR strategy takes a strategic look at the HR functions in line with the business needs and is a never ending journey with a rolling six step sequential approach. The HR strategy evolution process is a complex series of activities which needs to consider the stake holders' expectations, systematic practical approach without overlooking intintive approach about sustainable corporate growth and customer satisfaction HR strategy should not only serve the basic and essential needs of HR function and should be designed to inspire awe among the successful and powerful organisation and to give them glory and recognition through the excellence of their HR assets.

Building the HR Vision: Vision is not a mere dream, but something that you can fulfil and realise. Vision is a grand futuristic view of what the organisation would look like in the future as well as a statement of the great policies of the organisation. Mr. Dhirubhai Ambani, the former chairman, of the Reliance group of industries dreamt of making his company a global player. He said "Our dreams must be bigger our ambitions higher our commitment deeper and our efforts greater". From a small company reliance has grown to be a number one play in the Indian industry and a strong Competitor in the global market place. Any vision is a written or implicit model of a desirable or idealistic future for the organisation, it is a sign post pointing the way to those who need to understand where the organisation tends to go, it incarnate the possibility of a realistic, credible attractive future plan for the organisation, it provides a goal to be achieved. The HR vision identifies and reiterates an organisation's long term views and directions towards its human resources to build their competencies and commitment to remain competitive in its business, defining what values are central. HR vision is the transformation of beliefs to goals, culture to strategy, dreams into reality, by keeping in mind the interests of stake holders and providing a long term direction towards building the competencies of the employees and motivating them. HR vision should value the dignity and diversity of the people, honesty, integrity, honouring commitment, team work and collaboration, open communication, innovations and risk taking, job enjoyment, technical expertise and personal accountability. Shri. K.B. Dadisith, Former Chairman Hindustan Lever Ltd., at the company's AGM held in Mumbai on April 25, 2000 said:

"Vision for Hindustan Lever is that of a company where people are given unparalleled power to generate new ideas that have high impact; a climate which encourages them to be passionate about those ideals; and then the support they need to make these ideas a reality. In fact, today we are planning to go a step further by giving them a stake in the wealth that they create through these ideas".[10] A well conceived HR vision not only contain the basic HR Philosophy but future dream with commitment for HRD of the stakeholders of the HR function.

Scanning the Environment - Scanning the environment calls for facilitating the analysis of the organisation's external and internal environment so that we may understand our strengths and weakness as well as various threats and opportunities for helping us to determine how to be winners. The external environment is the interplay of social, political, legal, economic and technological forces while the internal environment is a harmonious balancing of culture, structure, HR processes and systems. The concept of scanning the environment assumes importance in the light of the dynamic HR activities because human beings change continuously and their changing continuously and their changing dynamics change with the change in the business environment. Organisational culture is generally the pattern of beliefs, knowledge, attitudes, customs and traditions that exist within an organisation. The HR strategy formulation process in closely intertwined to the organisations structure and work culture. The components of external and internal environment can be depicted by the figure given below.

Fig. 4. Showing External and Internal Environment of Indian Companies

External	*Internal*
1. Economic	1. Structure of Org.
2. Social/Caste/Race	2. Work Culture
3. Constitutional	3. Value System
4. Political	4. HR Processes and Strategies
5. Legal	5. Competencies and skills
6. Technological	6. Professional level skills
7. Cultural	7. Extent of Commitment
8. Emotional and Psychological	8. Level of urge to achieve excellence
9. National/International	9. Passion to win and complete
10. Ecological	10. Org Health
11. Spiritual	11. Industrial nature and temperament

Environment factors of HR are prime influences of change in HR strategy and give HR professionals adequate time to anticipate opportunities in HR areas and time to plan optional responses to these opportunities by aligning the organisational strengths to the changes in the environment. JRD Tata regarded employees as human resource and believed in giving employees a better understanding of their role and importance in the working of the industry and in the process of production. It is essential for all the HR strategists to keep up with changes in educational and societal levels in order to assess the potential impact on their strategies. Assessing internal environment is quite difficult and various techniques like critical incident analysis, HR surveys and questionnaires and research studies by outside agencies, can be used with profit. Organisational health is reflected in various dimensions of the organisation through profitability, growth of capital, organisation culture, level of productivity and HR strategies. Wage level of workers morale, absenteeism level, educational professional structure, promotion policies, pension and old age provisions, Medical insurance, etc influence organisational health.

Audit of organisations competencies and resources:- The concept of audit refers to a holistic, strategic and thorough assessment and evaluation of a part of the whole functioning of an organisation. Auditing, which is generally a part of control function, can be defined as the examination and evaluation of policies, procedures and practices in all phases of a business to achieve the most effective administration of the organisations.[11] Outlining the need for HR audit Gordon states that a major objective of personnel management is to "Improve productivity of individual employees and thus increase organisation effectiveness by better utilization of a firm's human resources".[12] The primary purpose of the audit should be to assist the rest of the organisation and the serve the purpose of identifying the gaps between objectives and results, for the end product of evaluation should be plans for corrections or adjustments.[13] During audit, each aspect has to be analysed and evaluated to view the components as fulfilling a whole. HR competence can be broadly comprehended to include (*a*) Knowledge, (*b*) Attitudes, (*c*) Values and (*d*) Skills. All competencies are interlinked and the sum total of an individual competencies is his potential. Corporate competencies can be broadly classified under the following groups:-

1. **Intellectual Competencies:** Analytical ability, ability to solve practical problems, organisational ability, communication skills, creativity, and innovativeness, ability to take decisions.

2. **Emotional Competencies:** Initiative, emotional skills, self confidence tolerance of pressure and ambiquity, leadership skills. Interpersonal relationships empathy, teamwork, tolerance of others viewpoint.

3. **Social Competencies:** Inter personal skills, team spirit, sense of responsibility, integrity self-insight.

4. **Motivational Competencies:** Achievement drive, will power energy level, risk taking ability.

HRD Managers

Human resource managers must develop new competencies to face the challenges of global economy. The new competencies can be broadly classified into four groups. Managerial competence should include (1) Knowledge of business; (2) Aligning HR with organisational functions; (3) Cross functional exposure and (4) Involvement in strategic planning and architecture. Functional competencies of the HR managers would include (1) finding out ways to retain talent; (2) new methods to assess effectiveness of training' (3) creating HR value for business; (4) facilitator of organisational transformation; and (5) Business driven HR activities rather than vice-versa. HR manager need specific skills in the 21st Century which include; (1) Managing change; (2) building organisational culture; (3) E learning design and development; (4) IT Savvy (5) Computer driven testing, (6) global benchmarking and (7) tools for managing large scale change in HR. HR manager need attitude will change by (1) being pro-active; (2) Be open to change and (3) Willing to stay focussed or business objective. On the whole HR managers should be able to facilitate organisational transformation and be periodical HR audit.

For audit of competencies of HR professionals performing HR functions, a five point scale with the following scores can be useful as given below :

1. Does not have this competence, needs to start developing, 2. Need to develop this competence substantially, 3. Has this competence but can develop some more, 4. Has this competence adequately, 5. Has this competence in abundance.

For purpose of HR competence audit HR Competencies can be broadly classified into the following three groups:

1. HR Knowledge : HR philosophy, Policies, Practices and system; performance appraisal systems and practices; career planning and development systems and practices; organisational diagnosis and intervention strategies; learning theories; training methods, techniques and systems, org structure and their functioning, group dynamics and group functions, Inter-links between org. goals, plans, policies, strategies, structure, technology systems, people management systems, and styles;

power-dynamics and net-working in the org; org plans, manpower and competency requirement; social science research methods; job analysis, job enrichment, job redesign and job evaluation, manpower planning methods; role analysis techniques, employee relation practices role of rewards, methodology, of behaviour modification and attitude change; quality circles; recent development in management systems; personality theories and measurement, personal and managerial effectiveness; inter-personal relations; organisational health, Instruments and measurement of human behaviour, personal growth and its techniques, methods, turn around strategies, problem solving and creativity techniques, conflict management strategies.

2. HR Skills: Articulating HRD philosophy and values; Designing skills for designing HRD systems; communication skills, skills needed to influence line managers and employees; Oral and written abilities, skills to monitor the implementation of HR systems (designing questionnaires) data gathering, feed-back and evaluation. Inter personal sensitivity, feed back system, consoling skills, Ability to inspire; leadership and initiatives; creativity; problem solving skills.

3. Personal attitudes and values: Empathy and understanding; positive and helpful attitude to others, faith in people and their competence; introspective attitude, openners; interpersonal trust; Pro-activity; Respect for others; self-confidence, sense of responsibility, sense of fairness; self discipline; honesty and Integrity; willingness to experiment; learning orientation; perseverance, work motivation super-ordination of goals, empowering attitude, stress tolerance, change management attitude.

1. Personal profile analysis, 2. Behavioural characteristics of the individual, 3. Individual competencies, 4. Job analysis, 5. Behavioural characteristics of the job, 6. Job needed competencies. Competence profiling is more effective in some organisations and depends on three factors:-

1. The nature of the industry that a company operates in;

2. The stage of the life cycle if is in;
3. The depth of the talent proof it can hire and retain.

Competence profiling is a technique that requires substantial investment in terms of time, money and commitment.

Managing people in the complex environment of modern business in the global context is a challenge and hence requires special capabilities and competencies enumerated above. The Human Resource Department is a major player in the company's climate change efforts and HR has established a core competency of change management skills and processes competence building in HR has two components basic competence and competence to manage HR systems and processes; innovation and leadership. HR people need good leadership skills and some operational exposure, proper HR audit needs an analysis of the strongly held beliefs and values. Inspite of all efforts, no company can avoid attrition in India where there are many reasons and problems related to it. A research study on employee attrition has grouped the problems causing employees attrition in broadly following groups: 1. Dissatisfaction with compensation package; 2. Insecurity over career growth; 3. Lack of recognition; 4. Technological preferences; 5. Dissatisfaction with the work culture; 6. Unfulfilled promises; 7. Conflict with superior and problem of loss management; 8. Regional, linguistic and racial preferences; 9. Personal and family reasons; 10. Miscellaneous including lack of professional mentors and suitable guidance to employees including counselling. Long terms strategies towards organisational culture building, leadership development and inculcation of the spirit or mentorship for people development and inculcation of the spirit of mentorship for people development will provide resilience to the organisation for withstanding the menace of employee attrition.[12a]

Resources: Resources are mainly financial, physical and human and all audits are to be viewed as pro-active tools of identifying the present state of being and the flaws and gaps in the strategy. The values audit is the most important and the most difficult process because values are "the beliefs of an individual which are chosen by oneself over other beliefs over a period of time." A value audit is an examinations of the values of the HR professionals and not of the organisational values. For conducting audit, gaining a fuller understanding of the strategic requirements of business and entails gaining a clear understanding of the business environment, corporate mission and the business strategy being perceived. Resource audit is the stock taking process of various dimensions of resources such as human, physical and financial. Infrastructure such as books, computer, technology and so on is audited as physical resources which financial resource audit related to badgetary assessment, clear allocation and utilization of funds. Competence profiling is a complete understanding of an individuals organisational, managerial and behavioural competencies and not just in terms of skills, abilities and intelligence—Devendra Nath G.M. (Personnel and HR) says; "Only HR that is rooted in competency based management can help a company bridge the gap between vision and implementation". There are four models of competence-profiling in tandom the job competency model, the role competency model, the functional competence model and the core competence model. The job competency model is built around specific tasks. It lays down the skills an individual will need to possess to perform a particular job. The role competency model looks at the role of an individual in the org and studies the past played by the employee in activating the organisation's super ordinate goals. The functional competency model is built around specific tasks. It lays down the skills an individual will need to possess to perform a particular job. The role of competency model looks at the role of an individual in the org and studies the part played by the employee in activating the organisation's super ordinate goals. The functional competency model is built around key business functions like finance, production and marketing. The core competency model in base on the value systems, vision and mission of the org and defines the set of soft skills that should be possessed by the employee. HR audit has to do profiling of its managers and employees. Audit leads to evaluation and various factors on the HR goals should find their relevance in the context of culture building; overcoming skill shortage; effective communication; competitive benefits, rewards; recruiting and retaining a quality work force;

leadership and team building; systematic performance audit training and development of employees and increased workforce productivity. HR audit and evaluation need to be integrated into the main HR strategy by identifying the gaps on the various areas enumerated above with a view to introduce and effectively utilise all resources which can enhance value additions to the organisation. Audit is a brutal but necessary activity and the process traverses through the conduct of the audit, carrying out the evaluation and integrating the results into the main HR strategy of the organisation.

Strategic Business Plans and Their Link to Human Resources

Andrews divided corporate strategy into four elements which definitely illustrate the integrative nature of business planning: 1. What an organisation might do; 2. What an organisation can do; 3. What an organisation wants to do; 4. What an org should do: Resources, Competencies, technological capacity's, product lines, market share, and position and financial capital are all given close consideration in strategic business planning process for an organisation are as under:- 1. Identification of org's capabilities, 2. Learn to Beat competition through capabilities, 3. Aim at value-additions, 4. Strengthen the value-addition process, 5. Encash on value addition.[14]

The quality and quantity of HR available at a given situation to run a business is very critical although these aspects are generally ignored. Effective HR planning involves long range career development of talent and optimum utilization of human resources. The main dimensions of HR in strategic business plans (SPB) can be as follows:

1. General HR profile in terms of competencies, qualifications, attitudes, values, etc. to attain the targets set in the strategies, 2. HR stock taking and forecasting, 3. Competence levels, 4. Training and HRD Strategies, 5. Productivity Parameters, 6. Potential Appraisal, 7. Succession Planning, 8. Compensation systems.

HR dimensions must be properly coordinated with the main strategy of business. While formulating and implementing the

SBPs of the business groups, it is essential to diagnose, define and consolidate all the HR issues and properly integrate the results into the HR strategy.

Define HR Objectives

Micheal Porter has asserted that survival strategy and indeed success in business depends upon improving employee effectiveness and increasing productivity as well as profitability through collaboration and team work. HR objectives can be as under:-

1. Organisational development, 2. Org. Structure, 3. Managing change, 4. Conducive environment, 5. Strengthening communication, 6. Internal customer service, 7. Competence building and developing skills, 8. Productivity with enhancement, 9. Aligning with Business goals.

HR objectives are the targets needed to translate an organisations HR vision statement into measurable, concrete and specific terms. To fulfil the HR vision, an organisation has to carryout specific HR tasks and certain critical factors can be as under:- 1. Retaining good talents and allowing them to achieve self-actualisation, 2. Increasing employee productivity by better motivation, having and HRD interventions, 3. Creative a healthy org climate and internal customer satisfaction, 4. Building up employee morale, 5. Building team work and trust.

We, in India, have huge human resources potential that can conquer the world economic stage. India is becoming a global economic power. According to S. Gurumurthy, by 2015, India will have 20 million student coming out a higher learning every year with 1.4 million engineers; 60,000 doctors; 50,000 PhDs; 250 universities; 1500 research institutions; 10,000 institutions; of higher education with annual intake of 10 million students. In India 5 millions graduate enter the workforce every year as against only 1.2 million graduates in China. Proper human resources management of these young people is ground to build up a strong economically super power India. As India gains economic strength, the entrepreneurs are acquiring companies overseas. In the first 8 months of 2005, Indian companies paid US $ 1.7 billion to acquire 62 foriegn business (Business

Mandate - Madras Management Association, December 2005, Vol. XXXIV No. 3).

Integrated Action Plans

In a dynamic business environment HR action plans need to be changed with the changing organisation's HR needs and defining HR action plans becomes an extra ordinarily plans can be defined as the detailed steps to achieve HR objectives practicability, measurability, feasibility are key factors in HR action plans. The action plans should be relevant and correlated to the defined objective and must be feasible. The HR action plans must be stated in measurable terms such as: 1. Our employees will have higher productivity by next year; 2. The employee satisfaction level should reach a scale of 4 by the next year.

HR action plans must identify appropriate HR systems to fulfil the objectives and following can be some of the main systems:

(1) Man power planning; (2) Recruitment and selection; (3) Induction; (4) Training & Development; (5) Promotion; (6) Appraisal; (7) Succession planning; (8) Mentoring; (9) Counselling; (10) Career planning; (11) Reward system and Recognition's; (12) Team Work; (13) Personal growth and self renewal; (14) Learning opportunities; (15) Welfare of employees; (16) Review and feed back; (17) One year to five year calendar for establishing systems not existing - drawing a long term time chart.

The goal of strategy should be clear to make and implement action plans that lead to greater value and excellence and ultimately, integration with the organisation. A primary element of successful strategy is effective integration of the resources, competencies, markets, opportunities, organisational structures, culture, environment, innovation, technology, processes, decisions and actions in a most harmonious manner. The most effective way of integration in the cascading process which involves the interlinking of HR action plans to the activities of the employees down to the lowest. The management can effectively cascade—the strategic framework process and subsequently key performance measures of the employees.

Linkage of HR Dimensions to Business Strategy

According to Athreya, corporate development is the balance synergy of strategic management and organisation development in the HR development system. (Athreya; Annual conference 2 STD 1980). HR philosophy is generally expressed in statements defining business values and culture and it expresses how to treat employees. HR policies are expressed as guidelines and shared values and provide guidelines for action on people related business issues and HR programmes. HR programmes are generally articulated as HR strategies which coordinate efforts to facilitate change and address major people related business issues. HR practices articulate leadership, managerial and operational roles and generally motivates needed people behaviour. HR processes are for the formulation and implementation of other activities and generally define how these activities are carried out. Several challenges are evident in implementing a new HR strategy and some of important challenges can be:

1. Re-engineering and its impact assessment, 2. Supporting HR employees in changing their roles from generalists to specialists, 3. Balancing the internal HR focus with pressing needs of the business, 4. Marketing the changes to line managers.

The important pre-requisites for the success of HR strategy are:-

1. Top management commitment and mandate, 2. Concerted efforts by the HR team, 3. Inter-functional involvement of HR and business, 4. Existence of an appropriate forum and appex council, 5. A conducive environment characterized by healthy climate, value of openness, proactivity, trust and collaboration.

Integration of HR strategy to business strategy has been gradually gaining acceptance. According to certain estimates, less than 20 percent of HR strategic plans in the United States are formulated and integrated into the total business strategy of organisation. In India at the corporate level few models exist of integration of HR strategy with business strategy. The O.N.G.C. experience is keeping pace and worthwhile HR initiatives have been taken. In O.N.G.C. productivity linked honorarium and performance incentive schemes automatically tend to align HR strategy with business strategy. India has to evolve a scientific integrated strategic HR model as given in Fig. 5.

Fig. 5 Integrated Strategic HR Model

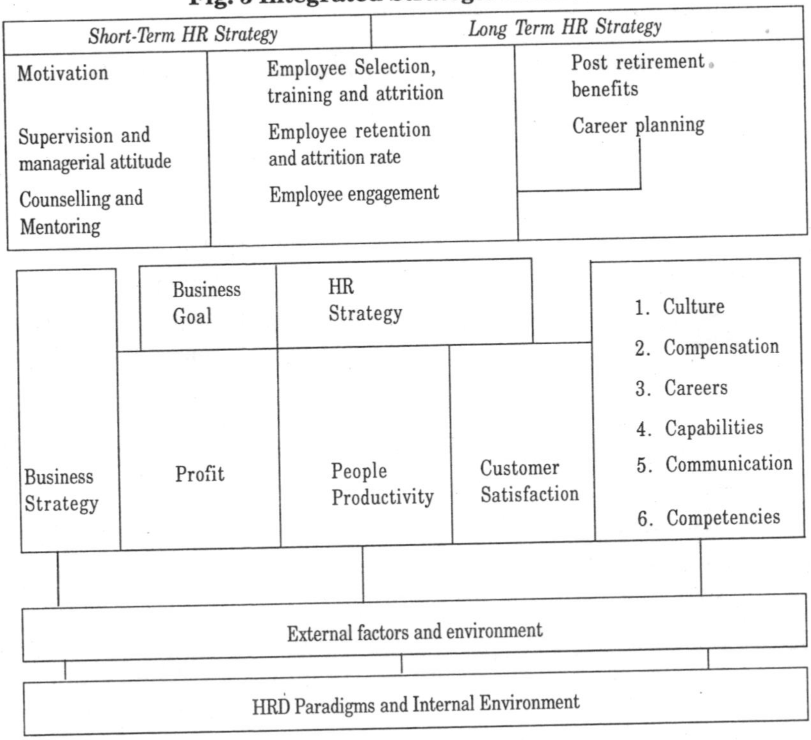

Best Practices strategy human Resource management: High commitment models.

The adoption of certain best human resource practices result in enhanced organisational performance, manifested in improved employee attitudes and behaviours, lower levels of skills and therefore higher productivity, enhanced quality and efficiency. During the last two decades there has been much work done on defining sets of HR practices that enhance organisational performance. One of the models most common cited is Pfeffer's (1998) seven practices for building profits by putting people first. These practices have been adapted for the U.K. audience by Marchington and Wilkinson. (2002) Table 1. It explains how changes in the external environment have reduced the impact of traditional sources of competitive advantages and increased the significance of new sources of competitive advantage, namely human resources that enable an organisation to adopt and innovate.

Table 1 HR practices for 'Competitive advantage through people'

Building profits by putting people first	*'High-Commitment' HRM*
Employment security	and internal promotion
Selective hiring	and sophisticated selection
Extensive training	and learning and development
Sharing information	Extensive involvement and voice
Self-managed teams/ teamworking	Self-Managed teams/teamworking and harmonisation
High pay contingent on company	High compensation contingents on organisational performance
Reduction of status differentials	mentoring and counselling

Many authors have offered models which focus on enhancing the skill base of employees through HR activities such as selective staffing, comprehensive training and broad developmental efforts like job rotation and cross-utilisation. Table 2 gives the list of best practices which vary intensely in their constitution and in their relationship to organisational performance.

A single set of best practices may indeed be over stated, it is actually distinctive human resource practices that help to create unique competencies that differentiate products and in turn drive competitiveness.

Table 2 Comparative Lists of Best Practices

Pfeffer (1998)	*Kochan and Osterman (1994)*	*MacDuffie (1995)*	*Huselid (1995)*	*Arthur (1994)*	*Delery and Doty (1996)*
Employment	Self-directed	Self-directed	Contingent pay	Self-directed	Internal career
Security	Work teams	Work teams	Hours per year	Work teams	Opportunities
Selective	Job rotation	Job rotation	Training	Problem solving	Training
Hiring	Problem solving	problem solving	Information	groups	Results oriented

Extensive	groups	groups	sharing	Contingent pay	appraisals
Training	TQM	TQM	Job analysis	Hours per year	Profit-sharing
Sharing		Suggestions	Selective hiring	training	Employment
Information		Forum	Attitude surveys	conflict	Security
Self-Managed		Hiring Criteria,	Grievance	resolution	Participation
teams		Current Job	Procedure	job design	Job descriptions
High pay		Versus learning	Employment	percentage of	
Contingent on		Contingent pay	tests	skilled workers	
Company		Induction and	Formal	supervision span	
Performance		Initial training	Performance	of control	
Reduction of		Provision	appraisal	social events	
Status		Hours per year	Promotion	Average total	
Differentials		training	Criteria	Labour costs	
			Selection ratio	Benefits/total	
				labour costs	

Source: Adapted from Becker and Gerhart (1996, Vol. 39, No. 4, pp. 779-801.

Strategies and Innovations in human resource management by Indian corporate sector:- The business today (March 2002) has carried out the best employers in India survey to find out how best employers align their HR strategy with business drivers and to understand what distinguishes best employers, effective HR systems, Philosophies and practices and emerging workplace trends for the future. According to the survey the following were consistent across all best employers.

"1. High degree of employee satisfaction commitment and morale.

2. A sense of ownership and belonging a collective relationship fostered by the organisations.
3. Opportunities for accelerated growth and development.
4. Depth, breadth and consistency in application of HR practices.
5. Unique HR practices-many of which were home grown and based on employee suggestions.
6. A sensitivity towards a balance between work and personal type.

7. Effectiveness of HR practices in meeting needs of employees.
8. Allignment of HR practices with business context.
9. Stature of organisations in the business community as evidenced by employee and corporate initiatives.[15]

According to the BT survey, referred above, the top employee motivators have been defined as under.[16]

S.No.	*Motivators*	*Satisfaction Score*	*Negative Drivers*	*Positive Driver*
1.	Culture	81%	46.7	10.9
2.	Quality of Work life	81%	17.9	8.4
3.	Work Activities	77%	40.5	11.5
4.	Managers	76%	29.9	10.3
5.	Senior Management	73%	29.0	12.2
6.	Compensation	70%	22.6	10.2
7.	Opportunity	69%	28.2	13.7

The negative drivers depict adverse impact on employee satisfaction in the absence of the activities which are included under this column, *i.e.*, by reducing activities in this area, a change up to the depicted percentage in the negative direction is possibly expected. Thus, a culture that is not conducive to work and improper work practices are key negative drivers and indicate negative impact. The positive drivers show the main impact of engagement, *i.e.* by increasing activities in this area, a change up to the depicted percentage in the positive direction is possible. Thus, career opportunities and the level of senior manager's involvement are key drivers culture, work-life issues, work activities, career opportunities, the level of senior management involvement, compensation, the immediate managers supervisory role are some of the matters which play important roles in making employees happy. The best employers in India who have been packed up out of a list of 204 employees who have practiced unique HR strategies and ensured high level of satisfaction of employees:[17]

Table 4 Showing Best Employers in India

Rank	*Name of Company*	*Existence in India years*	*Employee Strength*	*Ratio of HR staff to total employees*	*Average Trg Hours (Year)*
1.	Infosys Technologies	20	10,206	1:102	47
2.	Procter and Gamble	35	660	1:80	56
3.	Hewlett-Packard	12	1590	NA	35
4.	Smithkine Beecham Consumer Health care	41	1079	1:100	64
5.	Satyam Computer Services	14	6661	1:60	66
6.	Agilent Technologies	12	106	1:40	40
7.	Bharat Heavy Electrials	45	10293	NA	59.5
8.	American Express (India)	7	1052	1:200	88
9.	Colgate Palmolive (India)	65	687	NA	24
10.	Gillete India	15	655	1:100	36
11.	Highes Software Systems	9	1669	1:60	40
12.	Tata Steel	95	4766	NA	86.32
13.	Dr. Reddy's Laboratories	17	2178	1:80	60
14.	Sasken Communication Technology	10	1029	1:49	
15.	Oracle India	8	1612	1:161	72
16.	Reliance	30	9603	1:50	95
17.	Indian Oil Corporation	43	32266	1:50	24
18.	Compaq Computers (India)	7	460	1:77	48
19.	Microsoft Corporation (India)	10	193	1:54	40
20.	Maruti Udyog	18	1614	1:104	80
21.	Polaris Software	14	2278	1:90	57.3
22.	Johnson & Johnson	50	180	1:40	80
23.	LG Electronics India	5	415	NA	120
24.	S.T. Micro-electronics	14	804	1:98	53
25.	Tata Engineering	56	3957	1:182	71

Practices and HR Strategies of Best Organisations of India

The best employers have over the years evolved innovative HR strategies which make the difference[18]. Infosys Technologies

(Rank 1) has exhibited resilience enough to cope with the slow down with its business going on as usual as if nothing has really changed due to its excellent HR strategy and ability to cope with recession. Infosys was given the Best Employer award in 2001. Mr. Dinesh, Cofounder and director of Infosys explained the people-centric policies and practices at Infosys, has said: 'We have a very good human resource system. In our business the key, the only variable and the only asset we have is people. So to manage that very efficiently, we have a very good human resource system......... The employees' stock offer plan is also there, where people who have created wealth for the organisations they also get rewarded. 'People have three hierarchies of needs' (the need for) learning, emotional bonding and financial stability. And Infosys provides them very well." Infosys is a company by the people, for the people, and of the people. The strategy of grooming employees to be leaders has ensured dynamic emergence of successful executives. The senior most leaders of the company spend high percentage of their time at leadership development centre in Mysore for grooming future leaders, by conducting workshops and active involvement in training programmes. The ratio of HR staff to total employees is 1:102 and average training hours per year is 47. In Procter and Gamble (Rank 2) all initiatives are driven through taskforces. Principle based approach where practices and policies are aligned to employee needs and not directly to their levels, differentiates it from the rest. Employee task forces have both the budget and the power to take decisions and HR being only a facilitators. In Hewlett-Packard India (3rd Rank) HR Innovative practices include additional leave of 10 days for marriage, five days peternity leave, five days for bereavement in the family, 10 days if the employee is preparing for higher education and eight days for adopting a child. Work life balance is a well known HR practice of Hewlett-Packard India, besides providing flexible work arrangements. Smithkline Beecham consumer health care (Rank 4th) has provided all area sales managers with laptops enabling them to work from home and work life balanced is south through practices such as compressed work - week and flexiture SKB consumer Health care has 1:100 Ratio of HR staff to total employees and have 64 hours per year average training schedule. Satyam Computers Services (Rank 5) has its own "Suggestions" mileage card and the more the suggestions offered they points are more and thus offer attractive rewards to their employees, depending on the number of points that have been accumulated. The ratio of HR staff to total employees is 1:60 and average training hours per year are 66 within organisation. At Satyam some one who joins as an assistant on the help-desk has the opportunity to grow into a billable employer and this company gives lot of emphasis on career planning. The Agilent Technology (6th rank) has 1:40 ratio of HR staff to total employees and continuously ensure a highly satisfied and motivated work force. The employee satisfaction gets very high priority and it is tracked on a weekly basis through "Pulse"—an online survey and immediate action plans are undertaken to ensure that areas of employee concerned are adequately looked after. Bharat Heavy Electricals (7th Position) ensures complete lifelong medical coverage with no cap on expenditure to not only its all employees but also to retired employee of the company, critically ill employees needing treatment abroad are sent with an escort wherever required to ensure a highly satisfied work force. American Express India (8th rank) has "Blue box values" that drive people policies and provides structured forums for effective communication. 360 degree feedback for the employees, cross-functional training and freedom to apply for a job anywhere in the American Express network of 130 countries, flexible 12 optional holidays from a basket of 26 days, a healthy balance between the work and personal lives are some of the HR innovations in American Express. Colgate Palmolive India (9th rank) provide cross functional move for developing competencies of the employees. For providing global exposure, swap assignments are permitted and all employees are required to work the market irrespective of the grade or function and thus people development remains the key HR strategy. Colgate has placed over 50 people overseas over the past four five years. Gillette India (10th Position) is well known for exposure of employees to international assignments which provide opportunities to widen business perspective, strengthen functional expertise, transfer best practices and operate in a diverse back ground and thus representing "world class brands, products and people". The Hughes Software Systems (11th rank) gives high priority to employees family members and employees are encouraged to be in touch with their families while on travel. Family get together Parties are held every quarter and children's school admissions are facilitated by the company. To facilitate functioning at the workplace on line help desks for separate functions are present which take care of queries on an immediate basis. New year cards are made using the children's paintings open house sessions chaired by HR head makes every one a willing participant in the cost of head count reduction exercise. Tata Steel (12th rank) provides employees and their families perfect spots for rest and reapportion through their holiday homes which span the country. Tata Steel's value - set was laid down by Jamsetji Tata himself; fairness, honesty and ethical behaviour. It is one of the most "Caring" unit which demand high performance levels from its employees, measure these objectively and reward them accordingly. Over the last six years it reduced its work force from 73000 to 48000 but it still lays emphasis on creating a "great workplace". It spends average 86.32 training hours per year for its employees. Tata Steel is well known for a series of libraries, which not only provide an exhaustive and latest collection of books but also allow children of employees to borrow toys, music and children books. Dr. Reddy's Laboratories (Rank 13) is one Indian - born Pharma Company that best reflects greater growth opportunities to their employee than their MNC counterparts. CEO G.V. Prasad believes that "Work is the biggest motivator" and he says "good office space is just a hygiene issue, but what is crucial is the freedom to work, sharing of information and encouraging informality". DRL has over the past three to four years been working towards organisational transformation in a big way through a HR policy facelift with focus on learning and development talent management and performance orientation. Its ratio of HR staff to total employees is 1:80 and it has 60 average training hours per year DRL believes in the over all development of its employees and organises regular outward bound training programmes such as mountain climbing and river rafting offering fun and adventure. The company boasts of a number of interest clubs such as music forum, performing art club etc which encourage and exhibit talent of its employees in different areas. Sasken Communication Technologies (14th rank) observes organisation wise Christmas vacation from December 25 to January 1, every year and sends its employees to leading international management programmes. The Sasken Communication Technologies does whatever it can to ensure that its employees are constantly developing other unique practices include every one, right from the CEO to the most recent recrint sits in the same physical workplace, no attendance logging mechanism is used, employees can choose their designation from a flexible basket, on completion of 4 years an employee is eligible for six weeks of paid leave called libernation leave. It also gives attention to the competence building and employ ability of its employees. In, Sasken, the company decided on an across the board pay cut rather than to lay off people. Oracle India (15th rank), encouraging career opportunities for employees, has pioneered "the Oracle caller line" in which employees interested in a career in a company can call in and get information on the career opportunities, work culture, policies, practices and recruitment methods of the company. The staffers at the company's Bangalore development centre manage to give the phase work life balance a whole new meaning though various development activities and a toll-free number for information about career opportunities. Reliance Industries and Reliance Petroleum (16th Options) ensue that all employee needs are taken care of housing, schooling, medical, recreational, sports, shopping and temples. They have an integrated township at Gamnagar that takes care of all the needs of the employees, from telecommunications to entertainment, and from sports to worship. In Reliance there is a strong performance orientation system wherein every year managers, along with their team, make performance commitments which are kept on managers tables. On achieving this target, the chairman sends a letter complimenting the team. Indian Oil Corporation ranks 17th and provides the freedom to the employees for choosing their training programmes followed by action plan to ensure transfer of learning to the job. Learning and development are critical in the organisation and regular feedback from the supervisor assesses the benefits and effectiveness of the training. Surveys are commissioned to evaluate the effectiveness of the training surveys are commissioned to evaluate the effectiveness of their big programmes. In Compaq Computer India (Rank 18th) the HR postal facilitates multi-source feed back self pace learning, self nominations to development programmes with technology at the cutting edge. This cost provides online resources which include learning centre, training on sale management and inter-personal skills Micro-Soft India ranks 19th believes in practising planned diversity promotes a cultural rich work force that enhances product development and employee performance. For CEO Rajiv Kamal and HR head Debasis Patnaik, the big challenge is to keep their employees charged all the time since it is a dynamic, engaging, fast paced and informal company. Maruti Udyog values personal life of its employees and provides a golden week which is shut-down for two weeks in June and December to match the holidays of the children. It provides paid maternity leave beyond the statutory provisions of 36 weeks. Maruti has moved to an appraisal system where only the performance and potential of the employee are the criteria for promotion. Polaris Software Ranks 21st and employees are encouraged by the organisation to have fun through birthday, bashes, parties, family celebration and the Polaris days. This highly result oriented company ensures that a "Bonzer" man works with different work groups playing quizes and games to facilitate bonding and teamwork. Johnson & Johnson Ranks 22nd position among best employers provides unlimited sick leave to employees. The "Credo" (Creed) reflects the mission and values of the coy is practiced and lived by all employees. L.G. Electronics India (23rd Place) provides assistance to the employees on marriages and death of a family member. Representatives from the company visit employee homes and inform them about what the employees do at work thus ensuring family support to work life stress. Family members are welcome to visit office premises and work place to have a feel of where their beloved ones work and thus ensure better family support. The S.I. Micro-electronics (24th Rank) provides a full-fledged university which trains employees both in technical and behavioural areas. It has an attractive employee refersal scheme where a refersal award can go upto Rs. 1.6 Lakh and ensures that the desired talent is tapped through efficient and cost-effective means. This coy is operating in recessionary industry but it rules out lay offs, and thus its employees can afford to relax. Tata Engineering is 25th in the rank and is one of the rare companies where HR serves not as a cost centre but a revenue generator. It offers an innovative "leave Bank where employee credit their leave to the bank and a needy employee can debit the accumulated leave at any pourt.[19] The best 25 companies employees constantly carry out new innovations in people, programmes and ensure a healthy work environment having efficacy in delivery of HR services, including the used of technology. In ICICI around 33 percent of all employees are women. Apart from the three of the seven members on the executive management at the Board level-Lalita Gupta, Kalpana Morparia and Chand Kochhar, there are five women among the 22 executives who constitute ICICI's senior management. Infosys has 17 percent women executives.

With Strategic Organisations, people are the Prime Assets:- "Today's employees want career tracks that offer real opportunities for advancement. Mentoring programmes help diverse workers break through barriers like negative stereotypes, exclusion from informal and influential networks and lack of access to high visibility assignments. Work life balance is a key issue nation-wide".20 Organisation must develop a unique organisational culture and corporate saga as powerful symbols with meanings that help or reinforce communication. They can be used to promote and reinforce organisational commitment, convey a philosophy of management, rationalize and legitimate activity, motivate workforce and facilitate organisations socialization. Many management practioners believe that corporate leaders must build up a corporate culture with symbols, rituals, organisational stories company songs, dress code, and extended family system of Indian Culture. Rafacli and Workline (2000-73) consider symbol to be "Visible, physical manifestation of organisational life." Symbols reflect underlying aspects of culture, generating emotional responses from organisational members and representing the organisational values and assumptions.[21] Organisational leaders must create and sustain strategic organisations for achieving success and excellence. Ford Motor company and AT & T used strategic human resource management to unstil in their employees innovating entrepreneurial and risk taking skills and could master the new technologies, invent new products and complete with well settled gaints in new fields. In most of the leading corporations of India like IT Card L & T, their structure is conducive to promoting team work and a high degree of openness. HLL has attained/ reached outstanding level of effectiveness in personnel management, / management training and promoting soft skills. Cross disciplinary team work is becoming a pattern of strategic advantage building in Amul, Asian paints and ITC. These strategic organisations. Motivation is a very important condition that builds a working bond between the people and their organization. Hoick-Larsen, the founder of L & T always asserted need for an excellent work force having proper motivation. "We have always recriuted the best engineers and professionals without paying an attention whatsoever to extra neous social social or political considerations. "L & T is conspicuous for its highly committed work force and merit based promotion policy what makes companies like L & T, Asian paints and Hindustan levers head and shoulders above others is their human resource strategies which place a heavy emphasis on continued training, upgradation of skills and motivation.

Shifting Paradigms of HR Management

Tom Peters has said: "We have transitioned from an asset based economy to a talent based economy. The new definitions of lay off is untalented go, talented stay leaders must realise that talent *is* equal to Brand." His new theory is EVP - Employee value proposition—"Your brand is as good as your people". Rosabeth Moss Kanter said. Human beings are good raw material. They become assets when you train them to increase their knowledge and skills". In September 2001, from 83 countries 12,000 HR managers converged on Orlando, Florida, to attend the ASTD (American Society for Training and Development) Conference and exposition to understand and learn the global trends, techniques and methods of fostering change through shifting paradigms of HR management in the fast changing environment (22). HRM strategies are expected to play a pivotal role in successfully handling the emerging business requirement and leading the transformation for creating value and generating wealth as a partner of business.

References

1. Peter F. Drucker—Management tasks Responsibilities, Practices, Allied Publishers Ltd., New Delhi, 1996, p. 308.
2. Jauch, Lawrence R and William F - glueck - Business policy and Strategic Management - Mc Graw Hill Singapore 1988, p. 11.
3. R.S. Dwivedi - Managing Human Resources - Personnel Management in Indian Enterprises. Galgotia, New Delhi, 1997, p. 15.
4. Michael Porter - Competitive strategy - (1999). Also - Poseter, Michael E - Competitive Advantage creating and sustaining superior performance - Free Press. New York, 1985.
5. Johnson - Gerry - exploring corporate strategy Text and cases, 4th edition, prentice - Hall of India, New Delhi, 1997, p. 4.

6a. "Competing on Human capital" Sumantra Ghosal abd Lynda gratton - Corporate dossier - Economic Times 11-17 June 1999.

6b. S. Sudarshan - Time for wake up call - Indian Management— The Journal of the All India Management Association Oct., 2005. Vol. 44, Issue 10, pp. 28-32.

7. Gupta M.L. Business led HR strategies, All India Management association, Excel Books. New Delhi, 1998, P. 81. Also Sadler, Tony Human Resource Management, Developing a Strategic Approach. Kogan Page, London, 1995.
8. Ashok Chanda and Shilpa Kabra - "Human Resource strategy Architecture for change" Response Books - New Delhi 2000 P. 50. Also Mabey, Christopher - Strategic Human Resource Management. For change, Development and performance. Beacon Books, New Delhi, 1998.
9. G. Seybold—"Personel Audits and Reports to Top Management." Studies in Personnel policy No. 191 National Industrial conference Board 1964.
10. K.B. Dadiseth Business growth through people growth or blue print for the Next Millennium. The Economic Times, New Delhi, 24th April 2000, p. 5.
11. M.F. Gordo—"Three ways to effectively evaluate personnel programmes" Personnel Journal—Vol. 51 (7) 1972, pp. 498-504.

11a. Pradeep Kumar Ekka—Managing Employee Attrition—Indian Management. The Journal of All India Management Association, June 2005. Vol. 44—Issue 6, pp. 80-84.

12. R.D. Gordon - evaluating the personnel department - personnel 1965. 42 (2).

12a. S. Sudershan—Time for wake up call - Indian Management October 2005, Vol. 44-Issue 10, p. 32.

13. Ashok Chanda and Shilpa Kabra - Human Resource strategy-Architecture for change. Response Books. New Delhi, 2000, p. 147.

14. B.T. Hewett best employers in India Survey—The Hewitt Core Team Ravi Virman, Purva Misra, Sumer Datta and Madhavi Misra-study coordinator Sapna Khurana and Satish Dhasmana, Business Today, March 3, 2002, p. 59.

15. Source—Business Today - 51 March 3, 2002, p. What makes the Best the Best Madhavi Misra and Purva Misra.

16. Business Today March 3, 2002, p. 38-39. The Best employers in India.

17. Author is grateful to Madhavi Misra and Purva Misra for their cover page story—"Innovations that make a difference" in Business Today March 3, 2002, pp. 54-56 and reports of Seema Sunkla, Ashntosh Sinla, Nitya Vardharajan, Venkateshan Babu and E. Kumar Sharma for their inputs in Business Today. March 3, 2002, pp. 42-49.

18. Author gratefully acknowledges the research carried out by Madhavi Misra and Purva Misra and cover page story of Innovations that make a difference—Business Today, March 3, 2002, pp. 38-56.

19. Christina Eggert, Omid Nodoushani and Patricia Nodoushani—"Strategic Management of work force Diversity in the 21st Century" Business Journal—Fall Spring 2002, p. 21.

20. Rafacli, Anat and worline, Monica (2000) symbols in org. culture in "Handbook of Org culture and climate" Thousand OAK—Sage, pp. 75-84.

21. Ashok K. Maitra-Shifting Paradigms of HR management. Learning human lessons. "The Learning Curve—The Economic Times, New Delhi, Monday 17 September 2001.

Useful Books Suggested further reading for Strategic Human Resource Management

(*i*) Drucker—(1968) The Practice of management. London: Pan.

(*ii*) Watson K.—(1977) The Personal Managers: A study in the Sociology of Work and Employment. London: Routledge & Kegan Paul.

Wernerflet, B. (1984) 'A resource based view of the firm', Strategic Management Journal, Vol. 5, No. 2, pp. 171-180.

Whittington, R. (1993) What is strategy and Does it Matter? London: Routledge.

Wittington, R. (2001) What is Strategy and does it Matter? 2nd edn. London: Thomson Learning.

(*iii*) Leggee K (1978) Power, Innovation and Problem - Solving in Personnel Management. London: McGraw-Hill.

(*iv*) Purcell J. (1985) 'Is anybody listening to the corporate personnel department?', Personnel Management, Sept., pp. 28-31.

(*v*) Beer M. Spector B, Lawrence PR, Quinn Mills, D. and Walton, R.E.(1984). Managing Human Assets. New York: Free Press.

(*vi*) Legge K (1998) 'The morality of HRM', in Mabey, C., Salaman, G. and Storey, J. (eds) Strategic Human Resource Management: A Reader. London: Open University/Sage, pp. 18-29.

(*vii*) Keenoy (1990) - 'HRM: a case of the wolf in sheep's clothing', Personnel Review, Vol. 19, No. 2, pp. 3-9.

(*viii*) Fombrum C. (1984)—Tichy, N. and Devanna, M. (eds) (1984) Strategic Human Resource Management. New York :
Wiley. Schular, R.S. and Jackson, S.E. (eds) Strategic Human Resource Management. Oxford: Blackwell Business, pp. 142-158.

(*ix*) Schular and Jackson—(2000) Managing Human Resources. A Partner Perspective 7th edn. London: Thomson Learning. Schuler, R.S. and Jackson, S.E. (eds) (1999) Strategic Human Resource Management. Oxford: Blackwell Business.

(*x*) Guest D. (1997)—'Human Resource management and performance: a review and research agenda', International Journal of Human Resource Management, Col. 8, No. 3, pp. 263-276.

(*xi*) Legge K - (1995) Human Resource Management: Rhetoric and Realities. London: Macmillan.

(*xii*) Keenoy, T. and Anthony, P. (1992) 'HRM: metaphor, meaning and morality', in Blyton, P. and Turnbull, P. (eds) Reassessing Human Resource Management. London: Sage.

(*xiii*) Blyton and Turn bull P. eds (1992)—Reassessing HRM. London: Sage. Boxall, P. and Purcell, J. (2003) Strategy and Human Resource Management. New York : Palgrave Macmillan. Butler, J.E., Ferris, G.R. and Napier, N.K. (1991) Strategy and Human Resource Management. Cincinnati, OH: Southwestern Publishing Co. Chandler, A.D (1962) Strategy and Structure: Chapters.

(*xiv*) Kochan and Barocci (1985) Human Resource Management and Industrial Relations. Boston, MA: Little Brown.

(*xv*) Miles, R.E. and Snow, C.C. (1984) 'Designing strategic human resource systems', Organisational Dynamics, Summer, pp. 36-52.

(*xvi*) Pfeffer, J. (1994) Competitive Advantage through People. Boston, MA : Harvard Business School Press.

(*xvii*) Pfeffer, J. (1998) The Human Equation : Building Profits by putting people, First Boston, MA: Harvard Business School Press.

(*xviii*) Huselid M.A. (1995)—'The impact of human resource management on turnover, productivity, and corporate financial performance', Academy of Management Journal, Vol. 38, pp. 635-672.

(*xix*) MacDuffie, J.P. (1995) "Human resource bundles and manufacturing performance" Industrial Relations Review, Vol. 48, No. 2, pp. 199-221. Mahoney, T. and Deckop, J. (1986) 'Evolution of concept and practice in personnel administration/human resource management', Journal of Management, Vol. 12, pp. 223-241.

(*xx*) Guest, D. (2001) 'Human resource management: when research confronts theory', International Journal of Human Resource Management, Vol. 12. No. 7, pp. 1092-1106. Hamel, G. and Prahalad, C. (1993) 'Strategy as stretch and leverage', Harvard Business Review. Vol. 71, No. 2, pp. 75-84. Hamel, G. and Prahalad, C. (1994) Competing for the Future. Boston, MA: Harvard Business School Press. Henderson, B.D. (1989) 'The origin of strategy', Harvards Business Review, November-December, pp. 139-143. Hubbards, N. (1999) Acquisitions strategy and Implementation. Basingstoke: Macmillan.

(*xxi*) Kochan T.A. and Osterman P. (1994) The Mutual Gains Enterprise. Boston, MA: Harvard Businesss School Press.

(*xxii*) Arthur, J. (1994) 'Effects of human resource systems on manufacturing performance and turnover', Academy of Management Journal, Vol. 37, No. 3, pp. 670-687.

(*xxiii*) Dolery, J. and Doty, H. (1996) 'Models of theorizing in strategic human resource management', The Academy of Management Journal, Vol. 39, No. 4, pp. 802-835.

(*xxiv*) Becker, B. and Gerhart, B., (1996) 'The impact of human resource management on organizational performance: Progress and prospects', Academy of Management Journal, Vol. 39, No. 1, pp. 779-801.

(*xxv*) Merchington, M. and Wilkinson, A. (2002) People Management and Development, 2nd edn. London: CIPD.

9

Towards—Global Leadership

Introduction

"Awake Arise and stop not, till thy goal is reached."

Swami Vivekanand's above given slogan should be a source of inspiration for all individuals and organizations who want to achieve excellence in their respective fields. Globalisation is nothing new for India. It was Swami Vivekananda in the Nineteenth Century who first illuminated the western world with leadership through spirituality. Later India's first Prime Minister Jawahar Lal Nehru enhanced the Indian brand of global leadership when he spoke of "Panchsheel" at international forums. Indian Inc could now see the entire world—as their market place. With a thriving domestic market and growing exports, sky is the limit for Indian corporates in this global era. The Tata-Corus deal and Dr. Reddy's acquisition of Betapharm are only further indicators of Indian corporations entering the world market. "Can India become a global leader in next twenty years" is a question which is often discussed and analysed. As a result of globalisation and economic reforms during the last few years, India has made rapid strides in various fields. In India globalisation has resulted in high rates of growth, unprecedented prosperity and above all, a sense of optimism about the future shared by its citizens and many business houses. The fall of the Berlin Wall, the I.T. and communications technological revolution and the emerging transformation of Indian economy have opened new opportunities for Indian business leaders. In order to achieve global leadership - surviving, thriving, innovating, excelling and leading in today's global economy, it calls for hard work, passionate execution, significant contribution of not only from leaders at all levels but also from the entire work force. In the process of globalisation the economic power is inevitably shifting in favour of non-western players—particularly India and China. India is in the global spotlight and could assert its claim for global leadership. A Gold Man Sachs report predicts—that India will become the second largest economy in the world, after China, by 2042. Indian companies must acquire a very good reputation for its quality of products and earn recognition for "Made-in-India brand" overseas. A brand becomes truly global when the consumers of the world embrace it. India is even today a global leader in the field of Insurance and has the largest number of Life Insurance policies in the world. With the Insurance industry booming like never before, the career opportunities in insurance sector are plenty. The Insurance Regulatory and Development Authority (IRDA) bill 1999 allows private insurers to operate in the market. At present with a growth rate of over 20 percent and with off-shore delivery poised to take off in this sector, the Insurance business in India stands at the threshold of a brilliant future, both in terms of growth and careers. Globalisation is more than just about economics. It is not only about the ratio of exports to GDP but also about culture, society, politics, people and human values. India is at present having boom time and current growth rate is constantly rising.

Table Showing Boom Time Current Growth is Higher

Period	*Growth in GDP at factor cost at constant prices*
1993-94	6.0
1994-95	7.0
1995-96	7.3
1996-97	7.5
1997-98	4.8
2002-03	3.8
2003-04	8.5
2004-05	7.5
2005-06	9.0
2006-07*	9.2

*Estimated *Source:* CSO, CMIE

Growth Indicators—Emerging Trends

According to Dr. P. Chidambaram, India today is the largest milk producing country with over 90 million tonnes of milk a year with a per capita milk availability of 231 gm per person per day (2003 - 04). Per capita availability of eggs has increased from 15 in 1980-81 to 40 in 2004-05. These and other allied sectors provide livelihood for about 11 million in principal status and 8 million in subsidiary status. India is the world's largest gold jewellery market and producer. The remittances by non-resident Indians are the single largest flow in the world, reflecting the strong human capital base. India has to become a hub for innovation on a global scale. Peter Drucker saw invention as "the change that creates a new dimension to performance." We have already seen a number of business entities succeeding with new and innovative approaches. There are many case studies - Amul, the Mumbai dabbawala (Lunch carrier) system, shampoo in a sachet to reach the rural poor market, the Cellphone explosion-illustrating India's unique innovative approach and creating new opportunities for growth and global leadership. The large size of the Indian domestic market makes product development in India an attractive proposition. The globalisation of product development is the inevitable development in recent years. According to the NASSCOM study, even if India aims at 20 percent of the total size of the ESO market by 2020, the volume of the business can be in the range of $60 billion which can match the revenues from the I.T. services. India is the fastest growing market for wealth creation. The net worth of India's 40 richest people according to Forbes Asia in 2006 was $ 170 billion (Rs. 7,65,000 crores). The figure in 2005 was $ 106 billion. The rate of growth of India ITES and BPO sector in 2006 was 38.5 percent. The size of the sector was $7.2 billion (Rs. 32,400 crore) and it employed 4.15 lakh people. India is a successful growth story with MNCs looking to participate and reap the rich benefits. Capital formation as a percentage of GDP has gone up.

Table Showing Funds galore (Capital fomation as a percentage of GDP has gone up)

Period	*Gross domestic capital formation as % of GDP*
1993-94	23.1
1994-95	26.1
1995-96	27.2
1996-97	24.6
2002-03	25.0
2003-04	27.4
2004-05	30.2
2005-06	32.2

Source : CMIE, CSO.

During the last ten years capital formation and money supply have gone up. Table showing Money Supply in abundance growth is much higher now compared to the growth in nominal GDP.

Period	*Growth in money supply (%)*	*Growth in nominal GDP (%)*
1993-94	18.4	16.1
1994-95	22.3	17.3
1995-96	13.7	17.0
1996-97	15.2	15.9
2003-04	16.7	12.5
2004-05	12.3	12.0
2005-06	21.2	13.8
2006-07 (Till Feb)	21.3	14.4*

Source : CMIE, RBI. *Estimates.

India has been the largest democracy of the world for last 57 years and thus can be called the global leader of the democratic countries of the world. To start with let us take a look at the framework of value and purpose of Infosys and some other relatively new leading Indian Companies in the IT and pharmaceutical sectors that have built brand equity for India and changed the image of India and Indian products in the world markets. In some ways such companies have done for India what Sony and Toyota did for Japan.[1] "India could be a global leader in education and financial services to name just two possibilities but not until it opens up to the world.[2] The basic issue is : Do Indians have the mindset to be global leaders in today's globally integrated economy. In many ways India is today well prepared to be a global leader: with a vibrant democracy, a free press and the global expansion of Indian multinationals. There are many positive signs indicating the changing nature of the Indian nation. Today India has a great opportunity to make a significant contribution to the global economy in view of its large size of the population, democratic system of governance, multi ethnic plurality and large consumer base. It is the power of Indian minds that can make it globally prosperous. India needs to develop as a nation a unique mindset of doing its very best in all spheres of life to be recognized as a leader. As commented by Gurucharan Das in "India unbound" India will never be a tiger, it is an elephant that has begun to lumber, it will never have speed, but will always have stamina. "Our Prime Minister Dr. Man Mohan Singh has stated in an interview (McKinsey Quarterly 2005 Spl Edition): "One must understand that economic policy and decision-making do not function in a political vacuum. It takes a lot of time to take basic decision we are a federal set up. The state governments come in.... the local authority comes in. It gives our system the label that it is slow moving yet the roots of Indian political system are very strong and dependable." India's best known corporate leaders like K.V. Kamath, Deepak Parekh, Ratan Tata, Shiv Nadar, Suresh Krishna, Nandan Nilekani, Indra Nooyi, have transformed their corporations as global leaders. Globalisation is the new corporate mantra and the new young leaders must figure out how to manage organizations that span different countries, cultures, and regulatory frame works. Performance orientation, learning ability global mind-set and team building ability are the most essential requirements of the corporate global leaders. Ratan Tata believes that Business must be based on values and Ethics.[3] India must not only focus on the big push forward but also focus on sustaining current gains. Indian financial sector has been supporting the growth by bank credit. The figures below will speak for itself.

Bank lending goes up (growth in bank credit) has been noteworthy

Period	*Growth in bank credit in (%)*
1993-94	7.4
1994-95	27.2
1995-96	20.1
1996-97	16.0
2004-05	26.2
2005-06	38.0
2006-07*	29.6

*Till Feb

Source: CMIE, RBI.

(II) India Can Do It

India can do it is a very explosive, controversial and thought provoking topic for any Indian manager. The ever growing consumption, the explosion of new jobs, the avalanche of investments ("both foreign and Indian") the speedy emergence of rural India are all indicators. Three consecutive years of almost 8% growth rate have clearly heralded the era of India's Global Leadership. India is with steady steps moving towards greater goals to trigger a leadership role, and achieve world-class benchmarks in various fields. Globalization, diversification, wider customer interface, changing organizational structure and government regulations, each of these factors increase diversity and the organizational pluralities are becoming growing realities. Indian multinational corporations are increasing reflecting a multinational workforce and leadership ability of managing people diversity. The increasing diversity is seen along gender, age, regional, educational and nationality lines. Managing a global workforce is a key aspect of 'Infosys Technologies' diversity agenda. As Infosys increases its footprint across the world the need for a global workforce assumes greater significance. Towards this Infosys has a Global Talent Inclusively Programme (GTIP), that aims to recruit software engineers across undergraduate schools in the US. Infosys global internship programme attracts interns from- top universities and colleges like MIT, Harvard, Standford and Wharton.[4] Is India ready to lead the world into a wisdom based civilization? Everything we need, we already have: Technology, education, cultural diversity, a collective imagination from a vibrant living mythology and a historic context which has drawn upon every possible spiritual and religious tradition. The Vedas, Upanishads, Bhagwad Gita, Ramayan and other religious scriptures are our greatest treasures. The information age, according to Deepak Chopra, has made India an emerging economic giant. Today India has the largest diaspora spread out through the world and they bring their entire culture, spiritual and historical context with them. We have a very long tough journey ahead, a mountain to climb but all ingredients for that recipe are there and turning the great Indian Dreams into reality is a matter of time, determination and courage.

(III) Challenges of Global Leadership

Today corporate diversity is a global phenomenon as companies across the world take a global course to growth. For in depth analysis of global leadership, there have to be some yardsticks and criteria. In the context of globalization, the following issues emerge.

1. Where are we in terms of world class Bench Marks today?
2. What needs to be done differently in our sector?
3. What mental blocks/road blocks need to be removed to move towards being world class in their journey towards global leadership?

Twenty first century modern India is gradually building an image of a world leader in various fields particular in IT sector. India's emergence as an economic powerhouse has captured the world's attention in a way not seen since the opening of the China's economy. India's superb demographics, the quality of its manpower, the birth of new industries, new consumer aspirations and a radical pro-market shift in the thinking of young Indian has unlocked India's enormous potential as global leader. Based on the results of more than 1990 companies in manufacturing sector, the net margin for nine months of 2006 - 2007 stands at 7.53% more than 2 percent points higher than the FY06 margin. Manufacturing is the latest toast of India Inc. and its score-board is as under—

Table Showing Score Board Net Margins in Manufacturing Sector over the Years

2.15% 1989	3.46% 1994	1.44% 1999	4.31% 2004
3.11% 1990	5.25% 1995	1.25% 2000	5.32% 2005
2.86% 1991	5.25% 1996	1.13% 2001	5.44% 2006
2.50% 1992	3.33% 1997	0.93% 2002	7.53% 2007*
2.35% 1993	2.57% 1998	2.46% 2003	*(Till Dec. '06)

Manufacturing sector of India is gradually increasing its efficiency, performance and output. Indian Inc. will have to achieve corporate excellence for building global leadership but it demands continuous hard work, effective quality control, global mind-set, global competitive edge, strict adherence to ethical values and norms, effective team work, visionary and committed employees and innovative spirit at all levels in the organizations. It is a matter of great optimism to note that Indian stock market is the fastest growing in the world. Global stock exchanges and financial institutions interest in the Indian stock exchange goes to show growth potential for India Inc.

Table Showing Top of the Stocks Best - Performing indices in the last one year (% increase since February 7, 2005)

BSE Mumbai	50
Nikkei, Tokya	47
Bovespa, SAO Paolo	45
Nifty Mumbai	43
Kospi, Seoul	42
IPC Mexico City	40
FTSE London	17
STI, Singapore	15
Hang Seng, Hong Kong	13
Dow Jones New York	1

Source: TOI New Delhi 8/2/06.

India has global leadership for consumer goods and could reach $400 billion by 2010, making it one of the fifth largest in the world. According to Prof. C.K. Prahalad the real source of market promise is not the wealthy few in the developing economy or the emerging middle income consumers. It is the billion of aspiring poor who are joining the market economy for the first time. The size of the particular market is around 4 billion people living on less than $2 per day. According to Prof. Prahalad creating the capacity is based on three simple principles—affordability without sacrificing quality and efficacy, accessibility and availability.[6]

Ranbaxy Laboratories, Asian Paints, Tata Motors, Moser Baer, Sundaram Fasteners Ltd., and Bharat Forge can be cited as case studies who have achieved global success as leaders.

Ranbaxy laboratories have made five acquisitions abroad in 2006 alone. In the Year 2006 there were 170 outbound deals worth $9.57 billion as against 80 inbound deals of $5.5 billion. In 2005 there were 56 inbound deals with $5.1 billion and 136 outbound deals worth $4.3 billion. Some unique deals are shown in table below:

Table A trip through 10 Complex and Interesting Transactions M & AS in 2006

Deal	*Transaction*
Mylan's acquisition of Matrix	First major acquisition of Indian Pharma firm by a Western player/DSP ML, ABN Amro, UBS
Tata Tea's 30% stake buy in Energy brands for $677 mn	Big ticket cross-border deal marks entry of Tatas into the global water business/Rabo, Stanchart
KKR's $990-m buy of Flextronics' software arm	Largest leveraged buyout and technology investment into India/DSP Merrill Lynch, Citi
Acquisition of Aircel by Maxis and Reddy's	Deal completed after many false starts. Marks the Malaysian company's entry into India/Stanchart.

Deal	*Transaction*
Dr. Reddy's 480m acquisition of Betapharm	Two Indian players fought over a European firm. Largest overseas pharma acquisition/ Rothschild, Citi
Suzlon Energy's acquisition of Hansen Transmission	Indian player acquires overseas company roughly of its own size/YES Bank, UBS
Holcim's acquisition of GUJ Ambuja for over $1 bn	Made the Swiss MNC the second-largest player in the Indian market/DSP Merrill Lynch
Lord Krishna Bank's merger with Centurion	Despite opposition from union, LKB ties the knot with CBoP/ Ambit, DSP Merrill Lynch
Dubai Investment's acquisition of Thomas Cook India.	Marks Dubai Investment Group's entry into India. Deal turns Thomas Cook from target to an acquirer/HSBC, Kotak.
Zee acquires stake in Taj Television's Ten Sports	First for an Indian broadcaster to buy stake in a global channel/Ambit

Global Tech firms are now relocating top management functions to India and India is now seen as a big opportunity. India must innovate and build at least 500 super brands for getting global leadership. Stephen P. Smith a brand expert underlines; "A great brand is not merely a maker's mark. It is almost a heraldic symbol carrying with it a whole web of positive associations. If consumer won't normally go quite that far for a particular brand (people die for them) they will certainly go to considerable lengths to buy the brand they have come to know and trust". Indian managers must climb to super brandom though it is a tough, long and winding journey to the hilltop. Super brands are the economic pillars of a nation, its global ambassadors and nation's status symbols.

The Emerging Models of Indian Inc, becoming the Global Leaders?

There are 21 Indian companies which have become global

challengers. There are mainly the following six primary models of global leadership as shown below:-

S.No.	*Sector*	*Company*
1.	Automobile	Bajaj Auto, Tata Motors, Mahindra and Mahindra, TVS Motors, Bharat Forge.
2.	IT / BPO	Infosys, Satyam, Tata Consultancy Services, Wipro
3.	Engineering and Construction	Larsen and Toubro
4.	Health care/Pharmaceutical	Ranbaxy, Cipla, Dr. Reddy"s Laboratories
5.	Steel and industrial goods	Hindalco, Tata Steel, Crompton Greaves
6.	Other sectors	ONGC, Reliance, Videocon, VSNL Tata Tea.

(*Source:* Boston Consulting govt. report—"The new global challengers : Now 100 top companies from rapidly developing economics are going global and changing the world).

India is marching ahead on the basis of the following six models of global leadership. Model one is related to internationally growing companies by taking their established home market product line and brands to global markets. Amul, Infosys, Old Monk, Tata, Kingfisher Beer and Oberoi hotels are Indian brands, corporate which have world class acceptance. The second model companies are pushing their international clout by marketing innovative technology based solutions to leverage their strength in engineering and research. For example, Wipro of the IT services group has expanded rapidly by providing software coding support. From a $545 million company in 2000, it has developed to a $1.8 billion company in 2004. Wipro is making R & D service their next battle ground by building extensive engineering capabilities. The third model consists of companies which are growing by establishing themselves as specialists and global leaders in one specific, relatively narrow product category. Companies like Bharat Forge and Crompton Greaves principally follow the engineering led innovation approach (like Wipro too) they have managed to establish strong positions in their category. Bharat Forge has become the second largest forging company in the world. The fourth model consists of companies who leverage their home country's natural resource advantages. In India, Hindalco and Tata Steel followed this model. The $2.5 billion Hindalco is Asia's largest producer of finished aluminium and alumina. In steel making India has access to some of the richest supplies of iron ore which gives Tata Steel a competitive edge. The fifth model consists of organizations which are rolling out new business models to multiply markets. Indian companies adopting this approach include Reliance and VSNL. The sixth model consists of companies which are acquiring natural resources for their home markets. ONGC comes in this category. It has expanded globally to access oil resources and has committed investments of $4.3 billion in overseas exploration projects. Although above mentioned strategies are distinct in principle, they often overlap in practice. Tata Steel monetises natural resources of its home country, it is also rolling out business models that are perfected in the home country in its acquired business abroad. On 31st January 2007, Tatas have acquired the Anglo-Dutch steel firm Corus for £6.7 Billion. Tata group chairman Ratan Tata says that acquision of Corus marks Tata Steel's first expansion outside Asia and this merger would create the world's fifth biggest steel company. Success of the deal, given the world prices of steel, will depend on how the synergy planned actually works. If steel prices drop, Corus will be a liability for the Tatas, otherwise it is an opportunity well captured. Bangalore based software giant Infosys has joined the likes of E-Bay, Yahoo, Microsoft, Google, Dell and Cisco as a member of Nasdaq 10 Index on 18th December 2006. This will give greater branding, visibility and global recognition to the company. While India Inc. is basking in the glow of overseas conquests, A.T. Kearney ranks India 61st in its list of the most globalised nation in its Foreign Policy Magazine. Index across 12 variables across four broad areas. Economic Integration, person-to-person contact, political engagement and technological connectivity. Table 1 and 2 given hereafter indicate position of various nations. Whatever the tables may show, India is one of the fastest growing world economies and one of the few whose corporate sector is recording robust double digit growth.

Table 1. Showing India Inc. Going Global, But still long way to go

Target Nation	*Value ($ Million)*	*Market Share (%)*	*Number of Deals*
US	181,330.1	16.3	1,392
UK	125,228.9	11.3	674
Canada	90,048.9	8.1	447
Spain	84,775.3	7.6	189
Germany	62,425.9	5.6	642
Italy	56,979.9	5.1	169
The Netherlands	56,928.9	5.1	179
Luxembourg	45,057.9	4.1	23
France	35,416.8	3.2	388
Australia	34,791.7	3.1	372
Sweden	32,437	2.9	220
Switzerland	30,294	2.7	138
Brazil	19,315.2	1.7	100
Hong Kong	16,108.8	1.5	274
Turkey	15,766.5	1.4	69
China	14,971.7	1.4	558
Russian Federation	10,274	0.9	155
Israel	9,262.6	0.8	53
Greece	9,202.1	0.8	34
India	9,059.6	0.8	286

Table 2. As an acquirer, India makes up just 0.7 percent of the cross-border action in value

Acquirer Nation	*Value ($ Million)*	*Market Share (%)*	*Number of Deals*
US	186,347.6	16.8	1,878
Germany	168,825.9	15.2	433
France	110,465.7	9.9	456
UK	103,817.2	9.3	1,007
Spain	82,821.5	7.5	196
The Netherlands	68,678.9	6.2	259
Canada	42,961.2	3.9	643

(Contd.)

Switzerland	37,352.3	3.4	219
Australia	35,543.4	3.2	450
Brazil	26,906.5	2.4	33
Mexico	20,957.4	1.9	31
Italy	20,634.7	1.9	173
Singapore	16,845.5	1.5	258
Japan	15,484.7	1.4	221
Belgium	13,272.2	1.2	126
China	12,963	1.2	132
Hong Kong	12,529.5	1.1	365
South Africa	10,902.9	1.0	63
UAE	10,881.8	1.0	40
Norway	10,857.1	1.0	129
Sweden	10,418.5	0.9	283
Denmark	7,745.5	0.7	96
India	7,553.6	0.7	192

India Inc's confidence in the government is increasing and most sectors are optimistic of the centre's ability to manage economic growth as reported by ET-NCAER Business confidence survey.

Table Showing Holding on Political Confidence Index (PCI)

	Jan '06	*Apr '06*	*July '06*	*Oct '06*	*Jan '07*
Govt's Ability to manage:					
Over all Economic growth	55.3	62.5	41.0	52.0	56.6
Government Finance	43.4	49.5	32.6	39.3	43.0
Inflation	22.1	28.8	19.8	22.1	25.1
Unemployment	15.1	22.9	19.9	18.2	20.1
Exchange Rate	29.7	32.4	18.4	29.0	29.2
Conducive Political Climate	19.2	25.4	18.1	19.1	23.4
External Trade Negotiations (both bilateral/multilateral)	40.8	49.3	35.8	38.7	38.2
Pushing Forward Economic Reforms	53.4	51.6	38.0	44.7	45.5
	110.1	127.3	88.3	103.9	111.0

Source: ET Chennai 23 Jan 07.

India's Incs confidence has touched new heights due to favourable investment climate and over all economic conditions of the country. Indian companies are generally in very good financial health today. This is the result of confidence among Indian promoters. We are gradually achieving competitiveness at the global level. Business confidence by sectors in shown below:[17]

Table showing all over Business Confidence by Sectors

BCI components	*Consumer Non-durables*		*Consumer Durables*		*Intermediates*		*Capital Goods*		*Services*	
	Current	*Previous*	*Current*	*Previous*	*Current*	*Previous*	*Current*	*Previous*	*Current*	*Previous*
Overall Economic Conditions	73.9	52.2	70.0	77.3	74.4	76.0	76.7	78.2	81.9	74.1
Financial Position of Firms	71.0	64.2	71.7	71.2	72.4	71.4	80.8	75.0	66.0	74.1
Investment Climate	58.0	46.3	63.3	68.2	68.5	61.8	61.7	54.8	63.8	61.2
Capacity Utilization	98.6	95.5	98.3	96.8	98.8	97.6	98.3	100.0	98.9	100.0
Business Confidence Index	152.2	130.3	153.1	158.2	158.6	154.9	160.3	155.5	156.8	156.2

There are basically many risks for out bound deals. Regulations in global markets could be a damper particularly in industries like pharma, health care, and energy. Factors like language, culture and seller employees resistance to new owners can be great hurdles in integration. There are dangers of making acquisitions when an industry is on an upswing and buyer could take a long time to recover investments if the cycle turns. Economic down turn in the global market could create serious risks. The Cumulative effects of Indian reforms ever since 1991 have reached a tipping point that has pushed India into a virtuous cycle of higher growth and savings. Indian global leaders have to pro-actively analyse the rapidly changing business environment trends and analyse how they will affect their organisation. Mc Kinsey quarterly global survey of Business Executive (March 2006) had identified the following global trends:

1. Growing number of consumers in emerging economic/ changing consumer tastes.
2. Shift of economic activity between and within Asia and with European union.
3. Greater ease of obtaining information, developing knowledge.

4. Increasing global and talent markets.
5. Increasing constrainsts in supply or usage of neutral resources (*e.g.*, environmental regulations).
6. Increasing communication/inter-action in business and social networking as a result of technological innovation.
7. Shifting industry structures/emerging forms of corporate organisations.
8. Application of scientific techniques and approaches to business management.
9. More intense social backlash against business.
10. Growth of public sector.

Global trends form tangled webs that require their indepth analysis and strategic planning for identifying new growth strategies. Mergers and Acquisitions are great vehicle to put up a global outpost virtually overnight but the exercise can be a one way ticket to disasters. Indian promoters must take care to (i) to approach the local government and take them in confidence; (ii) approach the worker counsel and assure them security and growth prospects; (iii) Spend time on predeal integration planning (iv) gain the confidence of the customers and suppliers; and (v) keep a close watch on competitors. A clutch of Indian corporation is foraying overseas via a judicious mix of joint ventures, greenfield forays and acquisitions. India cannot become a global leader solely through services. It needs to leverage available opportunities in the manufacturing sector with grade employment and income benefit. There is a need for shifting to a market creating mindset.

(IV) Core Competencies required to be Leaders of the Future

According to Stephen H.Rhimesmith (1993) the core competencies required for global managers in the post-liberal economy can be summarized as under:

1. Managing competitiveness by constantly scanning the environment for change in market, socio-economic and political trends and global competition conditions.

2. Managing complexity by managing trade-offs of many competing interests as well as the inherent conflicts and contradictions of various global organizations.
3. Managing adaptability by developing a global culture with the values, beliefs, systems and norms of behavior.
4. Managing teams with multi-cultural sensitivity demands cultural - sensitivity and management skills to lead, supervise and manage people coming from wide range of different nationals.
5. Managing uncertainties to deal with constantly changing environment.
6. Managing learning on a continuous basis and building a learning organization. Liberalization requires administrators to put due emphasis on productivity, quality, effectiveness, efficiency, latest technology, skill development and customer satisfaction. In a liberal economy, globalization throws the following main challenges: (a) Technology and machinery upgradation, (b) Attracting maintaining and developing efficient, competent and trained professionals, (c) Competitiveness in terms of product and cost. Emerging Mega trends India's dormant and vigorous entrepreneurial genes have been resurrected due to recent economic reforms. There is a ravishing hunger to be competitive through increased focus on enhancing productivity in the manufacturing sector. These indicators given below clearly point to India's increasing presence in the global economic scenario. Today India is among the top Five-bulk drug manufacturing nations in the world. India's pharmaceutical industry is worth $ 6.5 Billion, the fourth largest in the world in volume terms. Over the last decade corporate India has been restructuring itself making management more professional in increasing efficiencies. The Indian consumer is the world's emerging engine of demand. Private consumption accounts for 64% of the Indian GDP, compared to 58% for Europe and 42% for China. During the last ten years India has rediscovered its

self-confidence and can do it spirit. India has huge potential for global leadership in various fields of life. India has huge and daunting challenges and the following are few which need immediate attention: (i) Providing greater labour flexibility, (ii) Capacity building through medical care and attention, (iii) Achieving higher growth in agriculture, (iv) Improving the urban and rural infrastructure, (v) Overcoming the Xenophobia of FDI, (vi) Getting the fiscal deficit under control, (vii) Controlling and targeting subsidies.[8]

India can overcome all the daunting challenges because today it has the youngest and most ambitious population in the World. 65% of the population is below 35 years of age and 50% below 20 years. The world class success record of 25 years of Infosys has shown that it is possible for a group of highly talented professionals to come together, share a common vision and collectively contribute to the success of an enterprise without the ego clashes. Infosys, along with a few other software majors, rewrote the rules of the outsourcing game, primarily moving those modules of software development that could be executed outside the borders of a customer's home country. Indeed ever since Infosys began operations in 1982; its sales have grown at a compounded annual rate of nearly 60 percent.

(VI) India's Swot Analysis

(a) Strengths

- Skilled Manpower.
- Power to leverage IT.
- Low operating cost.
- Becoming Hub for Global sourcing for auto components.
- Sound banking system.
- Mature and strong democratic system of governance.
- Ancient Indian wisdom inherited from Vedas, Upnishads and other scriptures.
- Plural, multi-ethnic, secular society.
- Abundant natural resources.
- Emerging entrepreneurship.

- Indian Railways is the world's largest employer and one of the biggest and basiest rail-networks in the world, carrying 17 million people every day.
- The incredible India as a tourist paradise. The foreign visitors to India have been rising and reached a record 3.92 millions in 2005 and 4.44 millions in 2006 as shown below:

Table Showing Tourism Statistics

Year	*Arrivals*	*Growth (%)*	*Mumbai*	*Delhi*	*Chennai*	*Kolkata*
2002	2,360,000	-6.98	25.40	28.60	11.50	3.80
2003	2,726,000	15.51	24.10	30.80	10.5	3.70
2004	3,406,623	24.97	25.10	32.20	10.30	3.30
2005	3,915,324	14.93	24.90	32.00	9.90	3.10
2006*	4,443,893	13.50	25.00	32.10	10.00	2.90

Figures for the four metros indicate percentage share of total arrivals
*2006 figures are from HVS Estimates
Source: HVS International.

(*i*) India is the third largest market for diamond and diamond jewellery after the U.S. and Japan. India will grow atleast five times the current growth rate over the next five years says Cherie Tandon Saldanhe, Managing Director, Diamond Trading Corporation Marketing India.

(*ii*) Hero Honda is the world's largest two wheeler manufacturer for five consecutive years.

The future of India is in the entrepreneurial spirit of the twenty five year old and fifteen years old says Tom Peter; he further says we are now at the very beginning of an enormous telecom and information revolution of which India is going to be one of the biggest beneficiaries. Louis V. Gerstner. (Former IBM CEO) has said "Elephants can dance, Big matters, size can be leveraged, breath and depth allow for greater investment. greater risk taking and longer patience for future pay off". This holds good for India as an emerging leader.

The National Stock Exchange has created a conducive climate for Indian Investors to invest in the opportunity economy. National Stock Exchange (NSE) is the unchallenged market leader since

October, 1993. Approximately 90% of capital market volumes in India were routed through NSE in 2006-07. NSE has around 50,000 terminals across 1500 plus locations in India. NSE is the world's largest stock exchange in terms of number of traders in equity shares. NSE is the world's largest stock exchange in terms of Single Stock Futures. The NSE Index-NIFTY 50 is universally considered the barometer of the Indian Economy.

(B) Weakness. Nearly 200 million people who are poor have to be lifted by upgrading their quality of life in both rural and urban areas before India can call itself a developed country. Dr. Man Mohan Singh has said: "There is a long road ahead for India. The backlog of poverty, ignorance and disease continue to hold India and Indian back. We have to invest more in education, health care, and labour-intensive sectors that generate employment and so on to bridge the development divide in India." The infrastructure constraints—power, roads, ports, lack of adequate management professionals with adequate funds are to be overcome by strong political will power, and support of Foreign Direct Investors and local business houses. We have to work intelligently and continuously towards harnessing all available opportunities to build and create India as a global leader in its own right. The infrastructural weakness are as under:-

(*i*) Power Sector

- Over 90,000 MW of new generation capacity is required in the next seven years. A corresponding investment is required in the transmission and distribution networks. Power costs need to be reduced from the current high of 8-10 cents/unit by a combination of lower AT & C losses, increased generation efficiencies and added low cost generating capacity.

(*ii*) Telecommunication

- The telecommunications market in India is projected to grow 30-40% per annum to reach 250 million subscribers by 2009-2010. Over 5 million new users are added every month-in wireless.

(*iii*) Rural Sector

There is lot of under employment, unemployment, poverty, starvation, under nutrition and illiteracy even today in Indian rural areas. According to National Sample Survey report (61st round July 2004—June 2005) thirty seven percent of the rural and 18 percent of the urban women usually carry out some economic activity in addition to their principal and subsidiary status in a household. One year National Rural Employment Guarantee Programes are pointers of real human stories of development as can be seen from table below.

Table Showing NR EGA one year performance

1.	No. of states covered	-	27
2.	No. of districts covered	-	200
3.	Job cards issued	-	3.47 Crore Households.
4.	Employment demanded	-	1.51 Crore Households.
5.	Employment provided	-	1.47 Crore Households.
6.	Funds released	-	Rs. 671497.57 Lakhs
7.	Total Expenditure	-	Rs. 503395.65 Lakhs
8.	Employment generated	-	Rs. 5365.37 Lakh man days
9.	Employment generated	-	A. SC - 24.58%
			B. ST - 38%
			C. Women - 39.38%

India has about 650 million people living in the villages and agriculture accounts for 26% of India GDP which is $ 162 billion. We should gradually reduce the number of people dependent on agriculture and national rural employment guarantee scheme is aiming to improve the economic lot of the rural poor masses. The impact will be noticeable in 5 years if scheme is properly implemented all over the country. No Indian youth should be without either a world - class higher education or without world class skill sets.

(*iv*) Roads

- The roads sector requires US$ 50-60 billion investment over the next five years to improve road infrastructure.
- Passenger Traffic is projected to grow at 12-15% and cargo traffic at 15-18%.

(*v*) Ports

- Cargo handling at all the ports is projected to grow at 7.7% per annum till 2013-14 with minor ports growing at a faster rate of 8.5% compared to the 7.4 for the major ports.

- Port Traffic is estimated to reach 960 million tonnes by 2013-14.
- Containerized cargo is expected to grow at 17.3% over the next nine years.
- The New Foreign Trade Policy envisages doubling of India's share in global exports in the next five years to US $150 Billion.

2. Lack of political consensus and political will.
3. Bureaucracy—Affecting FDI—Red Tapism and lack of commitment.
4. Corruption at different level in system.
5. Negative perception of Indian products—Poor Quality.
6. Barriers to growth Economic recession slow down, inability to hire needed talent, regularly changes, insufficient financing for investment, rising cost of natural resources and major currency shift on financial market crises, are considered main barriers to economic growth.

Table given below shows barriers to growth Executive Perspective.

Which of these factors will be the biggest constrain on your company's growth during the next three years?

	Increasingly competitive environment	*Economic slowdown/ recession*	*Inability to the needed talent*	*Regulatory Changes*	*Insufficient Financing for investment*	*Rising cost of natural resources*	*Major currency shift on financial market crises*
India	59	28	55	35	9	30	26
Asia	54	47	46	31	12	14	21
US	53	54	48	21	16	10	17
UK	62	49	45	23	13	9	18
Western Europe	52	41	39	19	14	12	18
Eastern Europe	51	26	40	37	16	20	14
China	40	35	45	43	19	14	28
Latin America	39	42	20	44	31	13	31

Figures are per cent of respondents who selected given factor.
All data weighted by GDP of constituent countries, excludes respondents who answered don't know or other.
Source: Mc Kinsey Survey of 1,338 executives in 100 countries.

Opportunity

- Global sourcing hub for various mergers and acquisitions
- IT-ITES, BPOs operations
- Medical tourism—Traditional schools of Indian Medicine—Ayurveda
- Leverage agricultural produce
- Project India as a country-Incredible India—a tourist paradise.
- India as teacher and trainer of the world - in fields of spiritualism, yoga academics and business management.

Threats

(*i*) Emergence of China as a LCC (low cost country), (*ii*) Protectionist Policies of USA and European Union, (*iii*) Environmental Changes and Its Disastrous Consequences-Tsunami, (*iv*) Political pressure to slowdown Economic reforms and globalization policies, (*v*) Environmental disasters—earthquakes, floods. (*vi*) Global Financial Crisis.

(VII) The Journey ahead

On the eve of the 58th Republic Day, 26th January 2005, President Dr. A.P.J. Abdul Kalam, addressing to the nation said that India could become a developed country and could have a global presence in strategic sectors. According to him there are many important tasks like making education accessible to every citizen, uplifting citizens below the poverty line through a focussed mission and accelerating agriculture reforms in a mission mode and with transparency. "In order to achieve 100 per cent literacy, near zero number of people below poverty line, tele density of 75 percent, quality power supply to all villages, equitable distribution of drinking water and water for irrigation and the industry, a national movement for development is essential in which every citizen, every constituent of our democracy, has to participate. The corporate sector has to rise to the occasion and should think of reaching the "Unreached" as an essential component of corporate social responsibility. The Indian youth should take up politics as a career in large numbers and citizens should proactively cast their votes to select candidates with proven performance, with honesty as the focus. There should be proper representation of women in all decision-making institutions." India has a multicultural multiethnic society with a vibrant democracy and a free press. In 2004, it accounted for 1.62% of the global GDP and only 1.07% of world trade. Despite the great strides in globalization during the last few years, India is still perceived in some global pockets as a country where wild elephants roam the streets.[9] The major road blocks are briefly enumerated as

1. Domestic Diversified Business
2. Lack of global mindset
3. Lack of scale
4. Lack of capital
5. Lack of global strategy
6. Government rules and regulations
7. Ethnocentric culture
8. Limited Experience in International Marketing.[10]

The National Manufacturing Competitiveness Council (NMCC) has identified factors that impinge issues of competitiveness, like tariffs and taxes, cost of capital, innovation and technology, infrastructure and the regulatory environment.[11] The journey is tough ahead. In India there are about 850 million poor who earn less than $ 2 a day and 370 million people living in extremely poor conditions earning less than one dollar a day.[12] According to UNDP report. In India, 79% of the rural people have sustainable access to cleaner water and 95% of people in urban areas have access to cleaner water. 61% of the urban population has access to improved sanitation. The back of rural household (56 percent) are still without electricity (2004-05) India's onward journey towards economic development is tough and very challenging.

Can India overcome the challenges to become a global powerhouse? Both the perceptions and the reality of manufacturing in India have shifted radically during the last one year. India has created the National Manufacturing Competitive Council (NMCC) for developing a national strategy with regard to academic leadership, talent management, and technology. Growth strategies for manufacturing should be viewed through the lens of the four forces framework of enablers, which encompasses modularity of products and supply chains, connecting technologies, economic integration and resource management. India is maturing as a global expert hub with exports growing from 3.5 to 7.4 percent of total sales. However, Indian suppliers must deploy strategies compatible with those of their OEM (Original equipment manufacturers) sourcing companies. Fortunately India is becoming the top destination for Research and Development investment. Buying houses in India are emerging as a link between Indian manufacturers and global retailers. In health care and medical electronics, India is leveraging information technology. A road map needs to be prepared to enable Indian manufacturing in becoming global.

A Case Study of Indian Global Leader

(*i*) Brief Snapshot about Bharat Forge

Bharat Forge Ltd is one of the most innovative and exciting companies to emerge in the history of the forging industry. The Indian Automotive Industry in the 50's was more like the story of imported kits. Ancillaries were nominal and infrastructure was scarce and inadequate, it was then, that Bharat Forge came into existence in 1961 to meet the forging needs of the Indian Automotive Industry. Bharat Forge Ltd (BFL) the flagship company of the $ 1.5 billion Kalyani Group, is currently a full service supplier of chassis and engine components. It is one of the leading chassis component manufacturers in the world and it is the largest exporter of auto components from India. It has manufacturing facilities spread over eight locations and five countries—two factories in India, three in Germany, one in Sweden, one in Scotland and one in North America. The company manufactures a wide range of critical components for commercial vehicles, passenger cars, and diesel engines. It also makes specialized components for the railway, and the construction equipment, oil and gas and other sectors. It is capable of producing large volume parts in both steel and aluminium.

(*ii*) BFL Before Going Global

The 70's witnessed a spurt in the Indian forging industry with more and more units coming up. For Bharat Forge, it was a period of consolidation and growth. With the largest integrated facilities in Asia and an unbeatable track record, Bharat Forge emerged as the undisputed leader—the first name in the forgings industry in India. With an emphasis on diversification, the 80's saw Bharat Forge grow from a primarily automotive ancillary to an engineering enterprise focusing on technological supremacy, resilience and total customer-orientation.

(iii) The Need to go Global

Until a few years ago, it led a very sedate existence. Today, this company based in Pune (160 km south of Mumbai, India's financial capital) is fighting for market share globally. "In 1997, it worked with the Tata Strategic Management Group (TSMG) to draw up a five-year strategic plan for the company," "Part of the objective was to aggressively grow the business by accessing global markets, and to be among the top three global players in the industry segment." What made BFL abandon its earlier sedentary style? A host of external factors spurred the international foray-aligning of interest rates with global rates, lowering of import barriers, and easy access to international funding. However, to stay competitive, Indian companies have to build a global workforce, integrate various operations, and successfully manage their global business. And this is the blueprint that BFL has etched for itself to keep to the road while speeding up even further. Today, it is the world's second largest forgings manufacturer. It has a presence in every important part for passenger cars and commercial vehicles. Part of this success story is because of the freedom allowed by the new India. The other half lies in the opportunities thrown up because the big boys failed to read the writing on the wall. Rising costs, a capacity glut and stiffer competition forced car-makers such as Daimler Chrysler, General Motors and Ford to cut costs. This pressure was passed to parts suppliers, forcing them to either seek cheaper manufacturing locations or shut shop. Some of the these companies, based in the US and Europe, were up for sale at bargain prices. Enter Bharat Forge. After moving from its traditions Russian and East European markets, BFL trained its sights on the US, Western Europe and China. The pick of the beleaguered pack was snapped up. Part of the production was moved to India, where low cost labour gives a pricing edge.

(*iv*) How it has gone Global

Baba Kalyani has spent nearly $ 120 million in acquiring companies in the UK, the US and Germany. When asked he says: "We believe that to serve customers better across geographies, capacities need to be spread across the globe. The concept revolves around creating 'dual shore' manufacturing facilities that complement each other," he explains. Baba Kalyani says : "We are following a strategy to achieve global leadership partly through expansion and partly through acquisitions" BFL's trophies include Kristall Forge of the UK (acquired in 2000 at $ 4.5 million), and two German companies—CDP and CDP Aluminiumtechnik (in 2003 - 04 at $ 50 million and $ 8 million respectively). In early July 2005, the company announced its acquisition of Michigan-based Federal Forge Inc ($10 million) and Imatra Kilsta AB and its subsidiary Scottish Stampings ($ 55 million). Today, BFL derives 64 per cent of its consolidated revenues of around $ 445 million from the international markets. The acquisition of CDP has been particularly advantageous. BFL's total forgings capacity has gone up 40 percent to 190,000 units. Production, which was heavily concentrated at its plant in Pune, is now segregated in a volume ratio of around 2:1 between India and Germany. However, Kalyani wants more. He is targeting a consolidated turnover of $1 billion by 2008. According to him, it will be achieved by leveraging existing relationships with global automobile companies and their Tier I suppliers to become a development partner, where BFL can play an active role in product design and development, offering solution from conceptualization to product delivery. This will also give BFL a captive market, as automobile companies have deep relationships with such suppliers Analysts are bullish. "Despite its seemingly high valuation, we remain positive on the stock owing to the company's competitiveness, export scalability and proven delivery capabilities, "Says auto analyst S.Ramnath from SSKI India, one of the country's leading brokerage firms. It plans to set up technology development centres in Europe and the US, while using its production base in India for lower cost output. Kalyani has also invested wisely in technology and has understood its importance from early on. He roped in foreign collaborators like Rockwell International and Bendix Corporation for axles and brake systems. At present, the company is planning to set up technology development centres in Europe and the US, while using its production base in India for lower-cost output. Technology investments have been accompanied by a focus on quality.

(v) BFL—The Way ahead

Automobiles are the Future—BFL's long-term strategy is to increase sales to car companies physically close. Second, existing companies come with contracts, networks and relationships. It is possible to replicate that, but it takes time. If you are in a hurry, takeovers are the only option. BFL is currently focused on creating a position of global leadership in engine and chasis components for passenger and commercial vehicles and has embarked upon a three pronged strategy to offer customers dual - shore design capability, dual-shore forging manufacturing capability, and dual-shore machining capability. That means offering these facilities from different centers, whichever is the most appropriate in each individual case. It has also set up a center of excellence in Germany with a specific focus on frontline product development capability and participation in the product development initiatives of customes. BFL is convinced that it needs to reconfigure its product mix. Both domestically and globally, the car and sports utility vehicles market is about four times the size of the commercial vehicles market. However, currently, only 9 percent of the company's sales are to car companies while 60 percent are to truck companies. The Company's long-term strategy is to increase sales to car companies.

BFL has already got initial orders from Daimler Chrysler, Ford and Renault and now hopes to make the long journey from initial orders to bulk orders from these global OEMs. Automobiles are the future. Meanwhile, BFL continues to pay special attention to the truck segment. The company is already a supplier to Arvin Meritor, Dana, and Cummins in the US, and to Caterpillar and Perkins in Europe. BFL also became one of the first Indian companies to bag large orders from China. Last year, it signed an agreement with First Auto Works for $ 25 million worth of forgings annually for the next five years and

$ 15 million annually for the next three to five years with Second Auto Works. Both these Chinese companies produce a large range of vehicles from cars to trucks. There's more happening in China. In December 2005, BFL entered into a joint venture (JV) with FAW corporation. The Indian Forging major will hold a majority 52 per cent stake in the JV.FAW Bharat Forge will manufacture highly engineered forged auto components. "We are following a strategy to achieve global leadership, partly through expansion and partly through acquisitions, says Kalyani. "We have made acquisitions in Europe and the US, and we will now have a presence in China, which will give us an entry into the world's third -largest car market. "The FAW group has ties with Volkswagen, Toyota and Mazda. A new world deserves a new look. BFL has recently unveiled a new identity. The baseline is "Driving Innovation". And, if Baba Kalyani has his way, it will be a drive across the world.[13]

(*ix*) Recommendations and Suggestions for Indian Companies for becoming Global Leader

1. The time to develop global competitiveness is when the company has resources and capacity of introducing change for improvement in balance sheet, sales performance and profitability. Team work, time management and accountability are three essential requirements for achieving success. Proper succession planning and career planning of global players are important factors in sustaining global leadership.
2. The will and determination to set ambitious goals for the organization and the passion to achieve such goals against all odds differentiate the global leaders who build outstanding organizations in the global context.
3. A proactive mindset and a positive attitude, not withstanding the forces working against such approach and behavior, lead to success in achieving global leadership in the long run. Prof. Rooshi Kumar Pandya, globally renowned guru of behavioural skills has said: "Having a positive self image, awareness of one's strength and weakness, seven to eight hours of sound sleep with lights off, nutritional diet,

maintenance of weight, no tobacco, regular exercise and practice of relaxation techniques/meditation by methods by shavasana, Transcendental meditation and sudarshan Kriya will enable a healthy life style and prepare themselves to fight frequent burn outs.

4. Clear purpose, vision and mission evolved through participatory process and widely shared across the organization with a high level of open communication, commitment and involvement among members of the organization for goals and targets will achieve and establish global excellence.
5. Indian firms must develop world class competencies, best practices, superior technology and management know how for achieving sectoral global leadership.
6. Indian multinational organizations must be extremely meticulous in translating any strategy into action-oriented plan and implement the same with high speed and efficiency to achieve global competitive edge. India can achieve global leadership in industrial and economic sectors if managers can adequately focus on the following items (*a*) High productivity (*b*) Quality control (*c*) Efficient performance of managerial and supervisory effectiveness (*d*) Use of update technology (*e*) Production and distribution of manufactured goods with speed (*f*) Customer management with best practices (*g*) Periodical human resource development (*h*) Diversification and specialization (*i*) Getting employee committed to organizational goals and missions (*j*) Commitment of all employees to achieve maximum result with speed and quality, (*k*) Ensuring vertical and horizontal communication.
7. Indian Companies should seriously consider internationalization route as strategy for developing competitiveness and tapping larger markets.[14] Based on a study of 150 strategic moves spanning more than a hundred years and thirty industries, Kin and Manborgne in their book "Blue Ocean Strategy" (Harvard Business School Press, Boston 2005.) argue that tomorrow's leading companies will succeed not by battling competitions but by creating "blue oceans" of uncontested market space ripe for growth. Such

strategic moves termed "value innovation" create powerful leaps in value for both the firm and its buyers, rendering rival obsolete and unleasing new demand. W. Chan Kin and Renee Manborgne have enunciated Six principles to formulate and execute above mentioned blue ocean strategies. The six principles show how to reconstruct market boundaries, focus on the big picture, reach beyond existing demand, get the strategic sequence right overcome organizational hurdles and build execution into strategy.

8. Transparency, meritocracy and professionalism in management and governance are important for becoming a world-class, internationally competitive organization.
9. Modesty humanity, access and informality in dealing with people are pre-requisite for success in business organizations. Career planning for all employees with good HR practices can help organizations in becoming global.
10. Passion to win and sustain international competitiveness has to be a continuous process and inspiring transformational top level leadership alone can lead Indian firm to global leadership.
11. Victor Menezes, Senior Vice-Chairman Citigroup In. has said: "At the end of the day, what is going to drive our business is top line growth, is innovation." A land mark study conducted by Pricewater House Coopers (PWC) found the most innovative were those firms that generated well above average shareholders returns (greater than 37 percent) and also had more than 75 percent turnover from products and service introduced within the last five years.[15] In today's global economy to deliver breakthrough results, business need to maintain a strategic focus on innovation.[16]
12. Indian business should gear up for tougher corporate governance standards.

13. TATA's cheap ear NANO project should complete its manufacturing on target dates and become world leader for small car production.

14. There are essentially the following eight factors which will make India succeed as a global leader in the 21st Century.

    (*a*) Global mindset; (*b*) Global acquisition and integration; (*c*) Quality reputation; (*d*) Difference through design and innovation; (*e*) Nurture world wide talent and leadership; (*f*) Global branding and positioning; (*g*) Global segmentation and targeting; (h) World wide supply chain.[17] Instead of becoming fiercest rivals in the global economy over next decade in terms of market, capital and investment, India and China must become great partners and become the most effective bloc in world trade.

15. For achieving global leadership the excellence in execution enables us to grow better that competition, produce at lower costs, meet customer expectations and become consistently successful. Success lies in getting the product or services out at a line when there is an opportunity, while making sure that pricing, advertising and everything else in the mix is right.[18]

16. India has to increase its manufacturing share to 40 percent to create employment for its millions of the people, while encouraging local manufacturers to become MNCs.

The 3D Model for Global Leadership

The goal of global leadership has to be actualised by continuous, ongoing sustained, all inclusive development of the nation for a reasonable period of time. 3D model for global leadership constitutes three different dimensions as given below:-

D1—Domains (Dominant infrastructure) include manufacturing sector, services territory sector and agriculture, mining and water resources. Land, capital and nature come under this category.

D2—Drivers include macro economic stability, infrastructure, demographic factors, Tourism, Efficient institutions, pro-active policies and govt. regulations, innovations, Health care and HRD Sector.

D3—Distant on going journey aimed at the targeted economic development and growth all be inclusive, plural, equitable and sustainable over a period of decades. The people below the poverty line should be brought to zero level within a decade. India has to lead the nations of the world in various fields and continue its superiority. Destination has to be a strong, vibrant, sustainable, democratic. India with high democratic value, secular base, tolerant plural society based on federal constitutional set up. Zig Ziglar says : "Success is not a destination, it is a journey."

India's progress during the last ten years or so indicates the following achievements:—(1) The contribution of services domain shot up from 41.1% to 53.64% of economy from 1990-91 to 2005-2006, (2) The contribution of manufacturing sector increased from 13.24% to 15.89% of economy from 1990-91 to 2005-2006, (3) Share of agriculture sector reduced from 28.52% to 17%, (4) Indian I.T. Services export (including BPO Services) touched 1,04,130 crore from mere 250 crore in 1991 (showing 41552% increase) and is stated to become 2,70,000 crore by 2010. India now commands 65% share of global offshore market and 46% share of BPO market, (5) The teledensity has increased from abysmal 0.69% in 1991 to 16% in 2006, (6) Organised retail is likely to occupy 14,00,000 crore sector (about 40 percent of GDP) within next five years, (7) Mutual funds manage Rs. 2,31,862 crore and banking system with assets of 12,11,760 crores and deposits of 9,87,360 crore, (8) India's contribution towards infrastructure is only 4.1% of its GDP. We must ensure $325 billion investment in infrastructure in the next five years. Figure given on the next page depicts the suggested 3D model of global leadership. Global leadership is dynamic ongoing process and continuous efforts and full utilisations of all resources are needed to remain on the top. Other nations will continue to make efforts to reach the top and therefore it is maintaining a competitive edge over other countries. Global leadership in various fields can be a continuous race for getting competitive edge over other countries by adopting various strategies. Balanced economic development of the nation having sustained growth, equity and all inclusiveness can be by itself a worth while pursuing goal.

Figure 3D Model for Global Leadership.

Factors	Dimension
1. Strong and vibrant India 2. Plural, secular, Tolerant India with strong spiritual base 3. Constitutional, federal, democratic system. 4. Spirit of Entrepreneur and innovativeness. 5. Equitable, Sustainable and inclusive economic development 6. Political stability and maturity. 7. Incredible India—a tourist paradise 8. Resources availability and optimum utilisation.	Distant onward Journey for global leadership D-3
1. Higher GDP growth 2. Manufacturing and IT performance 3. Demographic factors and huge HR Capital 4. Infrastructural developments 5. Increasing consumerism and high income 6. Cheaper and easier financial schemes 7. Economic development in rural sector 8. HRD and education sector 9. Innovations and new strategies 10. Health care and Medical tourism 11. Pro-active economic policies drivers of growth. 12. Macro-economic stability.	Drivers for Higher growth D-2
1. Manufacturing Sector 2. Service and Tertiary Sector/logistics 3. Agriculture mining and food processing 4. Human resources land/H.R.D. activities 5. Capital and Financial System 6. Land, Capital and other resources.	Domain (Dominant Infra-structure) D-1

India must strengthen its roots of democratic governance by more active participation of women by granting 33 percent seats in parliament and state legislative assemblies. Jagadish Bhagwati, university Professor Economics and law at Columbia

University believes that democracy is a big asset when it comes to sustainability of growth. Peter F. Drucker has said: "The most valuable asset of a 21st Century institution, whether business or non-business, will be its knowledge workers and their productivity." For Indian companies going global in a big way and MNCs hiring Indian professionals for global assignments-international immigration or relocation of senior executives overseas is proving a big challenge and a great opportunity. The challenges of global leadership are mainly cross-cultural and getting acclimatized to the new country's environment, learning local customs, traditions and language besides other cultural issues. India needs to be competitive and for that we take inputs from Porter's theory of Competitive Advantage. In his most famous work the competitive advantage of the nations 1990 Michael Porter has said "There are four broad attributes that are the main determinants of competitive advantages these are:

1. Factor conditions—Skills infrastructure so on
2. Demand Conditions
3. Related and supporting industries
4. Firm strategy structure and rivalry

India's future is in the hands of young, dynamic and forward looking Indian and will be what Indian make of it. India can become a global leader in the economic and industrial sectors only when we have totally dedicated young entrepreneurs and managers who want to make a difference by making company great and build a future where customers, employees, shareholders and society find win and win relationship. We are not saying it is easy, but it is worthwhile. Jagdish Bhagwati University Professor Economics and Law at Columbia University has recommended a porfolio of assets to the people to built up national human capital. Government would have to change institutional structure of educational institutions to build up national human capital. In order to operate in a global economy with lots of players every company will have to be prepared to innovate down the line technologically to remain a global leader. In a highly globalised economy, security can come to workers not from a specific job being given for life but from learning more skills. Only a porfolio of assets can give security to a person and this will need intensive and extensive human resource development strategies. Azim Premji, Chairman of Wipro Corporation has said: "No one bats a 100 runs every time. Life has many challenges and also many failures. We win some challenges and lose some. You may enjoy winning but do not let success go to your head. Instead learn your lesson from failures". These words of wisdom also apply to the leaders of the Indian Corporation who alone can make India a global leader by their dynamic leadership, transparency in working, global competencies and ethical conduct with firm commitment to values.

Concluding Remarks

A correspondent from the Economist magazine came to India with the object to take stock of the changes in India after the economic reforms started. He went to India's Silicon Valley (Banglore) and spent sometime in the gleaning, glass walled office of a software company to get the feel of the "New India". Then he looked through the window and saw a construction site. Hundreds of Sari-class women worker were carrying a mixture of cement and sand on buckets placed on their heads. He thought that nothing much has changed outside the software enclave. Then he took a closer look. He found that these women were all wearing hard-hats on their heads. He noticed the change! workers have become aware of international safety standards. Looking closer, still, he discovered that the hard hats, unlike those used in the west, had a flat top, specially designed to hold the bucket in place. He recognised innovation adapted to Indian reality. This anecdote shows that if you have eyes and proper perception, you can perceive significant changes occurring beneath the apparently placid exterior.[19] India is becoming a global leader in many fields and you can perceive it, if you have the right perception. Globalising Indian business is both the challenge and opportunity for India.

India can be really proud of its performance at global level but there is a need for cautious approach to mergers and acquisitions by Indian Incorporates. India needs to be cautious particularly in allowing Foreign Direct Investment in Education, retailing and banking sectors. A stable political scenario, thrust on infrastructure development and private public initiative will herald a new era in real estate developments, retail sector, banking and manufacturing sectors but there is need for cautions 2006 will go down in Indian corporate history as a year that saw Indian companies and entrepreneurs stepping onto the world stage in a definitive way;[20] but all this hyper activity masks some crucial challenges that the key players will face problems of manpower, real estate, customer shift and strategic redirection. What bothers, indeed alarms, the increasing number of top level managers is that integration efforts regarded as beneficial by the standard of synergy targets met (or even exceeded) may justifiably be reckoned as failures from a wider and long term perspective. Dr. Man Mohan Singh has said: "I am convinced that the 21st Century will be an Indian Century. The world will once again look at us with regard and respect, not just for economic progress we make but for the democratic values we cherish and uphold and the principles of pluralism and inclusiveness we have come to represent which is India's heritage."

References

1. Abad Ahmad and D.P. Chopra—Passion to win—How winning companies develop and sustain competitive edge—Research study by All India Management Association, Excel Books Private Ltd., New Delhi, 2004, p. 295.
2. Raghuraman G. Rajan—Economic Counsellor and Director of the Research Department at the International Monetary Fund—India—A hub for globalization—January 7, 2005 and article Speech at the Pravasi Bharat Divas Conference in New Delhi. Indian Management November, 2005, Vol. 44, Issue 11, p. 40.
3. Ratan Tata—Interview Indian Management, Aug 2006, Vol. 45, Issue 5, p. 8.
4. Tarun Narayan, Govind Krishna Seshan and S Lakshmi Chopra-Harmony in Diversity, Indian Management—Aug. 2006, Vol. 45 Issue 8, p. 19.
5. Tarun Narayan—Core Competencies for Indian CEOs-Source Joint Study by Hay Group, BPCL and Public Enterprises Selection Board-Indian Management—May 2005, Vol. 44, Issue 5, p. 8.
6. C.K. Prahalad—The fortune at of the Pyramid—eradicating Poverty through profits—Wharton—Wharton School Publishing—Indian reprint 2005.

7. A.V. Vedpurishwar—Replicating Global Success - How are smart companies creating a winning formula across countries—Indian Management, May 2005, Vol. 44, Issue 4, p. 43.
8. R. Gopalkrishna—Executive Director TATA Sons Ltd.—A Manager's view of India Business Mandate March 2006, pp. 4-8.
9. Prasad Sangameshwara—How COO matters—Indian Management, June 2006, Vol. 45, Issue 6, p. 19.
10. Priyanka Sangani—Global Brandwidth—How are Indian companies taking the "Made In India" brand, p. 25.
11. Tarun Narayan and S Lakshmi Chopra—Reddy for the Next Leap? Indian Management—March 2006, Vol. 45, Issue No. 3, p. 16.
12. Percy Barnev—The making of an Indian Social Entrepreneur Indian Management—March 2006, Vol. 45 Issue 3, p. 71.
13. Website : www.bharatforge.com
14. Abad Ahmad and DP Chopra—Passion to Win—How new winning companies develop and sustain competitive edge—Excel Books Publications Pvt. Ltd—A study of AIMA, New Delhi, 2004, pp. 295-296.
15. Robert B Tucker—Driving Growth Through Innovation - East West Books (Madras) Pvt. Ltd. Chennai, 2002, p. 16.
16. Nandan M Nilekani - Winds of change in Strategic sourcing-Indian Management 2006, p. 25—January 2006.
17. Priyanka Sangani—Global Brand Width—Indian Management, June 2006, Vol. 45, Issue, p. 32.
18. G Dhananjayan—The Challenge of Execution—Excellence Indian Management, June, 2006 Vol. 45, Issues, pp. 69-70.
19. Alok Ray—Why is India such a growth story—Hindustan Business Line, Quoted in Business Mandate February 2007, p. 7.
20. Promise and Peril—Indian Management, Vol. 46, January 2007, p. 6.

10

Preparing Leadership For Future

"Leaders of society should have the moral strength to proclaim truth fearlessly". (Rig Veda S.48.14)

The term leadership refers to a driving force that determines the direction and destiny of an organization. It refers to the orientation and behaviour of the persons who have the capacity to transform the organizations. Leadership is like the hologram of an organization. Just as any piece cut out of a hologram reflects the full picture, the leadership reflects the characteristics of an organization. Good leaders see the future. They don't only have vision. They see the future trends. Jack Welch says: "Tomorrow's person leads through a vision, a shared set of values and a shared objective." Leadership is an ability to look at things from a multiplicity of perspectives. The business world has become more competitive and more volatile. Faster technological change, greater international competition, the deregulation of markets, over capacity in capital intensive industries, an unstable oil cartel and the changing demographics of the workforce are among the factors that have contributed to uncertain future. Since the function of leadership is to produce change, setting the direction of that change is fundamental to leadership. The global nature of India Inc. is undergoing rapid changes and there is need for appropriate leadership for tomorrow. Are our leaders ready to take on the tomorrow's needs and aspirations? Leaders for tomorrow must have global mindset, with adequate core competencies. Every organisation in India needs to create a culture of kaizen within the company. All organisations must become learning organisations. Leader for tomorrow must build and sustain a conducive corporate culture in the context of globalisation. The future is in our hands. Let us make the future bright, prosperous and dynamic by building our leaders. Leadership development must keep pace with the new emerging challenges and big question of today is how to groom new leaders, those who will lead India into a new tomorrow. The changing environment of twenty first century is characterised by: (1) liberalisation (increasing competition); (2) aware and demanding customers; (3) educated and impatient employees; (4) high mobility, careerism and declining organisation loyalty; (5) growing unemployment and unemployables; (6) glamorization of designations and consequent meaningless promotions; (7) resistance to radical thinking. (1) Peter F. Drucker, the eminent management guru says that most organisations are being managed too much and not led enough which brings us to the question; Can all managers be leaders and all leaders managers? A leader is one who influences the beliefs and behavior of a given community, formulates visions, takes risks, explores new territory, initiates change, transforms, enpowers, encourages diversity, invokes passion and takes a long term view. A manager merely manages the given community, takes the short term view, makes plans and budget, avoids risk, maintains existing patterns, stabilizes, transacts, controls, enforces uniformity and invokes rationality. "Leadership is a process of inter-personal interaction. It is not a personality trait, leaders inspire people and people inspire leaders. It results in extra ordinary performance". Says Sam Pitroda, CEO World Tel. The big question of the day is how to groom the new managers to become leaders who will lead the people and the nation into a new tomorrow, it is all about preparing and making of young, dynamic, professional leaders. We need a group of leaders at the top not just one or two. Leadership is like conducting an orchestra and creating beautiful creative and the best symphony. Leadership is all about high performance, meaningful motivation and complete communication. Organisations that do not attempt to build new dynamic leaders for tomorrow at all levels are likely to be left behind in the race for excellence and competition in the present global liberalised era. The complex and fast changing realities of the 21st century require faster and high quality leaders who can perform both transactional and transformational functions effectively. Policy-making, Planning, Developing Systems, Monitoring performance, coordinating, Rewarding and coaching are the seven well accepted transactional functions. Visioning, Modelling, setting standards, building culture and climate, boundary management, synergizing, searching out and nurturing talents are the transformational functions of a leader.[2] The 21st Century with uncertain future throws the following serious challenges to various organisations:-

(*a*) Achieving high quality organisational leadership' (*b*) Sustainability in a changing environment; (*c*) creating an organisational culture that enables high performance; (*d*) the ability to retain and develop high quality talents and (*e*) retain competitive advantage through people, culture and business strategy. Every leader needs to face the prospect of an uncertain future characterised by global change and unpredictability. Leadership for tomorrow and beyond is necessary to anticipate changes based on the process of technological forecasting concepts of the scenario and the Delphi technique and is now considered to be a staple in the planning inventory of most organisations.' (3) Leaders have to prepare themselves for tomorrow and beyond because; (*a*) The world is complex and chaotic; (*b*) change is inevitable and (*c*) the future cannot be predicted. Therefore leadership has to prepare themselves for the changing future scenario. Shifting demographics, new global markets and competitors, industry consolidation, product proliferation, changing distribution channels, increased state and federal regulations and crisis of confidence on the part of both customers and investors are recent trends of the present business world. Leaders today find themselves continually challenged by the constant change, flux instability and uncertainty of the contemporary business world. The contemporary economic scenario is characterized by complexities and uncertainties due to transnationalisation of business, geometrical advancement in the areas of technology and service and large scale upheavals in societal values, generational aspirations and monolithic ethos in the enterprise system. These changes demand a very dynamic leadership for tomorrow. Policy-making, planning, developing systems, monitoring performances, coordinating, rewarding and coaching are the traditional leaders functions. Leaders for tomorrow will be those who perform transformational functions of visioning, modeling, setting standards, building culture and climate, boundary management, synergizing, searching out and nurturing talents. The main characteristics of transformational leaders are mainly six—(1) Empowering, (2) Risk-taking, (3) clarity of mission, (4) Team building, (5) Equanimity and (6) Evolving trust.

The Different Leadership styles

Daniel Goleman, well known for his two books "Emotional Intelligence" and "Working with Emotional Intelligence", refers to a research conducted by HAYMCBER which revealed different leadership styles springing from a different component of emotional intelligence. The coercive leaders want things to be done and employees work as they are instructed. The coercive leadership style helps people break unsuccessful business habits or make them work to achieve desired results in a given time frame. The authoritative leadership is needed in organizations like armed forces where there are given tasks with little discretion. The consultative leadership style strives to create harmony among his people. It shares ideas, builds trust and communicates frequently. It promotes egalitarianism within the organization. Laissez - faire leadership is a rather complete delegation of authority into the hands of the subordinates so that they may plan motivate, control and be responsible for their own actions. Bureaucratic leadership shows minimum concern for both people and work and wants to control the situation by the rules. Manipulative leadership is done by people who want to get power, money and credit for things done by others. Expert Leadership comes from a person's capacities, skills, talents and experience of the past life. Leadership styles are generally classified as under:-

"1. Autocratic leadership, authoritarian leader or the Coercive leader;
2. Consultative, participative, democratic or group centred leadership;
3. Laissez-faire, free-rein or non-interfering leadership;
4. Bureaucratic or rule centred leadership;
5. Manipulative leadership;
6. Expert leadership."[4]

However leadership is a dynamic process and situational.

The Different Faces of Leadership

In future there is likely to emerge a grand unifying theory of leadership where leaders will have different faces although at times these will be overlapping.

1. The Purposeful Leader/Inspirational Leader

The purposeful leader helps the organization and its members to develop a clear sense of values, beliefs, attitudes, guiding principles and philosophy. The corporate history suggests that only value driven organizations are capable of enduring beyond a decade or two—if their values and cultures are with custom needs, the competitive environment and the regulatory climate. The preservation of core values is one of the key reasons why successful companies endure.[5] The purposeful leader helps the organization to arrive at an empowering expression of purpose and answer questions like "what do we stand for? and what are we doing?. The purposeful leaders are sources of motivation and inspirations for members of their organization by clearly identifying the significant purpose of the organization and attend to values purpose and meaning of the organization. DUPONT, for example, proclaims that they produce "better things for better living through chemistry". David Packard, cofounder of the computer equipment giant Hewlett-Packard (HP) assets, "H.P. does not exists to make a contribution". The leader must understands that the mere attainment of short-term economic goals is not enough—an organization needs a deeper, a redemptive purpose and mission for its existence. Leaders go to great effort to build clarity of purpose and it "takes a combination of energizing forces and a consistent and carefully planned effort that raises the aspirations of the organization.[6] There are four key requirements for clarity of purpose and direction (*a*) creating a compelling picture; (*b*) establishing credibility; (*c*) developing connections within the business and (*d*) communication about company's business direction and goals. Inspirational Leadership is about change, transformation, improvement and challenging the status quo with positive and optimistic outlook.

2. The Visionary Leader

A vision represents an ideal end state; it describes the future dreams of the organization and where the organization are reaching within a given time frame and also implies a set of principles that govern its working culture and human resources management. Vision statement has to be action oriented and act as a plumb line against which decision and resource empower and envisage the employees. A visionary leader produces a series of scenarios that support the creation of a vision and plan for the future of the organization. Leaders first identify the driving forces—the trends or conditions (social, political, economic, regulatory and technological) that will affect the organization. Leaders then imagine alternative futures and entertain multiple scenarios. The visionary leaders, in the corporate world, who developed realistic vision are Henry Ford at Ford Motors, Edwin Land and Poloroid and Bill Gates at Microsoft. The visionary leader proposes an inspiring set of future goals. In India leadership of the Infosys has been visionary and could enable the organization to compete, survive and thrive in the global competitive world.[7] Visionary leaders in the early 1980s, like Jack Welch of GE and Lee laccoca of Chrysler, through sheer force of personality and brilliance of vision not only transformed their companies but carved out incredible results. The problem, though, is that there are not enough Jack Welches to go around.[8] Visionary leaders often go against odds to sell customers on their ideas and win market place acceptance. A leader has to bring about an organizational transformation with the help of higher value system. An effective leader must take to develop congruent successors. A visionary leader must develop his Antarjyoti (the light within) which will provide him the spiritual strength to lead the organization. Due to the efforts of the visionary leaders, India has become a member of trillion dollar club from April 2007. India's GBP has more than doubled in the last six years. India has now become the 11th largest economy in the world in nominal dollar terms. The 20 million strong NRI community has a financial wealth of over $ 500 billion. A study by the world Resources Institute has found that companies can tap a market of Rs. 54 trillion in India. The average Indian is presently only 23 years old as opposed even to China's current age which is 32. Young and visionary leaders of India will alone drive economic growth. The following prominent visionary Indians have their names in the Forbes list figures in world.

Sl.No.	World Ranking	Name	$Billion
1.	5	Lakshmi Mittal	32
2.	14	Mukesh Ambani	21.1
3.	18	Anil Ambani	18.2
4.	21	Azim Premji	17.1
5.	62	Kushal Pal Singh	10.1
6.	69	Sunil Mittal & Family	9.5
7.	86	Kumar Birla	8.0
8.	86	Shashi and Ravi Ruia	8.0
9.	114	Ramesh Chandra	6.4
10.	137	Pallonji Mistry	5.6
11.	210	Adi Godrej & Family	4.1

3. The Strategic Leader

Strategy determines the specific directions in which the organization will move and how the organization will allocate resources to attain its desired end-state in a given time frame. The strategic leader first looks outside the business, at the industry, the markets, and the competition and then analyses the strength and weaknesses of the organization. Strategy is the art of deploying resources towards market opportunities in a way that distinguishes a business from its competitors. Before leaders formulate strategy, they involve key managers in the formulation process for it is they who will be ultimately responsible for implementing strategy. Some leaders adopt the use of the concept of core competency, a set of core skills than can be combined to yield competitive advantage[9]. The classic illustration of this concept is HONDA's extension of competency in engines to business in automobiles, motor-cycles, outboard motors and lawn mowers. Insightful leaders incorporate one more parameter of elegance—a quality. A strategic leader generally adopts the following steps in effective strategy development. 1. Planning process management commitment and participation, 2. Effective resource allocation for products, services, markets and functions, 3. Data analysis, 4. Differentiation in applying strategies for different business, 5. Linkage to programmes, schedules and budgets, 6. Monitoring of implementation and control systems. Management education and effective internal communication.

The strategic leader should not only dictate strategy but must give equal attention to the quality of the strategy and the process used to generate the strategy. In Mahabaratha, Lord Krishna has displayed the role of a strategic leader. In order to win war against Kauravas, he guided Pandavas as a strategist who could effectively manage Bhisma Pitamaha's temper, to make even Yudhistar mislead Dronacharya, managing the illusion of the sun being still there to managing the killing of great warrior Jaidrath, from managing the guile of Shakuni to the anger of Dhritrashtra by strategically orchestrating the whole war of Mahabharata in a most successful manner like a specialised conductor. Lord Krishna has enunciated in Bhagwat Gita Bhaktiyog, Karmayog and Gyanyog to suit the different types of workers and members of the organization.

4. Emotionally Intelligent Leader The Beneficent Leader

Numerous studies suggest that it is emotions, properly managed, that drive the greatest productive gains, innovations and accomplishment of individuals, teams and organizations. (Cooper and Sawal 1997). Goleman (1955) defined Emotional Intelligence as a capacity for recognizing our own feeling and those of others, for motivating ourselves, for managing emotions well in ourselves and in our relationships. Emotional Intelligence as a capacity for recognizing our own feelings and those of others, for motivating ourselves, for motivating ourselves, for managing emotions well in ourselves and in our relationships. Emotional Intelligence is the ability to sense, understand and effectively apply our power and acumen of emotions as a source of human energy, information, connection and influence. The BT-Hewlett Association (2001) study on India's Best employees to work have identified the following ten organizations which really charged "the emotional and intellectual energy" of their managerial employees : (1) Infosys; (2) Procter and Gamble, (3) Hewlett-Packard, (4) ICICI, (5) Hughes Software Systems, (6) LG Electronics, (7) Hindustan Lever, (8) Compaq, (9) Asian Paints, (10) Bharat Petroleum. Emotional intelligence can be learnt and developed. Beneficial leaders help the organisation and its members to achieve their collective needs and aspirations and also implement strategies to achieve the mission of the organisation. The pre-requisite to implement a strategy is the collaboration of the individuals in the organisation in a concerted joint initiative as a community. Beneficial leaders must create communities that meet the criteria; strong boundaries; shared values, purpose and identity; and trust and loyalty. The beneficent leaders catalyse, they behave in ways that enable the organization to realise more of its potential, they transform droves into effective follower workers. The beneficent leader's programme begins with clear values and purpose and follows with an inspired strategy and vision by building a strong community. The beneficient leader shows the values and joys of life and enriches life by sharing his skills, knowledge expertise, experience and his understandings with learners and subordinate. "The leader has considerable confidence and trust in his subordinates".[10]

5. The Adaptive Leader/Resilient Leader

Resilience calls for elasticity, adaptability, buoyancy and strong life energy. The resilient leaders have a definitive personal profile which integrates the following characteristics in their behaviour pattern.

1. Clarity of purpose embedded in values
2. Strong personal identity
3. Action-Orientation
4. Active professional and personal networks
5. Self-motivated, self-driven
6. Well articulated internal standards.
7. Deep commitment to continuous life-long learning.

Dr. Anji Reddy, CEO of Reddy's Lab, Colonel S.P. Wahi of ONGC, Yogi Deveshwar, former Chairman of ITC, Narayana Murthy of Infosys, Azim Premji of Wipro, Rajat Gupta, of McKinsey & Company are some of the outstanding resilient leaders. Resilient leaders create resilient organizations.

The pervasiveness of change is not a new phenomena and adaptive leaders continuously address the challenges of change. The adaptive leader's goal is to achieve dynamic equilibrium as the organisation adjusts to external variables-customer needs, competitive initiatives or economic, social, technological and political changes or to internal variable, the changing aspirations of individuals as a result of their development and maturation. Adaptive leaders strive to be the first to understand change and to position the organisation where it can benefit from the new conditions. Adaptive leaders stimulate vitality and enthusiasm for the challenge of confronting change and the evolution of the organisation through its life cycle of growth, maturity and decline.[11] The adaptive leaders must understand the concept of a disruptive technology.[12] Disruptive technologies have the potential of sudden and drastic change and adaptive leaders must look hard and continuously for early warning signals, clues to what may become major discontinuities. Prof. Stan Abraham of USA has given an effective nine step change process: (1) create a vision, clear plan and case for change; (2) Identify actions that generate quick wins; (3) specify a new set of strategic values; (4) Communicate the vision and change strategy, (5) Overcome resistance to change; (6) begin taking strategic actions; (7) begin sustaining the change; (8) inspire change throughout the organisation; and (9) create a culture of continuous change.[13] The adaptive leaders recognise that change is inevitable and need to prepare the organisation to recognize the importance of continual adaptation.

6. The Guiding and Transformational Leader

The guiding leader has to develop future leaders by initiating various leadership programmes. The guiding leaders must first select those individuals who have the potential to become leaders. The future leadership roles must meet the three criteria: (*a*) motivations; (*b*) attitude; (*e*) morality. The guiding leaders nurture others in the art of leadership. Guiding leaders have the role of mentoring. The mentors simply act as role models. The guiding leader motivates, educates and leads by example. The transformational leaders achieve organisational goals by evolving a new organisational ethos, redefining organisational goal, and creating a new vision, meaning and hope for people.[14] They demonstrate enormous strengths by guiding followers to transcend the limitations of their self interest for the sake of the team, the organisation and the large society. The transformation functions include visionary, modelling, setting standards, building cultures and climate, boundary management synergising, searching and mustering talents and ensuring organisational learning.[15] The main focus of transformational leadership has to be on HRD institution building, norm building, team building and boundary management. Bernard Bass, the pioneer author of transformational leader has given four key characteristics of such leaders which are as under:

1. Charisma which provides vision and sense of mission
2. Inspiration and communicates high expectations.
3. Intellectual stimulation
4. Individualized consideration which provides personal attention, coaching and counselling to all team members.[16]

Transformational Leaders translate their vision into reality, mission into action and philosophy into practice by employing the four 1's : (*i*) Idealized influence, (*ii*) Inspirational motivation, (*iii*) Intellectual stimulation; and individualized concern for situations and persons. According to Howell and Avolio (1993) transformational leaders concentrate their efforts on long-term goals; place value and emphasis on developing a vision, change or align systems to accommodate their vision rather than work within existing system; and coach followers to take on greater responsibility for their own development of others. Transformational leaders may put special emphasis on certain values. The Tatas put strong emphasis on complete trust in the people chosen. The Bhilwara group emphasizes human and spiritual values combined with dedication. Telco Jamshedpur puts great premium on the dictum that to be a good leader one has to be a good man.

7. The Virtuous/Dynamic Leadership

The virtuous leader has to develop and strengthen both the intrinsic and extrinsic qualities. There is no such thing as a perfect and virtuous leader. Character, creativity and compassion are the three cardinal leadership qualities. The character traits of such leaders include integrity, morality and authenticity. For assessing corporate leadership, Fortune magazine has given the following eight attributes for most admired organisations: Innovativeness; Quality of management; Employee talent; Quality of products/services; Long term investment value; Financial soundness; Social responsibility; and Use of corporate assets. Walter Lippman, talking about the legacy of the leaders has said "The final test of a leader is that he leaves behind him the conviction and will to carry on. The genius of a good leader is to leave behind him a situation which common sense without the grace of genius, can deal with successfully. In India Infosys is a successful organisation because of "(i) Stability of senior leaders (ii) results-focused plan and action; and (iii) value-based management and leadership[17]. Only virtuous leadership can attain self discipline; self awareness and self realisation. They need dedication, and nurturing leadership qualities so that they may energize their team and organisation at the following four levels:

Attitude at mind level, (*ii*) Usefulness at body level, (*iii*) Mastery at thought level, (*iv*) Spirit at conscious level. They can achieve work excellence by acquiring emotional intelligence by acquiring emotional intelligence and spiritual commitment, based on a healthy value system.

8. Team Captains/Global Leaders

N.R. Narayan Murthy, Chief Mentor of Infosys Technologies has said: globalization is about producing where it is most cost effective, sourcing capital from where it's cheapest and selling it where it is most profitable: As Mr. Murthy says: globalization forces organizations to accept the best practices in their industry drawn from different parts of the globe. They (global leaders) have to adopt to and embrace global standards, practices, systems and procedures if they are to remain competitive. Global leaders see four factors behind the scene in the environment - globalization; liberalization customers and technology. For multinational organisations, there is a top management team for top management tasks—It requires at least four kinds of human beings: "the through man", "the action man", "the people man" and "front man" and there is need for a team captain to lead the team. In modern global economy, there are very large multinational companies like IBM, General Motors, where top management work is work for a team. As Peter Drucker has said "A team needs a captain. The team captain is not a "boss", he is a leader. "Alfred P.Sloan Jr was the undoubted head of General Motors with moral authority within GM's general management and had the legal power to over rule his colleagues on the management team but he almost never used it. According to Peter F. Drucker, there has to be a team captain and in times of extreme crises he has to be willing and able and have to have the legal power to take over. In time of common peril, there has to be unity of command. The multinational corporation raises diversity and complexity to new levels and makes new and unprecedented demands on top management with respect to business strategy as well as structure and behaviour. Tomorrow's management structure of the multinational will be different from today's and therefore dynamic and forward-looking team captain will be needed for such multi-nationals. India Inc. needs to become more self-critical and must create a policy-frame work that allows all clusters to flourish.

Need of Future Leaders

Erich From has coined a personality type called marketing personality; marketing personality excel at selling themselves to others and are less driven by conscience than obsessives. Instead, they are motivated by a radarlike anxiety that permeates everything they do—Unproductive marketing type lack direction and ability to commit themselves to people or projects. Marketing types generally make poor leaders in times of crisis. They lack the daring needed to innovate and are too responsive to current rather than future, customer demands. Such personalities should not be made leaders. Leaders of future should be people with balanced personality traits and should a blend of have emotions, intelligence. Leaders must be aware of the approaching threats and should be ready to take on change initiatives. Future leaders, according to Prof. Rooshikumar Pandya need team work, time management and accountability, when working in a team, leaders should share credit, resources and information. Leaders need to have a positive mind-set, regular physical exercise and practice of relaxation methods like shavasana, Transcendental Meditation, the sudarshan Kriya and proper balance between life work and quality of life. Leaders of tomorrow, of course need to know about markets, information technology, strategic planning, emotional intelligence, decision making, global environment and customers but they must be well trained in Brahma Vidya and spiritual experience of the witness (Drista). Future leaders must develop proper vision ensure organisational transformation and accept social responsibilites of the organisations. If India is to become fifth largest economy in dollar terms by 2010 AD, fourth largest by 2015 AD and the third largest by 2025 AD, we need not only well organised committed organisations but must ensure to nurture and develop congruent successors. Organisations must select the potential successors who are value-conscious, path-makers, committed to the grand mission—Swami Vivekanand has said "Tell everyone about her/his real nature and see how the sleeping soul awakens. Power, glory and purity will come, all that is excellent will come when the sleeping soul is aroused to self-consciousness by the powers of words, by the power of behaviour. Vedanta teaches us to give respect and recognise dignity in human beings. Success, wealth, glory and self-pride will come in the business world and India will become a world leader. We must nurture leaders who have vision, mission, action and devotion (Commitment)". Out future leaders must have adequate knowledge of turn around management, transformational management, empowerment, motivational techniques, financial management, international trade and human resource management along with India ethos of management. Leaders have to understand and activate the soul of their employees. Prof. Y.K. Bhushan has identified the following abilities and characteristics for future global managers in the context of liberalisation of economy:

1. The outbound skill—It refers to the instinctive quality of looking out and ahead keeping a tab on developments to the various regions of the world with global perspective.
2. Scanning skills with which they can see and seize business opportunities.
3. Ability to relate to diverse culture.
4. Capacity in relation to the swings in the environment through strategic thinking and scenario building skills.
5. Negotiation skills with other countries to drive hard bargains.

6. Analytical skills to identify the cost drivers and the factors responsible for high costs and low productivity for building up competitions.
7. Obsession for quality and skills of total quality management.
8. Skills of skimming study and reflections leading to autonomous learning "skills of learning to learn".
9. Linguistic skills and knowledge of foreign languages.
10. People management skills for team working and integration of ethnic diversity.
11. Information management with computers so as to access data base for quick decision making.

Building Future Leaders

To groom and buildup great future leaders, organizations must do the following:- (1) Launch a formal, high level succession planning conference for senior executives, facilitated by outside professional experts and corporate HR; formally outline the leadership development process and start properly designed leadership course for potential leaders; (2) Implement leadership development programmes to develop their capabilities and skills; (3) Like General Electric (GE) set the standard potential leadership programmes for churning out future leaders; (4) Involve HR official to create tools/systems for developing career planning for junior leaders for succession planning; (5) Have the board over see all leadership development initiatives and insist on continual communication and support by senior managers and CEOs on their commitment to leadership development; (6) Reshuffle star performers and potential leaders to give them varied experience; (7) Ensure that leadership development programme are properly aligned with strategy of the organization; (8) HR mandated mentoring programmes copied with 360 degree appraisal system and subsequent regular counseling. The core competencies required for global managers and leaders of tomorrow according to Stephen R. Rhinesmith (1993) can be summarised as follows:

"(*i*) Managing competitiveness by constantly scanning the environment for changes in market, socio-economic and political trends and global competition conditions; (*ii*) Managing complexity by managing trade-offs of many competing interests as well as the inherent conflicts and contradictions of various global organisations, (*iii*) Managing adaptability by developing norms of behaviours, (*iv*) Managing teams within a multi-cultural sensitivity and demands, managerial skills to lead, supervise and manage people coming from a wide range of different nationalities, (*v*) Managing learning on a continuous basis and building a learning organisation".[19]

Above core competencies have to be built in future leaders by various HRD Strategies. Leaders for tomorrow will have to learn holistic management which would include managing men in teams, tasks, time, targets, territory, trends materials and life-management. Managers and leaders have to learn to manage purpose, policies, plan programmes, people, processes, projects, production, products, profits, progress and prices. They have to uplift their perceptions and develop their personalities. Human being have four aspects—Body, Mind, intellect and self (spirit) and leaders of tomorrow will have to learn manage all these aspects of human beings for having a winning management strategy. These four aspects of human beings are related to actions, feelings, thoughts and consciousness. Conscience is the light of the soul that burns within the chambers of our psychological heart. It raises the voice in protest whenever anything is thought of or done contrary to the righteousness and morality. Future leaders must learn to listen to their inner conscience and should not indulge in corruption, lust or other immoral acts. A virtuous man alone can use the instrument of conscience. Future leaders must be upright, honest, committed to their job and role model for others. Leaders will also have to learn "Environment management and cross-cultural management. They have to develop emotional intelligence competence in their work style. This will be possible only if they develop their self and constantly make efforts towards self elevation, self-reliance, self-awareness and self-realisation. This will need self discipline, self motivation, self dedication, self confidence, self study and self reliance.[20] Great leaders have 4 Es: (*i*) personal energy (*ii*) they energise others (*iii*) they have an edge when it comes to being strong competitors, and (iv) they execute various business strategies superbly.[21] These can be supported by the well known case studies related to James Mc.Nerny at 3 M, Larry Bossidy at Honeywell and Robert Nardelli at Home Depot. Another case study is that of Vivek Paul who helped Wipro emerge stronger from the technical wreck. Leadership skills critical to success in the global economy includes the following:- (1) Cultural flexibility, (2) Communication skills, (3) HRD skills-skills of developing a learning climate, designing training programmes, providing career counseling, creating organisational change and adopting learning materials, (4) Creativity, problem solving and innovative skills, (5) Self management of learning.[22] Future leaders must learn above mentioned skills to be successful as global leaders.

Transformation to Transcendence—Break through Ideas-Indian Perspective for Leadership

Future leaders must develop unique Indian style of managerial leadership Shri G.Narayanan has given the following interpretation of the four methods of managing people. Sama - Persuasion, Dana - reward, Bheda -Discriminationa and Dand - Punishment. Persuasion (Sama) is treatment as equal, discussion, reasoning, reflection of goodwill and friendly approach. Reward (Dana) is appreciation, awards, doing good deed, giving material benefits, giving money and developing skills. Discrimination (Bheda) is challenge, talk, silence and showing dislike. Punishment (Dand) is reprimand, criticism, imposing fines, taking away things, restrictions, rough talk and anger (showing displeasure). Leadership for tomorrow have to be transcendental leaders instead of mere transformational leaders. Each human being is potentially divine. According to Swami Vivekananda the goal is to manifest this divinity within, by controlling nature, external and internal. Each individual, as a leader has to transcend to higher levels of consciousness and inculcate new approaches of leadership to utilize time, resources and potentials of the people. Man moves in physical space, man feels in mind space. Time is another dimension of physical space when purity, love, empathy and higher consciousness comes from leaders, it can introduce a unique value system in organization.

Developing Common Sense Management

Common sense, according to Michael Dillon, is rather uncommon ability to do the right thing without a lot of fore thought; as close connection to intuition. Common sense management comes from life experiences, it is about understanding people, communicating and working together to build a future. Common sense management is more of an unstructured, flexible, ongoing process. For developing common sense management the following are some of the factors that need to be taken into account.

1. Developing the habit of seeking updated information and using them to make decisions.
2. Avoiding prolonged data search and analysis.
3. Focusing on key issues by keeping your mission and targets together.
4. Generating a culture of shared information at all levels and build consensus before decision making.
5. Constantly scan the environment, look around for opportunities and learn to capitalize on them.
6. Develop skill in visualizing the future environment and learning to be intentive. Future leaders must learn to use common sense management.

Power Enhancers in Leadership—Transformational

Transformational leaders should believe in empowerment. Leaders should be prepared to shed their own power by withdrawing somewhat from controlling functions and confer people with power and routine tasks. Professor Udai Pareek has enunciated the following list as significant power enhancers:

"1. Developing the competence of employees, 2. Laying down clear rules and procedures, 3. Developing systems to generate feedback for individuals, 4. Providing intrinsically satisfying tasks, 5. Undertaking advisory and staff functions, 6. Giving rewards determined objectively by a team rather than by an individual, 7. Maintaining optional spatial distance between different key functionaries, 8. Building strong and cohesive teams, 9. Encouraging self government of teams (such as self sufficient branches), 10. Encouraging self definition of tasks, 11. Defining a formalized and clear organizational structure, 12. Initiate schemes to reward employees for ideas/suggestions/ creativity, 13. Nuture a professional orientations, 14. Developing systems."[23] Future leaders have to learn the art of empowerment and thus promote a healthy environment. The future leaders should be vision driven and develop competence, take moderate risks, learn from various sources and empower their people to experiment and take responsibility. The new leaders of tomorrow should be able to make things happen as they want then to happen and their internal focus of control should be very high. In Indian Times strategy Summit, R. Stephen Covey said: "Today's leaders are servant leaders and leadership is measured by their humility. (Times of India 17th October, 2003). Proper understanding and practicing the messages of different religions lead to the realization that all religions have one and the same goal - the attainment of the Godly qualities of being good and doing service to the poor, needy and deserving people. Swami Vivekanand said: "The Vedanta as a religion must be intensely practical. The fictitious differentiation between religion and the life of the world must vanish, for the Vedanta teaches oneness - one life throughout". Leadership, for future, have to become dutiful, supportive, devoted, empathetic and value adding leadership. In Bhagwat Gita, Lord Krishna talks about people who gain supreme knowledge. "Shining like the sun, knowledge reveals the supreme in them, in whom ignorance is destroyed by self-knowledge. Man of self knowledge are same - sighted on a Brahmana with learning and humility (5-16-18). In such leaders knowledge concentration leads to the realization of excellence. The Indian ethos in Management asserts the basic principles of "Tat-Tvam-Asi" (you are that (The Supreme) and Aham Brahmasmi - I am Brahman (the God). The transcendental leader has the service ideal-solving others problems by seva (Service). Sychronizing private and public gains by cooperation and Yagna and his self-motivation comes from svadhenta. Leaders have to work as inspired missionaries and act as humble servant leaders. Conflict to confluence and transforming to "transcending" should be the journey of leadership process. Leaders nurture love, manage material, lead to results and make path towards harmony. Leaders have to show dedication and commitment to programmes, principles, persons and processes to ensure excellence. Leaders exhibit attitudes at mind level, usefulness at body level, mastery at thought level and spirit at conscious level for achieving results beyond ordinary management. Leaders have to manage the following—which includes Men, Material, Machines, Money, Methods, means, movements, minds in an effective and integrated manner. Leaders have to be role models and have a well-integrated personality. Swami Vivekanand once said: Man-making process—the transformation service is available to mankind -The Bhakti Yoga (path of emotion and devotion), Gyan Yoga (The path of knowledge and analysis), Karma Yoga (the path of action and duty), and Raj Yoga (the path of gaining mastery over the mind) and every one is free to choose any one or more of all these for building and developing human beings of character, purity and excellence. The choice is before the future leaders. "The most important and urgent task before our leadership is to get all the forces for constructive change together and deploy them in a mission mode. The task of casting a strong India is in the hands of a visionary political leadership".[18] The holistic Indian approach to character building is most important for building the future leadership. Management education without character building can not produce the right type of leaders for tomorrow Leaders for tomorrow will be required to undergo intensive practical training in emotional intelligence self-realization, self-motivation and dedication to the higher goals of life. It is very gratifying to note that MNCs are now picking up Indian managers for global jobs. "Managerial strength, willingness to stretch working hours and proven track records in the complex Indian market have put the global spotlight on Indian managers more than ever before."[25] Not only are an increasing number of Indian executives being hand picked from global assignments by MNCs, even expat CEOs are for an "Indian experience on their CVs. Coca-Cola, Nestle and Whirlpool, continuously review performances of managers to post Indian talents at global or other key regional offices. Pepsi Co. has recently placed four middle level managers across sales, finance, quality control and manufacturing at its headquarters in New York and the Asia Pacific region. Pavan Bhatia Pepsi Executive Director (HR) says: Indian Managers are naturally accustomed to a cross cultural way of working and willing to work 12-16 hours a day and on weekends which gives them cutting edge, "India is perceived as a market with complex challenges, so Indian managers are more exposed." Indian

Managers need to be developed and transformed by expanding their creativity and developing their character and conduct. We have to nurture and build up Ethics - Moral leadership with positive virtues of truthfulness, sincerity, humility, purity, endurance and other ethical values of life.[26] Vedantic education can bring noticeable transformation at the following four levels:

(1) Spiritual level; (2) Personal level; (3) Social level; (4) Organisational level.[27]

Net-Working is an art that needs to be mastered with time. Ideally it should be perfected as one progresses in the career of one's choice. Net working is important in modern daytime. Social net working can be developed by making contacts with people and later strengthening it. Phone calls make a difference but meeting face-to-face, and attending informal meetings can do the job. Building new contacts and maintaining it over years is important. Networking is an activity that can be nurtured at all times. Leaders for tomorrow will have to be accountable for attracting and retaining skilled manpower to keep the wheels of business running in a global context. Long term strategies for surviving and growth will require leaders who will be able to manage the following dimensions of human resource management "Talent retention; Compensating knowledge workers; Recruiting skilled, trained and young personnel at all levels in today's context and tomorrow's needs; Creating high performance culture; Training for growth; Human capital practices ; HR system's implementation ; Managing global mindsets; Building inter-personal relationships; Building a learning organization; Career planning; Periodical counseling and mentoring; Synergising values, goals and mission of the organization; Building and promoting an ethical organisational culture; Responsibility of the leaders for organisational transformation of HRD and HRM through redesign of organisation.[28] Corporate leadership of India is gradually getting recognized all over the world due to its good performance. On Forbes elite list of 2000 corporate giants around the world, 34 Indian companies find their names. ONGC leads the pack of Indian companies (at 239), followed by Reliance Industries (No. 258), State Bank of India (No. 326) and Indian Oil (No. 399),

Tata Consultancy figures at 1047 on the list. Bharti Airtel is the only telecommunications company to find a place among the 2000 gaints with a rank of 1149. India has come to be known as a nation producing value enhanced superior, trained human power and leaders Indians have made their marks in the fields of management, information technology, bio technology, pure science and economics. India is known for spiritual master, yoga trainers and management leaders. Michael Usam, Director for leadership and change management and Professor of Management, Wharton has advocated the implementation of "Upward Leadership" concept where middle managers could be critical change agents in guiding the top management in leadership and strategic issues. It requires an ability to articulate and be persuasive. Bringing leadership down to frontline and middle managements, the change process in Indian companies can take a truly new meaning. Leaders for tomorrow must develop proper perspectives on strategy, strategic execution and strategy in alliance. "Strategy is about being different. It means deliberate choosing a different set of activities to deliver a unique mix of values", say Hammel and Prahalad. The reality of strategy is the pattern of resource allocation. "A Strategic alliance is a cooperative arrangement between two or more organisations designed to achieve a shared strategic goal". Strategic execution is a very important aspect of leadership responsibility. Strategic implementation fails because of the inability to appropriately reward and incentivise the very management of change. They have to know how to understand the following important issues and how to arrive at correct solutions through proper perception and consultations at various levels:-

(*i*) What should be our Corporate mission?

(*ii*) How do we gain a competitive edge?

(*iii*) How do we deliver results and desired performance?

(*iv*) How do we cope with change and uncertainties?

(*v*) How do we build effective teams and keep them motivated?

(*vi*) How do we make future business plans, strategic and resource management?

All these issues need a very close scrutiny and constant consideration of our future leaders. Management education in India must prepare new incomers for the great future challenges, leadership for tomorrow and beyond in India needs to be selected trained, nurtured and mentored in the Indian context with the spiritual and moral background. Such leaders will surely reach great heights, making their unique place in international world. Future leaders must have the quality of optimism. They should never indulge in negative or cynical thinking and should always exhibit self confidence and optimism. Future leaders must have self-restraint and self-discipline. Leaders of tomorrow should be value-driven and aware of dignity of work. Leaders for tomorrow should be well versed in transformational functions which include going beyond the immediate task, building up the competencies of individuals and groups and enabling them to achieve targets that the organization or individual would not have expected to achieve otherwise. The leaders for tomorrow have to ensure culture building for promoting initiative, empowerment, team work, and control through a vision. Culture building should be done by adhering to the following six principles. Organise work around and integrated process, not around segmented tasks. Create flatter structures, with parallel (instead of squential) teams. Make teams (not individuals) accountable for the task as a whole; empower teams to take all relevant decisions pertaining to their work. Make organizational boundaries permeable in order to bring teams in contact with the customers, suppliers and each other. Evaluate the performance of the teams on the basis of customers feedback. Reward acquisition of new skill by the individuals.

Indian leaders must have knowledge of not only the global markets and trends but also their self (inner contents). They have to integrate various available models of leadership and evolve the unique style depending on various internal and external factors. In his insightful book. "The fifth discipline:- The Art and practice of Learning organizations" Peter Senge has identified the following three learning disabilities:

1. The delusion of learning from experience; 2. I hit him because he took my ball, 3. The myth of team work. Peter Senge has enunciated the following laws:-

1. Today's problems come from Yesterday's "Solutions".
2. The harder you push, the harder the system pushes back.
3. Behaviour grows better before it gets worse.
4. The cure can be worse than the disease.
5. The easy way out usually leads back in.
6. Faster is slower.
7. Cause and effect are not closely related in form and space.
8. Small changes can produce big results - but the areas of highest learning are often the last obvious.
9. You can have your cake and eat it too - but not alone.
10. Dividing an elephant in half does not produce two small elephants.
11. Systematic thinking shows us that there is no outside: that you and the cause of your problems are part of a single system.

Future leaders must build learning organizations. The core disciplines that go into building learning organizations are : (1) Personal mastery; (2) Mental modes; (3) Shared vision; (4) Team learning; and (5)Systems thinking. Future leaders must thoroughly understand laws enunciated by Peter Senge.

Values and Beliefs for Indian Leaders

The Matsusluta experiment was so pioneering and spectacularly successful that all over the world, it sets a new trend for transformation of the tradition manager (emphasizing economies, wealth, profit and material satisfaction) into value-based management emphasizing human dignity, credibility, integrity and the social culture of peace and happiness. Corporate values and beliefs of Indian groups of industries are gradually eroding in practice although family groups such as Murugappa and Tatas are still strictly adhering to their proclaimed values. Murugappa group has the following proclaimed values and beliefs:-

1. Adhere to ethical norms in all dealings with shareholders, employees, customers, suppliers, financial institutions and government.
2. Provide value for money to customers through quality products and services.
3. Treat our people with respect and concern, provide opportunities to learn, contribute and advance; recognize and reward initiative, innovativeness and creativity.
4. Maintain (*i*) an organizational climate conducive to trust, open communication and team spirit (*ii*) a style of operation befitting our size, but reflecting moderation and humility.
5. Manage the environment effectively for harnessing opportunities.
6. Discharge responsibilities to various sections of society and preserve environment.
7. Grow in an accelerated manner, consistent with value and beliefs, by continuous organization reward.

The western model of modern management has been gradually moving from the profit oriented, utilitarian and materialistic practices in the direction of internal ethical resource and value-oriented corporate practices. Kenneth Good Paster of the Harvard Business School, Peter Drucker, John Ladd and Peter French believed that corporate bodies need to have a high level of moral awareness and morality of conscience (good moral conduct). Every corporate leader must listen to his conscience which reveals itself daily to every human beings but we shut our ears to the "still small voice" of wisdom. Corporate character is the inevitable result of understanding business as a community of relationships and the virtues of corporate character ethics include fairness, trust, respect and empathy. Personal character ethics involves primarily emotional virtues like self discipline, reliability, authenticity, sincerity, caring and empathy. Social character ethics covers virtues like tolerance, loyalty, supportiveness and trustworthiness. Professional character ethics entails public service, collegiality, impartiality and independence of judgement. Character ethics is also dependant on the corporate environment, legal frame work and politico-socio-economic frame work of the country and the place. A study by R. Sekhar found that

(1) Over 86% of the MBA students agreed that businesses have a responsibility towards society and responsibility is not limited to statutory requirements.

(2) Over 92% agreed that the primary goal of an organization is earning profit and maximizing share holder value.

(3) Over 73% believed that unethical practices are not justified in the name of performance.

(4) More than 56% believe that to achieve success in business dealing one may occasionally have to indulge in a certain degree of dishonesty and half truth and they would not hesitate to pay a bribe in a business situation, if needed.

The world is toasting the rise of women managers in the corporate world. Naina Lal Kidwai and Kiran Mazundar Shaw are two shining examples in India. India is among the countries which have seen a rise in women's participation in senior management levels. The latest findings from Grant Thornton International Business Report reveals that 38% businesses globally do not have any women in senior management. Philippines with 97%, China 96%, Malaysia 85% lead when it comes to having women in senior management positions as leaders. India has 56% with Japan 25%, Netherlands 27%, Luxumbourg 37%, Germany 41% and Italy 56. In India while there are many women in middle management, the number tapers off at the senior level. The over all pattern has not changed since 2004. It is disappointing that the participation of women in senior business management hasn't increased more drastically over the last few years because of work culture and nuclear family system. However, hopefully the coming years may see the pattern change as more women like Pepsi Cola's Indira Nooyi and E-Bay's Margaret Whitman take change and lead. During the last few years. India has seen a rise in women's participation in senior business level rising by 14%. Women leaders are competent and can lead business well.

A research survey by Siemensma found that the pursuit of corporate profit is incompatible with total honesty. Indian managers experience a clash between corporate values and present day socio-political and economic environment of the business world. The corporate values are being influenced by the market forces, changes in technology, financial constraints and misplaced incentive schemes, changes in social concepts, employee empowerment and over all liberalization of Indian economy. A research paper by Seema Sangli has found that the Indian managers experience tension between their private ethical beliefs and those they are required to apply at work. In some contexts, Indian managers adopt western corporate values. Regarding Indian managers scores on Hofstede's found dimensions (power distance, uncertainty avoidance, individualism and masculinity) Singh found that the scores on Hofstede's dimensions of Indian managers in internationally owned firms were comparable to the scores of Hofstede's western samples. Khan and Atkim son's study showed that 71 percent of the Indian and 69 percent of the U.K. companies made no specific budgetary provision for social responsibility activities. Indian managers regard family and social connections as important aspects of conventional ethical thinking. There is a need for reconsidering some of the corporate values of various business organizations. Indian managers have also to develop required courage, conviction and commitment to their personal ethical values. Many Indian business organizations like Infosys, NIL, NICCO, PSEDPCL, SRF, IFCI, STC, Phillips, Centaur etc. have identified their corporate values and have started rewarding people who live with them. National Instruments Limited asserts corporate values of transparency, honesty and innovation. Infosys technologies stress on values such as transparency, team work, innovation, dedication to customers and respect for the individuals. The liberalization, privatization and globalization of Indian economy have created new opportunities for increased collaboration between Indian managers and those from the collaborating countries. In this connection the importance of corporate values has become more important for the Indian managers who want to become global managers. By and large Indian managers are more business-oriented, self-oriented and performance-oriented with little emphasis on idealism. There is a lot of ground to cover through business ethics education and emphases on adherence to corporate values. Dr. Man Mohan Singh has asked the confederation of Indian Industry's annual general meeting "to resist excessive remuneration to CEOs, Promoters, senior executives and discourage conspicuous consumption". The emergence of India's first trillionaire in Reliance Chief Mukesh Ambani has brought pride to India. Expressed as a percentage of Profits, Indian company heads are far above their global counterparts. For every Rs. 1 Crores earned as profit, the Indian CEOs take home Rs.16,800, while global CEOs take home Rs. 9,900. Presently the average package of the top five Indian CEOs is around Rs.13.5 crores while the lowest paid workers in their own companies would earn 15,000-20,000 times less. Such gross inequality does more than breed resentment, destroys millions of lives and devastates the access of the poor to basic needs. Such inequality undermines democracy itself.

Leadership and Strategic Thinking

Leaders for tomorrow must prepare people and teams to make strategic decisions and align them with organizational goals. In a dynamic market global environment, future leaders must ensure strategic thinking permeating across the organization by following steps:

1. Communication from leadership must be clearly understood.
2. High credibility established earlier on goes a long way in others accepting and understanding strategic decisions.
3. Constant sharing of knowledge, information and experience helps others in effective decision-making.
4. Empower teams to make strategic decisions.
5. It is essential to develop allies to help you carry out your strategy.
6. Build teams that can perform under pressure/stress.
7. Design organizations to support leadership capabilities.

8. Leading up is as important as leading down.
9. Focus on long term and look at the short term.
10. Thinking like a multi-functional manager is important in strategic thinking and management.

In India, leadership at large diversified groups has shown capability in pulling strategic decisions and their implementation together.

Values in the Context of Management and Personnel Policies

Indian managers need a realistic value system. In the context of personnel policies, the following set of values are particularly relevant in the Indian context.

1. Humanistic and supportive approach.
2. Competence and expertise value.
3. Right environment-least control.
4. People-imaginative and creative.
5. People-honest and trustworthy.
6. Participative management.
7. Achievement recognition for growth.
8. Grace.
9. Money is not the only incentive.
10. Compensation/remuneration to keep body and soul together.
11. A socialistic approach - class less policies.
12. Growth is merit - based.
13. Trust.
14. Openness.
15. Respect for individual.
16. Participate management.

Prof. S.K. Chakraborty has highlighted humility, gratitude, self-discipline, respect for elders, piety and religiosity and renunciation as uniquely Indian values. Patriotism has to be a necessary value but not to the exclusion of consideration for other nations. According to Yogendra Singh, the dominant traditional values of India are characterized by hierarchy holism, continuity and transcendence. Post independent India has ushered the values of democratic republic, secularism, socialism, abolition of untouchability, rule of law, social justice and planned economic growth of the society. The conflict between the old and the new values system poses a real challenge to the administrators, bureaucrats and managers because the two have not been integrated or synthesized. The general picture however, continues to be one of twilight of transition; old values persist and the new ones are being added to them. Much of the Indian development depends upon the values system and attitudes of the top administrators, bureaucrats and managers in the rural sectors/infrastructural bases.

Leadership Skills for Future Leaders

To conceptualize the future leadership domain is to think of it as 5 QS: the intelligence quotient, the emotional quotient, the financial quotient the relationship quotient and the spiritual quotient. David A Whetten and Kirn S.Cameron have developed models for both personal and inter-personal leadership skills required for future global leaders identified through research.

Model of Personal Skills

1. Developing self awareness (*a*) Determining values and priorities, (*b*) identifying cognitive style, (*c*) assessing attitude towards change.

2. Managing stress—(*a*) coping with stressors, (*b*) Managing time, (*c*) Delegating.

3. Solving problems creativity—(*a*) using the rational approach, (*b*) using the creative approach, (*c*) foresting innovation in others.

Models of Interpersonal Skills

4. Communicating supportively—(*a*) coaching (*b*) counseling, (*c*) listening.

5. Gaining power and influence—(*a*) gaining power, (*b*) exercising influence, (*c*) empowering others.

6. Motivating others—(*a*) diagnosing poor performance, (*b*) creating a motivating environment, (*c*) rewarding accomplishment.

7. Managing conflict—(*a*) Identifying causes, (*b*) selecting appropriate strategy, (*c*) resolving confrontations.

Above mentioned leadership skills can serve as useful guidelines for needed skill development in the future. Leaders for tomorrow must develop soft skills, time management, communication skills, maintaining successful relationship with customers/professionals and colleagues and effective ways of dealing with stress of the corporate world. The ten fundamentals practices of exemplary leadership are as under:

(1) Challenge the status quo; (2) Inspire a shared vision; (3) Enable others to act; (4) Model the way forward by setting an example; (5) Tap individual inner drivers by linking rewards and performance; (6) Ensure training and development of all employees, constant organizational learning and updating core competencies; (7) Career planning and successive leadership planning; (8) Strategic long term human resource management and planning; (9) Sensitivity to future macro-economic factors, environmental and social issues; 10) "The future is not about financial strength or heritage. The future is about innovation and how nimble you are. The future is all about how open minded you are to learn from other people"—says N.R. Narayan Murthy.

Beliefs in Management

In the present day world of management values ultimately call for beliefs as operational imperatives. In Indian context some of the prominent beliefs can be enumerated as under:-

1. Belief in upholding the higher principles of life.
2. Belief in participation, collectivization, involvement and sharing.
3. Belief in modernity, change and newness.
4. Belief in tradition, status quo and maintenance orientation.
5. Belief in constant exploration of new possibilities and risk-taking.
6. Belief in creating meaning in life and art of living.
7. Basic belief in Atma (SELF) and positive live principles.

8. Belief in doctrine in Rebirth and Nishkam Karma Yog (good work without expecting reward).
9. Belief in socially evolved stands of fairness, equity, justice and truth.
10. Belief in goodness of mankind and trust in people.
11. Belief in constant hard work and perpetual pursuit of action to reach higher and higher goals of life.
12. Belief in democracy, socialism and human rights.
13. Belief in mutual support, acceptance and cooperation.
14. Belief in God as the creator, sustainer and destroyer of this universe.
15. Belief in self, self-development and self-control.

In a global economy, leaders have to build unity out of diversity. According to Peter F. Drucker. "A business can be highly diversified and yet have fundamental unity if its business and technologies, its products and product lines and its activities are embraced within the unity of a common market. Further a business can be highly diversified and have fundamental unity if its business, its markets and product lines and its activities are held together in a common technology. Leaders for tomorrow have to learn the art and science of managing the multi-national corporation". Peter F. Drucker has said: "The multinational corporation raises diversity and complexity to new levels and makes new and unprecedented demands on top management with respect to business strategy as well as structure and behaviour. For managers of tomorrow managing growth will be a survival need and there leaders will have to be constantly trained for their tasks. In management there is a well accepted belief that formal training can play an important role. It provides manages with insight into the company's culture and established processes as well as opportunities to receive systematic feedback on their performance. Equally important, training enable new managers to forge developmental relationships with 'peer managers' who are also attending the same sessions.[31] Shared values of supra ordinate goals refer to asset of values and aspirations that go beyond the conventional formal statement of organizational objectives and mission. These fundamental values give rise to a certain spirit among organizational members which is reflected in their values attitudes actions and philosophy. Shared values become beliefs in such organizations. Sometime in 1983 the Ministry of Education, Govt. of India, had published Report of a committee on values of Educational and teaching. Among other things, the Report emphasized on the understanding and propagation of "uniquely Indian Values".

Need for Emotional Intelligence

Leaders for tomorrow are required to have a very high degree of emotional intelligence. Globalisation is another reason for the rising importance of emotional intelligence at work. Daniel Goleman has suggested the following components of emotional Intelligence.

Sl.No.	*Components*	*Definition*	*Hall marks*
1.	Self-Awareness	The ability to recognize and understand your moods, emotions and drivers, as well as their effect on others.	(*a*) Self confidence (*b*) realistic self-assessment (*c*) Self-deprecation sense of humour
2.	Self-regulation	The ability to control or redirect disruptive impulses and moods and the propensity to suspend Judgement to think before acting	(*a*) Trustworthiness and integrity (*b*) Comfort with ambiguity (*c*) Openness to change
3.	Motivation	A passion to work for reasons that go beyond money or status—a propensity to pursue goals with energy and Persistence	(*a*) Strong drive to achieve. (*b*) Optimism—even in the case of failure (*c*) Organizational commitment.
4.	Empathy	The ability to understand the emotional makeup of other people—and skill in treating people according to their emotional reactions	(*a*) Expertise in building and retaining talent (*b*) Cross-cultural sensitivity (*c*) Service to clients and customers.
5.	Social Skills	Proficiency in managing relationships and building network—an ability to find common ground and build rapport	(*a*) Effectiveness in leading change. (*b*) Persuasiveness (*c*) Expertise in building and leading teams.

(*Source*: Harvard Business Review, Nov. Dec 1998.

Emotional intelligence can be learned although the process is not easy. It takes time and commitment, but benefits that come from having a well developed intelligence, both the individual and the organization, make it worth the effort. The emotional intelligence will be the sine qua non of future leadership.

On Joining a New Organization

When a leader joins a new job, there are certain useful tips. Bob Eckert has given the following ten tips of leaders who are joining a new organization.

1. Call on customers - learn how the organization in viewed.
2. Watch consumers - spend sometime in store.
3. Find retirees and find out the culture.
4. Read everything about the organization.
5. Talk to a mentor.
6. Phone a friend/old colleague.
7. Keep notes from every conversation.
8. Before taking, the job, write down your goals for the first 100 days.
9. Follow your heart - let your get feeling be your final guide.
10. Commit fully and always look forward with optimist and confidence.

On joining a new organizations, new entrants must learn the culture and value of the organization. Leaders must learn rules, regulations and managerial skills and other procedures prevalent in the new organization. He must meet people at all levels and learn the customs and traditions of that society.

According to Shri N.R. Narayana Murthy "Rules cannot substitute for character. It is ethical behaviour that will ensure that the CEO and the internal members of the board or the senior management behave properly. Remember that the rule of law cannot defeat the perversity of the heart". In the present day democratic system, a manager in the government needs a value system which is flexible in operation, is pragmatic, is laden with human values of service to the people and encourage transparency in decision making processes. Shri.N.R. Narayana Murthy of Infosys believes that a clear conscience and a high level of professional ethics are the values, a manager must inculcate and imbibe. Infosys is a role model company - an Indian brand. It stands for integrity, honesty, a value system and ethics. It is an inspirational brand for millions of young employees and for aspiring entrepreneurs. From a customer perspective, it stands for transparency, shared values. Unless character and human values are given the right place, the present crisis of leadership cannot be overcome.[31] Role models and mentors have played a crucial part in the success of India's top business leaders. Mentoring has became on effective method for career advancement, problem solving, coaching and support providing benefits to both mentors and proteges. Successful Indian business leaders like N.R. Narayana Murthy of Infosys and Azim Premji of Wipro are role models and mentors to a generation of business managers in India and overseas. Jack Welch is Kiran Mazumdar's role model for his unconventional approach to business. Azim Premji admires Mahatma Gandhi for his self confidence and leadership qualities. Dhirubhai Ambani always inspired Deepak S.Parekh for his towering business achievements. Infosys' Narayan Murthy admires JRD Tata for his leadership qualities. Thus leaders for tomorrow must draw inspirations from the galaxy of leaders which India has produced over the years.

Preparing Leaders for Tomorrow

For preparing leaders for tomorrow, both internal and external sources have to be fully utilized by the nation. Major general G.K. Nischol, Director General AIMA has said: The annual surveys conducted by AIMA have been able to facilitate introspection and redesigning of Business schools, creating healthy competition among them and bring transparency in their functioning. "Management education has to be reengineered and reinvented in India as the country is fast emerging as a global hub. Integration of global economies, implementation of WTO regime and FDI in India have thrown open new challenges and opportunities to the leaders who are to be provided required skills and knowledge to cope with the demands of the time. India has more than approximately 1200 management education institution recognized by the All India Council for Technical Education (AICTE). Indian Institute of Management Ahmedabad, Bangalore, Kolkata, Lucknow, Indore and Kozhikode have their own place of recognition due to very high levels of intellectual capital, admissions, placements, infrastructure, industry interface, governance and location. It is necessary that Business schools must keep pace with the changing economy and should manage to inculcate the qualities of leadership in the trainees that one feels to be the best. In order to prepare leaders of tomorrow, the faculty of the management institutes should be able to equip them with most updated knowledge, skill and case studies prepared from the real life situations. Today management education is going through a metamorphosis and facing innumerable challenges relating to quality of faculty members, performance appraisals and placement of students after their completion of post graduate management education. There is a need for having a vision of internationalizing quality management education, bench marking excellence and setting high standards in management education programmes. Improving infrastructure of training institutions is also needed for providing high quality training to future leaders. IIM Lucknow is leading the initiative to set up a full fledged campus at NOIDA near Delhi primarily as a centre to develop "Global Managers". It is initially a 50 crore project and will cater for the needs of those leaders who have work experience of seven to ten years. Alliance Business Academy Bangalore is the first Business school in India to be accredited by the International Assembly for Collegiate Business Education (IACBE) USA, one of the three premier management education accrediting bodies in the world and has international exchange opportunities with other business schools of USA, France, Switzerland, and the Russian Federation. Gradually many other management institutions are now entering into international exchange opportunities. India is gradually becoming the intellectual hub for the world and the there are opportunities to became forerunners in high quality international management education. However, there are many problems and challenges. With a strong push from the government to implement 27 percent reservation in educational institutions management institutions have to gear up for this reality. An overall expenditure of over Rs.16,500 crore is needed to increase seats in Institution of higher learning funded by the centre. With the possibilities of expansion due to increase quota, all management institutions will need additional physical space, constructions of new class rooms and hostel buildings, library facilities, and other state-of-the art infrastructure like computers, video conferencing and other technological support. The biggest challenge is to find out and retain qualified, dedicated and experienced faculty members. Quality of faculty is the key factor that the adds to the brand equity of business schools. Compensation perks and other working conditions of students passing from management institutes now-a-days are much higher than those of faculty members. Moreover there is a portion of faculty members who are increasingly going overseas with much better offers from foreign management institutions. In India the supply side of the faculty as a whole is quite tight as not many people opt for doctoral programmes. Good faculty is needed not just for teaching purpose but also for students overall personality development. There is a need for more synergy between industry and management institutions. The corporate world needs are constantly changing and the focus now is increasingly on leadership and analytical skills, problem-solving ability and adaptability. Management schools have to constantly upgrade themselves to suit the ever changing corporate needs of the global economy. Therefore a very detailed and exhaustive understanding of mergers and acquisitions with techniques of negotiations, internal settlement and integration process should find suitable place in the curriculum with specific case studies. Another need is of leaders for tomorrow who have the knowledge and art of managing different cultures in India and abroad. Management education for the 21st Century has to include globalization, diversification, wider customer interface, changing organizational structure, government and international regulations and changing business environment with stress on growing realities and how to bring harmony in diversity. The management education has to invent tools and techniques to understand the mind sets of the people of diverse nationalities and cultures and bring harmony and integration for achieving the common objectives of the organizations. For faculty member of the management schools the focus for global leaders training should be to change the mindset of people and help them realize that the employees from different background, cultures and nationalities could do the same job and acceptance of diversity should become a unifying force for the people. Leaders for tomorrow have to be prepared by the management institutes to develop a vision around tomorrow's industry, tomorrow's competition, tomorrow's market and tomorrow's society. Kumar Mangalam Birla has said: "The challenges of going global are mainly cross - cultural. The key challenges for future are managing people, consolidating core business and building the strategic architecture for the future growth of the group". Rata Tata has given the following message for leaders of tomorrow. "Business must be based on values and ethics, sometimes you lose, as we did, but is worthwhile. It bothers me that many MBA's want to win business at any cost. But I tell them I want you to go home and sleep peacefully. "The emphasis on values and ethical conduct needs to be emphasised all the time while preparing leaders for tomorrow. Leaders for tomorrow need to be given proper appreciation of work-life balance and about quality of life balance and about quality of life. Meditation, daily exercise/yoga for good health, maintaining happiness, peace and contentment in family life are also important things of life and need not be ignored. Training for leadership must explain the role of failure. Prof. Vijay Govindarajan says: "Create several pilot projects before scaling up, experience failures and then learn from those failures to build a more successful model." Leadership for tomorrow must equip people with their attitudinal change and be a constant learner. Training "must bring out the critical role. Senior executives must play in managing the inevitable tensions that arise between today's business and tomorrow's"[32] Corporate Social responsibility is now a well accepted doctrine in global business and leaders for tomorrow must get adequate inputs of CSR. Future leaders will need to ensure not only a healthy bottom line, with share holder satisfaction but also improve the quality of life for employees and local communities who help them generate wealth and business. Indian corporations are increasingly realizing this as they create the core of a new corporate soul. Dr. Abad Ahmad and Dr. O.P. Gupta in their path breaking research study. "Passion to win—How winning companies develop and sustain competitive edge" have noted the following characteristics and pattern of Inspiring leadership in India :-

1. Pro-active and positive mind-set.
2. Passion and ambition.
3. Competence building and winning paradigm.
4. Clear vision and mission.
5. Institution building and continued outstanding leadership.
6. Openness, learning and change.
7. Thorough knowledge, attention to details and holistic view.
8. People centric, team based approach, empowerment and commitments.
9. Simplicity, values and character.

Future leaders have to imbibe the above mentioned qualities and characteristics of leaders.

Abraham Zeleznik has said "What is the ideal way to develop leadership? Every society provides its own answer to this question and each is groping for answers, defines its deepset concerns about the purposes, distributions and use of power".[33] In considering the development of leaders, we have to examine two different courses of life history. (1) Development through socialization, which prepares the individual to guide institutions and to maintain the existing balance of social relations, and (2) development through personal mastery, which impels an individual to struggle for psychological and social change[34]. Leaders for tomorrow have to learn about emotional intelligence "The process is not easy. It takes time and most of all, commitment. But the benefits that come from having a well developed emotional intelligence, both for the organization, make it worth the effort. But leaders need to have motional intelligence to succeed. The importance of developing leaders through out the organization makes it imperative for the organization to take all necessary steps and measure to develop leaders. Specialised advanced training for synergy building boundary management, customer orientation, network competence and implementation, negotiations skills value orientation culture building, etc, have to be imparted to leadership. Warren Bennis noted: "Given the nature and constancy of change and transnational challenges facing business leadership, the key to making the right choices will come from understanding the leadership qualities necessary to succeed in the volatile and mercurial global economy". These qualities have to be cultivated and developed by all available techniques of training and bearing. Adler and his colleagues have identified the following skills namely global perspective, local responsiveness, synergistic bearing transition and adaptation, cross-cultural interaction, collaboration and foreign experience as necessary skills to be developed through various HRD strategies, mentoring counseling and personal examples.[35] Case study method is a very useful training methodology for leadership training and development. Various O.D. techniques like grid training, Laboratory, Seminar training, team development techniques, Conference, Video-conferencing are to be utilized for leadership development training. Kurt Lewin's procedure of unfreezing moving and freezing O.D. techniques can be used for various leadership development programmes. O.D. interventions are very useful techniques, for organizational development. Internal resource building is especially important to make O.D. a self renewing process. Leadership development is a continuous on-going process. Tata group of companies have developed specific leadership programmes for transformational leaders and distinct skills such as anticipatory skills, visionary skills, value empowerment skills and self understanding skills their in-house training.[36] In India, a number of management schools are having management development programmes for future leaders. IIM Ahmedabad has introduced innovative courses like PGPX for executives. Many institutes have started PGD or fellowship programmes for doing research on applied management subjects. Corporate giants such as Wipro, Infosys, HCL and Ranbaxy, have in fact embraced mentorship as a comprehensive business strategy that utilises the expertise of skilled and experienced professionals to train their future leaders and green horns. Using mentors for new employees results in faster promotion rates, increased job satisfaction, accelerated career mobility and most of all, increased productivity.

Preparing leaders for future requires a system's approach. A suggestive blue - print is given below.

A Blue-Print for preparing future leaders :

1. Develop job standards.
2. Identify needs of future leaders.
3. Determine training objectives.
4. Develop curriculum.
5. Select method and material.
6. Obtain instructional resources and experienced trainers, mentors and counselors.
7. Conduct training and development of trainees and periodical refresh courses.
8. Evaluation and feedback.
9. Develop HRD facilities and institutions with adequate training infrastructure.
10. Build up HRD environment.
11. Ensure adequate financial and other resources.
12. Work out Time schedule, durations of training.
13. Library and Book / Magazines for updating knowledge.
14. Interaction with global leaders, conferences, seminars etc.
15. In-service plant training and on the job experience with mentors and counsellors.
16. Exposure to global environment by short visits to some foreign countries.

Future leaders have to be deeply concerned with and acutely aware of the importance and centrality of effective execution, implementation, monitoring and measurement of results. Outstanding execution has become a big issue around the economic world. HRD specialists have to give great emphasis on the following core personality dimensions:-

1. Extroversion—assertiveness, sociable, outgoing and talkative.
2. Agreeableness—good natured, cooperative and trust worthy.
3. Conscientiousness—responsible, dependable, achievement oriented, committed to the job.
4. Emotional stability—relaxed, secure, stress free.
5. Openness to experience—broad minded, intellectual imaginative.
6. Creative—constructive in approach innovative.
7. Self discipline—control over anger, fear, greed and jealousy.[37]

A future leader has to don the role of a cognitive tuner, a people catalyser, a systems architect, a transformational leader and a servant leader, and an efficacy builder, in order to be a successful navigator through the rocky process of altering mindsets. Leaders of the future will have to consciously develop some traits of extraordinary courage if they want to be recognised as global leaders. It is gratifying to note that the Indian CEO is unique for including larger sociated good as part of business decisions, deriving strength from spiritual sources and in his compassion for others.[38]

References

1. Udai Pareek, Understanding Organisation Behaviour, Oxford University Press (2004), p. 376.
2. Udai Pareek (2002) Training Instrument in HRD and OD, New Delhi, Tata McGraw Hill.
3. The term was introduced by Herman Kalm and Anthony J.Wiener, The year 2000. A Frame work for Speculations on the Next Thirty three years. The Mac Millan Company 1967.
4. Uris, A. How to be a successful leader—McGraw Hills, 1953, pp. 32-39.
5. James Collins and Jerry Porras—Build to last—Harper Business, 1994.

6. Mick Bennett and Andrew Bill - Hewitt Associates—“Leadership Talent in Asia” John Wiley and Sons (Asia) Pvt. Ltd., Singapore—2004, p. 35.
7. Narayan Murty It is all in the mind, stupid”—Business Today, 19 January 2003.
8. Robert B Tucker - Driving Growth Through Innovation - How leading firms are transforming their future East West Books (Madras) Pvt. Ltd., 2002, p. 38.
9. C.K. Prahalad, Liam Fahey and Robert M.Randall. “A strategy for growth. The Role of core competencies in the Corporation”. The Portable MBA in Strategy, Wiley, 1994.
10. Dr. Krishna Mohan Mathur - Towards Effective Management Path ways to excellence, Gyan Publishing House, New Delhi, 1992.
11. Arnold J.Toynbee, A study of History - Oxford University Press, 1934 also Andrew S.Grove, only the Paraboid Survive-Doubleday 1996.
12. Joseph L.Bower and Clayton M.Christensen “Disruptive Technologies : Catching the wave” Harvard Business Review - January-February, 1995.
13. Stan Abraham “Conference Report” strategy and Leadership May 2002.
14. P. Singh and Asha Bhandarker - Corporate Success and transformational Leadership - Wiley Eastern Limited, New Delhi 199 Preface X.
15. Dr. Krishna Mohan Mathur - Managing Human Resource Development—An Indian Perspective - Gyan Publishing House, New Delhi-2001, p. 23.
16. Bernard, M. Bass—From Transaction to the Transformational Dynamics Winter 1990, pp. 19-31.
17. Narayana Murthy—“The Infosys Way”. The Times of India June 20, 2001.
18. Carla-Harvard Business School—Working Knowledge - Sharing the Responsibility of Corporate governance - 24/05/2005, p. 5.
19. Stephen H. Rhinesmith—A Manager’s Guide to Globalisation (1993).
20. Narayan—Transformation to Transcendence—Break through Ideas for leadership in the new millennium—Ahmedabad Management Association 2000, pp. 100-120.
21. Jaffery A. Krames—Jack Welch and The 4E’s of Leadership-Tata McGraw Hills, p. 250.
22. Michael J. Marquart and Dean W. Engel—“HRD Competencies for a shrinking world. Training and Development, May 1993, pp. 62-64.

23. Udai Pareek - Training Instruments in HRD and OD. (New Delhi—Tata McGrowthful (2002) and understanding organisation behaviour (2004).
24. Shri G. Narayana - Transformation to Transcendence - Breakthrough Ideas for Leadership in the New Millennium- Ahmedabad Management Association, Ahmedabad 2000, pp. 33-35.
25. Dr. A.P.J. Abdul Kalam—Ignited Minds—Penguin Books New Delhi-2002, p. 117.
26. Ratna Bhushan/TNN-MNCS picking up for Indian Managers for Global Jobs, Times of India, 28 May 2005, p. 19, Delhi Edition.
27. For Similar views see Dr. Krishna Mohan Mathur—Towards Effective Management—Pathways to Excellence—Gyan Publishing House, New Delhi, 1999, p. 46.
28. Dr. Krishna Mohan Mathur—The Relevance of Vedantic Wisdom in Aid to Contemporary Management. Indian Journal of Public Administration—Quoted in "Towards Effective Management—Pathways to Excellence—Gyan Publishing House, New Delhi, 1999, p. 85.
29. Aneeta Madhok—Managing People Tomorrow - Indian Management, October 2009, p. 67.
30. Purvi - Sheth - Executive Education learning @ Wharton - Indian Management March, 2006.
31. Daniel Goleman - What make a Leader? Harvard Business Review, November - December 1998, p. 95.
32. Dr. Krishna Mohan Mathur, Towards effective management. Pathways to Excellence—Gyan Publishing House, New Delhi, 1999 , p. 45.
33. Vijay Govindarajam and Chris Trimble—"10 Rules for strategic innovations (From Harvard Business School Press).
34. Abraham Zalezink Managers and Leaders: Are they different? Harvard Business Review. March-April 1922, p. 2. HBR Classic.
35. Abraham Zalezink—*Ibid.,* p. 9.
36. Nancy J. Adher and Susan Bartgolonew : Managing Globally competent People. Academy of Management Executives, August 1992, p. 54.
37. Dr. Krishna Mohan Mathur—Managing Human Resource Development. An Indian Approach—Gyan Publishing House, New Delhi, 2001, p. 175.
38. Signe M. Spencer et. al-The Indian CEO-Response, Saga, p. 206.

Appendix–A
US Financial Crisis and Its Impact

The Year 2008 will go down in the economic history of the world as a year of economic recession. The suddenness with which some of the biggest Wall Street firms like Lehman Brothers and American Insurance Group collapsed like a pack of cards is unbelievable. Lehman Brothers after 158 years of high flying filed for bankruptcy. Merrill Lynch, Wall Street's third largest Investment Bank worth more than $ 100 billion last year was bought by Bank of America for $ 50 billion. AIG (American Insurance Group) had to be bailed out by US Govt. with a 85$ billion loan in exchange for nearly 80% shares of the company. By far the biggest act of nationalism in Wall Street's history. The world Investment Report 2008, a publication of UNCTAD, has highlighted certain deleterious consequences of the US financial crisis for the capital flows, especially foreign direct investment. UNCTAD expects a 10% drop in the aggregate flows across the globe. The global economy is slowing down and the world has forecast weaker growth in the developed world as compared with developing countries like India. According to reports a struggling US economy lost 159000 jobs in September 2008 as the weight the housing collapse and credit crunch hit a broad swath of industries. Inevitably comparisons are drawn with the Great Depression of 1929. The crisis started from the retail banks lending enormous housing loans to borrowers with inadequate securities and uncertain credit histories. These banks repacked these doubtful loans as tradable securities and sold them to investment banks, such as Merrill Lynch and Lehman Brothers. Inevitably when these borrowers defaulted the market for these securities crashed. The fate of 60000 employees of Merrill Lynch and 50000 workers of Lehman Brothers across the world is uncertain. American President Bush in a 12 minute prime time address in the White House East Room said "Without immediate action by the Congress America could slip into a financial crisis and a distressing scenario would unfold." On 24th September George Bush further said "The law makers risk a cascade of wiped out retirement savings, rising home for closures, lost jobs and closed business if they fail to act on a massive financial rescue plan. Our entire economy is in danger." He said "Our country could experience a long and painful recession." The US economy reeled under the news of the biggest bank failure in its history as federal regulators seized the largest American Saving and Loan Institution, Washington Mutual Fund and broked an emergency sale of its assets to JP Morgan for $ 1.9 billion. With assets worth $ 307 billion. WAMU was the sixth largest savings and loan US bank after Bank of America, JP Morgan, Wachovia and Citibank. Previous largest failure was Continental Illinois which had about 40 billion in assets when it failed in May 1984. JP Morgan will now have about $ 900 billion in deposits making it the largest US bank.

"The greed of the Wall Street investment bankers and the dangers of a totally unregulated system are to a large extent responsible for the current US financial crisis. According to Shyam P, the US housing market went into a classic speculative bubble when every one in the US could get a home loan worth $100,000 (45 lakh INR) or more without income proof, without other assets and without credit history, sometimes even without a proper job. These loans were called NINA "No income no assets".[1] This US financial crisis has resulted in slowdown of the world economy. How bad is it? Which companies and sectors are worst affected? How long will it last? What are the lessons that India can learn from this US Crisis? These questions are bound to be asked but there are no easy answers to these questions. On 28th September Sunday, Bush Govt. submitted a $ 700 billion bail out for the financial industry paving the way for enactment of the large US Govt. intervention in the markets since the Great Depression of the 1930's. According to Mc Clathcy Washington Bureau, the bail out deal is briefly as under—The grand plan of funding treasury has been authorized to spend $700 billion, starting with $250 billion to be given now and rest will be given later. Regarding Executive pay, treasury department will set standards to prevent excessive executive compensation for participating companies. Tax payer Equity will be guaranteed by tax payers share in the profits of the firms that benefit. Oversight board and independent Inspector General will be established and regular reports will be given to Congress. Government has been barred from acting contrary to Congress. Efforts will be made to modify mortgages for homeowners at risk of foreclosure. There are many precedents when bank failures were rescued by the Federal Deposit Insurance Corporation, as can be seen by the figures of top 10 US banks since 1934 based on the size of their assets to prevent widespread economic collapse. Table showing top 10 US bank failure since 1934 bail out by Federal Deposit Insurance Corporation.

1. Washington Mutual 2008 - $307 billion
2. Continental Illinois 1984 - $40 billion
3. First Republic Bank 1988 - $32.5 billion
4. Indy Mac Bank 2008 - $32 billion
5. American S & LA 1988 - $30.2 billion
6. Bank of New England 1991 - $21.7 billion
7. M Corp 1989 - $15.6 billion
8. Gibraltar Savings 1989 - $15.1 billion
9. First City Bancorp - 1988 - $13 billion
10. Home fed Bank 1992 - 12.2 billion (Source - Federal Deposit Insurance Corp 2008 MCT)

The first bail out plan made by Henry Paulson and Bernake was rejected by the US Congress by defeating the legislation in a 228 to 205 vote, sending the Dow Jones Industrial Average tumbling 777 points to its biggest drop ever and erasing more than $ 1.2 trillion in the market value. However on 2nd October 2008 the US Senate cleared the $700 billion revised package which was called "essential to the financial security of every American".

J. P. Morgan has been accused by its Wall Street rivals of giving the final blow that forced Lehman Brothers to collapse. The giant American bank is alleged to have frozen $ 17 billion of cash and securities belonging to Lehman and this precipitated the liquidity crisis that forced Lehman Brothers into chapter 11 bankruptcy protection on the morning of September 15 2008. JPMC on 12 September, 2008 froze LBHI's account as potential offset against any claims JPMC may have against

LBHI. This crisis has become a clear global crisis and echoes in Iceland, Ireland, Denmark, UK, Germany, Benelux, France, and Russia. The cost of global bail out plans is pegged at approximately $2 Trillion. The US takes the top spot with bail out package of $990 billion till 6 October 2008, followed by Ireland government which put in around $572 billion as part of guarantee for liabilities of the country's banks. German administration pumped in $ 50 billion to shore up mortgage lender Hypo Real Estate while Belgium government invested $16 billion in banking and insurance major Fortis. Belgian Major Dexia was saved by the country's government by throwing a lifeline to the tune of $9.2 billion. In Denmark, Danish National Bank takes over Roskilde Bank. In Russia Govt. pumps in 13.8 billion Euros in bank sector and lowers Interest rates.

The US slowdown will have varying impact on various sectors in India and abroad. Crisis, the research and credit rating agency has estimated that a substantial investment will flow in the Indian infrastructure, despite the financial crisis gripping the world. Estimates suggest that eight sectors like oil and gas, power, roads, ports, railways, urban infrastructure and telecom are expected to draw more than Rs. 16 Lakh crore investment in India between 2007-2008 and 2011-12. The Crisil study shows that during this period, growth in power sector will be 60%, while roads will expand 100%, airport 400%, ports 160% and Railways at 250%.

Table showing eight sectors and their estimated growth

S.No.	*Name of Sector*	*Achievement 02-07($bn)*	*Estimated 07-11 ($bn)*
1.	Oil and Gas	26	69
2.	Power	52	85
3.	Roads	31	64
4.	Ports	4	11
5.	Airports	1	6
6.	Railways	16	57
7.	Urban Infrastructure	25	46
8.	Telecom	26	52

(*Source:* Crisil).

A consultation paper was prepared by the Planning Commission says that a $500 billion investment during 2007-11 is required in infrastructure to sustain India's high growth rates. The projected sector-wise shares are: 30.4% in electricity, 15.4% in roads and bridges, 13.7% in telecom, and 12.4% in railways. 30% of the total investment is expected to come from the private sector. Tight liquidity might create a short term crunch for the core sector but in the medium term there will be no impact. The crisis in the global economy could turn out to be an opportunity for India. The chaos in the US economy has affected investor confidence in the developed economies. It is possible that investors would prefer an economy like that of India and China. However Union Commerce and Industry Minister Kamal Nath giving cautious approach has said : "The ripple effect from a really big event can also be seen as waves. There will be a shift in the balance of financial power to the east. The world can not do without India—not as a recipient of policy but as a shaper of the new financial architecture." According to Kumar Manglam Birla he was worried about the impact of the crisis on his group company Novelis, which makes flat rolled aluminium sheet used in beverage cans. On the positive side speculative funds will back off and oil prices should drop. But given that we are closely integrated with the rest of the world there will be a significant impact. Indian firms lost $ 10 billion market cap in US bourses. With IT sector Infosys witnessing the maximum erosion of $2 billion upto 6 October 2008. The 16 Indian firms listed on the NYSE and Nasdaq saw their collective market capitalisation dip to $78.9 billion, from $88.7 billion within a week. However internet firm Sify Technologies posted a modest gain of $3 million. While Wipro shed $ 1.69 million in its valuation, Satyam Computer Services saw a drop of $ 938 million in its valuation and Patni Computers witnessed a decline of $ 7.2 million. India's two largest private sector lenders - ICICI and HDFC Bank together saw their market cap plunging by nearly two billion dollars. Tata Motors lost $ 489 million while Tata Communication shed $ 266 million during the week ending 5th October 2008. According to Meera Vankipuram and Kumar Shankar Roy top five Indian IT service providers which derive nearly $ 9 billion revenues each year from US may continue to face harder times as the flow of business from US is likely to be hampered in the coming months. TCS, Infosys, Wipro, Satyam and HCL are the Indian IT providers whose revenues will be under pressure as shown below:

Table showing revenues of IT firms under pressure from US financial crisis:

S.No.	*Name of Firm*	*BFSI (Rs. Crores)*	*Total Revenue in America & North America*
1.	TCS	10161	11471
2.	Infosys	5972	10349
3.	Wipro	3410	8594
4.	Satyam	2311	4911
5.	HCL	2150	4262

Source : 2007-2008 Annual Report.

Analysts believe that the growth from highly profitable BFSI segment is likely to be muted and may even hit a plateau. The margin of Indian IT vendors will be under pressure and profitability will tend to decline. Global turmoil may maul some Indian companies. Bankers are blaming input costs, tight credit and redepreciation and global churning for loan defaults. India has started noticing the impact. In September 2008 quarter, five new cases with total debts of 1,600 crores have been added to the Reserve Bank of India (RBI). Corporate debt restructuring cell (CDR) gave a signal that more corporate loan defaults on borrowings could be in the pipeline. According to the Citigroup report due to the US financial crisis and tightening global liquidity, India ranks the second most vulnerable Asian economy after Thailand.

For the FMCG industry the impending credit crisis is unlikely to have a major impact in the near future. During the last four weeks of Sept, 2008 Indian investors have lost a whopping Rs. 6.60 lakh crore on the bourses. Prime Minister has rightly asked the Finance Minister to closely monitor and watch the state of investments in India and overall financial strength of the nation. Swaminathan S. Ankelsaria has given a positive picture of India. He says "we are much better prepared for this downturn than we were in the 90's. Our foreign exchange reserves are almost $ 300 billion, cushioning our Balance of Payments. Corporations have not gone on a borrowing spree paying 20% interest as they did in 1990's - they have large cash reserves, modest debt equity ratios and interest rates are much lower today."

P. Chidambaram, Finance Minister of India, has said "we have built a system for Indian people that can withstand any storm that blows across the world." The situation is being closely monitored by the Reserve Bank of India and SEBI. Dr. Man Mohan Singh has said : "India should be prepared for a temporary economic slowdown since like other countries, it also faces the ripple effect of the world crisis". He assured the Lok Sabha that deposits in both PSU and private sector banks were entirely safe. Our banks are financially sound, well-capitalised and well-regulated.

Appendix–B
Indo-US—Nuclear Deal-2008

October 2008, will go down as a historic landmark in the history of India as the United States India Nuclear Cooperation Approval and Non-Proliferation Enhancement Act was finally approved by the United States of America. Congress President Sonia Gandhi hailed the final agreement of the 123 agreement by the United States Congress as a "landmark" development. "It marked the successful culmination of a bold initiative taken by Prime Minister Dr. Man Mohan Singh in July 2005. It has opened the door for India entering into civil nuclear cooperation with the US. and other major countries with advanced technologies including France, Russia and U.K.". Never before has any country been given this special, unique status that is given to India, without signing CTBT, NPT and FMCT. The bill says that 123 agreement would be subservient to the Hyde Act. The core of Hyde Act is the nuclear waiver for India. Three decades of nuclear apartheid has ended appropriately on a day on which the apostle of ahimsa Mahatma Gandhi was born. The nuclear deal finally crossed the last hurdle when the US Senate passed it with 86-13 majority. India has become the only country to not sign the NPT and yet keep its nuclear weapons. According to President Bush the deal will strengthen non proliferation, protect the environment, create jobs and assist India in meeting its energy needs in a responsive manner.

On 1st Oct., 2008 Dr. Manmohan Singh said: Today we have added a new dimension to our strategic partnership by signing an inter-governmental agreement on civil nuclear cooperation. France is the first country with whom we have entered into such an agreement after the lifting of international restrictions on civil nuclear cooperation with India by the Nuclear Suppliers Group. France today generates 80% of its electricity from atomic energy and is willing to offer its latest

EPR technology under the agreement. France and India have wrapped up the civil nuclear energy agreement which will form the basis of wide ranging bilateral cooperation from basic applied research to full civil nuclear cooperation including reactors, nuclear fuel supply, nuclear safety radiation, environmental protection and nuclear fuel management cycle.

India's power requirements are massive and it needs to enhance its energy generation. The Indo-US nuclear deal ends 34 years of nuclear isolation for India and opens up the way for India to trade in civilian nuclear technology not just with US but also nations such as France, Russia etc. According to CII the deal could attract investment to the tune of $27 billion in 18-20 nuclear plants over the next 15 years. According to the Planning Commission the deal will enable India to set up generation capacity of 15,960 MW by 2017 taking the total installed capacity to around 20000 MW. At present India has 3779 MW but most of the plants are operating at half the capacity because of the non-availability of raw material uranium.

FICCI Secretary General Amit Mitra has said that India has the potential to generate 60000 MW of nuclear power over next 25 years - This requires an investment of over $100 billion. According to Assocham a minimum investment of Rs. 2 lakh crore would come in nuclear power generation sector in next 15 years. Companies like NTPC, Reliance Energy, Tata Power, L&T and BHEL can now partner international companies like GE, Westinghouse & Areva in the field of nuclear power generation. Around 200 medium and small companies are expected to get into the act as ancillary producers with large companies thereby giving a new direction to efficient and cheaper power production of the country. However, the government will have to amend laws to allow private players to enter in the nuclear power sector.

Dr. Man Mohan Singh, Prime Minister of India, said on 27th September at the United Nations "NSG waiver for India was a vindication of its impeccable record on non-proliferation .... India is registering rapid economic growth "India can now enter into bilateral agreements with a number of other advanced countries to mutually benefit from economic cooperation.

There has been a lot of criticism, debate and protests about the above mentioned Indo-US nuclear deal. According to A.N.

Prasad former director of Bhabha Atomic Research Centre and Member Atomic Energy Commission "The Indo-US nuclear deal is all about lucrative commercial interests limited to trading in power reactors with conditions attached and not about full civil nuclear cooperation. Having failed to contain India through embargoes, denials, restrictions, isolation, an attempt is being made to rope us (India) as a strategic partner through the deal. It appears that the non-proliferation bogey is a ploy for capping India's nuclear deterrence capability prematurely." A careful study of the deal in its proper perspective reveals that the terms and conditions fall short of expectations and India is not a gainer in the ultimate analysis India has neither achieved parity with advanced states nor full civil nuclear cooperation. This is a colossal lapse in the deal; while actually the civil nuclear cooperation should have occupied centre stage, the issue of testing has hijacked the debate. In the Indo-US deal the Hyde Act, the 123 agreement, the NSG waiver has dominated the issue leaving India as a subservient state. Parity of India with other weapon states has not been.

Non Proliferation bogey is a ploy for capping India's nuclear deterrence capabilities prematurely at a qualitatively nascent level by depriving further tests forever without themselves committing on the same. The Hyde Act will hang like an albatross. India has failed to play its cards well. India has been relegated to the position of a recipient state not of a state treated at par with advanced countries. The diplomatic language of the 123 text has been a master stroke of US and India is a clear loser. The embargoes on the crucial parts of the nuclear fuel cycle will continue, a variant of the nuclear apartheid. The left parties and BJP have been opposing the deal citing national interest and loss of sovereignty.

Finally on 10th October 2008 US President George Bush signed the nuclear deal bill into domestic law and in a separate statement stated that the agreement grants India advance consent to reprocessing which will be brought into effect upon conclusion of arrangements and procedures for a dedicated reprocessing facility under IAEA safeguards. In addition the legislation does not change the fuel assurance commitments that the US Govt. has made to the govt. of India as recorded in the

123 agreement. US President asserted that the agreement is consistent with Atomic Energy Act and other elements of the US law. The Indian Cabinet Committee on Political Affairs has approved the 123 agreement for signing and formally the US Secretary of State and India's External Affairs Minister have signed the bilateral agreement of the 123 agreement. This marks a significant landmark in Indo-US relations and provides India access to global markets. This agreement has immense potential for the development of the Indian power sector and the economy in general.

Index